Rufus Cope

The distribution of wealth

The economic laws by which wages and profits are determined

Rufus Cope

The distribution of wealth
The economic laws by which wages and profits are determined

ISBN/EAN: 9783337232818

Printed in Europe, USA, Canada, Australia, Japan

Cover: Foto ©Suzi / pixelio.de

More available books at **www.hansebooks.com**

THE

DISTRIBUTION OF WEALTH;

OR, THE

ECONOMIC LAWS BY WHICH WAGES AND PROFITS ARE DETERMINED.

THE LIMITATIONS ON WEALTH, THE CORRELATION OF
WEALTH AND POVERTY—INTEREST—TAXATION
—MONOPOLIES—PROTECTION AND
FREE TRADE.

BY

RUFUS COPE.

PHILADELPHIA:
J. B. LIPPINCOTT COMPANY.
1890.

CONTENTS.

3

CHAPTER IX.

CHAPTER X.

CHAPTER XI.

CHAPTER XII.

THE

DISTRIBUTION OF WEALTH;

OR, THE

ECONOMIC LAWS BY WHICH WAGES AND PROFITS ARE DETERMINED.

CHAPTER I.

INTRODUCTION.

THE first extended and systematic treatise on the subject of political economy was Adam Smith's "Wealth of Nations," published in 1776. Smith was followed, in 1803-17, by Malthus and Ricardo. These writers gave form and direction to the current of thought on political science, and what are now known as the orthodox views of political economy may be found definitely formulated in their writings. Their opinions, with little substantial modification, still hold sway, and continue to shape the views of modern authors.

Smith holds his position of authority by virtue of an ability which is unquestioned, a style that is forcible and clear, and the general soundness of his theories, to which he always applies the test of practical illustration.

Political science remained for many years in a stationary condition, and naturally fell into the custody of the college professor, who, for the most part, occupied himself with the task of interpreting what had already been written, rather than with new and original investigations. It appears to have been generally regarded as a completed science; and, as a consequence, the discussion of the subject more frequently degenerated into an inquiry into the exact limits of the

old doctrines, and the most appropriate formulas for their expression.   It had reached that stage in the history of a science
where terminology begins to overshadow substance, and hyper-
criticism busies itself more about modes of expression than the
thought expressed.   The schoolman has a *penchant* for definition.   One of his leading aims appears to be to crowd subjects
into formal definitions that exactly fit, touching at all points, and
slack at none.   It has in this manner come about that there are
a host of writers who assume to be scientific and thorough, who
are merely literary *valet de chambres*, supervising the verbal
wardrobe of other men's ideas,—a service necessary, perhaps, to
be attended to ; but it should not be forgotten that strained attempts at extreme accuracy of expression do not contribute to
perspicuity.   A writer who tasks himself with the work of
giving expression to the doctrines of a complex science, in terms
of such absolute exactness and completeness as to forestall
quibblers who detach words from their context, gains nothing
in clearness.

Writers on political economy are prone to attempt to subject the science to the limitations of scholastic formulas,
wrought out by processes of abstract reasoning in which
economic forces are regarded as accurately ascertained invari-
able qualities, or quantities, whose variations may be definitely
measured; but political science cannot be reduced to a code of
abstract formulas ; nor will it always yield to the precision of
mathematic forms of statement.   It deals with a multitude of
facts, and numerous and conflicting forces of varying intensity ;
and attempts at absolute precision of statement within the
compass of a sentence or a paragraph lead either to clumsy
obscurity, or to the omission of troublesome qualifications which
may not be packed within the limits of a symmetrical formula.

It is as impracticable to declare, in precise terms, the laws of
trade, or of the tenure of property, or to define methods of taxation adapted to all ages and conditions of social progress, as it is
to make one adjustment of the sails of a ship answer for a voy-
age across the sea.   There are principles that inhere in the nature of things which must ever remain the same ; but doctrines
which deal not with fixed conditions alone, but with all the
changing phases of a growing civilization, must be shaped and

fitted to new conditions as they arise. Political economy is not a stationary science; it was not embalmed in the writings of Ricardo, Malthus, and Smith. What is once true is always true; but that which is true of one condition of men, or of the relations of the people of one age, may be far from true of those of another.

Many publications upon the subject of political economy are freighted with the anæmic thought, whose vitality has been destroyed by the malaria of a stagnant science; and the most sickly localities are often to be found in the vicinity of ancient institutions of learning.

When the Talmud was produced, religious literature and religious science among the Jews had reached what political economists term the stationary state, and we have, therefore, in this remarkable religious miscellany, an illustration of a religion gone to seed,—that phase of development in which normal thought is superseded by idle speculation and quaint conceits arrayed in the garb of consequential pretence.

One of the curious whims that exhibits itself in that remarkable body of writings is the subjection of thought to the notion of numerical relation. In consequence, there is the book of Ones, the book of Twos, the book of Threes, and so on through a long series. When we read in the book of Ones that "The former Chasidim used to sit still one hour, then pray for one hour, then sit for another hour;" and that "Rabbi Chanina could put on and off his shoes while standing on one leg only, though he was eighty years of age;" or in the book of Sevens that "a dog in a strange place does not bark for seven years;" or in the book of Tens that "Moses, being ten ells high, seized an axe ten ells long, and, springing up ten ells, struck Og on the ankle and killed him;" we cannot avoid the thought, that possibly ideas came to be fashioned with a purpose of avoiding discords in this artificial system of numerical harmonies, to which, doubtless, both tradition and logic were often compelled to yield precedence.

Political economy has sometimes exhibited symptoms of the Talmudic tendency. At the risk of intruding upon what may have been intended as only a *tête-à-tête* between two collegiates in their chosen dialect, I quote from a recent number of the *Journal of Economics* the following:

"The first of these (two points) is the form of the curve of the price of wheat, which Jevons regards as asymptotal, and Mr. Wickstead as cutting both axes. Mr. Wickstead proposes to limit his curve to the prices of wheat considered as used for human food only. This limitation does not radically alter the problem, as the alternative uses at lower values only delay the approach of the curve to the axis, and do not prevent it reaching zero, if Mr. Wickstead's views are correct."

"There are other uncertainties in the data. Is the excessive supply supposed to be caused by an accidental large yield or acreage, or by the discovery of a new more prolific variety? Differences of this kind in the data would modify the form of the curve, but would not affect the main question, whether or not it is asymptotal.

Here are two astute professors of science, or else young men who have not yet been long enough out to have wasted their college-born enthusiasm for asymptotes along the jolting highway of practical affairs, who, having observed a certain analogy between the relation of a curved line representing the varying price of wheat and a line representing the product, and the definite mathematical relation of the asymptote to its axis,—an analogy which, if simple and easily comprehended, might serve the purpose of illustration,—imagine themselves to be discussing a great principle, possessing all the necessary qualifications of recondite novelty to render it worthy the title of a "doctrine" of political science.

The science of political economy has become prolific of learning of this character.

Asymptotes are the dumb-bells and Indian clubs of science, and should constitute a part of the furniture of every well-equipped intellectual gymnasium. But, very naturally perhaps, many of our worthy professors, when they go abroad as architects of political science, insist on employing the implements with which they have become most familiar, rather than the common, though more efficient, tools of the practical artisan. The consequence is, that the noise they make is sometimes altogether out of proportion to the number of nails they drive. That which most attracts the listening crowd, in the field of constructive science, is not always the sound of effective industry, but often only the resounding din of asymptotalism ; it is the professor abroad with his dumb-bells—driving tacks.

Science is simply the ascertained interpretation of facts. That interpretation may or may not be reduced to the form of an abstract generalization. But when it is so expressed, every fact must have a place in the theory ; since a theory which runs counter to any fact, however plausible or recondite may seem the formula in which it is clothed, must be unsound.

Within the present century new economic forces have come into play, and old tendencies have gathered increased power. There are conditions which were useful in an earlier stage of social development that have performed their service and exhausted their utility, and now remain only as burdens which society has not yet been able to cast off. There are forces which are essential to the growth of society that need to be harnessed with judicious restraints. Forms of government, methods of administration of the highest utility in one age, may become an insufferable evil in the next. Rules of political economy fitted to one condition of society, adapted to one day and age, may be wholly unsuited to other times and conditions.

Within the limits of the present century the producing power of the people, in every department of industry, has been greatly multiplied by new discoveries and inventions. According to Edward Atkinson, "the labor of one man, aided by improved machinery, will, in one year, produce five thousand six hundred and twenty-five bushels of wheat (in Dakota ?) ; the moving of four thousand five hundred bushels of wheat seventeen hundred miles represents the labor of one and a half men for one year ; the labor required for making this wheat into flour, and making barrels for the same, from the log, is equivalent to the labor of one man for one year ; add to this the labor of one man for six months for repairs of machinery, and one thousand barrels of flour delivered in New York represent only the direct labor of four men for one year ; the conversion of one thousand barrels of flour into bread and its sale represent the work of only three persons working one year. Thus seven men serve bread to one thousand persons. One man in a cotton-mill spins and weaves cotton cloth for two hundred and fifty persons ; one in a woollen-mill, cloth for three hundred persons ; one in a coal-mine, iron-mine, or iron-furnace serves two hundred pounds of iron each to five hundred persons; one in a men's boot and shoe factory makes two pairs a year of boots and shoes for eight hundred persons; one in a women's boot and shoe factory makes three pairs a year for one thousand persons; one in a shirt factory sews two thousand four hundred excellent shirts, or more of lower quality, or four a year for six hundred to eight hundred persons." *

In the manufacture of agricultural implements one man does the work of two men twenty-five years ago. In the principal labor involved in the manufacture of small-arms one man now does what it required forty-five to fifty to do by hand. In the manufacture of women's boots and shoes one person does the work which it would take five to do by hand. In other departments of the same industry one person has taken the place of two. With Goodyear's sewing-machine for turned shoes one man does the work of eight. In nailing on heels one man does the work of five; in sand-papering the bottoms one man does the work of four.

In the construction of carriages one man has taken the place of three. In 1879 a large broom-manufacturing concern with seventeen skilled men manufactured five hundred dozen brooms per week. In 1885, with but nine men and improved machinery, the same firm turned out twelve hundred dozen brooms per week.

In the manufacture of carpet one man now does the work which it required from ten to twenty persons to do in 1860.

In the manufacture of hats of a medium grade one man does the work of three. A hand-loom weaver used to weave from sixty to eighty picks per minute in weaving a cloth of good quality with twenty threads of twist to each one-quarter square inch. A power-loom now weaves one hundred and eighty picks per minute of the same kind of cloth, and one weaver minds all the way from two to ten looms, according to the grade of the goods.

In the manufacture of flour one man has taken the place of four; and in the manufacture of furniture, of two or three workmen formerly required to do the same work.

---

* Atkinson on Distribution of Products.

In nearly all departments of industry, by means of machinery and combination under the direction and control of capital, the power of labor has been wonderfully augmented. Naturally, we would expect a corresponding growth of general prosperity and of individual wealth. And of wealth there is indeed an abundance. But the conditions which have made rapid accumulations of wealth practicable are unfavorable to its equitable distribution. The accumulated product of the industry and skill of the people of a nation is owned and controlled by a comparatively small number of persons, many of whom have made to society no adequate return for the possessions which they have acquired, but which they did not create. The laws of inheritance, of finance, the laws of trade and of land tenure are such as to lead to the grossest inequalities of property and of opportunity for its acquisition; and, although there has been the most wonderful development of the power of labor to produce, there has been no corresponding increase in the wealth of the great majority of the people. The extremes of poverty and of affluence have grown wider and wider apart, and suffering and want have become more common. Each individual has become less and less an independent producer. All have become involved in a tangled net-work of commercial and financial forces, and, as they move on together in the hurrying, jostling crowd, some are pushed forward, some are thrust aside, and many are trampled under foot.

Mr. Henry George, in "Protection or Free Trade," says, "Five centuries ago the wealth-producing power of England, man for man, was small indeed compared with what it is now. Not merely were all the great inventions and discoveries, which, since the introduction of steam, have revolutionized mechanical industry, then undreamed of, but even agriculture was far ruder and less productive. Artificial grasses had not been discovered. The potato, the turnip, the carrot, the beet, and many other plants and vegetables which the farmer now finds most prolific, had not been introduced. The advantages which ensue from rotation of crops were unknown. Agricultural implements consisted of the spade, the sickle, the flail, the rude plough, and the harrow. Cattle had not been bred to more than half the size they average now, and sheep did not yield half the fleece. Roads, where there were roads, were extremely bad; wheel vehicles were scarce and rude; and places a hundred miles from each other were, in difficulties of transportation, practically as far apart as London and Hong-Kong, San Francisco and New York are now. Yet patient students of those times, such men as Professor Thorold Rogers, who has devoted himself to the history of prices, and has deciphered the records of colleges, of manors, and public offices, tell us that the condition of the English laborer was not only relatively but absolutely better in those rude times than it is in England to-day, after five centuries of advance in the productive arts. They tell us that the working-man did not work so hard as he does now, and lived better; that he was exempt from the harassing dread of being forced by loss of employment to want and beggary, or of leaving a family that must apply to charity to avoid starvation. Pauperism, as it prevails in rich England of the nineteenth century, was, in the far poorer England of the fourteenth century, absolutely unknown. Medicine was empirical and super-stitious. Sanitary regulations and precautions were all but un-known. There was frequently plague and occasionally famine; for owing to the difficulties of transportation, the scarcity of one district could not be relieved by the plenty of another. But men did not—as they do now—starve in the midst of abundance; and, what is perhaps the most significant of all, women and children were not worked as they are to-day; but the eight-hour system, which even the working-classes of the United States, with all the profusion of labor-saving machinery and appliances, have not yet attained, was then the common system."

John Stuart Mill, in his work on political economy, says, "Hitherto it is questionable if all mechanical inventions yet made have lightened the day's burden of any human being. They have enabled a greater population to live the same life of drudgery and imprisonment, and an increased number of manu-facturers and others to make fortunes. They have increased the comforts of the middle classes; but they have not yet begun to effect those great changes in human destiny which it is in their nature and their futurity to accomplish."

Professor Thorold Rogers, in his "Six Centuries of Work and Wages," speaking of the thirteenth and fourteenth centuries in

England, says, "All the necessaries of life, in ordinary years, were abundant and cheap; and even in dearer years the margin of wages or profits over the bare wants of life was considerable enough to fill up the void. Meat was plentiful, poultry everywhere, eggs cheapest of all. The poorest and meanest man had no absolute and insurmountable impediment put upon his career if he would seize his opportunity and make use of it. . . .

"I am well aware that such medical skill is now at the service of the poor as princes and prelates desired, but were entirely without, in the Middle Ages. . . . I know that four grains of wheat and barley or any other grain are produced by modern tillage, where one was with difficulty raised before; that the ox has been selected and bred and fed from four hundred pounds or less to twelve hundred or more; that sheep which once yielded a pound of wool precariously, now produce from seven to nine pounds; that the powerful cart-horse has taken the place of the wretched and stunted pony of the old English breed, and that other animals which are destined for the service of man have been selected till there seems nothing to desire in their shape, size, or utility. I see, in all directions, that human toil has been supplemented and sometimes superseded by mechanical agencies which genius has invented and patience has elaborated. . . . But I am convinced that modern civilization will be judged, not by what it has done, but by what it has left undone; not by what it has remedied, but by what it has failed to heal, or at least to have relieved; not by its successes, but by its shortcomings. It may be that the progress of some has been more than counterbalanced by the distress and sorrows of many; that the opulence and strength of modern times mock the poverty and misery which are bound up with and surround them; and that there is an uneasy and increasing consciousness that the other side hates and threatens.

"It may be well the case, and there is every reason to fear it is the case, that there is collected a population in our great towns which equals in amount the whole of those who lived in England and Wales six centuries ago, but whose condition is more destitute, whose homes are more squalid, whose incomes are more uncertain, whose prospects are more hopeless than those of the poorest serfs of the Middle Ages and the meanest drudges of the mediæval cities. The arm of the law is strong enough to keep them under, and society has no reason to fear their despair; but I refuse to accept the superficial answer that a man is an admirer of the good old times, because he insists that the wants of civilization should be examined along with and not apart from its failures."

Speaking of the earlier part of the nineteenth century, he says, " That the patents of Arkwright and Peel secured enormous fortunes to those inventors, or purchasers of inventions, we all know; that they ultimately cheapened production is equally clear; that they gave England well-nigh a monopoly in the supply of textile fabrics is as manifest; but it does not strictly follow that the English workman was better paid. The hand-loom weaver was undoubtedly impoverished; but I do not find that the machine weaver bettered his position. His wages remained low; his means were ever straitened; and the misery of the manufacturing districts was greater even than that of the agricultural."

Speaking of the agricultural classes, he says, " The condition of the agricultural laborer has been different from that of the artisan. Scattered and incapable of combined action with his fellows, bowed down by centuries of oppression, hard usage, and hard words; with, as he believes, every social force against him, the landlord in league with the farmer, and the clergyman in league with both, the latter constantly preaching resignation, and the two former constantly enforcing it, he has lived through evil times."

Speaking of the agricultural laborers in England, Mr. Adam Badeau, in his " Aristocracy in England," says, " In 1880 the average wages of the agricultural laborer, the man who worked the two thousand million acres of land and produced the three hundred and thirty million dollars of revenue, was fourteen English shillings a week, or about fifty cents a day; out of this he had to pay his rent to the earl or duke, which was two English shillings, or fifty cents a week. Bread was three cents a pound, meat eighteen cents, and butter one shilling and eight pence,—about forty cents.

" I heard viscounts and baronets, and bishops and earls,

lamenting the misery and depravity, the poverty and low wages of the wretches who lived on their estates. I heard them admit that in their part of the country a shilling (twenty-four cents) a day was often the wages of a strong, healthy man, who had a wife and six or seven children to support, out of which, I heard them say, at least a shilling a week was deducted for rent. I heard that whole families occupied a single bedroom. I heard of the ignorance and stolidity, often the brutality, of the English peasants, of whom there are several millions."

This is England, that for centuries has stood first among the nations in moral, social, and religious culture, and has led the world in the development of the practical sciences, in industrial growth, and the accumulation of wealth; England, whose people are practically as free as the people of the United States, whose policies, more than those of any other nation, have been shaped in harmony with the orthodox theories of political science, and where the doctrine of *laisser faire*, or free and unrestricted play of economic forces, so devoutly cherished by writers on political economy, has held the most complete sway. The people of the United States are travelling along the same highway, and are rapidly nearing the same end. American works on political science, which have been in no small measure our guides in legislative policy, have been given us by college professors whose characteristic function it is to perpetuate ancient languages and ancient doctrines. Orthodox by profession, conservative by habit, they stand like painted sign-boards, pointing down the old travelled road. It is a needed service well performed. But, knowing, as we now do, where that old road leads, it is time to stop and consider whether we will to go that way, or whether we shall alter our destination and change our course along some new highway, where the sign-boards have not yet been put up.

The statistics of our national wealth, our commerce, our manufactures, our agriculture, are constantly paraded before us to excite our wonder and challenge our admiration. It may gratify our pride to know that in the race for wealth and power we are outrunning the nations of Europe; but the question that concerns most the social philosopher, or intelligent patriot, is what progress the people are making towards a life unworn by exhausting toil, unfettered by needless anxieties,—that condition which shall extend and widen the opportunities for social culture and moral and intellectual growth.

Political economy has been most frequently discussed in its relation to the growth of the industries and the increase of national wealth. The classes by whose labor wealth is created have been considered along with lands and chattels as important factors in the production of wealth; but their own well-being has been too often regarded only in its relations to production, and without independent consideration of the moral and social welfare of the common people. But much attention has been given by recent writers to the study of economic questions, with the distinct purpose of ascertaining what, if anything, may be done to ameliorate the condition of the laboring classes. The growth of wealth in the hands of a relatively small number of persons has been so unprecedented, so out of all proportion to the services which these persons may be supposed to have rendered, the power which they have thus acquired over the fortunes of others has become so threatening, as to weaken faith in some of the dogmas which, for nearly a century, have been accepted as ultimate truths of political science. There is a feeling of alarm, a sense of something wrong in the adjustment of social forces.

Mr. Carnegie, in the *North American Review*, tells us that "the contrast between the palace of the millionaire and the cottage of the laborer, with us to-day, measures the change which has come with civilization." How much civilization has done for the millionaire, and how little for the laborer!

Mr. Carnegie devotes several pages of the *Review* to the consideration of the question as to what millionaires should do with their excesses of wealth. He decides that it is not to be bestowed in alms; since, out of every thousand dollars spent in so-called charity, nine hundred and fifty are unwisely spent; but that it should be devoted to the endowment of colleges or building of churches, or be bestowed on cities in the form of public parks and libraries; not forgetting to suggest that a community cannot "pay a more graceful tribute to the citizen who presents it than to give his name to the gift," nor failing to remind the beneficently-inclined millionaire of the " admiration of his fellow-men," which inures to the bestower of princely gifts. It is some satisfaction to learn that millionaires who regard assistance rendered to the weak and unfortunate, without recompense other than the fleeting gratitude of suffering women, or the cheap generosity of impoverished manhood, as wasted charity,—wasted because, poured into a sea of misery and want, it does not, like a palace of stone, or a public park, endure to proclaim to the world the generosity of the giver,—may, in consideration of a substantial guarantee of posthumous fame, be induced to devote to a worthy purpose a part of their surplus wealth. If Mr. Carnegie has not overestimated the vanity of those to whom his appeal is addressed, within the next half-century the names of dead millionaires may be as thoroughly advertised as medical panaceas are to-day, and their virtues as loudly and as truthfully proclaimed.

Mr. Carnegie does not mistake the tendency of popular thought, when he says, " There will be nothing to surprise the student of sociological development, if society should soon approve the text which has caused so much anxiety," " It is easier for a camel to go through the eye of a needle, than for a rich man to enter into the Kingdom of God." Not that society is, at present, disposed to unreasonable extremes, or to rest its claims upon the authority of scriptural texts; but the people are conscious that there is somewhere a grave wrong; they are in doubt as to the cause and uncertain as to the remedy. They are studying the symptoms in the old family almanac, and are confused by the number of sure cures; but they are going to try something.

The tariff, the railroads, the merchants, taxation, are each assailed in turn as the cause of the admitted evil. The farmer, who has been, perhaps, the greatest sufferer, organized first against the railroads. Freights have fallen until they are now less than half what they were in 1869, and a ton of freight is moved a mile for less than a cent; but the farmer has found no relief. Seeing in the retail merchant the enemy of his prosperity, he has organized co-operative stores and farmers' stores, where he may buy goods at an advance of ten per cent. above cost. This remedy, too, has proved a failure. He is now urged to an attack on the protective tariff, and, other remedies failing,

he may be persuaded to try the experiment. The silver man
and the paper-money man each has his special theory, which he
deems adequate to explain the cause of existing evils.

The workingmen in manufacturing and mining industries,
and those engaged in railway service, have sought relief in
strikes, and no doubt have thereby maintained wages in these
industries at a point above the rates to which wages would
have fallen, except for the organized protest of the wage
earners. Such remedies are, however, temporary in effect and
unsatisfactory in results.

The aggregation of wealth is not peculiar to any one country,
though, for obvious reasons, it has proceeded more rapidly in
the United States than in any of the older nations of Europe.
It is the effect, not of local or temporary causes, but the essential product of economic forces everywhere operative, and
producing the same results, except as counteracted by hindering
forces. It therefore becomes necessary to recur to the exami-
nation of first principles, the underlying laws which control the
creation and distribution of wealth, before we shall be prepared
to inquire as to the remedy, if there be any remedy, that would
be effective and practicable.

When Adam Smith wrote the "Wealth of Nations," the
important inquiry was how to create wealth. That question
has been fully answered by the invention of labor-saving machinery, the steamship, the railway, and the telegraph. The
inquiry now is, how may wealth be distributed, so that he
who creates it may enjoy it? how shall the labor of the nation
be distributed so that equal opportunities may be open alike to
all? Mill, in his "Political Economy," says, "The observations
in the preceding chapter had for their principal object to
deprecate a false ideal of human society. Their applicability to
the practical purposes of the present times consists in moder-
ating the inordinate importance attached to the mere increase of
production, and fixing attention on improved distribution and
large remuneration of labor as the two desiderata. Whether
the aggregate produce increases absolutely or not is a thing in
which, after a certain amount has been obtained, neither the
legislator nor the philanthropist need feel any strong interest;
but that it should increase relatively to the number of those

who share it is of the utmost possible importance; and this (whether the wealth of mankind be stationary or increasing at the most rapid rate ever known in an old country) must depend upon the opinions and habits of the most numerous class, the class of manual laborers."

Edward Atkinson says, "The production of what constitutes wealth or welfare is no longer at issue; modern science and modern instrumentalities of production are adequate to produce what would suffice for a good subsistence for every man, woman, and child in any and all countries. The whole question at issue is the distribution of this subsistence after it has been produced."

The inquiry pursued in the following pages will be confined chiefly to the question of the distribution of wealth, and the causes by which distribution is determined. It is impracticable, however, to consider distribution wholly apart from production. They are essentially involved together, and must be carried on, each in immediate relation to the other. The nature, extent, and effect of the aggregation of wealth, the limitations of wealth, commerce, protection, taxation, and interest on credits are necessarily embraced within the scope of the inquiry upon which we enter.

The subject of political economy is one which concerns the welfare of every citizen, but which, nevertheless, possesses little attraction, except for those who have made it the subject of special study, and most readers are disposed to avoid a discussion of abstract theories which impose the necessity of a sustained effort to comprehend and apply them. I have, therefore, in the following pages, sometimes departed from the usual methods pursued in the discussion of questions of economic science, and endeavored, by means of somewhat elaborate and sometimes commonplace illustrations, to bring the subject within the more ready grasp of those who are unfamiliar with the general principles of political economy. For like reason, the discussion has not been conducted throughout in that subdued monotone regarded as best befitting a calm and impartial logic. Nevertheless, care has been observed to avoid inaccuracy of statement, or argument which will not bear the test of analysis.

I believe that the working-people in the United States and

throughout Europe are suffering grave wrongs, for which there may be found an effective and practicable remedy. I believe that prevailing doctrines of economic science, although emanating from eminent writers who are both earnest and sincere, have been fashioned in harmony with the interests of the controlling classes. I do not believe that it is one of the essential requirements of civilization that the enduring products of the toil of millions of people, which represent the savings of labor from year to year, should be gathered and appropriated by a few. I do not believe that any man ever earned or was justly entitled to a fortune of millions. I do not believe in any law of inheritance whereby wealth without limit may be transmitted from generation to generation in uninterrupted succession. I believe in a policy which will tend to level down all those gross inequalities that spring from the accident of birth or chance opportunity. I believe in a free and fair competition as essential to a healthy social and industrial life, and in guarding the rights of every man to the acquisitions of industry, enterprise, and skill. But the scheme of social order, to which the industrial life of every individual must conform, is in part conventional and artificial, and is essentially imperfect; and he who takes advantage of its imperfections to gather to himself that which in equity belongs to others, should be held in check by limitations which leave room and scope enough for all the accumulations which may be fairly set down to the credit of industry, skill, or exceptional enterprise, but interpose an impassable barrier to the increase of wealth beyond that point where it represents only unjust gains gathered from the weaker members of a great industrial copartnership.

I am aware that the more wealthy members of society, sustained by the orthodox doctrines of political economy, are generally prompt to attribute the great existing inequalities of wealth, and the impoverished and dependent condition of the industrial classes, to the imperfections of human nature; but I am not aware that there ever has at any time been made manifest a disposition on their part to relieve the weaker members of society from the weight of unjust burdens. They hold on, guarding with tenacious vigilance all the advantages which they have secured. Never yet has there been made an earnest, persistent effort in behalf of the working-people, to place them on the vantage-ground of equal opportunity. Their advance is held in check by the operation of economic laws developed out of conditions which, except in the United States, they have been without the power to change. When they have been brought to understand the origin of the evils that weigh them down and obstruct their advance, it must not be expected that they will continue to endure burdens which they have the power to cast off. I do not believe that the working-people of the United States will long continue to permit the present aggregation of wealth to go on. They must perceive that their opportunities are growing less and less, and that they are rapidly nearing that condition of absolute dependence which environs the masses of working-people of Europe to-day.

Among recent contributions to the science of political economy in its modern phases, those of Edward Atkinson are deserving of special attention. Mr. Atkinson is a patient investigator of facts, whose conclusions are generally well supported, if not always satisfactorily demonstrated. But the final deduction which he draws, and which it appears to be his leading purpose to sustain,—viz., that the present distribution of the products of labor is, in the main, equitable, and that improvement in the condition of the laboring classes must await the slow process of education and social evolution, and may not be aided by legislative interference,—appears to me to be a leap beyond the legitimate conclusion of his argument.

Mr. Andrew Carnegie is the author of a swaggering book entitled "Triumphant Democracy," an exulting pæan to the progress of the young republic, in which, after properly humiliating the effete monarchies of Europe by a calcium-light display of our territorial bigness, he exhibits in one dazzling panorama a complete collection of our worldly possessions. Though the style is somewhat suggestive of the show-bills of the "biggest show on earth," the book is both instructive and entertaining. Mr. Carnegie is a domesticated Scotchman, who has chanced to draw a lucky number in the lottery of life, and like the countryman who, by a lucky turn of the wheel of fortune at an agricultural fair, has drawn the capital prize, he enjoys the show, and feels a swelling pride as he views the big pumpkins and fat

Berkshires which, however, fail to arouse the enthusiasm of the unfortunate wight who risked his money on the wrong number.

Mr. Carnegie organizes a street-parade. Says he, " Were the live stock upon Uncle Sam's estate ranged five abreast, each animal estimated to occupy a space five feet long, and marched around the world, the head and tail of the procession would overlap. This was the host of 1880; that of 1885 would be ever so much the greater; and still it grows day by day, and the end of its growth no man can foretell."

Mr. Carnegie's book is a complete and reliable exposition of the wealth and resources of the United States, and only serves to increase our wonder that, in a country whose resources appear to be unlimited, where the arts of production have reached their highest development, and where wealth displays its magnificence on every hand, penury and want should abide; that even here, above the joyous laughter of peace and plenty, above the hum of factories and the roar of furnaces, should be heard the discordant mutterings of discontent.

The phenomenal success of some who begin life as poor boys, and afterwards attain to the rank of millionaires, which is often cited as evidence of the possibilities of exceptional industry and worth, proves not that all may become millionaires, nor that the reasonable rewards of industry and skill are sure, but only this, that the hard-earned dollars of a thousand men, even in America, may become the booty of the daring brigand. Mr. Carnegie, like others who have written panegyrics upon the phenomenal growth of our national wealth, does not seem to realize that the larger the capital prizes are, which are drawn in the lottery of fortune, the greater the number of the blanks; and that those who have drawn blanks are not in the mood to join him in a wild and reckless dance of joy, inspired by a contemplation of the wealth whose magnificence is but a measure of the booty gathered by capital and cunning in a war against labor,—an honorable war for the most part, maybe, conducted according to the time-honored laws of trade, but a war of conquest and aggrandizement nevertheless, that has left sorrow and suffering and blasted hopes in its trail. The exultant shouts of the victors on their triumphal march may resound loud and far;

but the tumult and clang of all this boastful rejoicing are commingled with the moans of the vanquished.

The writings of Mr. Henry George upon economic subjects, "Progress and Poverty," "Social Problems," etc., are all worthy of attention. Mr. George's writings are often instructive and always entertaining; his argument is generally well sustained, and, although it may not convince, must command the thoughtful consideration of the candid reader. Logical in method and loyal to his own convictions, he offends neither the taste nor the intelligence of his readers by a resort to the shallow devices of the literary charlatan. His works possess value, not only on account of their literary merit, but also because of their vivid portrayal of existing evils.

I cannot, however, give assent to the leading doctrine, the conclusion about which Mr. George has grouped all his facts and arguments. He traces the unequal distribution of wealth, and the extremes of poverty developed under existing conditions, to monopoly in the ownership of land, and proposes as a remedy the abolition of private ownership, or measures which are equivalent thereto. He finds no fault with usury, nor with existing laws of finance, but, consistent with his idea of a single tax on land, he favors the abolition of all customs duties, and the removal of all restrictions on trade.

To one who stands beneath the glare of an electric light, those objects within the illumined space are rendered unusually vivid and distinct; while the darkness beyond looks all the more black and dense; and the figures in the shadows take on the shapes that fancy gives them. Mr. George possesses a keen perception and a glowing imagination; and his logic is sometimes dazzled by the glare of his brilliant rhetoric. He sees clearly, and portrays with fidelity, those objects that fall within the illumined space about him; but the dim, half-lighted gloaming that fringes the outer bounds of his vision he peoples with pessimistic spectres, weird and gaunt, to trouble and affright us; and the reader who follows him to the end may be somewhat in doubt whether he be a veritable seer, or only a man who has been startled by a ghost. But, whether seer or alarmist, or somewhat of both, Mr. George is an accomplished writer with the power to command attention, and intensely in earnest, and no writer has done more to push to the front the questions concerning capital and labor that are now claiming universal attention.

In the year 1849, Edward Kellogg published a book entitled "Labor and Capital," which has since been republished. It attracted little attention at the time of its first appearance, there being then no awakened interest on the subjects discussed. Mr. Kellogg exhibits the rapid growth of aggregated wealth up to the time of his writing, and the relative increase of poverty among the masses of the people. The remedy proposed by him is a practical abolition of interest; and he elaborates a scheme by which he claims that interest may be reduced to the rate of one and one-tenth per cent. per annum. The book is the product of the patient study and observation of a man of wide business experience, is clearly written, and deserves to be read. It was republished in 1874.

One of the best discussions of the tariff, from the stand-point of the protectionist, will be found in a work by Mr. Henry M. Hoyt, published in 1886, entitled "Protection vs. Free Trade." The opposing view is strongly supported in the work of Henry George, entitled "Protection or Free Trade," published also in 1886.

In all standard works on the subject of political economy the doctrines of protection and free trade are discussed, the argument being generally that of the English free-trade school with which the reading public have long been familiar. Henry C. Carey, who is a protectionist, treats the subject historically, and supports his view with an extended array of facts. The most complete historical treatise is perhaps the special work of R. W. Thompson, published in 1888. "The History of the Tariff," by F. W. Taussig, is well written and reliable. Horace Greeley, in his work on "Political Economy," contributes valuable thought to the discussion.

As a general treatise on the subject of political economy, "Elements of Political Economy," by Francis Wayland, recast by Chapin, although designed for a school-book, possesses much merit, and is as comprehensive in scope as many of the more pretentious works.

"Principles of Political Economy," by John Stuart Mill, pub-

lished in 1848, has perhaps received a wider acceptance than
any other work on that subject except that of Adam Smith's
"Wealth of Nations." Mill's style is clear and attractive, and
his views are comprehensive. As a general exposition of economic science his work is not excelled by that of any modern
author.

CHAPTER II.

CHANGED CONDITIONS.

In the United States, within the last fifty years, there has
been a development of industry and a growth of wealth wholly
unprecedented in the world's history. We are accustomed to
regard this inordinate increase of wealth as the measure of our
progress in the line of an improved civilization, and to speak of
the great gain as a blessing enjoyed in common by the whole
people.

That there have been secured to the masses of the people
opportunities for increased enjoyment as common privileges of
all, and that the average amount of toil required for the maintenance of the family has diminished, there can be no question.
But, with all the multiplication of wealth, and increased power
of labor through the employment of ingenious machinery and
the use of electricity and steam, there have come also changed
conditions and new relations. The entire country has been
interlaced with lines of railway; distance has been annihilated;
New York and San Francisco, Chicago and New Orleans speak
together as neighbors standing face to face; the products of
one section are carried a thousand miles as readily as formerly
they might have been hauled the distance of a day's drive, and
are distributed throughout the nation in universal competition
with the products of every other section. Dakota raises wheat
for Massachusetts; Massachusetts makes shoes for California.
Flour from the mills of Wisconsin competes with the flour of
the mills of Pennsylvania, ground from wheat grown within a
stone's throw of the latter, in the little stores in the village near
by. The clothing we wear is manufactured five hundred or a

thousand miles away; the wagons and ploughs, reapers and mowers of the farmers on the prairies of Kansas and Nebraska are built in the workshops of Ohio. On the same day, in any little village, may be found commercial travellers from places five hundred miles apart, competing with each other in the sale of the same articles of manufacture. The mechanic of New England finds his customers in Iowa and Illinois, and the farmer of Illinois finds a market for his grain among the hills of Vermont.

The independence of communities has been destroyed, and every man has become but a part, one of sixty million factors, in a universal system of production and exchange. His competitors are no longer his neighbors; they are men in New York, Massachusetts, Ohio, and Illinois. The power of individuals is no longer circumscribed within the limits of small localities. The people of a mighty nation have been woven together in a web of interdependent relations, that may be held in the grasp of a single hand, and converted into a tossing blanket by the Samsons of commerce.

Increased opportunities for trade have opened the way to unlimited acquisitions of wealth, and the fruits of a nation's toil are gathered by the skilful and the unscrupulous alike, and piled in heaps of imposing grandeur beyond the reach of a struggling crowd of dependent poor.

The Napoleons of commerce lay tribute at will on a nation's trade, and augment their stores of wealth with a speed that increases in accelerated ratio as their fortunes grow.

In the place where once sat the village shoemaker now sits the cobbler, sewing ripped seams and patching holes in old shoes. In the place of a dozen wagon-makers is a man putting new spokes in old wheels, tightening tires, or renewing worn-out axles.

The blacksmith has become a shoer of horses or a sharpener of ploughs. The tailor is almost extinct. He is still found in cities, from whence he goes forth at intervals, with his samples and his tape, to take the dimensions and estimate the superficial area of a few patrons, whose tastes are beyond the range of the ready-made clothing store, whose articles of apparel are cut to fit the composite man of the period. The chair-maker and the weaver are but faded memories; and the cabinet-maker has given way to the undertaker, who sells ready-made coffins, and rides in state on funeral days. The millwright was driven out by the roller process; and the ranks of the house-painter have been decimated in a disastrous war with mixed paints. The mason and carpenter are still on dry ground above the flood of progress that has swept away their brother artisans, though many of their possessions also have been carried away on the swelling tide. The horse-rake, the two-horse cultivator, the mower, twine-binder, and steam-thresher have taken the place of men; and the farmer buys his fence at the hardware store, in a roll of jagged wire.

Manufacturing industries have abandoned the country village, and gathered the people under the smoke of mighty cities. The city has grown and the village decayed. In the place of a host of artisans, who once clustered in every hamlet, breaking the dull uniformity of village life with a variety of employment and a diversity of experience, we have duplicates of the village merchant, who for twenty per cent. stands guard over a stock of foreign wares which he vends for cash or exchanges for butter and eggs; while the city has grown monotonous in its confusion of over-abundant variety that satiates and cloys the senses like a museum of curiosities gathered for show.

This is truly an era of material ideas, aims, and ambitions. Every man has become a factor in an immense money-making scheme,—a wheel in the great industrial machine. The life of each has become a part of an universal routine. He moves along well-defined paths marked out for him by the shaping hand of a material destiny, reading as he goes the familiar admonition, " Keep off the grass."

In the industrial world everything is now done by machinery. Each worker performs an assigned part; and his labor is of value only in unison with that of many others. His work is often one continued round of repetition requiring no thought and little skill. He learns no trade that can be carried on independent of costly machinery, which must form a part of a manufacturing establishment requiring large capital to own or to operate. He cannot work without permission; he must first be employed. He is one of a brigade, all moving together under the command of a single head. He works for stipulated wages, and has no control over the product of his labor.

For the opportunity to work he may be dependent on the will of a single man, who adds to or cuts from his working-force of men, according to the pointings of the index on the register of his own interests, as an engineer regulates the force of steam by the markings of the steam-gauge of his engine.

If the laborer lose his place, he may be compelled to change his residence, and to seek employment in a distant locality, without the certainty of securing it, except after such delay and expense as he is unable to afford.

In the place of the independent artisan in his own shop, the proprietor of his own labor, we have the dependent factory-hand or iron-worker, a single part of a great and complex machine whose place may be supplied in an hour, should he drop out.

Says Mr. Andrew Carnegie, " We assemble thousands of operators in the factory, in the mine, and in the counting-house, of whom the employer can know little or nothing, and to whom the employer is little better than a myth. All intercourse between them is at an end. Under the law of competition the employer of thousands is forced into the strictest economies, among which the rate paid to labor figures prominently; and often there is friction between the employer and employé, between capital and labor, between the rich and the poor. Human society loses ' homogeneity.' "

By the aid of machinery, the productive power of labor, in many departments of industry, has been multiplied from twenty-to a hundredfold; and it would be quite within bounds to say that, in this country, the total power of labor has been increased tenfold. In the production of food the increase is not so great; but it is two or three times as great as it was fifty years ago. One-half the labor power of the whole country is sufficient to produce all that the people consume, although the present consumption of the products of labor must be more than double what it was fifty years ago.

Flouring-mills run to their full capacity for three months could supply the flour for a year's consumption; our cotton-mills, woollen-mills, and iron-mills, in six months, could supply a year's demand for their products.

In every town or city there may always be found idle men and others who, though not idle, are ineffectively employed; and there is always a man ready for every vacant place. A single insertion in a metropolitan newspaper of a two-line advertisement for a coachman or a clerk wanted is often sufficient to secure the response of a hundred needy applicants.

What shall be done with all this labor? How shall be secured equal opportunities to each man in this pushing, surging crowd of workers, where each, per force of necessity, must rudely jostle his neighbor to save himself from being trampled upon?

If the labor that is performed, even at the prices that are paid, could be equitably distributed among all, so that each might have like command of the products of industry, there would be no difficulty arising out of the excess of labor. But what is to prevent A from working twelve months, while B finds employment for but six months of the year? If B receives only the wages of six months, he can consume only the products of six months' labor. When a great number of people are unemployed one-half or one-third of the time, the demand for the products which they consume is proportionally reduced.

The increase of the product at any time beyond the effective demand rapidly lowers prices; so manufacturers, being on guard against over-production, cut off labor to reduce the product; and since, by the very act of reducing production, consumption is reduced, the effect of this form of competition often is to defeat its purpose by distributing the equilibrium of the industries. These effects are not always quickly manifested, for the reason that those who suffer enforced idleness supply their demands for perishable products by drawing from their store of savings, while those who are continuously employed save a larger part of their earnings; but the effect is to continually increase the number and dependence of the poor, and thereby to narrow the market for the products of industry.

An equitable division of labor among all workers, and relatively equal wages, in conformity with the principles of a sound social economy, is one of the conditions essential to universal and continued prosperity. Individual misfortune, differences in individual economy, inequalities in the numbers who compose the families of laboring men, and the power of capital in unjust measure to absorb the earnings of the workers, would, however, still remain the potent factors of inequality.

An equitable distribution of labor among the workers is necessary for the general good. How is such distribution to be secured? Evidently not by artificial arrangement, nor by the direct application of legislative authority. The shutting down of iron-mills and factories from time to time, in order to prevent over-production, often is, under present conditions, a business necessity, essential to the welfare of both employer and employé. But it is a harsh and unsatisfactory remedy, attended with great loss of labor, and injurious in its effects upon other industries. It is a measure open to serious abuses; only temporary in its results; and, without combination among all employers in the same industry, which in itself is a menace to the welfare of other industries, impracticable. The only effective and permanent remedy must be sought in some measure or policy that will secure to the entire people the opportunity for constant employment. Some relief, no doubt, will be found in an extended field for the employment of labor. When the old-time occupations of woman were taken away she found new ones. When she put away the spinning-wheel, the distaff, and the loom, she found no time for idle leisure. The training of her children, the decoration of her home, and a variety of social duties made new requisitions on her time. When the sewing-machine multiplied the power of the needle, she increased her wardrobe, and added more elaborate ornament to her apparel.

The demand for a more universal education of the people, it is to be hoped, may, in the near future, claim the time of the young, and thus, in part, relieve the productive occupations from the force of that feverish competition through which first one industry and then, in turn, another is depressed by a fluctuating surplus that renders values unsteady, and thereby endangers capital, which, to guard against possible loss, demands a wider margin of profit, and secures it by reducing wages or by restricting production; that turns trade into speculation, and makes the earnings of labor the stake to be raffled for by the gamblers on 'change.

The nearer values can be kept to a definite standard, and the more gradual the changes, the better always for the people. In the earlier part of the century, before our present industrial civilization had swept away the old conditions, each family consumed a much larger share, than now, of the product of its own labor. The houses in which the people dwelt were the direct product of their own labor and that of local mechanics. The lumber was sawed at the neighboring mill, out of logs cut by their own hands, and hauled by their own teams. There were then no great yards stacked with sawed and dressed lumber shipped from distant localities. The flour consumed in each community was ground at the local mill, from wheat grown on the farm near by. The clothing of the farmer and of the mechanic was the product of his own household. The food of the farmer was supplied from his own farm, and that of the mechanic from the neighborhood in which he dwelt. Each community was, in great measure, an independent social and industrial organization forming a complete circle for the rounds of exchange ; and commerce did not then, as now, sweep in one unbroken tide from Maine to California, overleaping mountain ranges, gathering volume over a wide-extended sea of human industry, and commingling on its crest the products of New England and Illinois; it was then as but a wave on a little inland lake, which, ere it gathers force or volume, is wasted in ripples on the shore near by.

To-day the farmer and the mechanic buys his clothing ready made ; and the money he gives in exchange is carried hundreds of miles away.

The grocery store supplies him with flour, canned fruits, and cured meats brought from distant places, and sold at varying prices, the net result of the manipulations of two or three sets of middle-men, each seeking a profit out of whatever passes through his hands. Then the exchange of products was more direct, and relatively much smaller in amount. To-day every product of labor is tossed into the whirlpool of universal commerce, and each man is engaged in a struggle with every other man to get more out than he puts in.

Instead of sailing in small vessels over the placid waters of a quiet inland lake, commerce, in heavy-burdened ships, ranges over a storm-swept sea, where only the more experienced and skilful mariner can steer clear of hidden rocks, and only the old sailor is able to read the portent of a threatening sky, and reef his sails before the oncoming of the angry storm, which shall wreck the vessel and scatter the cargo of the inexperienced adventurer; where pirates ply their trade and rob the weak; and where greater fortunes are often gathered out of the salvage of sunken cargoes than from the profits of legitimate commerce. We may not wish for the return of the olden time, when privation indeed was more general than now, but the pinch of extreme poverty was less severe and more seldom felt; when there were no millionaires and no tramps; when there was less of luxury, but more general content; but we may invoke the return of one of the advantages then enjoyed. The producer and consumer were neighbors then; it would be better if they were neighbors now. If, instead of a few great manufacturing centres, manufactures could be so distributed as to bring producer and consumer into the nearest possible proximity, great benefit, both material and moral, would accrue to the people at large.

Capital is not interested in leading to this result, but the people are. Transportation for the sake of transportation, trade for the sake of trade, may furnish to surplus capital opportunities for profit; but labor bears the burden.

The spirit of American trade is best expressed in that slang proverb, "Business is business." A healthy social economy must be founded on nobler sentiments than those which gave birth to this maxim of commercial piracy.

Commerce for the purpose of supplying the wants of the people is a necessity; commerce for the purpose of supplying opportunities to middle-men is but an organized scheme to levy tribute. Under present conditions of production and trade, results like the following are possible.

Illinois is a State rich in agriculture, capable of supplying food for ten millions of people. Suppose she had, within her limits, cotton- and woollen-mills, and skilled workmen to operate them, enough to supply all the cotton and woollen fabrics required for the consumption of the people of the United States. Suppose that these industries in her midst had reached the highest degree of perfection, and that like industries had not yet been established elsewhere. Her manufactures supply the wants of the whole people. We will assume, further, that she is supplied with other manufacturing industries sufficient to meet the wants of her own people. Her cotton and woollen fabrics are sold in every city and village in the nation, bringing in a continual flood of money. As all her people need for home consumption is supplied at home, she has no need to buy beyond her own limits. Her trade with the people of other States is an exchange of cottons and woollens for money. The process goes on till other States are drained of money. Then comes financial pressure. The people who have been buying more than they have been selling resort to loans. They borrow from the capitalists of Illinois and pay interest. If an attempt be made to establish cotton and woollen industries in other States, first capital must be secured; then skilled labor must be brought in, and skilled labor is loath to emigrate, except on condition of assured employment and higher wages. Small mills, burdened with interest on capital and higher rates of transportation, and without the advantage of an established trade, are unable to compete with the strong and skilfully-managed establishments of Illinois. A condition of dependence is brought about, similar to that which exists to-day between England and Ireland.

Here are two islands, separated only by a channel of the sea, each enjoying all the advantages of a salubrious climate and a fertile soil. , Their industries have been developed under the same laws, both alike enjoying the advantages of a trade untrammelled by protective duties; and yet England is rich and Ireland is poor. The area of England is less than double the area of Ireland; yet the incomes of the English people are nearly thirty times as great as those of the people of Ireland; the houses of England average, in value, two and one-half times the value of the dwellings of Ireland; while the rental value of the lands of Ireland, per acre, is less than one-third the rental value of the lands of England. Why? England obtained an earlier start in industrial progress. Her manufacturing industries became established and strong. Ireland grew oats, and cattle and hogs, and potatoes; England made cloth and iron. Nature fixes no bounds to production in manufacturing industries, nor is consumption limited by fixed needs; while the product of agriculture is measured by the capabilities of the soil, and the number of people is the measure of the demand. A

3

manufacturing industry, in its infancy, in Ireland, could not compete with capital and skill in England, where every industry had become a part of an associated group of industries, thus securing the greatest possible economy of production in each; and so the Irish kept on raising oats and potatoes, cattle and hogs; while England gathered in the wealth of the nations, and her capital flowed abroad in the shape of loans and railway bonds, to burden the industries of poorer nations with perpetual tribute to the English people; and, having exhausted the field of most profitable investment elsewhere, is now absorbing the most profitable industries of the people of the United States. True, there were other causes; but they became effective, and produced results through the operation of the leading cause which I have stated.

In time, after the people of other States had sent their money to Illinois, and gotten it back in the form of loans, they would begin to ship their products abroad, selling at whatever price the market would command, or shipping to Illinois and selling in competition with the produce of the farms of Illinois, as the Irish sell the produce of their lands in England in competition with the English farmer, to pay for what they buy of the English manufacturer. The accumulated capital of Illinois would overflow into the other States in the form of loans; there would be an era of apparent prosperity, followed by years of adversity and commercial dependence. This, of course, is an overdrawn picture of what even might be in the United States; but, in its illustration of the operation of economic laws, under certain conditions, it is a true picture. It is essential to the welfare of States, and of communities even smaller than States, that the balance of trade be preserved with the world at large. The evil which I have illustrated is, in a great measure, self-corrective, at the expense, however, of permanent loss to individuals and communities. The people of a county, burdened with a foreign debt, may consume less food and less clothing, and live in meaner houses, and get out of debt; but when interest accumulates too rapidly, mortgages mature, and money goes out faster than it comes in, and prices of real estate go down, and farms begin to fall into the hands of the foreign creditor, it is not only those in debt who suffer, but the people of the county, except those who may be able to thrive upon the adversity of others. When such conditions are not confined to a county, but spread over a State, the evil is intensified and the period of adversity prolonged.

It has been claimed that the relative conditions which I have described exist between the New England and the Western States. It is not the purpose here to inquire whether or not this claim is well founded; what I seek to show is, that the way is open for such conditions to establish themselves.

It is to the interest of every community, so far as practicable, to maintain commercial and industrial independence. A policy shaped to this end will necessarily be subordinated to those controlling conditions which will confine its operation within somewhat narrow limits, yet it is a policy which should never be lost sight of nor abandoned.

Money accumulates in the centres of manufacturing and commercial industries, and goes out again in the form of loans on agricultural lands, until the whole country is laid under tribute to aggregated wealth at the great money-centres. Every great city is the body of an immense commercial octopus, whose innumerable arms reach out and gather in the wealth of the tributary area that surrounds and feeds it.

Until the prices of the products of agriculture have felt the effects of a limitation of the agricultural area, the capital employed in agriculture in the United States, except in some favored localities, will not bear the tax of even a low rate of interest, unless, in the mean while, the relations of the industries shall be somewhat changed by means of legislative modifications of conditions and tendencies that now prevail.

It is my purpose in the following chapters to pursue the inquiries suggested in this: First, to ascertain what are the facts with regard to the distribution of the products of labor; second, to consider the economic forces that control production and distribution; third, to ascertain what remedies there are that may be applied to the correction of industrial evils, if any are found to exist, which are not the necessary outgrowth of essential economic conditions.

CHAPTER III.

STATISTICS OF PRODUCTION AND DISTRIBUTION.

THE distribution of the products of labor can be ascertained only by consulting the facts disclosed by statistics.

The census of 1880 shows the number of persons of each occupation, and gives a carefully-prepared exhibit of all manufacturing and mechanical industries conducted in factory or shop, embracing each establishment whose gross annual product exceeds five hundred dollars per annum, showing amount of capital invested (both personal and real); the average number of workers employed during the year; the total amount of wages paid (including salaries of managers, etc.) during the year; the total cost of materials used, and the total value of all products.

The statistics of railways, telegraphs, telephones, steam navigation, fisheries, insurance, and mining are also given. The statistics of agriculture disclose the number of workers, the number of acres and amount of each crop, and the total value of the whole, as well as the values of farms and farm property.

The information contained in the census reports, with other statistics embraced in the following chapter, arranged and analyzed, enable us to determine with a sufficient degree of accuracy, not only the amount of the product, but also the manner of its distribution.

AGRICULTURE.

The statistics of agriculture of 1880 show the total value of the entire agricultural product for the year 1879, including that which was consumed on the farm, to be $2,212,540,927. In arriving at this estimate, the food of meat-producing animals was deducted from the gross product, otherwise this item would be twice counted, once in the form of corn and hay, and once in the form of cattle and hogs sold or consumed.

It has been contended that this amount is altogether too low. Edward Atkinson adds $1,000,000,000 *to cover amount consumed on the farm.* I am unable to find any warrant for this addition to the census estimate. The census purports to give the total value of all products, including the amount consumed on the farm and the amount on hand. The value of crops appears to have been estimated full high, and I am unable to perceive wherein there could have been omissions which, in the aggregate, would greatly alter the census figures. Atkinson, however, quotes a letter from Mr. Nimmo, chief of the Bureau of Statistics, dated October 21, 1884, in which Mr. Nimmo says, "The estimate of $3,600,000,000 for the products of agriculture was given me by Mr. J. R. Dodge a year ago, as the result of careful investigations, and he firmly adheres to that estimate. . . . The census of 1880 gives $2,213,402,564 as the estimated value of farm productions. This, however, does not include the increased value of live-stock, nor the value of the products of pasturage on the public lands. It also omits, to a very large extent, the products of horticulture."

The increased value of live-stock was properly omitted. The omitted value of horticultural products could not amount to any considerable sum. The orchard and market-garden products are included. The total product of pasturage on the public lands was relatively a small sum. The ranch business employs but a small number of persons and a large amount of capital. It belongs to the field of capital, rather than that of agricultural labor. But adding all these items claimed to have been omitted would not increase the census estimate ten per cent.

But an explanation of the manner in which Mr. Dodge reaches the result so at variance with the amount stated in the census reports is given in a table which he calls his corrected estimate of the value of farm products of the year covered by the census returns. That table is as follows:

TABLE No. 1.

THE PRODUCT OF AGRICULTURE FOR THE YEAR 1879.

Product.	Quantity.	Value.	Price.
Meat	. . . . .	$800,000,000	. . .
Poultry and eggs	. . . . .	180,000,000	. . .
Butter (pounds)	900,000,000	189,000,000	$0.21
Cheese "	300,000,000	28,500,000	.095
Milk consumed (gallons)	1,800,000,000	135,000,000	.075
		$1,332,500,000	

Product.	Quantity.	Value.	Price.
Corn (bushels)	1,754,591,676	$694,818,304	$0.396
Wheat "	459,483,137	436,968,463	.951
Oats "	407,858,999	146,829,240	.36
Rye "	19,837,595	14,992,686	.756
Barley "	43,997,495	29,302,832	.666
Buckwheat "	11,817,327	7,019,492	.594
Rice (pounds)	110,131,873	6,607,882	.06
		$1,336,538,399	
Hay (tons)	35,150,711	$409,505,783	$11.65
Irish potatoes (bushels)	169,458,539	$81,848,474	$0.483
Sweet potatoes "	33,378,693	15,020,412	.45
Peas and beans "	9,590,027	14,385,041	1.50
Market-garden products		21,761,250	
Orchard products		50,876,154	
Hops (pounds)	26,546,378	6,371,131	.24
		$190,262,462	
Cane sugar (hhds.)	178,872	$16,098,480	$90.00
Maple sugar (pounds)	36,576,061	4,754,888	.13
Cane molasses (gallons)	16,573,273	5,800,646	.35
Sorghum syrup "	28,444,202	9,386,587	.33
Maple syrup "	11,796,048	1,796,048	1.00
Honey (pounds)	25,743,208	5,663,506	.22
		$43,500,155	
Cotton (pounds)	2,771,797,156	$271,636,121	$0.098
Wool "	240,681,751	67,390,890	.28
Hemp (tons)	5,025	1,005,000	200.00
Flax (pounds)	1,555,546	391,387	.25
		$340,423,398	
Tobacco (pounds)	472,661,157	$38,758,215	$0.085
Flaxseed (bushels)	7,170,951	$8,963,689	$1.25
Grass seed "	1,317,701	1,976,552	1.50
Clover seed "	1,922,982	11,537,892	6.00
		$22,478,133	
Wines (gallons)	20,000,000	12,000,000	$0.60
Beeswax (pounds)	1,105,689	364,877	.33
Total value		$3,726,331,422	

In the foregoing table the meat product is estimated at more than double the value of the meat product of 1869, as given in the census report of 1870, when it was reported as a separate item. The value of poultry and eggs is nearly double the amount shown by the census estimates. The butter product is given as 93,000,000 pounds in excess of the sum of farm and factory product as shown in census returns, and the value is placed at twenty-one cents per pound, while the export value, as shown by the report of the Treasury Department for the second quarter of the fiscal year of 1879 and 1880, was fourteen and one-fifth cents. The price of oats is six cents more than the export value during the same period, and the price of cheese one-half cent more than the export value. Many other values are manifestly too high.

The estimates of the values of crops made by the Department of Agriculture are based on the prices obtained for that portion of the product which is sold. The unmerchantable part of the product which is consumed on the farm is for this reason valued too high. The estimates are made, as a rule, after prices have somewhat advanced beyond those obtained for the product which is sold early.

The average price is arrived at by averaging different localities in a State, and then by averaging the States. The result does not show the average price realized by the farmer. Where the prices of corn and oats are highest, there the largest proportion is consumed on the farm. Much of the corn sold is purchased and consumed by farmers elsewhere; shipments are made from where prices are low to where prices, owing to short crops, are high, thus adding cost of freight and commissions to a considerable part of that which is consumed on farms, in feeding meat-producing animals and work-animals. I have, in the following table, put wheat five cents, corn 3.6 cents, and oats four cents lower than the Agricultural Department estimates, but have valued the amount consumed on the farm at the average price of the entire product, whereas it is in fact considerable more. The per cent. of corn shipped from the county is, in the Western States, 24.7; in New England, 2.4; in Middle States, 10.8.

Of the total product of $2,212,540,927 for the whole United States for the year 1879, as exhibited by the census of 1880, the sum of $203,980,137, or $467.45 per capita for each agricultural worker, is credited to the State of Illinois.* Reports of the

---

* Report of Department of Agriculture for 1883.

Department of Agriculture of that State give the farm prices of agricultural products for that year of every product of importance. The quantity of product returned in the census is so much greater than that shown by the agricultural reports of the State, based upon assessors' returns, as to leave little room for doubt that the quantities shown by the census returns fully cover, if they do not exceed, the amount of the actual product.

Statistics of farm crops furnished by assessors are always incomplete, and the crop is always in excess of the amount shown by assessors' returns. The reason for this is not, as commonly asserted, a disposition among farmers to underestimate their crops and withhold information,—a disposition sometimes manifested by the most ignorant,—but the negligent manner in which the work of obtaining these statistics is attended to by assessors, whose principal duty does not relate to the collection of statistics of farm crops, and who are often indifferent as to the manner in which this incidental service is performed. The statistics of the census were obtained by persons specially charged with that work, which was carefully and conscientiously performed. Inaccuracies in reports given by farmers would naturally occur more frequently in over-estimates than under-estimates of the amount of crops grown.

In the following table of the agricultural products of the State of Illinois for the census year, the quantities given are taken from the census of 1880, while the prices of the cereals and of hay and potatoes are taken from the agricultural report of the State. Prices of other commodities are estimated.

TABLE No. 2.

PRODUCTS OF AGRICULTURE OF THE STATE OF ILLINOIS FOR THE YEAR 1879.

Product.	Quantity.	Price.	Value.
Meat product	. . .	. . .	$46,000,000
Poultry sold or consumed	. . .	. . .	3,000,000
Butter made on farms (pounds)	53,657,943	$0.15	8,053,690
Cheese made on farms "	1,003,069	.09	92,976
Milk consumed on farms	. . .	. . .	3,000,000
Milk sold (gallons)	45,419,719	.07	3,179,380
Eggs produced (dozens)	35,978,297	.15	5,396,745
			$68,722,791

Product.	Quantity.	Price.	Value.
Corn (bushels)	325,792,481	$0.32	$104,253,694
Wheat "	51,110,502	.87	44,166,136
Oats "	63,189,200	.22	13,901,624
Rye "	8,121,785	.47	1,467,239
Barley "	1,229,523	.46	565,580
Buckwheat "	178,859	.60	117,315
			$164,471,588
Hay (tons)	2,578,786	$6.37	$15,717,713
Irish potatoes (bushels)	10,365,307	.50	5,182,653
Sweet potatoes "	249,407	.50	124,708
Peas and beans "	69,248	1 50	103,872
Market-garden products	. . . .	. .	959,962
Orchard products	. . . .	. .	3,502,583
Hops (pounds)	7,778	.24	1,859
			$25,593,345
Maple sugar (pounds)	80,193	$0.13	$10,425
Maple syrup (gallons)	40,077	1.00	40,077
Sorghum syrup "	2,265,993	.33	755,331
Honey (pounds)	1,310,806	.20	262,160
			$1,067,993
Cotton (pounds)	8,928	$0.09	$803
Wool "	6,093,066	.28	1,706,057
Hemp (tons)	2¼	2.00	450
Flax (tons fibre)	61	5.00	30,500
			$1,737,810
Tobacco (pounds)	3,935,825	$0.08	$314,866
Flaxseed (bushels)	1,812,438	1.00	1,812,438
Grass seed "	213,329	1.50	319,993
Clover seed "	138,191	5.00	690,955
			$3,138,252
Wines (gallons)	326,323	$0.50	$163,160
Beeswax (pounds)	45,640	.33	15,200
Broom corn "	11,645,100	.05	582,255
Wood cut (cords)	1,763,334	2.00	3,526,668
Lumber	. . . .	. .	3,952,800
Hungarian seed (bushels)	43,776	.50	21,888
			$8,261,971

Product.	Quantity.	Value.
Horses sold		$2,800,000
Castor beans (bushels)	24,344	30,000
		$2,830,000
Total gross agricultural product		$275,823,750

On the 20th of December, 1879, the price of wheat was much higher than at the date taken for the estimate above given; the price of corn had not advanced; the prices of cattle and swine had declined; while the prices of hay, oats, rye, barley, and buckwheat had advanced.

From the gross product must be deducted the value of the food consumed by work and meat-producing animals, and the seeds required for the next year. Of the hay grown probably eighty-five per cent. was fed on the farm. The corn consumed on the farm was, according to the estimate of the Department of Agriculture of 1883, sixty-eight per cent. Probably sixty per cent. of the oat crop was consumed on the farm.

The amount required for seed is readily ascertained from the acreage of crops as shown by the census report of 1880 Basing our estimate on these ratios, we reach the following result:

Value of hay consumed on the farm	$12,860,056
" " corn " " " "	66,722,242
" " oats " " " "	6,340,974
Cereals, grass seed, and potatoes, etc., required for seed next year	5,730,800
Total	$91,154,072

Leaving a net product of $184,669,678,—a sum which is $19,310,459 *less than the census estimate.*

The report of the Illinois Department of Agriculture for the year 1880 shows:

		Value.
Sheep sold in 1879	191,398	$613,156
Cattle " " "	409,982	16,751,450
Swine " " "	1,984,294	16,640,061
Total		$34,004,667

Average weight of hogs sold, 210 pounds, and average price $3.99 per hundred, *net.*

But little beef or mutton was consumed on the farm.

The total population of the State was 3,077,871, forty-four per cent. of which, or 1,354,153, were engaged in agriculture, the number of agricultural workers being 436,371.

Mulhall's estimate of the consumption of meat in the United States is one hundred and twenty pounds per capita per annum. One hundred and twenty-five pounds of pork per capita to the agricultural population of the State would, at the prices at which that product was sold, amount to $6,670,765, which is probably sufficient to cover farm consumption of pork, beef, and mutton. This amount, added to the total above, gives a total meat product of $40,675,442. To cover omissions in the foregoing table I have put the meat product at $46,000,000.

In 1880 the total number of cattle in Illinois, as shown by the census, was 2,384,322. Of those, 865,913 were milch cows. The total number of cattle slaughtered or sold for slaughter in the State in 1879 probably reached 600,000; but those not embraced in agricultural reports, used in the home markets principally, and slaughtered on the farm, would not average a value of over thirty dollars per head.

The number of hogs in Illinois on June 1, 1880, was 5,170,266; the number in 1879 was less. The number reported as dying with disease in 1879 was 182,877. This number, added to the number reported as marketed, would make 2,167,171. Making allowance for the number kept over to the next year, and for the light weights and inferior quality of many slaughtered on the farm, it will be seen that the meat product cannot vary greatly from the estimate adopted in the foregoing table.

The proportion of corn shipped from the county in the Western State is given in the census report as 24.7 per cent. The amount shipped from the county in Illinois in 1882 is given by the Department of Agriculture as thirty-two per cent.

The cost to the farmers of Illinois for the year 1879, of agricultural implements, machinery, wagons, windmills, bagging, twine, tools, fencing wire, and salt, and the cost of commercial fertilizers, blacksmithing, and the annual outlay in maintaining barns and other out-buildings, was not less than $30,000,000. Subtracting this sum from the product already ascertained, we have a final net product to the farmers of Illinois of $154,669,718, or $49,310,419 less than the net product exhibited by the census.

This gives a per capita product to each agricultural worker of $354.45. Allowing one-third of this amount for rents or profits on capital, we have $236.30 to each worker, and $51,556,572, or five per cent. on the value of lands, farming utensils, and live-stock (the value of farm dwellings not being included), to the credit of rent or profit on capital invested. However, in the census estimates no deduction was made for expenditures. Food for cattle was deducted, but food for work-animals does not appear to have been deducted from the gross amount.

The estimates made of the products of Illinois are no doubt a fair standard of comparison by which to judge the estimates of the products of other States. Tested by this standard, the estimated total product for the United States is too high.

The total value of sheep, cattle, and swine, slaughtered at slaughtering establishments in the United States in 1879, was $256,738,906. To obtain farm values, freights and commissions must be deducted from this sum. The total value, in the hands of farmers, did not exceed $210,000,000. This amount does not include animals slaughtered by retail butchers. In the following table I have estimated the total product at $470,000,000. This may be an under-estimate; but I am unable to find any warrant for an estimate of over $500,000,000. I have adopted the value given by Mr. Dodge as to most products, many of which are too high.

TABLE No. 3.

PRODUCTS OF AGRICULTURE, 1879.

Product.	Quantity.	Value.	Price.
Meat	. . . . . .	$470,000,000	
Poultry and eggs: census, 456,910,916 dozen . . .	. . . . . .	95,000,000	
Butter made on farm (pounds)	800,000,000	120,000,000	$0.15 per pound.
Cheese made on farm (pounds)	30,000,000	2,700,000	.09 " "
Milk consumed, sold (gallons)	530,129,755	37,109,002	.07 " gallon.
Milk consumed on farm (gallons)	500,000,000	35,000,000	.07 " "
		$759,809,002	

Product.	Quantity.	Value.	Price.
Corn (bushels)	1,754,591,076	$649,199,918	$0.86 per bushel.
Wheat "	459,483,137	413,357,679	.90 " "
Oats "	407,858,999	130,514,859	.82 " "
Rye "	19,837,595	11,898,957	.60 " "
Barley "	43,977,495	26,386,497	.60 " "
Buckwheat (bushels) . .	11,817,327	7,019,492	.59.4 " "
Rice (pounds)	110,131,373	6,607,882	.06 " pound.
		$1,244,984,284	
Hay (tons)	35,150,711	$351,507,110	$10.00 per ton.
Irish potatoes (bushels) .	169,458,539	$81,848,474	$0.48.3 per bushel.
Sweet potatoes " .	33,878,693	15,020,412	.45 " "
Peas " .	6,514,977	3,500,000	
Beans " .	3,075,050	4,612,575	1.50 " "
Market-garden products	. . . . .	21,761,250	
Orchard products . . .	. . . . .	50,876,154	
Hops (pounds)	26,546,378	5,709,275	.20 " pound.
		$183,328,140	
Cane sugar (hogsheads) .	178,872	$16,098,480	$90.00 per hogsh'd.
Maple sugar (pounds) .	36,576,061	4,754,888	.13 " pound.
Cane molasses (gallons) .	16,573,273	5,800,646	.35 " gallon.
Sorghum syrup " .	28,444,202	9,386,507	.33 " "
Maple syrup " .	11,796,048	1,796,048	1.00 " "
Honey (pounds)	25,743,208	5,663,506	.22 " pound.
		$43,500,075	
Cotton (pounds)	2,771,797,156	$271,636,121	$0.098 per pound.
Wool "	240,681,751	67,390,890	.28 " "
Hemp (tons)	5,025	1,005,000	200.00 " ton.
Flax (pounds)	. . .	391,387	.25 " pound.
		$340,423,398	
Tobacco (pounds) . . .	472,661,157	$36,624,357	
Flaxseed (bushels) . . .	7,170,951	$8,963,689	$1.25 per bushel.
Grass seed " . . .	1,317,701	1,976,552	1.50 " "
Clover seed " . . .	1,922,982	11,537,892	6.00 " "
		$22,478,133	
Wines (gallons)	20,000,000	$12,000,000	
Beeswax (pounds) . . .	1,105,689	864,877	
Total		$2,995,019,376	

Brought forward $2,995,019,376
Add to cover sales of horses for use of
    others than farmers   100,000,000

    Total $3,095,019,376

From the above table should be deducted:

Value of seeds required for next year $87,700,000
Grain and hay fed to stock 880,000,000

    $967,700,000

    Net agricultural product $2,127,319,376

If we accept the figures of Mr. Dodge, we must deduct for seed and feed for stock, $1,049,600,000, leaving a net product of $2,676,731,422. To this sum should be added value of horses and mules sold, to be used for other than agricultural purposes, which, I think, I have estimated full high. The net result would then be, according to Dodge, $2,776,731,422.

In the census of 1880 the amount of cheese made on farms is given as 27,272,489 pounds; cheese made in factories as 215,885,361 pounds. Mr. Dodge gives the total cheese production as 300,000,000 pounds, and then adds an estimate of 1,800,000,000 gallons of milk consumed. The amount reported in the census, as sold to factories and others, is 530,129,755 pounds. The product given by Dodge would require the milk of about 16,000,000 cows. The number reported in the census is 12,443,120. He also embraces in his estimate about 4,000,000 bushels of cow-peas at $1.50 per bushel.

The total value of agricultural implements manufactured in 1880 is given in the census table of manufactures as $63,640,486; that of carriages and wagons, $64,951,615. The manufacturers' value of wagons, wheelbarrows, windmills, bagging, twine, tools, and salt sold annually to farmers and consumed in the process of agriculture is not less than $50,000,000. This would make the total amount of manufactured products annually consumed in agriculture $104,951,615. To this must be added cost of transportation and commissions and profits of middle-men, at least thirty per cent., making $136,437,099. The cost of commercial fertilizers used was $28,586,397. The cost of fencing purchased of manufacturers, the cost of blacksmithing, and the annual waste of capital invested in barns and other out-buildings (not counting the labor of the agricultural classes expended in building and repairs) was at least $50,000,000. The total amount of the expenses of agriculture in money paid to persons engaged in other industries, as here estimated, was $215,023,496. This leaves a net product of $1,912,296,880, or, if we accept the figures of Mr. Dodge, $2,461,607,926.

The forest product, consisting of wood and timber cut from farm lands, reported in table of product of agriculture, is not embraced in the above estimates. The amount is $95,774,735. A great part of this product probably represents the labor of persons returned in the census as laborers, and classed under the head of personal service.

The advantage of wood and fuel on the farm, not embraced in the amount returned as forest product, and the advantage of food without the intervention of railway transportation or middle-men, may be put down as equivalent to $50,000,000. Adding this sum, and the amount of the forest product stated, we obtain as the net value of the agricultural product $2,058,071,705. There are some products, the aggregate value of which is not counted, and some expenses—among others the cost of imported breeding animals—which are not included. But if we accept the figures of the census, $2,212,540,927, as the *net* product of agriculture for the year 1879, this sum is large enough to cover all possible omissions and under-estimates. I will, therefore, adopt that sum as the basis of subsequent estimates, although the amount is certainly too large, if treated as the net product.*

The number of laborers returned as engaged in agriculture is 7,670,497; omitting females and males under fifteen years of age, the number is 6,491,116. The total number of persons engaged in all occupations, not including females or males under

---

* Comparing the prices of agricultural products of the census year with those of 1889, it will be seen that the values of agriculture have suffered great reduction. The average price of wheat has gone down from ninety cents to seventy cents per bushel; the average price of corn from thirty-six cents to twenty-seven cents per bushel; the average price of oats from thirty-two cents to 22.6 cents per bushel; and there has been a corresponding reduction in the prices of hay and other products. The drouth of the present season will, however, reduce the product and advance prices.

fifteen, is 13,919,752. Of those persons classed as laborers under the head of personal service, a large number were employed, at least during part of the year, in some department of agriculture. We may, therefore, assume that the total population supported by agriculture was 25,000,000. This is Edward Atkinson's estimate, and it cannot vary far from the true number. This gives a per capita product of $88.50, or, $288.45 per capita for each person employed.

MANUFACTURES AND MINING.

I shall now endeavor to ascertain the value of the products of other industries.

Mr. Atkinson estimates the total value of the products of all industries at $10,000,000,000; and he gives the following table, furnished by Joseph Nimmo, chief of Census Bureau:

Agriculture	$3,600,000,000
Manufactures	5,369,579,191
Illuminating gas	30,000,000
Mining	236,275,408
Forestry (partly estimated)	455,000,000
Fisheries	43,046,053
Meat production and wool clip of ranches (est.)	40,000,000
Petroleum (manufactured product)	44,000,000
Total (materials out)	$9,817,900,000

Regarding the estimate of the product of manufactures, he quotes Mr. Nimmo, who says, "I conferred fully with acting superintendent of the census, Mr. Geo. W. Richards, an exceedingly intelligent and able man, who appears to have a thorough understanding of the whole census figures. Regarding the total value of the products of manufacture, he stated to me that, while there were some duplications in it, the omissions amount to very much more. It is certain that the values are, on the average, below the actual values, and that there is a considerable amount overlooked; besides, the census did not take into account the products of any establishment the value of whose products was less than five hundred dollars."

How far this statement is aside from the truth in regard to

the product of agriculture we have already seen. Now, as to manufactures. The total gross product of all manufactures, as shown by the census, was $5,369,579,191, the amount given in the statement of Mr. Nimmo *as the net product.* The total value of materials was $3,396,823,549 ; leaving a net or actual product of $1,972,755,642, a little more than one-third of the amount given by Mr. Nimmo and adopted by Mr. Atkinson. The materials consisted principally of manufactured products, which appear in the statement of gross products. For instance, the iron and steel product is $296,557,685. The iron and steel product is not an ultimate product, but enters into the manufacture of nails, forgings, castings, etc.; leather appears under seven different heads, and then again in boots and shoes and belting. Under the head of boots and shoes it appears at different stages of progress towards the ultimate product.

In vol. ii., "Census of the United States," 1880, page 2, notes on "statistics of manufactures," appears the following statement : " It is also evident that in estimating the contributions made by the manufacturing industries, as a whole, to the annual revenue of the country a similar deduction should be made. Thus, while the aggregate value of the manufactures of the United States is reported at $5,369,579,191, the value of the materials consumed therein is given at not less than $3,396,823,549. *It is the difference between these two sums,* $1,972,755,642, *which measures the net product of our manufacturing industries.* This deduction would be required to be made were all the materials of manufacture drawn in every case directly from agriculture; but, as a matter of fact, the product of one industry often becomes the materials of another, and the products of this perhaps, in turn, the materials of a third industry; and so the values of manufactured products are swollen by the repeated inclusion of the same original subject-matter. Thus, certain amounts of coal, iron-ore, limestone, and labor—not to speak of other elements—enter into and make up the value of pig-iron. All the latter may, a few months later, become the material of the manufacture of a certain quantity of bar-iron, the reported value of which, of course, includes the value of the pig-iron as well as the labor and other elements in the production of the bar. The bar-iron may again become the material for the manufacture of a certain body of machinery, the value of the latter including the value of the bar-iron, as well as the labor and other elements in its own production. In this way the value of the coal, iron-ore, and limestone reappears again and again through successive processes of manufacture. And this is statistically right. Only in this way can the facts of each industry by turns be exhibited. To omit these elements at any stage of production would be to misstate the facts of the particular industry concerned. But it is evident that this statistical condition renders it imperative not to consider the aggregated values of all products of manufacture as an addition to the wealth of the country, but, on the contrary, in all comparisons of the nature referred to, the value of materials should be uniformly deducted."

Edward Atkinson ("Distribution of Products," page 129) says that he reached the conclusion that the annual product of all industries in the United States was $10,000,000,000 in the following remarkable manner: "First, by converting that portion of the wheat crop which is consumed in the United States into bread, and a large portion of the corn into meal for final consumption; and to this secondary or final form I applied the average retail prices. I also ascertained, as nearly as possible, the ultimate value of dairy products and the like. Second, I converted the known quantity of textile fibres consumed within the United States into fabrics, and I then estimated these fabrics at their value in finished clothing at the average prices which are charged by shopkeepers. Third, I converted the known production of metals into machinery and other forms ready for final use, and valued them. Fourth, I valued the timber product as furniture, dwelling-houses, and the like. Fifth, I converted the sum of our imports into a value at its final point of consumption, by estimating the cost of distribution, and by other similar methods.

"Of course, this method is one which could not be made absolutely correct, especially by a private person working only in the intervals of active business."

Had Mr. Atkinson furnished an inventory of products showing the result of his labors in the imaginary *rôle* of farmer, miller, baker and butcher, spinner, weaver and tailor, blacksmith, carpenter and cabinet-maker, with a schedule of retail prices attached, it might have added to the interest and humor of the explanation. We would have then been advised how much of the iron he converted into watch-springs, and how much into stoves; how much into pins, and how much into pokers; how much of the timber was converted into joists and beams, and how much into matches and tooth picks; how much into pianos and fiddles, and how much into wheelbarrows and log wagons. It is not to be wondered at, that when Mr. Atkinson found that Mr. Nimmo's statistics brought a result corresponding to that which he had reached by a method of calculation so intricate and laborious, he was not in a mood to question Mr. Nimmo's figures. Mr. Atkinson and Mr. Nimmo having verified each other, their statements have been accepted as authoritative.

The following table gives the value of the products of the different industries as shown by the census report of 1880:

TABLE No. 4.

Industries.	Products.
Agriculture	$2,212,540,927
Manufactures	1,972,755,642
Coal	94,558,608
Salt	4,762,493
Petroleum	24,000,000
Iron-ore	23,156,957
Copper-ore	9,458,434
Lead	7,985,140
Zinc	4,240,006
Minor metals	3,387,444
Quarry products	18,000,000
Fish product	43,046,053
Gold and silver	203,141,764
Boat-building and repairing (including ships)	17,063,969
Lumber in logs not included in agricultural product	100,000,000
New railroads in 1879, 4746 miles, grading $5000 per mile	23,730,000
Railway and water transportation of freight	500,000,000
Total	$5,261,777,437
Total (agriculture omitted)	$3,049,236,510

The item of "lumber in logs" is an estimate, but is approximately correct. I have estimated the cost of grading new railroads at $5000 per mile, which amount, considering the location of the roads, will fully cover the cost. The cost of iron and steel is embraced in "products of manufacture," and of ties and timbers in forest products of agriculture, or "products of manufacture."

My statement of the amount of the petroleum product does not agree with that of Mr. Nimmo quoted above, for the reason that, in the figures given by him are embraced $13,000,000 worth of barrels and tin cans, and $1,200,000 worth of sulphuric acid, as well as other items which do not belong under that head.

INDUSTRIES NOT EMBRACED IN CENSUS REPORTS.

The employment tables of the census do not purport to embrace the product of the labor of retail butchers, tailors, dressmakers or milliners, nor of establishments yielding a gross annual product of less than five hundred dollars. Only the average number of employés is given; and the total number of persons employed is considerably larger. If we deduct from the number of persons set down in the occupation tables to each industry the number of those whose labor is embraced in the employment tables, the remainder will represent the number of those whose labor product is not included in the value of products already given. A large number of carpenters are in the employ of railway companies; and allowance must also be made for laborers employed in railway construction, the value of whose labor is included in the product already given.

Among those classed as carpenters, masons, plasterers, and painters, in the occupation tables, are many who are very irregularly employed, and many low-grade mechanics, whose average income is quite small. I present the following estimate of wages (or product which is the same in value) of those whose labor product is not embraced in the foregoing statement, except laborers in railway construction, and seventy-five thousand lumbermen embraced under head of laborers:

TABLE No. 5.

PRODUCT OF WORKERS NOT INCLUDED IN EMPLOYMENT TABLES OF CENSUS.

Occupation.	No. of Workers.	Wages or Product.	Average Wages.
Tailors and tailoresses	53,834	$21,533,600	$400 00
Milliners, dressmakers, seamstresses	181,662	49,957,050	275 00
Butchers, retail	90,000	36,000,000	400 00
Jewellers	15,000	6,600,000	400 00
Blacksmiths	59,812	59,200,000	400 00
Shoemakers	148,000	20,934,200	350 00
	548,308	$194,224,850	
Painters and paper-hangers	49,000	$17,150,000	$350 00
Plasterers	22,183	7,764,000	350 00
Masons	78,000	31,200,000	400 00
Builders and contractors	12,000	12,000,000	1,000 00
Carpenters	296,300	103,705,000	350 00
	457,483	$171,819,000	
Laborers	1,475,000	$442,500,000	$300 00
Clerks, salesmen, accountants . . .	445,513	. . . . .	. . . .
Agents	18,523	. . . . .	. . . .
Saloon-keepers, bar-tenders, etc. . .	68,461	. . . . .	. . . .
Traders and dealers	481,450	. . . . .	. . . .
Officials and employés of express companies	14,860	. . . . .	. . . .
Officials and employés of trade and transportation	9,702	. . . . .	. . . .
Others in trade and transportation .	159,389	. . . . .	. . . .
	1,197,898	$598,949,000	$500 00
Total	3,678,689	$1,407,492,850	

If we add this sum, less $53,730,000, the value of labor already counted in the items "lumber" and "railway construction," to the total product before ascertained, we have the sum of $6,615,540,287.

The number of workers whose labor product is now included in this total is 15,074,981. The number of workers in all occupations reported in the census, as shown in the occupation tables, is 17,392,099. The number whose labor is embraced in the foregoing estimates is therefore 2,317,118 less than the whole number of workers. The number of workers returned under the head of "telegraphs" and "telephones" is 18,256; under the head of "personal and professional service" is 4,074,238. Of these 1,859,223 are classed as "laborers." The nature of the work performed by the persons designated as laborers not being stated, it cannot be ascertained to what extent their work may be properly classed under the head of personal service. But if they should all be considered as engaged in some form of creative industry, the number already included in the foregoing estimate is only 102,103 less than the total number of workers engaged in constructive work, or in work the cost of which was added to the value of the product. The work of persons engaged in transportation or trade enters into the value of the product passing through their hands, just as the work of the farmer or manufacturer.

The cost of production and of transportation and the wages of merchants, clerks, book-keepers, travelling salesmen, traders, and all middle-men, are already included. There yet remains to consider the earnings of capital employed in trade, which enter into the price of the product as distributed at retail. There must be added a sum sufficient to cover the rent of buildings and the profits of capital employed in the wholesale and retail trade. There are no statistics which furnish adequate data for an estimate of the amount of the contribution to capital in this form; $500,000,000, which is ten per cent. of $5,000,000,000, will not exceed the true amount, and this we will assume to be the earnings of capital employed in trade. To this we will add $30,000,000, Mr. Nimmo's estimate of the value of illuminating gas, and $40,000,000, his estimate of the meat product and wool clip of the ranches,—items which have not yet been counted. This gives a total product of $7,185,540,287. This sum I regard as adequate to express the total product of all industries of the United States in 1879. The only way in which the amount can be materially increased is by raising the estimate of the earnings of capital in trade, or of the wages of those classes of workers whose wages are not embraced in the returns of the census. If we increase our estimate of the earnings of capital in trade, the share of the capital of the total product will be increased. If we increase the estimate of the wages of the workers whose wages are not embraced in the census returns, the actual earnings of capital will remain the same, while the share of labor will be increased absolutely and relatively. But no estimates within the scope of reasonable limits will greatly modify the general results arrived at.

There is no method by which the profits of capital employed in agriculture may be determined. The amount of capital employed in agriculture, including land, according to census estimates, is not less than $12,000,000,000. Three per cent. of this sum would be $360,000,000, leaving to the credit of labor employed in agriculture $1,852,540,927, or $241.52 to each worker.

WAGES.

TABLE No. 6.

WAGES IN INDUSTRIES OTHER THAN AGRICULTURE, AS SHOWN BY CENSUS.

Occupation.	No. Employed.	Total Annual Wages.	Average Wages.
Manufacturing and mechanical .	2,732,595	$947,953,795	$346.98
Mining coal and non-precious metals	229,475	71,992,502	346.73
Mining gold and silver	75,000 *	60,000,000 *	800.00 *
Quarries	39,000 †	15,000,000 *	384.61 *
Petroleum	9,869	4,381,572	454.10
Salt	4,289	1,260,023	293.77
Railway employés	418,957	195,350,013	466.27
Merchants' steam-craft	63,843	25,982,803	406.98
Fisheries	131,426	39,427,800 *	300.00 *
Boat-building	21,345	12,718,813	595.63
Telegraphs	14,928	4,886,128	327.30
Telephones , ...	3,338	901,400 *	300.00 *
Total	3,744,065	$1,379,849,849	$368.54
Omitting telegraphs and telephones	3,725,799	$1,374,062,321	

* Estimated.

† Census returns highest number employed during the year, not average number, as in other industries; the average number is much smaller. The total wages are much less than the amount given.

The total net product of the above-enumerated industries, telegraphs and telephones excepted, after deducting materials, and the product of the passenger traffic on railways, was $2,925,506,510. Deducting $1,374,062,321, the total amount of wages paid, from the value of the product, there remains the sum of $1,551,444,189 to cover any expenses which have not been deducted, to supply waste of capital, and apply as profits on capital invested.

I omit the receipts of railways on account of passenger traffic, for the reason that a large part of these receipts represents distribution and not production. The larger part, perhaps, should be credited to production; but it cannot be ascertained as a separate element, and is covered in the form of salaries of persons engaged in trade.

The earnings of railways were as follows:

Passenger traffic	$144,101,709
Express earnings	8,828,259
Mail services	10,472,813
Freight	417,047,813
Total	$580,450,594

Under the head of "freight" are included $902,055 of "earnings not analyzed."

The amount added to the value of the product by transportation is expressed in the amount of charges for freight, express, etc. The expenses of railway companies are not deducted from amount of product in tabular statement No. 7, which appear in this chapter, for the reason that these "expenses" cover cost of maintaining capital, and improvements as well. The cost of maintaining capital is not deducted from product of other industries in column showing product, and should not be, therefore, in case of railways.

The net product of the manufacturing and mechanical industries is $1,972,755,642. The amount of wages paid is $947,953,975. The product remaining is $1,024,801,847. The total capital employed in the manufacturing and mechanical industries is returned at $2,790,272,606, a little over $1000 to each worker. The claim has been made that this amount is not sufficiently large. It does not cover the value of rented buildings, and probably does not embrace the greater portion of borrowed capital; and yet a considerable portion of borrowed capital is no doubt included.

The annual consumption of capital occasioned by the wear and destruction of buildings, machinery, and tools, and in the destruction of stock by fire, and the waste of machinery occasioned by the progress of invention, cannot exceed ten per cent. upon the capital invested; it is probably very much less.

If we assume $3,000,000,000 as the actual amount of capital invested, and estimate the amount of taxes paid as one per cent., and the waste of capital at ten per cent., and deduct the amount of taxes and waste of capital from the manufacturers' net product after paying wages, we have remaining $694,801,847, or 23.16 per cent. on the capital employed.

It is claimed by Mr. Nimmo that the census valuation of products of manufacturing industries is too low; and the estimate I have made of the amount required to supply the waste of capital I believe to be too high.

The same rule applied to the cotton-goods industry gives a net profit of 13.26 per cent.; applied to the woollen-goods industry it shows a net profit of 13.45 per cent.; to blast-furnace industry, 7.13 per cent.; steel-rail industry, 55.9 per cent.*

In the aggregate iron and steel industries in the United States, the surplus, after deducting wages and materials, is 22.47 per cent. In the manufacture of flouring- and grist-mill products the surplus is 26.56 per cent., in meat slaughtering and meat packing the surplus is 51.22 per cent., in the manufacture of boots and shoes the surplus is 47.92 per cent., and in the manu facture of agricultural implements the surplus is thirty-five per cent.

The wear and the displacement of machinery resulting from new inventions in different manufacturing industries varies greatly; and a rate per cent. which would represent the average waste of capital in all the industries could not be applied to particular industries.

---

* Instead of saying net profit, it would be more accurate to say a net contribution to capital of the given per cent. of the capital shown to be invested. A portion of this amount goes to pay rent and interest on borrowed capital. What portion the census does not inform us.

The annual dividends of New England manufacturing companies, from the year 1877 to the year 1886 inclusive, range from nothing to twenty per cent. The average dividends made by seven different establishments showing the largest dividends, for this period of ten years, are 18.2 per cent., 14.9 per cent., 13.5 per cent., 12.1 per cent., 10.7 per cent., 9.2 per cent., and 8.6 per cent.

Since accrued earnings are often invested in new buildings and machinery, which represent an increase of capital, and do not in such cases appear in the form of dividends, dividends declared may represent only a portion of accrued profits.

The *Pall Mall Gazette* recently published the results of the quarterly stock takings of nineteen Lancashire cotton-spinning companies. The statement is as follows:

Company.	Per cent. per annum on Capital.	Dividends declared.
Dowry	14½	9
Equitable	9⅛	. .
Ivy	18	11½
Leesbrook	24½	10
Rigefield	18	11½
Rochdale	39	10½
Stanley	9¾	. .
Duke	19	12
Albert	9	9
Hathershaw	10	. .
New Earth	9	. .
Park Side	15	10
Royton	15	10
Hollinwood	20	10
West End	11½	10
Lees Union	18	7½
Grosvenor	20	10
Hope	17	. .
Oak	16	. .

If to the amount of the wages of those employed in the specified industries of Table No. 6 we add the wages of retail butchers, mechanics, traders, and others embraced in Table No. 5, we obtain the total amount of the earnings of labor in all the creative industries except agriculture. The result is,—

Wages of Table No. 6 . . . . $1,874,062,321
   "   " Table No. 5 1,407,492,850

Total earnings of labor except agriculture $2,781,555,171
Earnings of labor in agriculture 1,852,540,927

Total wages in all creative industries $4,634,096,098

Number of workers in all industries except agriculture . . . 7,404,488
   "   "   " agriculture 7,670,493

Total number of those whose earnings are embraced in product 15,074,981
Average wages to each worker in all industries except agriculture $375.65
Allowing three per cent. on capital employed in agriculture to the credit of profits, there remains to the credit of labor . . 1,852,540,927
Average wages in agriculture would be 241.52
Profits reserved to capital in agriculture 360,000,000
Portion of product reserved by capital in other industries . . 2,191,464,189

The expenses of railways, other than those included under the head of wages, were, not including taxes, $144,166,288. Fuel for steam-craft costs about $15,000,000; and $16,800,000 will cover the waste of capital not already covered under the head of wages. The waste of capital in all other industries besides agriculture, railways, and steam-craft, I have placed at $400,000,000, as a sum sufficient to cover the entire waste of capital employed in the production of the values embraced in the total product stated. Allowance has already been made for the waste of capital in agriculture.

The total amount of direct taxes for the census year is given as $312,750,721. $130,000,000 will closely approximate the amount of taxes paid by the capital (agriculture omitted) employed in the production of the values embraced in the foregoing total. The sum of $705,966,208 we will therefore assume covers the waste of capital and direct taxes. Deducting this amount from the product reserved by capital, we have remaining to the credit of capital at the end of the year $1,485,478,981.

The rewards of labor in agriculture are less uniform than in any other industry. While the average is given as $241.52, in some localities the average will not exceed one hundred dollars; and, as to individuals, the range will run from nothing to six hundred dollars or more.

SUMMARY STATEMENT.

Total number employed in agriculture	7,670,493
" " " other creative industries	7,404,488
" " " all creative industries	15,074,981
" " " persona land professional service, telegraphs and telephones . . .	2,317,118
Total number employed in all industries	17,392,099

Total value of product of agriculture	$2,212,540,927
Estimated product of industries not tabulated in census . . .	1,407,492,850
Product of manufacturing and mechanical industries	1,972,755,642
Product of other tabulated industries and timber not otherwise counted (see Table No. 4)	522,750,868
Railway and water transportation of freight	500,000,000
Cost of capital employed in trade, estimated	500,000,000
Illuminating gas	30,000,000
Wool clip and meat product on ranches	40,000,000
Total product	$7,185,540,287

Cost of distribution as included in foregoing statement (about fifty per cent. on value of product distributed)	$1,598,944,000

Total amount of wages or earnings of labor in all creative industries	$4 634,096,098
Portion of product reserved by capital	2,551,444,189
" " credited to capital in agriculture	860,000,000
" " reserved by capital in other industries . .	2,191,444,189
Earnings of railways in passenger traffic and mail service . .	154,574,522
" " capital in all industries except agriculture . . .	2,346,018,711

Amount of direct taxes and waste of capital, not including agriculture	$705,966,208
Balance remaining to the credit of capital in industries other than agriculture	1,640,052,513

Product to each worker in agriculture	$288.45
" " " all industries.	476.65
" " " manufacturing	721.93
Average wages in all creative industries	307.50
" " " " except agriculture	375.65
" " in manufacturing and mechanical industries	346.98
" " in agriculture	241.52
" " Table No. 5, estimated	382.60
" " in trade, estimated	500.00

Contribution to capital in agriculture, less taxes	$240,000,000
" " " other industries	1,640,052,513
Interest on national debt, paid in 1879	105,327,949
" " State and municipal debt, 1879	66,062,740
Rent of dwellings in excess of cost of maintenance, estimated	80,000,000
Interest on moneys loaned or sales on credit to farmers and others, not including money invested in manufacture, mining, trade, or transportation, estimated	70,000,000
Total contribution to capital in 1879	$2,151,443,202
Deduct labor cost of banking and brokerage paid by capital, herein embraced, estimated	25,000,000
Net contribution to capital in 1879	$2,126,443,202

Express, telephone, telegraph, and street-car companies have not been embraced in foregoing statement, it being impracticable to determine their additional contribution to value of product considered. If taken into account, general results would be little altered, but the relative share of capital would be increased.

Taxes on agriculture may be stated relatively too high. But if all corrections were made so as to conform strictly to true amounts, and all omissions were supplied, general results would not vary greatly from the figures here exhibited. The contribution to capital in the form of cost of distribution is probably greater than is here shown. The contribution to capital arising out of different forms of speculation is not shown.

It will be observed that the question as to what are the profits of particular industries is not essentially involved in determining the shares of capital and labor of the total product. We have ascertained with sufficient accuracy the amount of wages earned, and the total value of the product. What is not distributed as earnings of labor goes to capital.

The addition to product by reason of foreign importations would be the increase of value of imports over cost. The labor cost of distribution is counted. The increase would go to the share of capital.

The following table exhibits the industries in detail. Telegraphs and telephones are included, and passenger traffic is embraced in railway product. The figures are taken from the census of 1880, except as otherwise noted.

TABLE No. 7.

Exhibit of industries, in which capital appears as a separate factor in production, showing number of persons employed, capital invested, wages paid, product after deducting value of materials, estimated cost of maintaining capital, amount of taxes capital would yield on basis of one per cent., and product remaining to the credit of capital, after material, wages, and cost of maintaining capital are deducted.

	Number Employed.	Amount of Capital.	Product after Materials are Deducted.	Total Wages Paid.	Average Wages.	Cost of Maintaining Capital.‖	Amount of Taxes at one per ct.	Remaining to Credit of Capital.
Agriculture	7,670,493	$12,000,000,000	$2,212,540,927	$1,852,540,927	$241.52	....	$120,000,000	$36,000,000
Manufactures and mechanical industries	2,732,595	2,790,272,606	1,972,755,642	947,953,795	346.98	$390,000,000	30,000,000	694,601,847
Mining coal and non-precious metals	229,475	364,909,324	142,736,589	71,992,502	346.73	18,645,450	3,649,000	61,485,468
" precious metals	*75,000	400,000,000	203,141,764	60,000,000	800.00	60,000,000	4,000,000	71,141,764
Quarries	39,000	25,414,497	18,000,000	‡15,000,000	384.61	600,000	254,000	2,246,000
Salt	4,289	8,225,740	4,762,493	1,260,023	293.77	1,600,000	82,000	1,820,470
Petroleum	9,969	27,325,746	24,000,000	4,381,572	454.10	2,732,570	273,000	16,612,658
Fisheries	131,426	37,965,949	43,046,053	†39,427,800	300.00	1,800,000	379,000	1,439,253
Railroads	418,957	5,425,722,560	580,450,694	195,350,013	466.27	†144,166,288	¶18,283,819	227,650,470
Merchants' steam-craft	63,943	112,005,600	85,991,067	25,982,808	406.98	16,800,000	1,120,000	41,188,264
Boat- and ship-building and repairing	21,345	20,979,847	‡17,063,969	12,713,813	595.63	629,390	209,700	‡2,960,166
Telegraphs	14,928	76,068,747	‡16,669,623	4,686,128	327.30	6,882,151	760,600	‡6,478,344
Telephones	3,388	13,723,119	3,098,081	901,400	300.00	2,373,703	137,200	770,516
Logging, etc.	**75,000	...	100,000,000	80,000,000	400.00	...	...	...
Total, omitting agriculture	3,819,065	$9,302,603,185	$3,210,815,875	$1,409,849,849	$369.16	$554,579,552	$54,148,319	$1,118,395,420
Total, including agriculture	11,489,558	$21,302,603,185	$5,423,356,802	$3,262,390,776	...	$554,579,552	$174,148,319	$1,154,395,420

* Number of employés, wages, and capital estimated.
† Wages not given; amount shown is too great.
‡ Wages not given.
§ Gross receipts and net receipts given.
‖ No claim is made as to accuracy of estimate in this column.
¶ Census.
** Estimated.

From the statement of product furnished by Mr. Nimmo and adopted by Mr. Atkinson, the cost of distribution and the product embraced in Table No. 5 both appear to be omitted. The aggregate of these omitted products is $3,006,426,850. Deducting this amount from the total product as shown in this chapter, we have a remaining product of $4,179,103,437 against Mr. Atkinson's total of $9,817,900,000,—less than one-half.

The inequalities of distribution do not fully appear in the foregoing exhibit. While the average wages in the different industries are shown to vary greatly, the range of individual wages, which is not shown, is from one hundred dollars or less to the highest salary paid.

Among the causes of these wide differences is the fact that the number of skilled workers is relatively small. There were returned as "laborers" in 1880,—that is, persons without a trade or special occupation,—1,859,223 workers, of whom 1,616,504 were males between sixteen and fifty-nine years of age. The number of agricultural laborers (owners or proprietors of farms not included) is 3,323,876.

The excessive ratio of crude to skilled labor is in great measure owing to the following causes: (1) foreign immigration, (2) the natural immobility of labor, and (3) to the obstructions placed in the way of industrial education by the opposition of the workers in skilled industries.

In order to measure the full effect of the large contribution to capital, shown in the distribution of the annual product, we must take into account the fact that the capital which is most widely distributed—that is, capital employed in agriculture— receives but a small share of this contribution, and that the revenue-bearing capital of the country is owned by a comparatively small number of persons.

The effect is naturally and necessarily a rapid aggregation of the durable property and credits of the country, which represent the annual savings of industry, in the hands of the few, the loss of industrial independence on the part of the working people, and the administration of the wealth of the country without due regard to the interests of those who produce it.

The report of the Bureau of Labor of the State of Massachusetts for the year 1888 shows the following:

The average earnings to each worker in manufacturing industries were $402.02, ranging from $276.31 to $789.11 for the year 1888.

The wages paid amounted in 1887 to 66.02 per cent., and in 1888 to 63.92 per cent. of the total product of the industries (net product after deducting cost of materials) considered. The amount devoted to "profit and minor expenses" was, in 1887, 33.98 per cent., and in 1888, 36.08 per cent. of the product.

The percentage of the product devoted to "profit and minor expenses" in certain specified industries was as follows:

Industry.	1887.	1888.
Boots and shoes	23.20	20.93
Carpetings	41.47	40.45
Cotton goods	41.21	42.29
Leather	40.19	42.98
Metals and metal goods	48.39	42.68
Woollen goods	53.98	52.63
Worsted goods	33.98	36.08

The percentage ratio of "profit and minor expenses" to the capital employed was:

Industry.	1887.	1888.
Boots and shoes	22.33	18.30
Carpetings	15.67	15.42
Cotton goods	13.05	14.70
Leather	20.06	23.71
Metals and metallic goods	25.82	24.77
Woollen goods	22.15	20.77
Worsted goods	18.86	15.24

The increase of capital devoted to production in 1887 over 1886 was 9.43 per cent.; the increase in the value of the goods produced was 5.29 per cent.

The proportion of the product to the full capacity of the establishments was, in 1886, 77.48 per cent., and in 1887, 77.80 per cent.

The report of the Bureau of Labor of the State of Connecticut for the year 1889 shows the following:

Number of industries considered	22
Number of establishments embraced in report	241
Total capital employed	$85,863,552.26
Total product	85,929,133.43

Cost of stock or materials $45,368,405.47
Cost of manufacturing (less interest, rents, and taxes) 31,621,592.93
Rent, interest, and taxes 1,690,420.52
Net profits 7,248,711.51
Wages paid 22,482,824.66
Number of hands employed 53,147
Wages paid are per cent. of net product 55.8
Number of employés classed as superintendents, book-keepers, salesmen, and not included in "number of hands employed" 2,708

The number classed as superintendents are 5.08 per cent. of wage-earners. Cost of superintendence is 15.08 per cent. of wages paid and 4.32 per cent. of the cost of goods manufactured.

Average wages of persons classed under head of superintendence . $1251.80
    "   "   all other workers 860.30
    "   "   all employés 401.66

The net profits of capital in the specified industries are stated as follows:

Industry.	Per cent. of Profit.
Bakeries	15.51
Brass	9.68
Clocks	1.73
Corsets	13.32
Cotton goods	7.03
Cutlery	12.78
Carriages	11.39
Forgings	7.94
Hardware	7.64
Hats	13.11
Iron foundries	12.36
Iron, malleable	7.41
Knit goods	15.20
Machine-shops	10.31
Paper boxes	25.19
Paper-mills	12.58
Printing and publishing	8.80
Rubber goods	.86
Shoes	7.61
Silk goods	12.32
Silver plating	7.04
Woollen goods	7.41
General average	8.44

The net profit here given is after the payment of taxes, interest, and rents.

It would add to the value of these reports, if it were made clear just what is embraced under the head of capital, and what are the values placed upon land, machinery, buildings, etc. In Connecticut the information is furnished voluntarily, some manufacturers refusing to make statements; and, from the report of the commissioner, it appears that there existed among manufacturers the apprehension that the public might be misled in the direction of an over-estimate of the profits made, and that no account would be taken of the losses incurred by those who fail. So, in the absence of any showing as to the manner in which "capital" was itemized in the statements made, we may be excused if we express some doubt as to the entire accuracy of these reports. It is possible that borrowed capital may have been included under the head of "capital." The work of the labor bureaus in both Massachusetts and Connecticut is not lacking in accuracy or completeness. But the voluntary statements of private individuals are necessarily exposed to the suspicion of being more or less modified to accord with the purposes of those who make them. From the foregoing statistics of Massachusetts and Connecticut, it appears that the worker (including superintendence) receives as wages from fifty-five to sixty-six per cent. of the product. In these States less than twenty per cent. of the wage-earners in manufacturing industries own their own homes. Those who pay rent will, on the average, if heads of families, spend one-fifth of their earnings for rent. In paying out their earnings for articles of food, clothing, and other things purchased at retail, ten per cent. at least of the expenditure is a contribution to capital in the form of profits on trade and rent of buildings occupied for purposes of trade. And, considering all factors that enter into the problem, it is safe to say that over one-half of the labor product of the wage-earners in manufacturing industries is, in some form, absorbed by capital; and this in addition to the amount required for the maintenance of capital.

In agricultural industries the same relation between labor and capital does not exist, except in part. Such, however, is the association of the industries, that what touches one reaches all, as a chain of lakes is drained by an outlet from one of the number.

In order to obtain the measure of the profits on capital employed in agriculture, where the worker generally owns the capital which he employs, we may deduct from the value of the gross product the labor cost of production, estimating the cost of labor at the customary wages paid to agricultural laborers hired by the day or month. This method universally applied to the agriculture of the United States would exhibit no margin of profit. If we measure the profits of agricultural capital by the average rental paid, which ranges from one-third to one-half the gross product, the landlord paying taxes and maintaining improvements and defraying cost of supervising tenants, the margin of profit through a series of years will range from nothing to ten per cent., while the average earnings set apart to the share of labor will fall to two hundred dollars, or less, per year. This, however, is on the basis of the crops and prices of the year 1879. Prices during subsequent years have been on an average much lower.

It will be seen that in the division of the total product of the nation, agricultural labor and capital employed in agriculture have received the smallest shares awarded to any class of labor or capital.

WORKERS EMPLOYED IN PERSONAL AND PROFESSIONAL SERVICE.

The number of persons returned in census of 1880, as engaged in personal and professional service, is 4,074,238. Of these, 17,000 of those whose occupations are designated perform work the cost of which enters into the value of products. Of those whose occupation is given, whose labor does not enter directly into the cost of production, and whose earnings are therefore omitted from the estimate of value of products, the following is a complete list:

TABLE No. 8.
No. 1.

Actors	4,812
Showmen and employés of shows	2,604
Artists and teachers of art	9,104
Musicians and teachers of music	30,477
Billiard- and bowling-saloon keepers and employés	1,548
Authors, lecturers, literary persons	1,181
Journalists	12,308
	61,979

No. 2.

Chemists, assayers, etc.	1,961
Designers, draughtsmen, and inventors	2,820
Collectors and claim agents	4,213
Clerks and copyists, not otherwise specified	25,467
Watchmen (private) and detectives	18,384
Lawyers	64,187
Teachers and scientific persons	227,710
	339,692

No. 3.

Midwives	2,118
Nurses	18,488
Dentists	12,314
Veterinary surgeons	2,130
Physicians and surgeons	85,671
Clergymen	64,698
Sextons	2,449
	182,863

No. 4.

Barbers and hair-dressers	44,851
Launderers and laundresses	121,942
Janitors	6,763
Messengers	13,985
Domestic servants	1,075,635
Livery-stable keepers	14,213
Hostlers	31,697
	1,309,086

No. 5.

Hotel-keepers	32,453
Lodging-house keepers	77,413
Restaurant-keepers	13,074
Clerks in hotels and restaurants	10,916
Other employés of hotels and restaurants	77,413
	211,269

No. 6.

Officers of United States army and navy	2,600
Soldiers, sailors, and marines	24,161
Officials of government	67,081
Clerks in government offices	16,849
Employés of government	31,601
" " charitable institutions	2,396
	144,688

Total number of persons engaged in personal and professional service, the character of whose employment is designated 2,249,577

The support of the professional and personal service class is borne by those engaged in productive labor. Those designated in subdivision No. 6, of the foregoing table, derive their support from all classes equally, except in so far as our system of raising revenue may bear unequally on different classes. The support of those designated in subdivision No. 3 may be considered as resting about one-third on the agricultural, and two-thirds on other classes. Farmers "doctor" a good deal, but their spiritual wants are administered to by clergymen in receipt of small salaries. The agricultural classes may contribute one-fourth of those designated in Nos. 1 and 2, and one-fifth of the support of those designated in No. 4, and one-twentieth of the support of those designated in No. 5. On the basis of these assumptions, the support of those engaged in professional and personal service would rest, about one-eighth on the agricultural, and seven-eighths on the other classes. Assuming that the earnings of this class of persons amount to $700,000,000, the agricultural classes would, on this basis, contribute out of that portion of the total product set apart to their credit $87,500,000, and $612,500,000 would be derived from the other classes. But since "the other classes" include those engaged in professional and personal service, who employ each other, something like one-fifth of their earnings would consist of wages derived from their own class, and there would remain about $472,500,000 to be contributed by workers in other productive industries besides agricultural. The greater part of this amount is paid from the fund representing the total wages of labor and that portion of the product already assigned to the maintenance of capital, though a very considerable amount is derived out of the fund set to the credit of the profits of capital. If we assume that the amount of $172,500,000 is paid from this fund, the balance remaining to the credit of capital would be $1,954,943,202. What becomes of this fund?

First, there is that part which is consumed in the form of perishable products; second, that part which is converted into new factories, mills, and increase of machinery, new railways, and other forms of tangible and durable property; and third, that part which is invested in notes, bonds, and mortgages, and which reappears in the form of property in the hands of farmers, laborers, and other debtors; or is represented by the amount of the consumption of other classes beyond their incomes; to the extent of which they are necessarily in debt. The entire labor product, each year, is consumed in some form; if in the form of perishable products, it is destroyed; if in the form of investment in buildings, or like durable property, it represents so much added to the national wealth.

MANUFACTURES OF ONE HUNDRED LEADING CITIES.

The census of 1880 gives, separately, the statistics of manufacturing and mechanical industries in one hundred leading cities of the United States, from which I have deduced the following summary:

Total population of one hundred leading cities	9,100,745
Capital employed in cities	$1,399,619,618.00
" " outside	1,590,652,988.00
Total capital employed	$2,990,272,606.00
Materials used in cities	$1,925,987,807.00
" " outside	1,470,835,742.00
Total materials used	$3,396,823,549.00
Gross product	$5,369,579,191.00
Net product in cities	$1,119,381,024.00
" " outside	853,375,618.00
Total net product	$1,972,756,642.00
Product to each worker	$721.93
Per cent. of capital employed in cities, of net product . .	125.0
" " " outside	186.0
Number of hands employed in cities	1,451,177
" " " outside	1,280,788
Total number of hands	2,731,965
Wages paid in cities	$561,710,845.00
" " outside	886,242,950.00
Average annual wages	346.98
" " " in cities	388.45
" " " outside	301.55

Total number of workers in all occupations 17,892,099
   "   "   "   "   male 14,744,942
   "   "   "   "   female. 2,647,157
   "   "   "   "   males over fifteen . . 13,919,755
   "   "   "   "   " " sixty . . 933,644
Per cent. of females, of all ages, and of males under fifteen . . .   24.9

Total number engaged in agriculture 7,670,493
 "   "   "   "   females 594,510
   "   "   "   "   males under fifteen 584,867
   "   "   "   "   " over sixty 662,938
   "   "   "   "   " " fifteen 6,491,146
Per cent. of females, all ages, and males under fifteen 15.37

Total number classed under head of professional and personal service 4,074,238
Domestic servants 1,075,655
Per cent. of females, all ages, and of children under fifteen in pro-
    fessional and personal service 36.54
Per cent. of females and males under fifteen, domestic servants .   0.90
Number engaged in professional and personal services, about . . 2,300,000
Total number engaged in trade and transportation 1,810,256
Per cent. of females, all ages, and males under fifteen 4.7

Total engaged in manufacturing and mining 3,837,112
   "   "   "   "   males 3,205,124
   "   "   "   "   " over sixty . . . 139,602
   "   "   "   "   " under fifteen . . 86,677
   "   "   "   "   females 631,988
   "   "   "   "   " under fifteen . 46,930
   "   "   "   "   " over sixty . . 7,901

The following is a summary statement of Edward Atkinson's deductions and estimates of product and distribution for the census year 1879.*

Total annual product $10,000,000,000
Domestic consumption on farms, and domestic product of
    families not exchanged   1,000,000,000
Commercial product $9,000,000,000
Share of capitalists, five per cent. $450,000,000
Savings of people,   "   "   450,000,000
Addition to the wealth of the nation   900,000,000
Wages fund $8,100,000,000

---

* Atkinson, Distribution of Products, page 141.

Share of 1,100,000 persons engaged in mental and administrative work, $1000 each, including teachers, scientists,
authors, artisans, young lawyers and clergymen, merchants, tradesmen, officials $1,100,000,000

16,200,000 farmers, mechanics, artisans, operators, clerks,
dress-makers, laborers, and others at $432 each 7,000,000,000

      Total $8,100,000,000

Total assumed product accounted for above $10,000,000,000

He then adds 5 per cent. upon this gross product to account
for the larger consumption of well-to-do-farmers, tradesmen, shop-keepers, and other classes, making 500,000,000

                                       $10,500,000,000

He says ("Distribution of Products," page 109), "In general, it
may be said that the necessary qualifications by which the average wages disclosed by the census, in respect to all manufactures,
should be governed would lead to the conclusion that three hundred and forty-six dollars represented not over ten months' work,
and if then we added one-fifth of three hundred and forty-six
dollars to make up for the two months, we reach a general average, including the administrative force, of four hundred and fifteen
dollars each,—again substantially corresponding with the conclusion of the writer." Again, speaking on the same subject, page 108,
he says, "But this result must be subjected to very important
qualifications. The list of occupations, listed under the term of
manufactures, includes brick-making, which can only be followed
six months in the year. . . . The wages of cotton manufacture
appear to be only two hundred and forty-five dollars each, per
year, by far the larger portion of those employed being women
and children; but in his (Mr. Weeks') judgment, this sum should
be raised to at least two hundred and eighty dollars, and, including administrative force, to perhaps three hundred dollars a year,
in order that it may be made to correspond to the full year's
work of those who were continuously employed."

Now, if the purpose were to ascertain average *monthly* wages,
there would be ground for this statement. But, when we are
endeavoring to ascertain the total amount of wages paid to the
working-force of the country, the proposal to add one-fifth to
the amount actually paid, for the reason that workers were employed but four-fifths of the time, could never be made except

by some one zealous to verify estimates which cannot be verified in a more rational manner.

It is true that there are those who are employed but a part of the year in their special calling, who are employed in other industries during part of the year. But, if they engage in any of the industries reported, their labor and wages are counted. If they are employed at something else, what is it? Most frequently in agriculture. The product of that industry is counted. They are not carpenters, nor blacksmiths, nor merchants; what do they do, that Mr. Atkinson proposes to count full time and pay them at the rate of four hundred and fifteen dollars per year?

The truth is, as indicated, and as every person who looks about him knows, that the labor unemployed during the course of a year represents more than one-fifth of the entire labor power of the country. The product of the manufacturing industries could be doubled, without drawing from other industries, or from the common labor of the country, those who could not be spared.

Capital, in its struggle to maintain its margin of profit, checks production and hinders distribution; and Mr. Atkinson feeds idle labor on *a priori* estimates of what might be if labor were employed the year round.

The effect of the unequal and inequitable division of the product between capital and labor, in aggregating the wealth of the country, demands special consideration, which will be given in the following chapter on the Distribution of Wealth.

THE WEALTH OF THE UNITED STATES.

Forty-three billion dollars has been the generally accepted estimate in round numbers of the total wealth of the United States in 1880. How this amount is arrived at appears from the following, which is given by Mr. Atkinson as the *census* valuation of the wealth of the United States in 1880.

1. Farms	$10,197,000,000
2. Residence and business real estate, including water-power .	9,881,000,000
3. Railroads and equipments	5,536,000,000
4. Telegraphs, shipping, and canals	419,000,000
5. Live-stock on and off farms, farming-tools, and machinery	2,406,000,000
6. Household furniture, paintings, books, jewelry, household supplies of food, fuel, etc.	5,000,000,000
	$33,439,000,000

Brought forward	$33,439,000,000
7. Mines, petroleum wells, quarries, and one-half the annual product thereof reckoned as the average supply in the hands of producers or dealers	781,000,000
8. Three-quarters of the annual product of agriculture, manufactures, and annual importation of foreign goods, assumed to be the average supply in the hands of producers and dealers	6,160,000,000
9. Churches, schools, asylums, public buildings of all kinds, and other real estate exempt from taxation	2,000,000,000
10. Specie	610,000,000
11. Miscellaneous items, including tools of mechanics . . .	650,000,000
Total	$43,640,000,000

The statement that this is the census valuation is misleading. Several items are made up largely of estimates for which there is no reliable data. This is true of Items 2, 6, 9, and 11. Some of the estimates are evidently too high, and Item No. 8 is double what it should be. No. 3, railroads and equipments, is put down as the sum of the stock and indebtedness of railway companies. The net incomes of railways amounted to four per cent. on this valuation. Many railroads are mortgaged for fifty per cent. more than what would be the present cost of construction. The amount of earnings in excess of fixed charges was but $40,385,000, or five per cent. of $807,700,000. Adding this latter sum to the indebtedness, we have $3,620,000,000. But, estimated according to what would have been the cost in 1880, the valuation should not be more than $3,000,000,000.

Three-fourths of the products of agriculture and manufactures amount to but $3,140,000,000. Imported foreign goods ought not to be included, except the amount of the excess of value over exports, which is a small item.

The total capital invested in mining (except precious metals), petroleum wells, quarries, and salt manufacture, and one-half the annual product amounts to but $523,000,000.

Making the corrections here suggested, the statement would stand as follows:

1. Farms	$10,197,000,000
2. Residence and business real estate, including water-power, machinery, etc.	9,881,000,000
	$20,078,000,000

Brought forward	$20,078,000,000
3. Railroads and equipments	3,000,000,000
4. Telegraphs, shipping, and canals	419,000,000
5. Live-stock on and off farms, farming-tools, and machinery	2,406,000,000
6. Household furniture, paintings, books, etc.	5,000,000,000
7. Mines, petroleum wells, quarries, and one-half the annual product	525,000,000
8. Three-quarters of the annual product of agriculture and manufactures	3,140,000,000
9. Churches, schools, asylums, public buildings, and other real estate exempt from taxation	2,000,000,000
10. Specie.	610,000,000
11. Miscellaneous items, including tools of mechanics . . .	650,000,000
Total	$37,828,000,000

The total assessed valuation in 1880, including credits, was $16,902,993,543. The taxes assessed amounted to $312,750,721. A considerable amount of the property here enumerated is owned in foreign countries. Taking the fact into account, and allowing for over-estimate in Items 2, 5, and 11, I am of the opinion that the value of the property owned by the people of the United States in 1880 did not exceed $35,000,000,000.

DISTRIBUTION OF WEALTH.

In the collection of statistics hitherto, no effort has been directed towards ascertaining how the wealth of the nation is divided among individual owners. Statisticians have been content with general averages, and an exhibition of the relative wealth of States and counties. When the census of 1880 was taken, the subject of the individual distribution of wealth had not yet forced itself upon the attention of legislators and of government officials in charge of that work.

The doctrine that if property exists it is not a matter of public concern who owns it has been often announced, but more frequently tacitly accepted by those who would not care to openly avow it.

It is said, in behalf of the accumulation of wealth in great individual fortunes, that millionaires are but trustees holding title to property for the benefit of the people at large. And so doubtless in a romantic sort of way they sometimes regard themselves.

It would accord with the general principles of equity, were the immense acquisitions of some to be treated by the State as resulting trusts, properly subject to gradual distribution through the agency of graded income taxes and laws affecting the distribution of the estates of deceased persons.

Mr. Thomas G. Shearman, in an article in the November (1889) number of the *Forum*, enumerates by name a list of millionaires as follows, omitting names:

2	owners of	$150,000,000	$300,000,000
5	"	100,000,000	500,000,000
1	"	70,000,000	70,000,000
2	"	60,000,000	120,000,000
6	"	50,000,000	300,000,000
6	"	40,000,000	240,000,000
4	"	35,000,000	140,000,000
13	"	30,000,000	390,000,000
10	"	25,000,000	250,000,000
4	"	22,500,000	90,000,000
15	"	20,000,000	300,000,000
68	"		$2,700,000,000

Mr. Shearman gives the following exhibit from the Boston tax-list of 1888:

Individual Tax-Payers.	Average Assessed Wealth.
2	$4,600,000
4	3,205,000
3	2,732,570
8	1,840,000
39	930,000
133	500,000
1065	160,000

Mr. Shearman assumes that an assessment of four hundred thousand dollars represents an estate of one million dollars, and that an assessment of seventy-five thousand dollars represents an estate of one hundred and fifty thousand dollars, making a difference in the ratio of assessments to total wealth between very large estates and comparatively small estates, for the reason that, where estates are very large, the chances for under-valuations and omissions are greater than in smaller estates. This view is in accord with general observation and experience.

From English statistics showing gradations of wealth, and from the foregoing figures, Mr. Shearman reaches a basis of classification, which, applied to the ascertained facts, gives, as a result, the following exhibit of the distribution of the wealth of the people of the United States. A population of sixty-five millions and a total wealth of sixty-one billion five hundred million dollars are assumed. I regard the amount of estimated wealth as somewhat too large; but, as affecting the question of distribution, it is not necessary to attempt more than an approximate estimate of the amount. The rule of general averages applied by Mr. Shearman will doubtless yield general results approximately correct; but it can only be applied where large numbers are embraced.

DISTRIBUTION IN CLASSES.

No. of Families.	Total Wealth.	Average per Family.
70	2,625,000,000	$37,500,000
80	1,025,000,000	11,500,000
180	1,440,000,000	8,000,000
135	968,000,000	6,800,000
360	1,656,000,000	4,600,000
1,755	4,036,000,000	2,300,000
6,000	7,000,000,000	1,250,000
7,000	4,550,000,000	650,000
11,000	4,125,000,000	375,000
14,000	3,220,000,000	280,000
16,500	2,722,000,000	165,000
50,000	5,000,000,000	100,000
75,000	4,500,000,000	60,000
200,000	4,000,000,000	20,000
1,000,000	3,500,000,000	3,500
2,000,000	4,000,000,000	2,000
9,620,000	7,215,000,000	800
13,002,080	$61,582,000,000	

From this table it will appear that seventy families own one-twenty-fifth, or four per cent. of the wealth of the nation; eight hundred and forty-five families, or about one-fifteen-thousandth part of the population, own one-eighth of the total wealth, and less than one-fifteen-hundredth of the population own three-sevenths of the total wealth, and one-thirty-fourth of the population own over seventy per cent. of the total wealth.

A high degree of accuracy for these figures, in detail, cannot be claimed; but that the first half of the table approximates somewhat closely the actual distribution of wealth there is no reason to doubt. The distribution of wealth among farmers and in villages cannot be brought under the operation of the same rule, and is more equitable than is here shown.

The following, from Mulhall's table of incomes of the British people for the year 1883, indicates the distribution of wealth in that kingdom:

Class.	No. of Families.	Total Income.	Average.
Gentry	222,000	$1,665,000,000	$7500
Middle	604,000	1,205,000,000	1991
Trade	1,220,000	1,220,000,000	1000
Working	4,629,000	2,235,000,000	482
Total	6,675,000	$6,325,000,000	

One-thirtieth of the whole population absorb a little less than one-fourth the earnings of the British nation. The earnings of the gentry and middle classes are derived chiefly from rents, interest, and profits on invested capital.

The incomes of the British people in 1877, as given by Mulhall, are as follows:

Income.	England. No.	Scotland. No.	Ireland. No.	United Kingdom. No.
Over $250,000 . . .	71	15	4	90
$50,000 to 250,000 . . .	904	132	31	1,067
5,000 to 50,000 . . .	18,622	2,191	878	21,691
750 to 5,000 . . .	275,733	27,642	14,473	317,848
Over $750	295,330	29,980	15,386	340,696

A considerable portion of the revenues of Great Britain are obtained from income taxes, and statistics therefore furnish accurate information.

The average value per inhabitant of houses in England, in 1880, was $95; Scotland, $75, and in Ireland, $35.

In the United Kingdom of England, Scotland, and Ireland, thirty-four persons own over one-eleventh of all the land. The total number of land-owners is 180,524, and the average number of acres to each holding is 390. In Ireland, the average holding is 1120 acres; in Scotland, 2150; in England, 212. The number of holdings under fifty acres is, in England, 3500; Wales, 600; Scotland, 700; Ireland, 7800. The land of England comprises 72,000,000 acres, one-fourth of which, not counting owners of less than one acre, is owned by 1200 proprietors, and half the entire United Kingdom is owned by 2512 persons out of a population of 35,000,000.* The peers, about 600 in number, own 14,000,000 acres, yielding an annual rental of $66,000,000. The Duke of Devonshire owns four estates, amounting to 115,000 acres; the Duke of Bedford, 72,000; the Duke of Portland, 61,000; the Duke of Northumberland, 181,000; "and in every county there are properties ranging from 10,000 to 30,000 acres in the possession of the lords. Seven persons own one-seventh of Buckinghamshire, which has a population of 175,000." Five persons own one-ninth of the land in Cambridge, and sixteen persons own two-sevenths of the land in Cheshire, where there is a population of 561,000.

"In Ireland the situation is similar. In the province of Munster eleven persons own one-seventh of the land. In Ulster, a noble marquis, the grandson of George the Fourth's mistress, owns 122,300 acres; the natural son of another marquis owns 58,000; and still another marquis, married to a woman of the town now living, owns 34,000. In Connaught two persons own 274,000 acres; and, besides these, Viscount Dillon holds 83,000, and the Earl of Lucan 60,000. Lord Fitzwilliam has an estate of 89,000 acres; the Duke of Leinster one of 67,000; Lord Kenmare one of 91,000 and another of 22,000; Lord Bantry owns one of 69,000; Lord Lansdowne, one of 91,000, another of 13,000, and another of 9000; Lord Downshire, one of 26,000, one of 15,000, and another of 64,000; Lord Leitrim, three of 54,000, 22,000, and 18,000, respectively. The Duke of Devonshire, in addition to his enormous English properties, has one estate of 32,000 acres, and another of 27,000."

In Scotland, "the county of Sutherland contains 1,290,253 acres, of which the Duke of Sutherland owns 1,176,343. The population of the county is 24,317 souls. Six other potentates hold over 100,000 acres among them, leaving exactly 5295 acres

---

* Bateman's Great Land-Owners.

for the rest of the remaining 24,310 inhabitants. There are, however, only eighty-five of these with more than an acre apiece.

"Among the other great proprietors in Scotland are the Duchess of Sutherland, who owns an estate of 149,000 acres in her own right; and the Earl of Fife, who has one of 140,000, another of 72,000, and another of 40,000. The Duke of Richmond has one of 155,000 and another of 69,000; the Earl of Seafield, one of 96,000, one of 48,000, and one of 16,000. The Earl of Breadalbane owns one of 193,000 and one of 179,000; the Duke of Hamilton, one of 102,000 and one of 45,000; the Duke of Buccleugh, three of 253,000, 104,000, and 60,000, respectively. The Duke of Argyle is comparatively poor; he owns only 168,000 acres. . . . In Invernesshire, twenty men own 2,000,000 acres among them; and in Aberdeenshire, twenty-three lords and gentlemen own more than half the county, though the population is 244,000." *

Five men own one-fourth of Scotland. One duke, with estates all over England, has 300,000 acres in Scotland. "This nobleman's park is fifteen miles in circumference. Another duke has estates which the highway divides for twenty-three miles. A marquis there is who can ride a hundred miles in a straight line on his own land. There is a duke who owns almost an entire county, stretching from sea to sea. An earl draws $1,000,000 every year from his estates in Lancashire. A duke regularly invests $400,000 a year in buying up lands adjoining his already enormous estates. A marquis enjoys $5,000,000 a year from land. An earl lately died leaving to his heirs $5,000,000, and $800,000 a year income from land. The income from land derived by one ducal family of England is $5,000,000, which is increasing from year to year by the falling in of leases. One hundred and fifty persons own half of England; seventy-five persons own half of Scotland; thirty persons own half of Ireland." †

The average rental value of land in England (1880) is $7.70 per acre; in Scotland, $1.98; in Ireland, $2.45. The average

---

* Adam Badeau, in English Aristocracy.
† Quoted by Ruskin, in Fors Clavigera.

value of land in England was, in 1875, $210 per acre. The rental was a little under three per cent. on the value.*

The capital of the people of Great Britain, invested in stocks, bonds, and mortgages, outside of loans and mortgages in Australia, Brazil, and other countries, amounts to $17,455,000,000, and yields an annual income of $776,500,000, an average of 4.4 per cent. The capital embraced in this statement does not include lands or manufacturing industries. It is invested as follows:†

	Capital.	Rate of Interest, per cent.
National debt	$3,845,000,000	3.0
Railways	3,850,000,000	4.0
Banks	1,850,000,000	6.5
Mines and iron	1,075,000,000	5.5
Canals and docks	470,000,000	4.0
Gas and water	360,000,000	8.0
Telegraphs	150,000,000	5.7
Insurance	100,000,000	6.0
Shipping, etc.	965,000,000	5.0
British	$12,165,000,000	4.4
Colonial loans	740,000,000	5.0
Indian loans	770,000,000	4.0
Indian and colonial railways.	930,000,000	5.4
Foreign loans and railways	2,850,000,000	4.5
	$17,455,000,000	4.4

Making, in 1883, *a total interest-bearing capital of $17,455,000,000.*

Investments of capital in the United States, as shown by the census of 1880, are as follows:

---

* In France there are 10,426,368 proprietors who own less than five acres each; 1,894,847 who own from five to 12.35 acres each; and 1,754,305 who own 12.35 acres each and over; seventy-five per cent. of the total number of landed proprietors possess but ten per cent. of the entire area; thirteen per cent. of the proprietors own twelve per cent. of the area; and twelve per cent. of the proprietors own seventy-seven per cent. of the entire area. There are proprietors owning two hundred and fifty thousand acres devoted to the pleasures of the chase. Nearly one-fourth of the land is occupied by renters. About one-third is cultivated by proprietors with the aid of hired labor; and about one-tenth is cultivated and owned by the peasants themselves.

† Mulhall.

Railways	$5,425,722,560
Merchants' steam craft	112,005,600
Sail-vessels	50,152,950
Telegraphs	76,068,747
Telephones	13,723,119
Petroleum	27,325,746
Salt	4,762,493
Quarries	25,414,497
Non-precious minerals	364,909,324
Fisheries	37,955,349
Manufacturing	2,790,272,606
Insurance companies, fire	204,450,532
" " life	442,272,471
Loans of national banks	878,500,000
Public debt of United States	2,120,415,370
State and municipal debt	1,117,585,546
	$13,691,536,910

To this should be added estimates of private banks, savings banks, and mining precious metals.

Loans of private banks and savings banks	$1,000,000,000
Mining gold and silver	400,000,000
	$1,400,000,000

Other loans and credits	$2,000,000,000

The mortgage indebtedness of the people of the State of Illinois, in 1880, was $204,000,000. The wealth of the people of the State of Illinois was one-fourteenth part of the wealth of the nation.

If the mortgage indebtedness of the people of other States were as great in proportion to wealth, the total mortgage indebtedness of the people of the nation would be $2,856,000,000.

A portion of these loans represents assets of insurance companies, and the total estimate of $2,856,000,000 would be doubtless too great. The total amount, not including capital already enumerated, did not probably exceed $2,000,000,000, including private credits not secured by mortgage, other than bank loans.

The value of business houses used in trade, and of houses rented for dwellings, offices, etc., was probably $4,000,000,000.

Capital employed in trade, street railways, gas-works, and water-works, was probably $4,000,000,000 more, making a total of revenue-bearing property (besides that invested in agriculture) of—in round numbers— $25,000,000,000. This exceeds the amount of capital represented by property employed in productive industries. The excess grows out of the public debt and other credits which constitute a lien on the whole property and productive power of the people.

Further illustration of the distribution of wealth is found in the statistics of 1880, with regard to United States registered bonds.

Total amount of registered bonds	$644,990,400
" number of holders, 73,114	
Held in New York	210,264,250
" Massachusetts	45,138,750
" Pennsylvania	40,230,050
" Ohio	16,445,050
" District of Columbia	12,419,050
" California	11,601,100
" Illinois	9,118,950
" Connecticut	8,894,400
" New Jersey	8,104,150
" Maryland	6,989,600
" Rhode Island	4,717,100
" New Hampshire	4,658,100
	$378,580,550
Other States	38,958,300
" " insurance and trust companies . . .	227,451,550

Four hundred and ten million dollars are held in sums of fifty thousand dollars and over. Fifteen hundred persons hold two-thirds of the whole amount.

In the United States the growth of monopoly in land has not yet made great headway, except in the cities, where the law of "I got here first" is the foundation of many great fortunes. The following table shows the distribution of agricultural lands in the United States as exhibited by the census of 1880.

Total number of farms	4,008,907
" " " acres	536,081,835
" improved land	284,771,042
" unimproved land	251,310,793

Average number of acres of land in farms			134
"	"	" improved	71
"	"	" unimproved	63
Number of farms cultivated by owners			2,984,306
"	"	rented for money rent	322,357
"	"	" for share of crops	702,244
"	"	under 3 acres	4,352
"	"	3 to 10 acres	134,889
"	"	10 to 20 acres	254,749
"	"	20 to 50 acres	781,574
"	"	50 to 100 acres	1,032,810
"	"	100 to 500 acres	1,695,983
"	"	500 to 1000 acres	75,972
"	"	1000 acres and over	28,578

The increase of large farms from 1870 to 1880 shows a large per cent. of gain.

HOMES OF WORKINGMEN.

The Illinois Bureau of Labor Statistics has collected information showing the home and family relations of 47,287 workmen out of a total of 54,247 members of various labor organizations in the State of Illinois, in the year 1886. These statistics show that 23,764, or fifty-two per cent., are heads of families. The number who own homes is 6953, or twenty-eight per cent. of those who are heads of families. In Chicago the proportion of those who own homes is twenty-four per cent.; in the State outside of Chicago, the proportion is forty-two per cent. All having a proprietary interest in homes are included. The number of homes under mortgage does not appear. If all workingmen, including those not members of any labor organization, were included, these percentages would probably be somewhat lowered.

WAGES IN MASSACHUSETTS.

The report of the statistics of Massachusetts for the year 1888 shows the following:

The average annual earnings of the operatives in the manufacturing establishments of Massachusetts for the year 1888 were $402.45 for each operative. In 1887 the average to each operative was $394.79.

The averages in the several industries are as follows:

Agricultural implements	$516.59
Arms and ammunition	551.91
Artisans' tools	558.28
Boots and shoes	503.41
Boxes, paper and wooden	410.97
Buttons and dress trimmings	277.78
Carpetings	343.66
Carriages and wagons	634.41
Chemical preparations (compounded)	709.04
Clocks and watches	687.02
Clothing	406.76
Cooking, lighting, and heating apparatus	789.11
Cordage and twine	341.98
Cotton goods	324.41
Cotton, woollen, and other textiles	365.02
Flax, hemp, and jute goods	276.81
Food preparations	418.61
Furniture	436.23
Glass	416.77
Hose, rubber, linen, etc.	474.72
Hosiery and knit goods	338.41
Leather	512.87
Linen	302.29
Liquors, malt, distilled, and fermented	688.72
Machines and machinery	535.22
Metals and metallic goods	481.85
Mixed textiles	352.10
Musical instruments and materials	671.18
Oils and illuminating fluids	600.00
Paper and paper goods	407.46
Print-works, dye-works	411.13
Railroad construction	413.12
Rubber and elastic goods	552.32
Ship-building	630.19
Silk and silk goods	318.61
Stone	541.68
Straw and palm-leaf goods	388.21
Tallow candles, soap, etc.	451.72
Wooden goods	485.87
Woollen goods	351.98
Worsted goods	346.39
Average	$402.45

The average wages in the industries named for the United

States and for Massachusetts, during the census year, and for
Massachusetts during the State census year of 1888, were:

Industry.	United States for Census Year 1880.	Massachusetts for Census Year 1880.	Massachusetts, 1888.
Agricultural implements . .	$385.07	$376.05	$516.57
Carriages and wagons	418.30	481.29	634.41
Cotton goods	245.93	274.08	324.41
Food products	257.80	422.84	418.61
Glass	378.29	405.23	416.77
Mixed textiles	307.02	337.22	352.10
Woollen goods	298.51	329.65	351.98

WAGES IN EUROPE AND AMERICA.

The following tables are taken from Mulhall's "Dictionary
of Statistics," published in London in 1883:

ARTISANS' WAGES IN 1880—SHILLINGS PER WEEK.

	Great Britain.	France.	Belgium.	Germany.	Italy.	New York.	Chicago.
Printer	32	20	19	20	16	54	62
Painter . . .	32	21	18	16	19	54	38
Plumber . . .	33	23	25	15	16	62	66
Tailor	25	21	17	15	18	58	50
Shoemaker . .	31	20	14	13	18	62	56
Carpenter . . .	33	23	23	16	17	44	42
Mason	35	17	25	15	15	56	33
Smith	31	23	18	15	16	50	44
Tinsmith . . .	28	18	20	16	15	50	44
Baker	27	23	18	15	16	. .	42
Collier	24	15	14	16	. .	. .	. .

WAGES OF DAY-LABORERS IN AGRICULTURE IN 1880.

England	30 pence =	60 cents.
Scotland	18 "	36 "
Ireland	28 "	56 "
France	25 "	50 "
Germany	18 "	36 "
Russia	12 "	24 "
Austria	20 "	40 "
Italy	10 "	20 "
Holland	20 "	40 "
Belgium	20 "	40 "
Scandinavia	14 "	28 "

The rise in agricultural wages between 1835 and 1880 was as follows :*

	Per cent.
England	50
Scotland	75
Ireland	125
France	66⅔
Germany	125
Russia	100
Austria	100
Italy	150
Holland	122
Belgium	122
Scandinavia	86

COTTON-MILL OPERATIVES' WAGES—SHILLINGS PER WEEK.

	England.	United States.
Sizers	36	40
Weavers	30	35
Pickers	15	28
Strippers	17	28
Cardboys	14	10
Doffers	15	16
Warpers	15	16
Winders	15	16

WOOLLEN OPERATIVES—SHILLINGS PER WEEK.

	England.	France.	Belgium.	Germany.	United States.
Sorter	24	22	10†	5†	44
Carder	24	11†	8†	8†	25
Spinner	12†	11†	. .	12	26†
Dresser	24	16	12	7†	54
Weaver	30	24	18	12	35
Fireman	26	19	15	. .	35
Carpenter	33	27	15	. .	52
Engineer	40	27	18	16	75

* For the greater convenience of the reader, in statistics quoted from European authorities I have in many places substituted, in place of foreign denominations of money, their equivalents as stated in terms of American coin, counting the English pound as five dollars and the shilling as twenty-four cents. The exact equivalent of the British pound is twenty shillings sterling, equal in value to about four dollars and eighty-four cents.

† Females.

(The reference is to wages of artisans.)

It will be observed that, in the following table, the estimate of food consumed by the family of each worker in the United States is much greater than in Europe, although the cost of food is less, the food of the American working-man being of a different kind and quality.

	Wages.	Food.	Surplus.	Rates of Surplus, per cent.
Great Britain	31	14	19	55
France	21	12	10	48
Germany	16	10	6	38
Belgium	20	12	8	40
Italy	15	9	6	40
Spain	16	10	6	38
United States	48	16	32	67
Australia	40	11	29	72

WAGES IN GERMAN TEXTILE INDUSTRIES.*

In textile industries over fifty per cent. of employés are women, receiving a weekly wage of from ten to twelve marks ($2.50 to $3.00).

WAGES PER HOUR.

Hand workmen	$3\frac{3}{4}$ to 5 cents.
Factory operatives	5 to $7\frac{1}{2}$ "
Female workers	$2\frac{1}{4}$ to $3\frac{1}{2}$ "
Persons from fourteen to sixteen	$1\frac{1}{4}$ to 2 "
Children, twelve to fourteen	$\frac{1}{2}$ to 1 cent.

In Berlin a skilful seamstress is supposed to earn from $2.25 to $2.70 per week; an inexperienced seamstress about half as much.   Board of a sewing-girl about $2.30 per week.

Mr. Tom Mann, president of the Dockers' Union, London, in the May number of the *Nineteenth Century*, states that the chain-makers of Credly Heath, England, work for $2.40 or $2.88 per week; that the lock-filers of Staffordshire get less still, and that thousands of laborers in Lancashire, in towns like Bolton, get no more than $3.60 per week; that in towns like Ipswich, in

---

* American Consular Reports, February, 1888.

the eastern counties, many are working for $2.64 and $2.88 per week, out of which they have to pay eighty cents for rent and twenty-eight cents for coals; and that before the great strike in London, thousands of dock-laborers considered themselves fortunate if they averaged $1.92 a week.

The United States Commissioner of Labor, in a statement laid before Congress, of recent date, gives the following comparative statement of the average wages of certain classes of laborers in Great Britain and in the United States:

Class of Employés.	Great Britain.	United States.
Engineers, per day	$1.46	$3.22
Firemen "	.91	1.79½
Conductors "	.97	2.63
Switchmen "	.85	1.50½
Flagmen "	.81	1.13
Engineers' yearly earnings	457.00	1007.00
Firemen's " "	285.00	562.00
Conductors' " "	304.00	824.00
Switchmen's " "	266.00	471.00
Flagmen's " "	254.00	354.00

The average weekly wages of potters are:

United States	$10.00	Austria	$3.17
England	5.20	Japan	2.50
France	4.78	India	1.75
Germany	3.60	China	1.50

In China day-laborers are hired for ten cents per day, including meals. The average wages of a field-hand are twelve dollars per annum, with food, straw shoes, and free shaving. His clothing costs about four dollars. He may save eight dollars per annum. An acre of land is worth one hundred and fifty dollars. Ten years' savings will enable a young man to buy one-third of an acre and the necessary tools for farming. In twenty years he may save enough to purchase two-thirds of an acre, and in six years more enough to purchase a wife, with whose assistance he can maintain himself on his own land and consider himself independent.

Land in China is minutely subdivided, many holdings being as low as one-sixth of an acre.

The tenant pays the farmer one-half of the rice-crop. The crop on an acre is worth about thirty-nine dollars.

A family of six persons will consume about six pounds of rice per day, worth about ten cents. A farmer pays two per cent. per month for what money he may borrow. *

In Japan (1885) daily wages, without board, in agriculture, are 18.6 cents for men and 12.1 cents for women. The average monthly wages, with board, are $2.12 for men and $1.10 for women. Workmen employed in preparation of tea receive 25.8 cents per day. Day-laborers receive twenty cents. Domestic wages for women are $1.06 per month, with board.

I find in "Prisoners of Poverty Abroad," by Mrs. Helen Campbell, published in 1889, the following table of prices paid to working-women in London at the present time; the workers boarding themselves:

"Making paper bags, four and one-half pence to five and one-half pence per thousand; possible earnings, five shillings to nine shillings per week. .Button-holes, three pence per dozen; possible earnings, eight shillings per week.

"Shirts, two pence each, worker finding her own cotton; can get six done between 6 A.M. and 11 P.M.

"Sack-sewing, six pence for twenty-five; eight pence to one shilling six pence per hundred; possible earnings, seven shillings per week.

"Pill-box making, one shilling for thirty-six gross; possible earnings, one shilling three pence per day.

"Button-hole making, one penny per dozen; can do three or four dozen between 5 A.M. and dark.

"Whip-making, one shilling per dozen; can do a dozen per day.

"Trousers finishing, three pence to five pence each, finding own cotton; can do four per day.

"Shirt finishing, three pence to four pence per dozen."

WAGES ONE HUNDRED YEARS AGO.

On the Pennsylvania canals the diggers were paid six dollars per month from May to November, and five dollars per month

---

* Consular Reports, September, 1887.

from November to May. Hod-carriers and mortar-mixers, diggers and choppers, who worked on the public buildings and cut the streets and avenues of Washington, from 1793 to 1800, received seventy dollars per year. The hours of work were from sunrise to sunset. Wages at Albany, N. Y., and New York City, were forty cents per day; at Lancaster, Pa., eight to ten dollars per month; elsewhere in Pennsylvania, six dollars in summer and five dollars in winter. In Virginia white men received sixteen pounds currency per year. Slaves were hired at one pound per month. A pound, Virginia currency, was equivalent to three dollars and eighty-three cents. The average rate of wages all over the country was sixty-five dollars per year, with food, and sometimes lodging.

WAGES AND PRICES IN THE THIRTEENTH CENTURY, AS ASCERTAINED BY THE INVESTIGATIONS OF PROFESSOR THOROLD ROGERS.

Price for threshing was, for wheat, one-eighteenth part; barley, one-twenty-second part; oats, one-fourteenth part. In the eighteenth century the peasant got one-twenty-fourth part of wheat and barley, and one-twenty-first part of oats. The average crop of the eighteenth century was more than double that of the thirteenth century.

Prices of reaping in thirteenth century were: Wheat, five pence per acre; barley, five and one-half pence; oats and rye, four and one-half pence; gathering beans, peas, and vetches, five pence per acre; mowing hay, five pence per acre.

Meat was one-fourth penny per pound. Clothing consisted of homespun russet cloth, hempen or linen shirting, rude boots, worth about two shillings, and leather gaskins worth one shilling and six pence. Amount required for the support of a farmer and small family is estimated at three pounds per year, and the ordinary savings of a small farmer at twenty shillings per year.

Carpenters' wages were from three pence to three and one-half pence per day; in London, from four pence to five pence per day.

At the building of Newgate gaol, in 1281, carpenters received four, five, and five and one-half pence per day; masons, five pence; sawyers, nine and one-half pence per pair. Winter wages were about twenty-five per cent. less than for other seasons. A day consisted of eight hours' labor.

Board cost from one and one-fourth pence to one and one-half pence per day.

Threshing was three pence for wheat, two pence for barley, one penny for oats, per quarter.

Farm wages were two pence per day for men, one penny for women, one half-penny for boys. Wages per year, including harvest, two pounds fifteen shillings.

Hands hired by the year received a quarter (eight bushels) of wheat, worth four shillings, every eight weeks; six shillings in money during the year, and board in harvest and other exceptional times.

Domestic servants received thirteen to fourteen shillings and board per year.

An advocate retained to defend a will received six shillings and eight pence; and in another instance, noted by Mr. Rogers, a fee for conducting a case was six shillings and eight pence.

Advocates and clerks, as a rule, were poorly paid.

On account of the competition of manufacturing labor, wages were higher in the eastern counties.

In 1333 the income of a lord was estimated at twenty per cent. on his capital. Parsons received two-fifths of the income of the lord on each estate.

Weston Tower, Oxford, built in 1448–50, cost twenty-eight pounds eight shillings. It would now cost one thousand pounds.

In the thirteenth century a penny contained three times as much silver as now.

In 1260 money was worth twelve times as much as in 1760. And Rogers estimates that labor was better paid in the time of Henry III. than in the time of George III.

NOTES FROM CENSUS OF MASSACHUSETTS, 1885—MANUFACTURING INDUSTRIES.

Number of wage-earners employed during the year ending June 30, 1885, 419,966; total wages, $147,415,316; net time actually lost by *establishments*, 6.10 per cent. Greatest number of persons who could be advantageously employed at any one time, with present buildings, machinery, and capital, 438,229;

aggregate number of persons employed at the periods of greatest
employment of the several industries, 301,159; smallest aggregate employment, 177,381; number of salaried persons, 9590;
salaries, $10,846,367. Capital employed consists as follows:
Land, $34,412,516; buildings, etc., $84,474,127; machinery,
$100,955,619; implements and tools, $14,298,711; cash and
credit capital, $173,440,947; credit capital furnished by partners or stockholders, $19,481,405; bills payable, accounts on
long time, etc., $73,531,052; total capital, $500,594,377.

PROPORTION OF PRODUCT TO CAPITAL.

	Per cent.
1865. State census	291
1870. United States census	239
1875. State census	210
1880. United States census	208
1885. State census	185
1885. State census, credit capital omitted	166

COMPARISON OF WAGES FIFTY YEARS AGO AND AT THE PRESENT TIME IN ENGLAND (FROM "MISCELLANEOUS STATISTICS OF THE UNITED KINGDOM" AND PORTER'S "PROGRESS OF THE NATION").

Occupation.	Place.	Wages Fifty years ago, Per Week.	Wages Present Time, Per Week.	Increase, Per cent.
Carpenters	Manchester.	24s.	84s.	42
"	Glasgow.	14s.	26s.	85
Bricklayers	Manchester.*	24s.	86s.	50
"	Glasgow.	15s.	27s.	80
Masons	Staffordshire.	24s.	29s. 10d.	24
"	Huddersfield.	14s.	23s. 8d.	69
Miners	"	2s. 8d.†	4s.†	70
Pattern weavers . .	"	16s.	25s.	55
Wool scourers . . .	"	17s.	22s.	30
Mule spinners . . .	"	25s.	30s.	20
Weavers	"	12s.	26s.	115
Warpers and beamers	"	17s.	27s.	58
Winders and reelers	"	6s.	11s.	83
Weavers (men) . . .	Bradford.	8s. 3d.	20s. 6d.	150
Reelers and warping	"	7s. 9d.	15s. 6d.	100
Spinning (children) .	"	4s. 5d.	11s. 6d.	100

* 1825.   † Per day.

COMPARISON OF SEAMAN'S MONEY WAGES PER MONTH (IN ENG-
LAND) IN 1850 AND THE PRESENT TIME (FROM "PROGRESS OF
MERCHANT SHIPPING RETURN").

	1850, Sailing.	Present Time, Steam.	Increase Rate, Per cent.
Bristol	45s.	75s.	66
Glasgow	45s.	70s.	55
Liverpool (1)	50s.	69s. 5d.	88
" (2)	50s.	85s.	70
" (3)	45s.	60s.	88
" (4)	40s.	50s.	25
" (5)	42s.	60s.	40
London (1)	45s.	75s.	66
" (2)	50s.	77s. 6d.	55
" (3)	45s.	65s.	45
" (4)	45s.	70s.	55
" (5)	40s.	67s. 6d.	69
" (6)	40s.	67s. 6d.	69

PRICES OF VARIOUS ARTICLES FIFTY YEARS AGO AND NOW.

	1839-40.	Present Time.
Sugar (per cwt.)	68s. 8d.	21s. 9d.
Cotton cloth, exported (per yard)	5⅝d.	3¼d.

	1840.	1882.
Inferior beasts (per eight pounds)	8s. 1d.	4s. 3¾d.
Second class " "	8s. 6d.	4s. 9¾d.
Third class " "	3s. 11¾d.	5s. 7½d.
Inferior sheep " "	3s. 5d.	5s. 7d.
Second class " "	3s. 10¼d.	6s. 1¼d.
Large hogs " "	3s. 3½d.	4s. 6d.

The three foregoing tables are quoted from "Progress of the
Working-Classes of the Last Half-Century," by Robert Griffin,
LL.D., president of the British Statistical Society. He estimates that the rental paid by workingmen is now two and one-
half times what it was fifty years ago, and that houses have
improved in corresponding ratio. The prices of wheat have
ranged as follows :

1836. The highest price was . . . . . . 36s.   per quarter.
1838. " " " " . . . . . . 78s. 4d.   "
1839. " " " " . . . . . . 81s. 6d.   "

1840. The highest price was	72s. 10d.	per quarter.
1841. " " " "	76s. 1d.	"
1847. " " " "	102s. 5d.	"
1837 to 1846. The average price was . .	58s. 7d.	"
1872 to 1882. " " " " . .	48s. 9d.	"
1862 to 1882. The highest price (1867) .	70s. 5d.	"
1862 to 1882. " " " (1868) .	74s. 7d.	"

Of late years the price has been both low and steady. During the earlier half of the century prices were subject to extreme fluctuations. Fifty years ago the English workingman consumed but little meat. Bacon only was within his reach, and not much of that. The same writer estimates the reduction in the hours of labor in textile, engineering, and building trades at twenty per cent.

AGRICULTURAL WAGES IN ENGLAND.

"On the whole, the agricultural laborer, at any rate in the south of England, was much better off in the middle of the eighteenth century than his descendants were in the middle of the nineteenth. At the latter date wages were actually lower in Suffolk, Essex, and perhaps part of Wilts, than they were at the former; in Berks they were exactly the same; in Norfolk, Bucks, Gloucestershire, and South Wilts there had been a very trifling rise: with the exception of Sussex and Oxfordshire, there was no country south of the Trent in which they had risen more than one-fourth. Meanwhile, rent and most necessaries, except bread, had increased enormously in cost, while most of the laborer's old privileges were lost, so that his real wages had actually diminished. But in the manufacturing districts of the north his condition had improved. While nominal wages in the south had risen, on the average, fourteen per cent., here they had risen, on the average, sixty-six per cent. In some districts the rise had been as great as two hundred per cent. In Arthur Young's time the agricultural wages of Lancashire were four shillings and six pence, the lowest rate in England; in 1821 they had risen to fourteen shillings. It may be roughly said that the relative positions of the laborer north and south of Trent had been exactly reversed in the course of a century.

"Turning from the agricultural wage-earners to those engaged in manufactures, we find their condition at this period, on the whole, much inferior to what it is now. In spite of the widening gulf between capitalist and laborer, the status of the artisan has distinctly improved since Adam Smith's time. His nominal wages have doubled or trebled. A carpenter then earned two shillings and six pence a day; he now earns five shillings and six pence. A cotton-weaver then earned five shillings a week; he now earns twenty shillings; and so on.

"If the wages have, on the whole, very greatly increased, there were, on the other hand, some obvious advantages which the artisan possessed in those days, but has since lost; for the manufacturing population still lived, to a very great extent, in the country. The artisan often had his small piece of land, which supplied him with wholesome food and healthy recreation. His wages and employment, too, were regular. He was not subject to the uncertainties, and knew nothing of the fearful sufferings, which his descendants were to endure from commercial fluctuations, especially before the introduction of free trade; for the whole inner life of industry was, as we have seen, entirely different from what it now is. The relation between workmen and employers was much closer, so that in many industries they were not two classes, but one. As among the agriculturalists, the farmer and laborer lived much the same life,—for the capitalist farmers as a class were not yet in existence, and ate at the same board,—so in manufacturing industries the journeyman was often on his way to become a master. The distribution of wealth was, indeed, in all respects more equal. Landed property, though gradually being concentrated, was still in a far larger number of hands, and even the great landlords possessed nothing like their present riches. They had no vast mineral wealth nor rapidly-developing town property. A great number of the trading industries, too, were still in the hands of small capitalists. Great trades like the iron trade, requiring large capital, had hardly come into existence." *

Another important fact not to be overlooked in this connection, as bearing upon the relative amount of the actual earnings of labor, is that in the eighteenth century the production

---

* Industrial Revolution of the Eighteenth Century in England.

of fabrics, clothing, and other articles in the family of the laborer was far greater than in the nineteenth century.

On the other hand, the laborers of the nineteenth century enjoy many advantages in the way of public schools, postal service, and otherwise, which the eighteenth century did not afford.

The industrial growth of England was attended by two notable changes in the condition of the people. The first was the consolidation of lands through the purchase and extinction of small holdings; the second, the introduction of machinery. To these causes must be chiefly attributed the change in the condition of the laboring-classes, which is illustrated in the fact that the poor-rate gradually increased from three shillings and seven pence per head in 1760 to thirteen shillings and three pence per head in 1818, the highest rate ever reached.

In 1831 there were 1,243,057 adult males employed in agriculture in Great Britain; in 1841 there were 1,207,989; in 1851 the whole number of persons engaged in agriculture was 2,084,153; in 1861, 2,010,454; and in 1871, 1,657,138.

MONEY, STATISTICS OF.

The amount of gold and silver necessary for use as money, or for the purpose of facilitating exchange, is not an absolute quantity depending on the value of these metals according to present ratios of value, but a quantity sufficient to admit of division into pieces of sizes convenient for handling and numerous enough, when distributed among the people, to furnish measures of value in the number necessary to answer the purposes of convenience in conducting the business of exchange.

The value of gold and silver depends upon the quantity in existence. If the present quantity of gold and silver in the world were only one-half what it actually is, the value would be twice as great, except for the fact that these metals are used in the arts; and it may be, also, that the greater subdivision made necessary might extend somewhat the employment of credit, with these metals as a basis. But it may be laid down as a general proposition, that the value of the precious metals increases or diminishes in inverse ratio as the quantity increases or diminishes.

The principal element that gives value to these metals is their scarcity and the fact that the amount on hand can be increased but slowly, so that the quantity, as compared with the volume of exchange, remains the same from one year to another, and the fluctuations in the ratio, through the course of a decade or a century, are confined within a narrow margin.

Nevertheless, the variation in the value of these metals through long periods of time has been very great; and the fluctuations within comparatively short periods have, in a few instances, been quite marked. It is estimated that between 1800 and 1849 the purchasing power of gold, as measured in the ordinary necessities of life, increased about forty-five per cent., and between 1847 and 1858 the depreciation in the value of gold, resulting from greatly-increased production, was not less than twenty per cent. The increase in the product of silver within recent years has had a like effect in depreciating the value of that metal. Except for the demonetization of silver in Europe and in the United States, the depression in value resulting from the increased production of that metal would have extended to gold as well, and the two metals would have retained their relative values as before.

The relative depreciation in the value of silver is attributable altogether to demonetization of the latter metal. The effect of demonetization was, therefore, to increase the value of money, and, in like measure, to increase the amount of debts as measured in the products of labor.

From this demonetization of silver great advantage resulted to the holders of public securities and to private creditors holding paper payable several years later, with corresponding loss to debtors and to the people who are taxed to pay public securities.

The depreciation in the value of money resulting from increased production is a risk fairly assumed by the creditor. The depreciation in the values of other property, from whatever cause, is something which the government has never attempted to prevent, by increasing the amount of money in circulation, or by other special measure; and the favoritism shown to creditors is an injustice, for which there can be offered no valid excuse. But, under the plea of guarding the public credit, legislation has often favored the creditor at the expense of the debtor.

Prior to the eighteenth century the larger proportion of coin in use in England and America and throughout the world was silver.

From 1200 to 1420 the amount of gold coined in Great Britain was £35,000, while the amount of silver coined was £183,000; from 1420 to 1603 the amount of gold coined was £1,494,000, and the amount of silver coined was £5,649,000; from 1604 to 1688 the amount of gold coined was £13,432,000, and the amount of silver was £17,421,000; but from 1689 to 1760 the amount of gold coined was £26,058,000, and the amount of silver £8,239,-000; from 1760 to 1880 the amount of gold coined in Great Britain was £369,670,000, and the amount of silver was but £27,525,000.

The coinage in the United States from 1793 to 1840 was, gold, £32,000,000, silver, £11,100,000; from 1840 to 1850, gold, £19,800,000, silver, £4,500,000; from 1850 to 1860, gold, £66,-000,000, silver, £9,300,000; from 1860 to 1881, gold, £147,200,-000, silver, £37,100,000.

The following table shows the quantity of coin in the world since 1600, the amount of commerce and the ratio of coin to. commerce (foreign).

Date.	Coin.	Commerce.	Ratio of Coin to Commerce.
1600	£130,000,000	£35,000,000	371
1700	297,000,000	94,000,000	316
1809	380,000,000	286,000,000	133
1830	813,000,000	368,000,000	85
1880	1,128,000,000	2,650,000,000	42

AMOUNT OF COIN IN DIFFERENT COUNTRIES, RATIO TO COMMERCE, AND AMOUNT PER INHABITANT.

Year.	Country.	Gold.	Silver.	Total.	Per Inhabitant.	Ratio to Commerce.
1881.	Great Britain . .	£123,600,000	£19,300,000	£142,900,000	£4. 0.2	25
1880.	France	190,000,000	110,000,000	300,000,000	8. 0.2	90
1880.	United States . .	115,000,000	41,000,000	146,000,000	2.17.0	46

The paper money of the United Kingdom was £42,000,000; that of France, £100,000,000; and that of the United States, £144,000,000. Amount of money per inhabitant of the United

Kingdom, £5.6.0; France, £10.10.0; United States, £5.15.0. The banking power of the United Kingdom was four times that of France.

The extent to which credits, employed through the agency of banks, have taken the place of money is here illustrated. The amount of money per inhabitant in France is nearly double what it is in the United Kingdom, although the foreign commerce of France is only three-fifths as great as that of the United Kingdom of England, Scotland, and Ireland.

The amount of uncovered (by coin) paper money in 1880 was, in the United Kingdom, £10,000,000; France, £13,000,000; Germany, £20,000,000; Russia, £88,000,000; United States, £81,000,000.

At the close of the Franco-Prussian War, Germany exacted of France a thousand million dollars of gold indemnity; and on the 9th of July, 1873, gold was, by law, made the standard of value in Germany. Before this the metallic currency of Germany was silver. Denmark, Norway, Sweden, and the Netherlands, following the example of Germany, changed their currency to gold and threw their silver on the market. Coinage was restricted in Italy, France, Belgium, Switzerland, and Greece, and soon thereafter ceased altogether; and in 1873 the United States also ceased to coin silver, and made the gold dollar the sole unit of value.

In England, prior to 1816, the unit of value, the English pound, was silver. In 1816 gold was made the unit of value, and silver ceased to be a legal tender in sums over forty shillings.

From 1873 to 1878 there was no law authorizing the coinage of silver dollars in the United States.

Prior to 1873 the silver dollar, of the same weight and fineness as now, was a full legal tender.

The ratio in coinage between gold and silver was, in Europe, 1.15½; in the United States, 1.16.

Prior to 1873 silver was at a premium. From 1873 to 1876 the price of silver in the London market varied as much as thirty-five per cent., and on the 19th of May, 1887, it fell to eighty-three cents per ounce.

During the four years ending June 30, 1865, the average value of the silver in a silver dollar is officially stated as about three and three-fourths per cent. greater than the value of the gold in a gold dollar.

The amount of silver in our dollar is the same to-day as under the first coinage act of 1792; but the alloy has been changed, so that the dollar contains, since 1837, three and one-half grains less copper than before that time.

In July, 1876, our silver dollar, as a commodity, was worth but seventy-nine and one-fourth cents; in 1884 it was worth eighty-six and one-fourth cents.

From 1834 down to 1873, when silver coinage was stopped, silver, being at a premium, went abroad.

Silver is the coin of most Eastern countries.

The fall in the price of silver enabled England to purchase in India, with thirty-two cents, an amount of wheat that before the depreciation cost forty-eight cents. The effect was to stimulate imports from India and reduce the demand for American wheat.

The proportion of silver money to the amount of gold money in the world is as 9 : 11 ; or, for every fifty-four cents in gold there are forty-six cents in silver.

.The amount of silver coined in the United States since 1878, and prior to 1889, is $308,780,157.

The law enacted in 1878 authorized the Secretary of the Treasury to purchase silver bullion on the market, and provided for the coinage of an amount not exceeding four million dollars per month.

In 1792, silver dollars of four hundred and sixteen grains were authorized.

In 1793, Spanish milled dollars and parts of dollars were made a legal tender, and other foreign coins were made a legal tender until the expiration of three years after the establishment of the United States Mint.

In 1806, foreign coins were made a legal tender at certain defined rates. Limitation in act of 1793 suspended three years.

In 1834, foreign silver coins were made current at named rates.

In 1837, silver dollars of four hundred and twelve and one-half grains were authorized.

In 1851, three-cent pieces were authorized and made legal tender for amounts not exceeding thirty cents. They were three-fourths silver and one-fourth copper.

In 1853, half-dollars and other subsidiary coins were made legal tender to amounts not exceeding five dollars.

In 1857 it was enacted that no foreign gold or silver coin should be a legal tender.

The coinage act of 1873 authorized the deposit of silver bullion for the coinage of trade dollars of four hundred and twenty grains, and stamped bars, but no deposit was permitted for any other purpose. It provided for the purchase of silver bullion for coinage of fifty-cent, twenty-five-cent, and ten-cent pieces, and made silver coin a legal tender to the amount of five dollars.*

The act of July, 1876, authorized the Secretary of the Treasury to issue the silver coin in the treasury in exchange for legal-tender notes to the amount of not exceeding ten million dollars, provided that trade dollars should not thereafter be a legal tender, and authorized the Secretary to limit the coinage thereof to the export demand.

The act of 1878 made silver dollars of four hundred and twelve and one-half grains a legal tender, and authorized the Secretary of the Treasury to purchase silver bullion for coinage at a rate not exceeding four million dollars per month. It provided that silver should not be used in payment of gold certificates.

An act passed by the present Congress (1890) provides (1) that the Secretary of the Treasury shall from time to time purchase silver bullion to the aggregate of four million five hundred thousand ounces per month, or so much thereof as may be offered each month at the market price thereof at not exceeding one dollar for 371.25 grains of pure silver; (2) that payment for the bullion purchased shall be made in treasury notes, which are made a legal tender for all debts both public and private, except where otherwise expressly stipulated by contract, and are redeemable in gold or silver coin at the option of the Secretary of the Treasury, it being declared the policy of the United States to maintain gold and silver at a parity with each other in the ratio fixed by law; (3) that the Secretary of the Treas-

---

* The coinage of silver dollars had ceased prior to the repeal of the law authorizing their coinage in 1873, owing to the fact that silver was at a premium over gold. The higher value of silver was caused by the foreign demand. Silver was rated at a relatively higher value in the money of Europe, and was the standard coin in the East.

ury shall each month coin two million ounces of silver bullion into standard silver dollars until July 1, 1891, and after that time as much as may be necessary for the redemption of the treasury notes issued under this act; (4) the treasury notes provided for, after being redeemed, may be reissued, but the amount at any time outstanding is limited to the cost of the silver bullion purchased.

The purchase of silver provided for by this act is sufficient to absorb the silver product of the United States at present available for coinage. The value of silver is not forced to a parity with gold in the home market by an arbitrary act of government, but its value is raised to the extent of the effect of the increased demand. The treasury notes issued, being made redeemable in gold or silver at the option of the Secretary of the Treasury, and being based on the gold value of silver, will naturally remain at a parity with gold. While an increase in the volume of currency, substantially equivalent to that which would have been obtained by free coinage, is thus secured, it is sought to avoid the effect of an attempt to maintain the circulation of coin at a higher relative value than that fixed by the markets of the world, which in the past has been exemplified in the hoarding and the exportation of the dearer metal.

During the war which began in 1861 and ended in 1865, United States bonds were sold on the market to the amount of $1,163,769,611.89. Legal tender notes were received for the greater portion of this amount. On the third day of October, 1865, the total debt of the United States was $2,808,549,437.75, embracing bonds, compound interest notes, treasury notes, certificates of indebtedness, temporary loans, United States notes, and fractional currency. This debt was contracted on the basis of the value of the paper currency. The total circulation at that date, embracing all securities used as money, was $1,894,779,825.66.

The process of contracting the currency began during the year following the close of the war, and by July, 1870, the circulation had been reduced to $747,000,000. The consequent appreciation of credits and depreciation of property values resulted in the financial crash of 1873.

The war was a source of great profit to capitalists. The losses

have been borne by the workingmen. A financial policy may be
altogether sound from the stand-point of the money-lender, and
yet be but robbery disguised.

The policy of the government in financial matters is dictated
by the necessity of commanding the support of the money
power, which is stronger than the people and always on the
alert. The remedy will be found in that improved intelligence
of the people which shall extricate the government from such
necessity.

The following table exhibits the amount of the outstanding
currency of the United States and of national banks on January 1 of each year, and the estimated amount of coin in circulation and in the treasury for the years designated. The first
column, United States issues, embraces legal tender notes, old
demand notes, and fractional currency. The amount of demand
notes August 31, 1865, was $402,965. This amount was reduced
each year. The amount of fractional currency in 1874 reached
$48,544,792, the largest amount outstanding at any one time.

Year.	United States Issue.	National Bank Issue.	Coin.	Total Currency.
1865 . . .	$459,201,619	$176,213,955	. . . . . .	$635,415,574
1866 . . .	452,232,409	236,636,098	. . . . . .	688,858,507
1867 . . .	409,230,614	298,588,419	. . . . . .	707,819,033
1868 . . .	387,756,710	299,846,206	. . . . . .	687,602,916
1869 . . .	390,343,813	299,747,569	. . : . . .	690,091,382
1870 . . .	395,875,762	299,629,322	$40,000,000	695,504,087
1871 . . .	396,096,175	306,307,672	. . . . . .	702,403,847
1872 . . .	398,360,678	328,465,431	. . . . . .	726,836,099
1873 . . .	404,364,355	344,582,812	140,000,000	748,947,167
1874 . . .	427,026,131	350,848,236	. . . . . .	777,874,367
1875 . . .	428,462,917	354,128,250	. . . . . .	782,591,165
1876 . . .	416,053,934	346,479,756	. . . . . .	762,523,690
1877 . . .	392,468,752	321,595,606	. . . . . .	714,064,358
1878 . . .	367,771,417	321,672,505	. . . . . .	689,443,922
1879 . . .	362,851,210	323,791,674	· 398,541,683	686,642,884
1880 . . .	362,406,670	342,387,336	502,981,634*	704,804,006
1881 . . .	362,265,225	344,355,203	732,398,542*	706,620,428
1882 . . .	362,192,797	362,421,988	· 756,100,686*	724,614,785
1883 . . .	362,138,319	361,882,791	824,672,186*	724,021,110
1884 . . .	. . . . . .	. . . . .	861,347,311*	. . . . .
1885 . . .	. . . . .	. . . . .	894,386,614*	. . . . .

* November 1.

Since the above figures include amounts in the United States Treasury at the dates named, in order to ascertain the actual circulation the amount in the United States Treasury should be deducted. On October 1, 1883, the amount of bullion, coin, and currency in the treasury not represented by outstanding certificates was $311,590,769, and on October 1, 1887, the amount in the treasury was $469,977,945. The money in the hands of the people, not including that in banks, was, on November 1, 1881, $918,048,519, and on November 1, 1885, $829,792,777.

From the above table alone, it would appear that there had been no contraction of the circulation from 1865 to 1879, but, on the other hand, that there had been an increase. Besides United States legal tender notes there were issued, prior to 1865, compound interest notes, one-year, and two-year notes of 1863, and two-year coupon notes of 1863, all of which were a legal tender and intended to circulate as money. Of government legal tender currency there was outstanding, June 30, 1866, $608,870,825. But, in addition, there were other issues, not designed to circulate as money, but which, owing to early maturity and the small denominations in which they were issued, were extensively used as currency. Of securities of this class, there were outstanding, September 1, 1865, as follows:

Temporary loan certificates	$107,148,713
Certificates of indebtedness	85,093,000
Three-year treasury notes	830,000,000
State bank notes	78,867,575
Total	$1,101,109,288

Securities of the classes here enumerated did not enter into circulation with the same freedom as the ordinary legal tender note; nevertheless they were extensively employed as money, and tended greatly to the inflation of values. Counting these securities as money, the total circulation September 1, 1865, was $1,996,678,770.

Prior to December 1, 1873, the securities here enumerated were cancelled, and in their place were issued long-time interest-bearing bonds; and on the 1st of December, 1873, the circulating medium, exclusive of coin, was as follows:

United States notes $367,001,685
Fractional currency   48,000,000
Certificates of indebtedness (bearing interest) . .   678,000
National bank currency 350,000,000
                                             ────────────
    Total December 1, 1873 . . . . $765,679,685

Thus it appears that the amount of the evidences of indebtedness of the United States government used as a circulating medium was contracted over $1,200,000 in eight years. Owing to the fact that many of these securities were held as investments, and did not in fact circulate as money, the degree of contraction was much less than the amount measured, as here shown, by the reduction in volume. But, nevertheless, the contraction was sufficient to produce the panic of 1873 and the great depreciation in values of all classes of property which began with the reduction of the circulating medium, or as soon thereafter as financial pressure began to be seriously felt.

When there is a contraction of the currency there is a tendency to supply its place by the employment of credit, and values for a time are maintained. When the pressure continues, prices go down and credit is withdrawn, a financial crisis is brought on, and there comes a forced readjustment of values.

The contraction in values of farm products resulting from the contraction of the currency is shown by a comparison of the amount and value of the cereals grown in 1867 and 1868, with the amount and value of cereals grown in 1880, 1881, and 1882.

Year.	No. of Bushels.	Value.
1867.	1,339,729,400	$1,284,037,300
1868.	1,450,789,000	1,110,500,538
1880.	2,718,193,501	1,361,497,704
1881.	2,066,029,570	1,470,957,200
1882.	2,829,319,089	1,280,765,927

Agricultural exports in 1867 were $330,413,246, and in 1880, $823,846,353.

The increase in population from 1867 to 1880 was about forty per cent.

The great reduction in price of agricultural products must be attributed in part to the increase of the product per capita, but it was to a great extent the result of the contraction of the currency.

FLUCTUATIONS IN VALUES.

The following tables show the annual production of wheat and corn in the United States during a period of twenty years. The value of each year's product is given, and the average farm price per bushel. The population also is shown, and the number of cattle and hogs at certain periods. The number of miles of railway built each year, the product of pig-iron and the prices thereof, the value of exports of meat and dairy products, bread-stuffs, wheat, and flour are exhibited. The gold value of currency and the cotton product and prices, and the wheat- and rye-crops of the principal countries of Europe and the imports from India to Great Britain for a series of years are shown. The values of exports and imports are measured in gold. The statistics of cattle and hogs are given for December of the year designated, or for January of the following year, so that they represent the matured product of the corn-crop of the year designated. To ascertain the amount of the product of any year exported, reference must be made to the year following. The fiscal year ends June 30.

The low prices which prevailed from 1874 to 1879 were the result of the panic of 1873 and the industrial depression which followed and continued until the business of the country had readjusted itself to the new conditions. The resumption of business activity is marked by the increase in miles of railway constructed and the production of pig-iron. During the first half of the decade beginning in 1880 prices advanced, but during the latter half the excess of the agricultural product broke down prices in that department of industry, so that the per capita product to each agricultural worker, after deducting seed and food of work-animals, is only eighty-two per cent. of the average per capita product for the years 1870 to 1874, inclusive, if we accept the value of the wheat and corn crops as a basis of estimate.

While the reduction in the per capita product of agriculture was great, the indebtedness of the farmer had greatly increased. The immense amount of money borrowed by farmers and invested in agriculture resulted in an increase of the quantity of product; but the effect was to reduce values, so that these investments not only brought no returns to the farmer, but caused a reduction of the farmer's income while adding to his expenditure. Besides, the fact must not be overlooked that the great increase of product was not distributed among the workers, being largely the result of extensive farming in the Western States and the cattle industry in the Territories, the per capita increase in quantity east of the Mississippi being but small.*

It will be observed that the fluctuations in prices of wheat depend in part upon conditions which control the European market.

Europe requires, on an average, about 140,000,000 bushels of foreign grain; yet in 1881 there were 322,000,000 bushels to cover this demand, 186,000,000 bushels being from the United States alone.

From 1876 to 1879 the crops of Great Britain were a succession of failures, and Germany, Austria, Hungary, and other European countries had short crops in 1879.

Prices of agricultural products in Europe have suffered from foreign competition to such degree as to greatly depress that industry and lead to general embarrassment.

In England the price of hogs has fallen from forty-one cents per pound in 1868 to twenty-one and a half cents in 1888; the production of wool from 166,000,000 pounds in 1868 to 134,000,-000 in 1888; the area of grain culture is diminishing, and the rental value of lands has fallen to about one-half of former rates. Agricultural values throughout Europe have gone down as foreign competition increased.

The fluctuations in railway construction, and in the manufacture of iron, exhibited in this table, indicate the large numbers of workers who are from time to time thrown out of employment by the partial suspension of these industries, creating irregular and unhealthy competition in the labor market, reducing consumption and impairing values.

---

* In 1889, Kansas alone produced one-ninth of the total product of wheat, oats, and corn; and the wheat-crop of Dakota increased from 2,800,000 bushels in 1880 to 41,600,000 in 1889. In 1887 it was 62,500,000 bushels. The corn-crop of Kansas and Nebraska in 1889 was over 390,000,000 bushels, against 165,700,000 bushels in 1880.

TABLES SHOWING PRODUCTS OF UNITED STATES, AND AVERAGE PRICES FOR YEARS NAMED.

Year.	Population.	Bushels of Corn grown.	Value.	Average price per bushel, local market.	Bushels of Wheat grown.	Value.	Average price per bushel, local market.
1867	35,868,000	768,320,000	$610,948,390	$0.79	212,441,400	$421,796,460	$1.98
1870	38,558,371	1,094,255,000	600,746,996	.64.9	235,884,700	246,865,045	1.04
1871	39,555,000	991,898,000	478,275,900	.48.2	230,722,400	290,411,820	1.26
1872	40,596,000	1,092,719,000	435,149,290	.39.8	249,997,100	310,180,375	1.24
1873	41,667,000	932,274,000	447,183,020	.48	281,254,700	323,694,806	1.16
1874	42,796,000	860,148,500	550,043,080	.64	309,102,700	291,107,895	.94
1875	43,951,000	1,320,069,000	555,445,930	.42	292,136,000	294,580,990	1.00
1876	45,137,000	1,288,827,500	475,491,210	.37	289,356,500	300,259,300	1.04
1877	46,353,000	1,342,558,000	480,643,400	.36.8	364,194,146	394,695,779	1.08
1878	47,598,000	1,388,218,760	441,163,405	.31.8	420,122,400	326,346,424	.78
1879	48,886,000	1,764,591,676	657,971,879	.37.5	459,483,137	436,968,463	.95
1880	50,155,783	1,717,434,543	679,714,490	.39.6	498,549,868	474,201,860	.95
1881	51,495,000	1,194,916,000	769,482,170	.63.6	383,280,090	456,880,427	1.19
1882	52,802,000	1,617,025,000	783,867,175	.48.4	504,165,490	444,602,125	.88
1883	54,166,000	1,551,066,895	658,051,485	.42.4	421,086,160	388,649,272	.91
1884	55,550,000	1,795,528,000	640,735,560	.35.7	512,765,000	330,862,260	.65
1885	56,975,000	1,936,176,000	635,674,630	.32.8	357,112,000	275,320,390	.77
1886	58,420,000	1,665,441,000	610,311,000	.36.6	457,218,000	314,226,020	.69
1887	59,893,000	1,456,161,000	646,106,770	.44.4	456,329,000	310,612,960	.68
1888	61,690,000	1,987,790,000	667,561,680	.34.1	415,868,000	386,248,080	.98
1889	63,540,000	2,112,892,000	597,918,829	.28.3	490,560,000	342,491,707	.70

Year	Domestic Exports of Merchandise.	Average value per ton.	Tons of Pig-Iron made.	Miles of Railway built.	Average value.	Number of Hogs.	Average value.	Number of Cattle other than Milch-Cows.
1867	$279,786,809	$44.00		2,440	$4.55	24,317,258	$20.86	11,192,484
1870	376,616,473	38.25	1,865,000	6,070	6.19	29,457,500	22.81	16,212,200
1871	428,398,908	35.50	1,911,608	7,879	4.36		19.61	
1872	428,487,181	48.87	2,854,558	5,878	4.09		20.06	
1873	505,033,429	42.75	2,868,278	4,097	4.36		19.15	
1874	569,433,421	30.25	2,689,418	2,117	5.34		18.68	
1875	514,890,624	25.50	2,266,581	1,711	6.80		19.04	
1876	586,089,810	22.50	2,093,236	2,712	6.09		17.10	
1877	602,722,018	18.87	2,814,585	2,280	4.98		17.14	
1878	680,683,798	17.62	2,577,361	2,629	8.18		15.39	
1879	698,340,790	21.50	3,070,875	4,746	4.28		16.10	
1880	823,946,253	28.60	4,295,214	6,876	4.70	47,681,700	17.33	28,482,891
1881	883,925,947	25.12	4,641,564	9,796	5.98		19.89	
1882	783,239,782	25.75	5,178,122	11,568	6.75	43,270,086	21.80	28,046,077
1883	804,228,682	22.37	5,146,972	6,741	5.57	44,200,898	23.52	29,046,101
1884	724,964,852	19.87	4,589,618	8,825				
1885	726,682,946	18.00	4,529,869	3,608	4.48	44,612,836	21.17	31,275,242
1886	665,964,529	18.25	6,365,328	9,000	4.25	46,092,043		
1887	703,029,928			11,000			19.79	33,511,750
1888	683,862,104			8,000	5.79	50,301,592	17.05	35,082,417
1889	780,282,609			6,500		51,602,780		36,049,824

Year.	Meats, Dairy Products, Cattle, Sheep, and Hogs exported.	Bread-stuffs exported.	Bushels of Wheat exported.	Barrels of Flour exported.	Gold value of $100 in Currency on January 1 of each year.	Bales of Cotton produced.	Value of Cotton per pound.
1867	$26,602,170	$41,288,804	16,940,899 *	2,076,423 *	$76.18 †	2,019,774	.8159
1870	31,717,238	72,250,933	34,304,908 *	3,653,841 *	83.33	8,164,946	.2398
1871	40,300,565	79,381,187			90.29	4,852,817	.1695
1872	65,209,608	84,586,278			91.32	2,974,351	.2219
1873	84,602,717	98,743,151			89.28	3,930,508	.2014
1874	86,447,704	161,198,864			90.70	4,170,888	.1795
1875	85,126,255	111,468,265	66,073,122	3,935,610	88.89	3,832,991	.1646
1876	94,227,154	181,181,665	40,325,611	8,348,100	88.69	4,669,288	.1298
1877	121,106,416	117,806,476	72,404,961	8,974,550	93.46	4,485,423	.1182
1878	129,342,713	181,177,841	122,353,936	5,629,714	97.21	4,811,265	.1122
1879	130,020,092	210,355,528	163,252,795	6,011,419	100.00	5,073,581	.1084
1880	147,146,132	288,086,885	160,565,477	7,701,340	100.00	5,757,397	.1151
1881	172,449,018	270,332,519	95,271,802	4,137,900	100.00	6,689,329	.1208
1882	130,934,186	182,670,628	106,385,828	9,205,660	100.00	5,435,846	.1156
1883	118,985,922	208,040,850	70,849,012	9,162,260	100.00	6,992,234	.1188
1884	133,684,909	162,544,716	84,653,714	10,644,814	100.00	5,714,052	.1088
1885	121,330,897	160,370,821	57,759,209	8,179,241	100.00	5,669,021	.1086
1886	102,588,311	125,846,558	101,971,949	11,518,449	100.00	6,550,215	.0900
1887	102,774,910	165,768,662	65,789,261	11,963,574	100.00	6,518,628	.0940
1888	104,742,605	127,191,687	46,414,129		100.00	7,164,940	.1020
1889					100.00	7,177,930	.1020

* Year ending June 30, 1888.　† The values of exports are estimated in gold.

WHEAT- AND RYE-CROPS OF THE PRINCIPAL COUNTRIES OF EUROPE, ETC.

Year.	Wheat-crop of principal countries of Europe, bushels.	Rye-crop of principal countries of Europe, bushels.	Total Wheat- and Rye-crops, bushels.	Imports of Wheat to Great Britain from India, bushels.
1874	931,414,000	1,200,058,000	2,131,419,000	. . . .
1875	764,894,000	982,050,000	1,746,944,000	. . . .
1876	766,943,000	990,008,000	1,756,951,000	. . . .
1877	891,798,000	1,128,000,000	2,019,798,000	8,097,123
1878	894,455,000	12,272,523,000	2,166,978,000	10,698,518
1879	708,523,000	954,025,000	1,657,548,000	1,597,273
1880	810,900,000	956,075,000	1,766,976,000	3,037,022
1881	807,770,000	994,919,000	1,802,690,000	8,964,168
1882	. . . . . .	. . . . . .	. . . . . .	17,507,907
1883	. . . . . .	. . . . . .	. . . . . .	12,273,632

Year.	Total wheat-crop of Europe, bushels.	Total wheat-crop of the world, bushels.
1880	1,128,000,000	2,111,000,000
1881	1,160,000,000	2,025,000,000
1882	1,283,000,000	2,282,000,000
1883	1,553,000,000	2,054,000,000
1884	1,270,000,000	2,293,000,000
1885	1,183,000,000	2,095,000,000
1886	1,108,000,000	2,055,000,000
1887	1,245,000,000	2,188,000,000

PRICES OF LEADING ARTICLES FOR THE YEARS 1867, 1868, AND 1870, COMPARED WITH PRICES OF 1884, AND OTHER YEARS, AS DESIGNATED, THE AVERAGE PRICES OF THE FORMER YEARS BEING REPRESENTED BY 100.

	1867–68 and '70.	1884.
Cotton goods	100	56.3
Coffee	100	67
Coal (anthracite)	100	58
Iron (bar)	100	48.3
Iron (pig)	100	52
Leather	100	70
Sugar (refined)	100	70
		1884–86.
Mackerel	100	77
Wool	100	100
Rice	100	40.8
Eggs	100	60

Butter		100	60
Wheat		100	47.5
Corn		100	56.4
Mess pork		100	53
Beef (salted)		100	70
Hams		100	71

		1869.	1883.
Freight charges, Chicago to New York		100	46.6

		1867–75.	1885–89.
Yield of wheat per acre		100	94.23
" corn "		100	97

		1866–71.	1889.
Beef cattle (New York)		100	57.7

CHAPTER IV.

LIMITATIONS ON THE AMOUNT OF WEALTH—HOW THE VALUE OF LABOR IS DETERMINED—EFFECTS OF THE AGGREGATION OF WEALTH.

THE following chapter may be summarized as follows:

The wealth of a country is divided into perishable property and durable property.

Perishable property consists of those products which are of such nature as to be susceptible of preservation during only a short period, and which must therefore be quickly consumed.

Durable property consists of lands and other things possessing value which are not created by labor, and such products of labor as may be preserved in continued use from year to year.

The distinction here drawn is not marked by a clearly-defined boundary, but it serves the purpose of a classification exhibiting certain differences in character of different kinds of property considered in this chapter. Only a small part of the products of labor can be preserved from year to year, and there are but few forms of wealth which may be handed down from one generation to another. The amount of wealth which can be saved or preserved constitutes but a small portion of the annual product of labor.

The amount of perishable wealth which may be accumulated

at any one time is determined by the demands of consumption, and, in proportion to population, varies but little from year to year. The quantity of durable property which may be created, and which may exist at any one time, is likewise limited by the demand for use. The demand for durable property for any given time and population is determined by the natural and acquired wants of the people, and is therefore dependent on the degree of civilization by which the habits and tastes of the people are determined. The demand is further limited by established economic conditions which regulate the distribution of wealth. The capacity to produce being greater than the demand is not, at least in this country, an operative limitation. The variation in the demand from year to year is within narrow limits.

There are, therefore, limits upon the amount of wealth which a people, constituting a single industrial and social entity, may acquire, imposed, first, by natural laws; second, by economic conditions developed out of the growth of organized society, which restrain the productive power of labor and control the distribution of its products.

The savings of labor, during any given period, are represented by the total amount of the increase of durable property during that period.

The aggregate of such increase is small, and whatever part is absorbed by the increased wealth of a few is deducted from the amount which would otherwise be distributed among the people.

The value of property arises out of the demand for its use. The demand for property owned by one person for use by others arises out of the fact that those who desire it are themselves without it. The wealth, therefore, of one individual, to the extent that it consists of property in excess of that moderate amount which he may himself use, implies a corresponding want of wealth in others. Great fortunes are possible only to the few. One man may own a fortune of one million only by virtue of the fact that one thousand men own nothing, or a much larger number own less than they use.

The addition to the amount of durable property in any country is subject to the limitation of the demand, which increases but slowly, and in a diminishing ratio as the stationary state of wealth is approached; and as the rich grow richer, in more rapid ratio than the average increase of durable property, the poor grow poorer.

_____

Property, which is the right conferred by natural law and by the laws of society to the exclusive use, possession, and control of any article or thing, may exist in anything which can be made the subject of exclusive possession or control.

The conditions which give value to property are, first, utility; second, limitation of quantity. Nothing can possess value that is not useful, or of which the supply is without limit.

Air possesses utility, yet it is without value, for the reason that the supply cannot be made subject to human control. Fish in the sea possess no value, but fish in a private pond have value. In the one case they are not under the control of any person, while in the other case they are. Water possesses utility, but is without value except under special conditions which limit the supply and make it a subject of individual control.

In times of drouth, when it becomes necessary to transport water from one locality to another, water is reduced to possession and may acquire commercial value. In cities, where labor and capital are employed to convey water to the consumer, water acquires value. When water is conveyed through ditches for purposes of irrigation, it becomes property and acquires value.

The word useful in this connection is not employed in the limited sense of what is good for man, but in the broader sense of being an object in demand for use. Whatever meets any human desire or want is useful in the sense of the word as here employed. The fact that the only uses to which an article may be put are immoral, or even criminal, is immaterial, except as modifying the degree of utility. That it is in demand for such purposes may give it value as property.

It is quite evident that when the supply of an article is without limit, so as to be at the command of every person without exertion on his part, such article can possess no value, and cannot be made a subject of wealth. When the supply of a commodity is in excess of what can be used, the excess, being without use, is also without value.

The value of an article may be reduced or destroyed by the smallness as well as by the excess of quantity. The quantity may be so limited as to prevent its use for purposes to which it might be applied if more abundant.

Only such quantity of any commodity as can be used is useful; but many things not required for use at present, for the reason that the quantity is in excess of the demand, possess value because of the demand which will arise in the future; but the more distant the time when they will be called into use the less the value.

The value of perishable articles such as food or clothing depends upon their being called into use within a short time. The value of clothing is subject to destruction not only by decay, but also by change of fashion. The products of iron may be longer preserved; but even iron decays, and new devices destroy the value of old.

The value of perishable articles deteriorates rapidly in proportion as the quantity on hand exceeds the present demand; and the shorter the time within which they must be consumed the greater the reduction in value caused by an over-abundant supply.

The interest value of capital reduces the value of property held only for future use. In estimating the value of an article which in ten years will be worth one hundred dollars, but which cannot be used in the mean time, we must take into account the cost of storage, insurance, and interest, and risk of loss by theft or other destructive agency.

Any excess of the supply of articles produced by labor over the present demand must compete with the future product of labor, and therefore, in measuring the value of an excess of a product beyond the immediate demand, the probabilities of future production must be taken into account.

As there can be no demand for a greater quantity of any product than can be used within a period limited by the conditions which we have mentioned, an excess beyond that quantity can possess no value. An excess creates an eager and unhealthy competition, which rapidly diminishes the value of the entire product. The point of highest value of the whole product is within the limit of the normal demand.

When the supply of any product is equal to the normal demand for consumption, the limit of wealth as to that product has been reached; an excess not only does not add to the total value of the whole, but reduces the total value.

To illustrate: When the potato crop is sufficient to meet the demand for consumption, an increase of the potato product cannot give additional value to the entire product,—cannot increase the wealth of the nation. Suppose, for instance, that the American people have capacity to consume, in one year, twenty million bushels of potatoes, and require no more, and that this quantity of potatoes is worth $8,000,000. Now add to this product of twenty million bushels, five million bushels more, and we have a total supply of twenty-five million bushels. This twenty-five million bushels would be worth less than $8,000,000; how much less depends upon conditions, the effect of which can be determined only by the measurement of actual results. The possible modifying effect of a foreign demand is not here considered.

The price of an article is rapidly advanced by competition between consumers, and rapidly diminished by competition among producers. The highest pecuniary value of a crop is reached at a point much below the amount of the total possible consumption.

To illustrate: The amounts and total values of the corn, oat, and potato crops of the United States during a series of years, as reported by the Commissioners of Agriculture, are as follows:

CORN.

Year.	Product in bushels.	Value.
1879	1,754,591,676	$694,618,304
1880	1,717,434,543	679,714,490
1881	1,194,916,000	759,482,170
1882	1,617,025,100	783,867,175
1883	1,566,000,000	658,700,000
1884	1,795,528,432	640,735,560
1885	1,936,176,000	635,674,630
1886	1,665,441,000	610,311,000
1887	1,456,131,000	646,106,770
1888	1,987,790,000	677,561,380
1889	2,112,892,000	597,918,129

OATS.

Year.	Product in bushels.	Value.
1879	407,858,000	$146,829,240
1882	488,250,610	182,978,022
1883	571,302,400	188,529,792
1884	583,628,000	161,528,470
1885	629,400,000	179,631,860
1886	624,134,000	186,137,930
1887	659,618,000	200,699,790
1888	701,735,000	195,424,240
1889	751,515,000	171,781,008

POTATOES.

Year.	Product in bushels.	Value.
1879	169,458,539	$81,848,474
1882	170,972,508	95,304,844
1883	208,164,425	87,849,991
1884	190,642,000	75,524,290
1885	175,029,000	78,153,403
1886	163,000,000	73,350,000
1887	134,000,000	91,120,000

The total aggregate product, in bushels, of all cereals (corn, wheat, oats, rye, barley, and buckwheat), and the values of the same, as reported by the Department of Agriculture, are as follows:

Year.	Product in bushels.	Value.
1880	2,718,193,501	$1,361,497,704
1881	2,066,029,570	1,470,957,200
1882	2,699,394,496	1,468,693,393
1883	2,829,319,089	1,280,765,927

It will be observed that the value of the largest corn crop is less than that of the smallest; that the value of the oat crop diminishes as the quantity increases, subject to the modification resulting from a diminished or increased corn crop; while the small potato crop of 1887 is of greater value than the largest crop reported. The value of the potato crop depends much on how the crop is distributed; and the same is true, but in a less degree, of the corn and oat crops.

It will be observed that the total aggregate crop of cereals of

1881, the smallest of the four aggregates enumerated above, has the greatest value. The value of the crop of one year is affected by the amount of the crop remaining over from the year previous, and the gradual increase of population causes a corresponding increase in the demand, while the development of the cattle industry in the Western Territories tends to reduce the prices of both corn and oats, grass-fed cattle taking the place of corn-fed animals; but the operation of the principle stated very clearly appears.

The following table shows the estimates of the Department of Agriculture of the average yield per acre, and the average price per bushel of corn and oats during a series of years.

Year.	CORN.		OATS.	
	Yield.	Price.	Yield.	Price.
1871	29	48.2	30.5	40
1872	30.8	39.6	30	35.5
1873	24.3	48	28	37
1874	20.8	64.5	22	52
1875	29.3	42	29.5	36
1876	26	37	24	35
1877	26.5	35.6	31.8	29
1878	27	31.7	31.5	24.6
1879	29	37.4	28.6	33
1880	27.5	39.6	25.8	36
1881	18 5	63.3	24.8	46.5
1882	24.5	48.2	24.5	48.5

In 1881 the yield of corn was but 18.5 bushels per acre; the value of the product per acre was $11.71. In 1879 the average yield was 29 bushels per acre; the value of the product per acre was $10.84. In 1882 the average yield of oats per acre was 24.5 bushels; the value of the product per acre was $11.87. In 1878 the average yield of oats per acre was 31.5 bushels; the value of the product per acre was $7.75. In 1874 the yield of both the oat and corn crops was small; and the average value of the corn crop per acre was $13.41, and that of the oat crop $11.44.

The value of the oat crop depends upon the quantity of corn grown the same year and the year previous.

The variation in the area of crops grown, which is not here taken into account, affects the price, so as to somewhat vary the ratio between the yield per acre and the price. But the fact that as the product increases the value diminishes is clearly illustrated.

During the last eight years the value of corn, in many localities, has varied as much as one hundred per cent. from the lowest, or fifty per cent. from the highest price. The value of the total annual product has varied as much as twenty per cent. from the highest price.

What is here shown as to corn, oats, and potatoes is true also of the meat product. Where hogs were sold, in 1888, at five dollars per hundred to the shipper, at the same date in the year 1889 they were selling for three dollars per hundred.

About thirty per cent. of our wheat is exported, and the value of this crop is therefore subject to the variations occasioned by fluctuations in the amount of the total product competing in the same market.

It will be seen that our agricultural product, most of the time, has been in excess of that amount which would be of greatest value to the producer, and beyond which the returns for agricultural products cannot be increased.

Our farmers diminish their incomes as they increase their crops. Wet seasons, drouths, and early frosts have been to the farmers blessings in disguise; and the Hessian fly, the chinch-bug, and the potato-bug have been the farmers' loyal friends. The only cause for complaint lies in the fact that they have localized their operations in such manner that the general gain has been at the expense of the people of particular localities. Our manufacturers, who do not enjoy these natural advantages, have found a substitute in suspensions and lock-outs.

The fluctuations in the price of potatoes are greater than the fluctuations in the price of corn or wheat, generally and locally, not only because of the greater variation in the amount of the annual product, but for the further reason that the surplus, not needed for immediate consumption, cannot be carried over to another year.

What is true as here shown of potatoes is true of every other agricultural product, and also of every manufactured product. It is true of woollen fabrics, hardware, machinery, houses, mills, telegraphs, and railways. One railroad more than enough is ono railroad too many, and adds nothing to tho total value of the railway property of tho wholo country. When tho people are supplied with houses in sufficient number, that satisfy their wants and gratify their tastes, more houses can add nothing to the total value of the whole. An excess beyond tho demand is superfluous. When the market is glutted with houses to rent and houses to sell, rents and prices go down; and, as tho excess increases, prices fall in accelerated ratio.

Gold and silver are valuable chiefly as measures of value in commerce. Their usefulness in the form of money, and their value for every purpose, depends upon tho limitation of the supply. An increase in the quantity of gold and silver over tho present supply could not add to the total value of the product. An increase in the amount would lead to the use of a greater quantity in the arts; but the increased consumption would be the effect of lower values. An increase in the coinage of gold and silver reduces the value of money in the ratio of the increase in the volume of coin. If gold were as abundant as iron, it would lose its value as a medium of exchange, and its then value would be such as it might possess for uses to which it is not now applied.

Since, then, nothing except that which is useful can possess value, and only a limited amount of each species of property may be used, only a certain amount of wealth can exist in each of the several products of labor. The aggregate possible wealth of a people being the sum of a certain number of limited quantities, is itself limited. The people of a nation can create so much property and no more. When the supply is equal to the demand the limit of a nation's wealth has been reached, except as that demand may be increased.

The demand has its limitations in the number and in tho natural and acquired habits and tastes of the people. While, therefore, the demand is not stationary, but progressive, not unvarying, but elastic, its temporary variations are within narrow limits, and its permanent growth, though steady, is not rapid.*

---

* It must have been seen, more or less distinctly, by political economists, that the increase of wealth is not boundless; that at the end of what they

For the purpose of illustration, let us assume that, measured in dollars of the present value, the limit of wealth which can exist in this country at the present time, with its present population and under present conditions as to education and culture of the people, is $70,000,000,000. Let us then assume, further, that one-half of this amount is aggregated wealth, owned by one class of people and used by others, property bringing revenue to the owners in the shape of interest, rents, profits on capital invested in trade, railways, manufacturing establishments, etc. Let us further assume that one-half of this aggregated wealth—that is, $35,000,000,000—is amassed in fortunes varying from $100,000 to $200,000,000. It follows that the great body of the people own less property than they use. If the entire amount were divided among the whole people, allowing to each one the amount required for his own use, that amount being dependent upon the education, tastes, and habits of each individual, no one person could be the owner of a great amount of property. Interest, rents, and profits would be abolished if such conditions were established and could be maintained.

Supposing the distribution of property to be as assumed. When the people who possess little or no property seek to acquire it, they are confronted with the fact that there is a limit to the total amount of the wealth of a nation, and that

---

term the progressive state lies the stationary state; that all progress in wealth is but a postponement of this, and that each step in advance is an approach to it. We have now been led to recognize that this ultimate goal is at all times near enough to be fully in view; that we are always on the verge of it, and that if we have not reached it long ago it is because the goal itself flies before us. The richest and most prosperous countries would very soon attain the stationary state if no further improvements were made in the productive arts, and if there were a suspension of the overflow of capital from those countries into the uncultivated or ill-cultivated regions of the earth.

"The impossibility of ultimately avoiding the stationary state—this irresistible necessity that the stream of human industry should finally spread itself out into an apparently stagnant sea—must have been to the political economists of the last two generations an unpleasing and discouraging prospect; for the tone and tendency of their speculations goes completely to identify all that is economically desirable with the progressive state, and with that alone."—JOHN STUART MILL.

one-half of that possible total amount is already in the hands of a comparatively small number. They cannot create new wealth because the limit of wealth has been already reached. If they seek a larger share of that which already exists, they are confronted with the fact that those who are in possession carefully guard and preserve it, while they derive revenue from its use by others.

But it may be said that, notwithstanding there are enough dwellings to supply the whole people, those who do not own houses may build new ones for themselves. True, but by so doing they do not add to the total value of the houses in the country; they do not increase the amount of the nation's wealth. The effect is a distribution of property; one more owner has been added. By this method A, B, and C may force a division of the aggregate wealth of the nation. But what, if any, are the obstacles in the way? Let us see. A seeks to build a house worth one thousand dollars. He does not possess the one thousand dollars. He must therefore acquire it from those who have it. Those who own the property of the nation, through the revenues derived from its use, absorb the country's increase of wealth, and the aggregation of wealth continues in increased ratio. A must therefore obtain one thousand dollars of the aggregated wealth of the country, or one thousand dollars of property now belonging to others. He must do this through the medium of wages or of prices received for the product of his labor. He must exchange his labor, or the product thereof, with the capitalist for that one thousand dollars. His labor competes in the same market with the labor of others equally needy, who sell their labor for what they require to eat, drink, and wear, and pay the rents of the houses they live in. If A does better than the average, it is by habits of harsh economy to which he is little accustomed. The saving of one thousand dollars cannot be accomplished without years of patient self-denial. Sickness, misfortune, or want of employment may come at any time and waste his little store of savings. The chances are against him. His savings, in the first instance, must take the form of money. In order that A may save a dollar, B, C, and D must, at the same time, expend a dollar. Saving in the form of money means suspended consumption. Suspended consumption means a reduction in the demand for labor.

The more A saves the more difficult it is for others to save. Saving and spending are correlative acts. The amount of money in use is not sufficient, and in its nature cannot be sufficient, to enable a large number of people to store wealth in the form of money at the same time.

Every worker is therefore dependent upon conditions which restrict his power to save. In his attempt to do so he enters into competition with every other person who is endeavoring to save. Among them they strive each for a share of a limited quantity. Thus the working-people, in their efforts to accumulate property, are forced into destructive competition, while capital, in the form of credits or of revenue-bearing property, exacts its tribute of interest, rent, or profits on the product of labor, and draws to itself, in accelerated ratio as its volume increases, the property of the nation.

There may be said to be two principal reasons why the poor remain poor. The first is that the products of labor are absorbed by the profits of capital, and the money tribute which labor is compelled to pay to aggregated wealth prevents those small accumulations of money which, during the period intervening between the time of earning and the time of investing, must represent the savings of the working-people. The second reason is the great aggregate amount of unemployed labor.

As to the first. A possesses a fortune of a hundred millions. How did he acquire it? Assuming that labor is worth one dollar and fifty cents per day, that one hundred million dollars represents 66,666,666 days' labor, or four days' labor for each able-bodied man in the United States. What consideration did A give for all this wealth? Shrewdness and cunning in manipulating markets, skill in operations on the board of trade. He schemed for it, he played with loaded dice, and won.

As to the second reason. Labor under present conditions is unable to employ itself; it is unable to combine its power; without the aid of accumulated capital it can build neither mills nor houses; and when capital owns houses and mills enough to satisfy the demand, all that it can profitably use or rent, it has no interest in producing more.

The productive capacity of labor may be such that one-half or two-thirds of the productive power of the people is fully adequate to meet the demands of consumption. But the labor of the individual worker can be utilized only in combination with that of others. One worker is but a fractional part of the great industrial unit which combines in a relation of complicated interdependence not only many workers, but many industries, and, in a measure, the whole people of one country or of many countries who exchange in the same market the products of labor. The individual worker, therefore, can create wealth only by working in conjunction with the industrial and commercial forces of the community of which he forms a part. As a producer of wealth he is dependent on the co-operation of others, and from this dependence there is no escape. Production is limited by consumption. The production, distribution, and consumption of products are relative and dependent parts of an industrial unit. When production is restricted, consumption is likewise limited; when consumption is reduced, production falls off in corresponding measure; when distribution is hindered, production and consumption both suffer diminution.

Production and distribution are effected through the use of money, and the financial system of a people is brought in as a factor in every industrial or commercial operation,—a factor which, more than any other, is subject to the control of individuals or combinations of individuals.

The total savings of a people are represented by the amount of durable property created and used and the supply of perishable commodities on hand. Ninety per cent. of the products of industry are consumed as they are produced. The margin of savings is necessarily small; and to secure a part of this remainder, the worker competes with capital, and, where capital is centralized in great fortunes, always at a disadvantage.

The amount of interest, rent, or profit earned by capital in excess of the amount consumed by the owners of capital necessarily takes the form of durable property, or of credits, and absorbs the annual savings of the people.

Hitherto prices of labor have been sustained and increased by reason of the unprecedented growth of the permanent wealth of the country,—the construction of railways, factories, mills, dwellings, and every other species of durable property,—and because of the demand of the working-classes for better food and clothing. But the margin of savings has not increased in equal ratio. We have been rapidly moving towards the end,—that point in development where the supply of permanent property begins to overreach the demand and labor is deprived of its margin of savings.

Since wealth can exist only in the form of durable property and the necessary supply of perishable commodities for present use, the total savings of a people during a period of five years are represented by the amount of the aggregate increase of the permanent or durable property of the whole country during that period. When, at any given time, there are already enough railways, factories, furnaces, mills, tools, and other durable property to satisfy the existing demand, the growth of wealth during the ensuing year must be limited to the amount of the increase of the demand during that year. This amount will represent the aggregate amount of the possible savings of the whole people during that period. Dividing that amount, so ascertained, by the number of the population of the country, we have the average possible savings for each person.

The total increase of wealth in the United States during the period from 1870 to 1880, as shown by census estimates, was $13,573,881,493. In 1870 the wealth per capita of. the people of the United States was $780. The increase in population from 1870 to 1880 was 11,587,412. Allowing to this increased population the same per capita wealth, we have $780 × 11,587,412 = $9,038,181,360, which must be subtracted from $13,573,881,493, the aggregate increase, leaving a remainder of $4,535,300,133, which represents the total of the per capita increase of wealth during that decade; an increase of ninety dollars per capita in ten years, or nine dollars per year.

The total wealth of the United States in 1870 and in 1880 was much less than the amounts given out as estimates of the census bureau, but for the present we will accept these estimates as near approximations of the wealth of the country at these respective dates.

We will now inquire how this increased wealth was distributed.

During this period the capital invested in the leading manufacturing industries and in railways was increased in the amount of $4,626,550,502, ninety millions more than the total amount of the per capita increase of the wealth of the nation.   And, if we take into account the excessive valuation in 1870, this increase was much greater.   Nearly the entire amount of the increase of capital invested in manufacturing and railways may be set down as so much added to the aggregated wealth of the country; in other words, to fortunes already large.   This is all revenue-bearing property.   After deducting the increased aggregation in manufacturing and railway capital, there is left no margin of savings for distribution.

We must also take into account the wealth which was invested in telegraphs, telephones, street railways, commerce, banks, mortgage loans, and palatial dwellings, as well as the aggregation of landed property. · Could we ascertain the total increase of property in the hands of those holding more than the per capita amount of 1870, we would no doubt find that the amount owned by the remaining classes had greatly diminished.

To this, the answer readily suggested will be, that the increased amount of capital invested in manufacturing and in railways—that in railways alone being $4,080,950,502—was, in the main, withdrawn from other investments; that capital which had already been aggregated was absorbed in the creation of this new property, which therefore only represents old capital in a new form.   But from what sources was it drawn ?   In 1880 the entire credits of the country, not including the bonds which represented the new railway property, had increased in proportion to the population, rather than diminished.   The aggregations of real estate had also greatly increased, and every species of aggregated wealth had kept full pace with the increase of population.   And, while it is necessarily true that part of the money invested in railway construction is withdrawn from some other form of investment, and to an amount near the actual cost of construction aggregated capital merely assumes a new form, it is nevertheless true that, at the expiration of the period under consideration, when the net results of all the agencies of distribution and aggregation of capital are ascertained, it will be found that the increased wealth in railways, telegraphs, telephones, etc., has been brought about without any reduction of aggregated wealth in other forms of investment. It will be found that the bank loans and mortgage loans to the people at large have increased in full ratio to the increase of population.

The claim will also be made that the valuation of property in 1870, being based upon an inflated currency, was much too high, thus reducing the amount of the increase of wealth as shown by the census. The accepted estimate is that the valuation was about twenty-five per cent. higher in 1870 than in 1880. But the estimate of 1870 embraces credits to the extent that they were included in the assessments of property for taxation. And this is true also of the estimate of 1880, or else the estimate of 1880 is much too high.

As values contracted, however, the credits of the country relatively appreciated. If we deduct twenty-five per cent. from the amount returned as the aggregate wealth of the country in 1870, we must add twenty-five per cent. to the aggregate credits in 1880.

The increase in the number of acres in farms in 1880 over 1870 was 95,850,943 acres; the increase in the total value of farms, most altogether attributable to increased area, was $934,292,915. The increase in the total value of city real estate, aside from increased value of buildings, was also very great; so that the savings from 1870 to 1880 were probably not in excess of the census showing which I have assumed as the basis of this estimate.

It is not, however, material to this inquiry whether this estimate be too large or too small, since it is clearly evident that the process of aggregation is taking up not only the savings or increase of wealth, but also the wealth already acquired by the people. The distribution of wealth is year by year growing more unequal. In other words, the rich are steadily growing richer, while the number of those who are without any store of savings is increasing both absolutely and relatively,—a fact often asserted, and as frequently denied, but a fact, however, which the statistics of wealth clearly demonstrate.

The number of people without any store of wealth, people who are wholly dependent upon their immediate earnings for the necessaries of life, and the number who feel the pinch of poverty and want, is rapidly growing in ratio to the increase of population.

It is true that the average consumption of the working-people has increased, that labor is better paid, that the people are better clothed, better housed, and better fed; but they are more dependent, and the relative number of those who succeed in laying by a store of wealth as a provision against sickness, old age, or as a support for dependent families is diminishing, notwithstanding the increase in the capacity of labor to produce.

The rapid increase of wealth now going on in the United States is possible in a country only during the period of its industrial development. When our lands shall all be occupied and improved; when all the railroads required by the necessities of our commerce shall have been built; when our towns and cities shall have reached that stage of arrested growth at which they must soon arrive, then the present rate of increase in wealth will be no longer possible. Year by year the rate of increase will grow less and less, and the possible savings to each worker must diminish.

Herein lies the force of the objection to the policy of permitting foreign capital to invest in and absorb the revenue-bearing property of the country. Foreign investments in the durable property of the country represent so much subtracted from the opportunities of our own people to acquire wealth.

The margin of possible savings depending upon the increase of durable property must diminish as the rate of increase in durable property is reduced. If the supply of durable property at the present time were adequate to satisfy the demand during the next ten years, then during that period labor would be employed only in the production of perishable products, articles designed for immediate consumption, and there could be no savings. The average price of a day's work during that time would be the equivalent of the price of the food, clothing, etc., consumed per day by a worker and the non-producers dependent upon him for support. While, then, the people as a whole could save nothing, yet one worker, by earning as much as the average and consuming less, would be able to retain a portion of the money price which he received for his labor, to the disadvantage, however, of others. His savings in that case would represent not so much wealth created, but so much wealth acquired out of the total quantity already on hand.

The value of labor is the price of its product. If the product of labor be confined to perishable property, articles intended for present consumption, then, the total value of labor being equal to the total consumption, the wages of labor are all consumed and nothing is saved. If labor be employed also in the production of permanent or durable property, then the total value of labor is equivalent to the value of the perishable property consumed, plus the value of the durable property created. The durable property represents the amount saved, and the amount of durable property created during any period, less the amount of the increase of aggregated wealth, determines the margin of savings covered by the wages of labor.

Hence, in new countries undergoing the process of rapid development, where railroads, furnaces, iron-mills, and dwelling-houses are being constructed, wages are high, and property is easily acquired. The margin of savings is large. Rates of interest also advance, and encroach upon the margin of labor's savings, until, sometimes, the total amount of savings is absorbed by capital. In old countries and in old communities, where development has been arrested and labor is employed almost wholly in the production of perishable articles and maintaining in repair the durable property already created, wages tend to the minimum, and the margin of saving to labor, if anything, is very small. Interest, too, is low, since interest is deducted from the savings of labor, and represents the share of the product appropriated by capital. The fact that low wages and a low rate of interest generally go together, and high wages frequently accompany a high rate of interest, has led some writers to the opinion that a high rate of interest and high wages sustain to each other the relation of cause and effect; whereas they are each the effect of the same cause. The opportunity of labor for increased wages is the opportunity of capital for higher interest; but the more capital takes the less there is left for labor; the more labor saves the less there is left for capital.

A country may be devastated by war, cities may be swept

away by fire or destroyed by earthquakes, and the permanent wealth of a country thereby reduced in the amount of many hundred millions of dollars; yet it is but a few years until the loss is repaired, a new and more beautiful city springs up out of the ashes of the old, and the aggregate wealth of the country is even greater than it would have been had not the destruction taken place. New buildings and better ones replace old and inferior structures, which, for the time sufficing, checked improvement; the way is cleared to new enterprise, new fields of employment are opened, wages are advanced, and more labor is performed; but in the end a redistribution of property has taken place. Capital, by increasing its rate of interest, its rents, and its profits, has obtained a large share of the newly-created wealth; but much also has been stored as the net savings of workingmen. These savings are in small amounts and widely distributed, and the greater part may soon be gathered again by the absorbing power of capital; yet the distribution has its permanent results, and new owners have been admitted to a share of the national wealth. We cannot estimate the privations, the suffering, the anguish which the destruction of a great city inflicts upon its people. Homes destroyed, little fortunes, representing years of frugal living, swept away in an hour of flame; the feeble and the old, the young and helpless, the able-bodied and the strong, alike made dependent on the charity of strangers for food and shelter; but though the losses of those whose property is thus destroyed may never be restored to them, yet, in a short time, the loss to the aggregate of national wealth will be replaced by more and better buildings, and the total wealth of the nation will be even greater than it would have been had no destruction of property taken place.

A few months ago Johnstown, Pennsylvania, was carried away by flood, and Seattle and Spokane Falls, in Washington, were consumed by fire; idle labor, gathered from a dozen States, hastened at once to repair the loss; and it is probable that, at the close of the present year, the wealth of the nation will not be less than it would have been had neither flood nor fire occurred. Of the phenomena here described, John Stuart Mill offers the following explanation:

"This perpetual consumption and reproduction of capital

affords the explanation of what has so often excited wonder,—
the great rapidity with which countries recover from a state of
devastation; the disappearance, in a short time, of all traces of
the mischiefs done by earthquakes, floods, hurricanes, and the
ravages of war. An enemy lays waste a country by fire and
sword, and destroys or carries away nearly all the movable
wealth existing in it; all the inhabitants are ruined, and yet, in
a few years after, everything is much as it was before. The *vis
medicatrix naturæ* has been a subject of sterile astonishment, or
has been cited to exemplify the wonderful strength of the principle of saving which can repair such enormous losses in so
brief an interval. There is nothing at all wonderful in the
matter. What the enemy have destroyed would have been
destroyed in a little time by the inhabitants themselves; the
wealth which they so rapidly reproduce would have needed to
be reproduced, and would have been reproduced in any case,
and probably in as short a time. Nothing is changed except
that, during the reproduction, they have not now the advantage
of consuming what had been produced previously. Nor does
this evince any strength in the principle of saving, in the popular sense of the term, since what takes place is not intentional
abstinence, but involuntary privation."

Mr. Mill rests his explanation of the rapid recuperation from
losses occasioned by general destruction of property upon the
supposed fact of a diminished consumption during the period
of recuperation.* There may or may not be a diminished
total consumption during the period of recovery. But the main
cause of the quick return to, and rapid progress beyond, the
former condition of wealth is the more rapid creation of wealth
by means of the more general and more effective employment
of labor. The rapid increase of wealth in the United States
during the years immediately following our exhausting civil
war was attended by no privations; they were years of pros-

---

* This enforced economy affords an adequate explanation of the recovery
of a people from the devastations of war, of hurricane and flood, where the
period of recuperation is extended over a considerable space of time, and
before the advent of the present era of surplus energy. But restricted consumption is not the principal agency to which must be referred the phenome-
nally rapid building or rebuilding of American cities.

perity and of generous consumption, *but of unwonted industrial activity.*

The rapid growth of wealth is checked not by an increased consumption that keeps pace with the capacity of labor to produce, but by the limitations of wealth, which, being approached, the demand of capital for those forms of durable property which can be made to yield a revenue is satisfied, and labor goes unemployed. Convince capitalists beyond a doubt that a new railway from New York to San Francisco would pay a dividend of ten per cent. on the cost of construction, and it will be but a short time until a new railway will be built and splendidly equipped. Give satisfactory assurance of a permanent increase of profits in all the manufacturing industries, and within a few years the product can be doubled.

The labor of the people is of such capacity that, if it could be properly combined and directed, it might, in a short period, construct all the houses required for the comfort of the people, and then double the number. But it is not to the interest of capital to create that of which there is already enough to command the largest revenue.

Labor, without liberal savings, is without power to utilize surplus labor for the benefit of those who are without acquired capital. To do so would impair the value of existing investments. To construct houses for those who occupy rented houses, when there are already houses enough, is to deprive the landlord of his tenants, to make his houses superfluous. Here, then, arises a direct conflict between labor and capital,—a conflict in which labor is perpetually vanquished, since labor can do nothing without capital. With a capacity to produce far in excess of its wants, labor continues poor because unable to control the machinery by which wealth is distributed.

The agriculturist produces enough to supply the demand for consumption, yet the prices he receives for the products of his labor yield him little or no margin of savings. To increase his profits he increases his product, only to find that a surplus reduces values, and his profits are less than before.

A sufficient amount of woollen goods is manufactured to supply the demands of the market. The worker in this industry receives enough to defray the expenses of an economic living for himself and family, but not enough to enable him to save. If the product be increased, the price goes down, and nothing is added to his wages. He is unable to accumulate; he cannot acquire houses and lands; he must continue to pay rents.

The interests of labor require a greater distribution of wealth; the interest of capital is in the direction of the concentration of wealth. There being, as has been shown, a limit on the amount of wealth, the question is one of distribution,—what is owned by the few cannot belong to the many; two men cannot own the same thing, and the creation of a surplus impairs the value of the whole.

Wealth being a product of labor, when the supply is sufficient and the demand for the products of labor is satisfied, the demand for labor is satisfied. Labor competes not only with labor, but with the products of labor in the form of accumulated wealth. Wealth blocks the way to the creation of new wealth, and labor must continue to pay tribute in the form of rents, interest, and profits. When, in the accumulation of national wealth, a certain stage has been reached, and the demand for labor has been diminished by competition with its accumulated product, the tendency to lower wages, or at least to a smaller margin of savings, is inevitable.

Wealth controls production, regulates commerce, and fixes the conditions of labor. The interests of wealth are not in direct conflict with an increased consumption of perishable products by the workingman, nor with a demand for a rate of wages sufficient to supply him with such part of the perishable product of labor as he may consume; but its interests are in conflict with the savings of labor, which must take the form of durable property. For, when labor owns its own dwelling it pays no rent; when it acquires money it ceases to pay interest. If its savings are multiplied, and take the form of durable property,—and there can be no considerable savings except in the form of durable property,—values of existing property are destroyed.

It will be seen that an abundance of wealth in the hands of a few imposes conditions of hardship on the many. Wages, values, as we are so often reminded, are regulated by the law of supply and demand; but the law of supply and demand, in its operation and effects, depends upon conditions determined by the interests of accumulated capital.

Is there a remedy? None which is not in conflict with the interests of centralized capital. Because, in the nature of things, the remedy must be chiefly directed not to the creation of more wealth, but to the distribution of the wealth we have,— to a reduction of the tribute which labor pays to capital.

Wealth and poverty are correlative conditions; they are the ebb and flow of the same tide, the crest and the hollow of the same wave. The snow that lies in drifts along the hedges was gathered from the fields. There are no hills without valleys between.

It is true that capital, which is but the stored product of labor, competes with capital, and that labor is benefited by the competition. But, though the tribute may be reduced, the savings of labor are not materially increased. Labor requires food, clothing, and shelter; capital requires neither. A thousand dollars earns eighty dollars in a year; in ten years it has doubled. Its earnings consist of what it draws to itself of the product of labor. Capital creates nothing in the sense of that term as applied to labor. Money has no hands, it builds no houses, weaves no cloth; it handles neither spade, pick, nor plough.

Our late civil war withdrew from productive labor on the farm, in the factory, in the mines, on railways, and in the shop a million of men; yet, with the labor that was left, two magnificent armies were fed, clothed, equipped, and transported; the people at home were fed and clothed; houses, mills, and steamships were built, railways were constructed, and the wealth of the nation continued to grow. The census of 1870 shows not only a greater increase in proportion to population, but a greater aggregate increase of wealth than that which took place between the years 1870 and 1880. It is true that the relative valuation of property in 1870 was higher than in 1880, but, adjusting valuations to the same standard, the exhibit shows a marvellous growth of wealth notwithstanding a destructive and expensive war.

The reasons of this remarkable growth of wealth, under conditions apparently the most unfavorable, were, first, the unusual activity of the productive energies of the people, and, second, the employment of a greater per cent. than usual of the labor force of the country in the production of durable property, such as dwellings, mills, factories, and railways.

All this increased wealth was the product of labor, the work of hands and brains. The capital employed was the product of former labor. The only creative power is mind and muscle; capital in itself is inert.

Let us consider, further, the causes operating on the distribution of wealth.

No individual can himself use a large amount of property. If each worker were the owner of all the property used by himself and family, or an amount of property equivalent in value, the amount which it would be possible for any one person to own would be comparatively small. If the common people all enjoyed the higher comforts of our civilization, and were all provided with good homes, the necessary limit of property to the head of each family, under the conditions named, would probably not exceed the value of six thousand dollars. But if each one were supplied with all that is required for his own use, there would then be no use for property owned by any person in excess of what he might require for use; and, being useless, it would be without value. If A owns one hundred houses, he can occupy but one; and if every other person be supplied with a house of his own, such as fills the measure of his wants, then A's other ninety-nine houses, being without use, are without value. If A owns a hundred horses, and can use but two, the other ninety-eight are of no value, unless some other person be in need of horses. It follows, therefore, necessarily, that the accumulation of property by some in excess of the amount required for their own use, or, in other words, of property which derives its value from the fact that it is used by other people, diminishes the amount of property which may be owned by others.

If A owns a residence worth one hundred thousand dollars, occupied by himself and family, though the creation of this property absorbed a greater proportion of labor than what would be A's distributive share if each person were awarded the measure of his earnings, the ownership of this costly residence does not interfere with the acquisition of property by others. The erection of costly dwellings by men of wealth employs labor and, to the extent of the cost of construction, distributes values. If A, being worth one million dollars, builds for himself a residence worth the amount of one hundred thousand dollars, the cost of construction, one hundred thousand dollars, is distributed among the people. A's fortune remains the same, but has, in part, assumed another form ; and, as a result of the transaction, the people have acquired one hundred thousand dollars in property which they did not own before. And since this costly residence is appropriated to A's own personal use, and does not depend for its value upon occupancy by persons other than the owner, it cannot be employed as a means of aggregating wealth. It does not stand in the way of the construction of dwellings for others. But the ownership of property from which a revenue is derived— property belonging to one person and used by others, or of property in which capital is employed at a profit in the production of articles for consumption—reduces the amount of property which may be owned by others in the amount of the value of the property so employed. Those who do not own the property which they use, but who pay tribute to capital in the hands of other owners by way of interest on credits, rents on houses or lands, or profits on articles of consumption, can acquire property only by securing it out of the excess in the hands of those who hold the aggregated capital of the country ; that is, presuming the limit of wealth has been reached. And if that limit has not been reached, they may acquire permanent property out of the savings of labor, which under present economic conditions are absorbed by capital, leaving nothing for labor as a whole.

If the limit of wealth be reached in any class of property, as in woollen-mills, iron-founderies, flouring-mills, or manufactories of machinery, the same principle holds good as to these classes of property ; and those who are without can secure a part only by means of a wider distribution of that which already exists.

True, when, for instance, the demand for woollen-mills has been supplied, more woollen-mills may be erected, if capital can be diverted to such purpose ; but the effect is a destruction and distribution of values, and not an increase of the nation's wealth. This form of distribution, by means of the creation of a surplus of a certain kind of property, an excess beyond the demand, destroys values and reduces the total wealth.

Distribution in this manner is restrained by the fact that the creation of a surplus rapidly diminishes the value of the whole, and, the effect soon becoming apparent, capital avoids destructive competition.

If there were enough and no more than enough of woollen-mills to supply the demand for woollen fabrics, and the owner-ship were distributed among all the employés who operate them in proportion to the labor and skill of each, so that each employé would in effect use his own property, or would own an equivalent of the property used by him, this would be such distribution as would give to each worker the entire product of his labor; while the indefinite increase of the number of mills would destroy the value of both capital and labor employed in that industry. It will be seen, therefore, that an enforced distribution by means of that excessive competition which destroys values is not to be desired, even if it were practicable. Distribution by such means is, however, impossible. What is needed, and that which alone is attainable, is not more mills, more furnaces, more railways, when there are already enough, but a distribution of the ownership of the wealth we have.

The quantity of product may be increased to the full measure of the demand, but an increase beyond that point is not only a waste of labor, but a destruction of existing values. The consequence would be a general derangement of values, panics, hard times; the weak would succumb to the pressure, and the end would be an increased aggregation of wealth in the hands of those strong enough to break down weaker competitors and control markets.

Competition in any one industry tends to bring prices of labor and of the products of labor to the general level of prices in other industries. But excessive competition forces prices below the normal standard, first in one industry and then in another, to the disadvantage of all, except it be the creditor classes, whose dollars grow large as values grow small.

Any policy which tends to cheapen the price of the products of labor in general is detrimental to the people, for the reason that it increases the value of credits. The true policy for the general good is that which promotes high prices for labor and its products in all departments of industry and yet tends to an equitable equalization of values among all industries, having due regard to quality of labor and skill employed.

It is true that a generation hence the greater portion of durable property in its existing forms will have been consumed by use or wasted by decay. And it may be urged that this process of continual consumption opens the way for an equitable distribution of property. But, in answer, it is sufficient to say that revenue-bearing property perpetuates itself. New forms of wealth, which take the place of the old, represent only a part of the revenues derived from the property which they replace. So far as involved in the question which we have been considering, durable property may be regarded as though subject to neither wear nor decay.

Lavish expenditures of the wealthy in the erection of splendid palaces, or in the construction of steam-yachts, or for costly equipages, blooded horses, diamonds, paintings, statuary, servants in livery, or any object of personal comfort, or the gratification of extravagant tastes, are not always to be condemned as detrimental to the interests of labor. Such expenditures constitute an important agency in the distribution of wealth. They afford to labor the opportunity to reclaim what labor has lost.

Palaces for the wealthy may represent unjust gains; but they also represent so much wealth distributed among the people, so much reduction in the amount of revenue-bearing property. The costly mansion may overshadow, but it does not compete with, the cottages of the poor.

It is the tenement-house and the rented flat that hold the laborer in bondage and deny him a home of his own. It is not the rich prodigal, but the man of business that absorbs the earnings of labor and obstructs the way to prosperity. The rich young spendthrift may set a bad example in morals; he may bring grief to fond parents; and yet to the people he may be a blessing in disguise. As an agent in the distribution of wealth he is often an important and useful factor. In utter disregard of Dr. Franklin's frugal maxims, he tears down the mountain of wealth piled up by his worthy ancestors, and scatters the golden coin among the crowd of scrambling poor.

No enterprise, no business, can be established without the aid of capital, without paying tribute to capital. In any manufacturing industry, before a beginning can be made there must be expensive buildings, costly machinery, and money at command to pay numerous employés. Capital exacts its tribute; and the man who attempts to establish himself in any business cannot rely with confidence on success. If he add his own accumulations to the capital of others, he incurs the serious risk of seeing his own savings swallowed up in rents, interest, and the losses occasioned by fluctuating values. Speculation is an element in every business. Every enterprise is directed, managed, and controlled in the interests of capital. Labor cannot organize except under the control of capital. For the privilege of existing, labor must pay tribute to aggregated wealth. Wealth, it is true, cannot exist without labor, since all wealth is created by labor; but wealth, when created, becomes the proprietor of labor, the monarch of muscle, a king beneath whose golden sceptre toiling millions bow and cringe. But while they sweat and toil, they grow weary of a king who considers only the splendor of his court and the garnered wealth in the vaults of his royal treasury. The lords of wealth, who have been knighted by the touch of his royal wand, are loud in their praises of the king; but the millions whose faces are bronzed, and whose hands are hard, often complain of the heavy tithings, and murmur of the injustice of a king so preoccupied with the splendor of his retinue and the grandeur of his palace that his royal mind is little concerned for the cottages of the poor.

The people demand a charter of King John. They do not seek to uncrown him, they do not clamor for a new king, but they ask for some limitations on his royal prerogative. They have been too long deluded with the stale old maxim that prices are regulated by the law of supply and demand. They have found this law, under present changed conditions, wholly inadequate to reduce inequalities of opportunity and secure to them the earnings of their toil.

During a recent period the entire country has been covered with a net-work of railways; splendid cities have sprung up;

and of factories, furnaces, and mills the supply outruns the demand; agriculture has doubled its product; magnificent churches and splendid palaces everywhere attest the overflowing abundance of wealth; and yet millions still abide in rented cottages or huddle together in crowded tenements; many are idle for want of work, and many are hungry and meanly clad.

If labor could be utilized, if it could be combined and directed, its capacity is not only sufficient to feed and clothe the people, but within a short period to furnish every family with a home of its own. But money is required to put labor in motion, and money cannot be commanded, for capital cannot afford to destroy itself.

The problem is not now how to increase the effective power of labor,—that problem has been solved,—but how to employ labor so as to secure to every one the opportunity to work and to enjoy the product of his toil.

In the pursuit of this object it is evident that, without in some manner modifying the tendency of wealth to accumulate in the hands of a few, but little can be accomplished.

Mr. Carnegie has said that the contrast between the palace of the millionaire and the cottage of the laborer measures the change which has come with civilization. Does it not also suggest the change which is yet to come?

There must be some abatement of the tribute which labor pays to hoarded wealth. The workingman is deprived of the product of his industry; his savings are taken from him. He sees men in the possession of fortunes measured by millions which he knows they never earned, but which they are said to have acquired according to the time-honored usages of trade that are vouched for by all the professors of political science as in full accord with the laws of progress and of civilization. He is assured that the drawing is perfectly fair, "conducted in the presence of honorable gentlemen;" but he observes that the managers of the lottery of distribution have grown wealthy, while he has remained poor.

What can be done to secure to each worker a fairer measure of reward for his industry? Arbitrary distributions of wealth are of course impracticable, and, if attempted, they would afford no remedy.

The same forces continuing to operate, the same results would be repeated, and soon a second distribution would be required. The people would lose all incentive to industry and economy. The right of each to the product of his own labor would cease to be respected, and an utter demoralization of industry would ensue.

The remedy must be sought in restraints on the power of capital to absorb the earnings of the worker, and there must be such readjustment of economic forces as will equalize opportunities and give full play to the productive power of labor. The remedy must not ignore fundamental laws of trade, but make use of them; it must not destroy the incentive to the acquisition of property, but extend the opportunity to acquire a share of wealth to a greater number. In seeking a wider distribution, it must guard against the destruction of values; it must proceed on general principles along well-defined lines.

. The value, the necessity of very considerable accumulations of wealth must be fully recognized. In many industries large capital is essential to economic production. Great enterprises are not accomplished without those combinations of capital which are impracticable among a people where there are no persons of wealth. Social refinement, moral and intellectual culture, are the growth of leisure and opportunity, and no class of persons are more essential to the moral, social, and industrial welfare of a people than those possessing fortunes adequate to the demands of the highest culture. But accumulations of wealth beyond reasonable limit impose burdens upon the people *without corresponding benefits.* When centred in the fortunes of a few, society is deprived of the advantages which constitute the justification of wealth.

Extreme centralization of wealth is responsible for the spirit of communism and vulgar class antipathy now manifested by large numbers of people in both Europe and the United States; and, unless we are ready to deal with still graver evils, it were best to make speed in correcting those which give rise to the prevailing spirit of discontent.

I shall in other chapters set forth such remedies as I believe to be efficient and practicable, at least in great measure, to re-

move those causes which hinder the working-people from reaching that condition of independent thrift which, considering the
present productive power of labor, I believe to be attainable.

CHAPTER V.

SAVING—CREDITS.

THE suggestion is often made that the poverty of the poorer
classes is attributable chiefly to their own improvidence and
wastefulness, and that, if each would habitually save a small
portion of his earnings, all might accumulate wealth. Let us
inquire if this be true.

By saving, as that term is commonly understood, is meant a
diminished consumption. What are the effects of saving, in
this restricted sense of the term, upon the accumulation and
distribution of wealth?

Consumption treads close upon the heels of production.
Whatever is produced, to be of value, must be consumed, either
in the form of food, clothing, fuel, and the like, or in furniture,
dwellings, and other durable property. The question is, therefore, not how much the people shall consume, but in what form
the product of labor shall be consumed. Shall they eat it, wear
it out in clothing, or build houses to live in? "Do neither,"
says the strict economist; "sell it and save the money." By
this is meant, let some other fellow eat it, and give you his
money or his note. But where is the other fellow? Our free-
trade friends tell us that he works in a factory across the sea;
and our worthy Secretary of State insists that he is lolling in
the sun down in Mexico or South America. And we are told
that all we need, in order to accumulate wealth, is to open our
ports and send our ships abroad laden with the surplus products
of our labor. We must seek a foreign market. But when we
find the Englishman or Frenchman or Spanish-American we are
looking for, it is altogether probable that, instead of paying good
hard cash for the products of our labor, he will insist on swap-

ping either food or clothing, which we shall be compelled to eat
or to wear out, and there will be nothing saved after all.

The *capacity* of labor to produce is at present greatly in
excess of consumption. If all the labor and machinery in
the various industries of the country were steadily employed
throughout the entire year, the surplus product for which, at
the present rate of consumption, there could be no demand
would be very large. This is especially true in the manufacturing industries. Hence arises the incessant competition among
producers for a larger share of the market.

If the entire labor in any one industry of the country be all
the time effectively employed, the product chokes the market.
If a portion of the workers be for a time withdrawn from
production, while others continue steadily employed supplying
the market with the products of their labor and deriving whatever advantage may result from the withdrawal of other labor
from competition, the workers out of employment, pressed by
necessity, soon return to a fiercer competition. Thus it is
that, in order to secure their due proportion of employment and
of the product of labor, the whole body of working-people are
constantly striving against each other in heated competition,
while they are unable to maintain prices by means of such combinations as enable capital to maintain its margin of profits. If
consumption always kept pace with production, a glut in the
market could never occur. But when people attempt to save in
the form of money or credits; when, in other words, they put
into the market more than they take out, products accumulate,
production outruns consumption, prices are deranged, distribution is interrupted, and the demand for labor ceases, until, by
enforced idleness, production falls within the limits of the
demands of trade.

There is not a uniform distribution of labor nor of the
products of labor among the working-people. Some are employed the year round, while others may be idle half the time.
The result is that, notwithstanding the capacity of labor to
produce more than is wanted, there is always much individual
distress. Owing to excessive competition, the savings of labor
which take the form of durable property are absorbed by capital, the laborer shifts from place to place and lives in rented

houses, and the mortgage which aggregated wealth holds on his muscle and his brain grows and grows. It never can be paid off, extinguished, or evaded.

The uncertainty of permanent employment at any one place, or at steady wages, greatly hinders, when it does not wholly prevent, the acquisition of homes by workingmen, and opens to capital the opportunity for investment in the homes of the poor.

Saving, in the form of money, means deferred consumption. If, for instance, in the course of a year A saves one hundred dollars, he has put into the market one hundred dollars' worth of the product of labor more than he has taken out, while others have consumed that much in excess of their earnings, in excess of their contribution to the market. A's savings, in this form, measure an excess of consumption over production by other persons. It will be seen, therefore, that all persons cannot save at the same time, and that the total savings, in the form of money, are limited to a small aggregate. These accumulations must be constantly converted into other forms of property ; if into food or clothing or other perishable property, no permanent saving is effected. Accumulations of wealth are represented by property of more durable character. Durable property consists mostly of articles of considerable value. The small accumulations of money savings which represent only suspended consumption, and which are, in the nature of things, possible to any considerable number of workers, are in amount too small to pay for the building of houses or the purchase of machinery, or even of valuable furniture ; and for this reason such savings are less liable to be invested in any form of durable property, but are expended for articles of perishable nature, for the purchase of which small sums are available.

A general effort on the part of the people to save, in the form of money or of credits, means a general refraining from the purchase of the products of labor. To the extent that the effort succeeds, it means that the people have quit work. This form of saving, therefore, defeats itself. The only form of saving practicable to the people at large consists in the conversion of money savings into the forms of durable wealth. Saving, in the true sense of that term, is that form of expenditure by which the wages of labor are converted into property that is both useful and durable. The other form of saving, by which the individual may profit at the expense of his fellow-workers, consists in contributing the products of labor to the common market, and refusing to accept the products of other labor in exchange, but storing up wages in money and then in credits, not for the purpose of a consumption reasonably deferred, that it may take the form of expenditure for durable property, but that, by means of interest, it may grow into a future claim for a larger share of the products of labor than its present equivalent.

The total consumption of a people must be the equivalent of the total production; while the production and consumption of an individual member of society may greatly vary. To balance the sum of the accounts of all the individuals of a nation who contribute to one common market, so that the column which represents consumption will foot up the same amount as the column which represents production, requires that the industries in their several classes, as well as production in its individual subdivisions, by means of ever-varying quantities and fluctuating prices, shall so adjust themselves as to reduce the grand totals to equivalent amounts.

Industrial disturbances are in great measure attributable to competition in saving, using the term in its limited sense. Production and consumption must move together; when one halts the other must stand still. Industrial harmony requires that they keep step and move at a steady, unbroken pace.

Since articles of food and clothing cannot be stored for any great length of time, each year's production must provide for each year's consumption; and wealth, beyond the amount of perishable products required for consumption within the limits of a short period, must be stored in the form of houses, mills, railways, machinery, tools, and other like products. The title to wealth, however, or to the products of labor, may exist in the form of credits, and credits may accumulate to the amount of one-third or more of the aggregate wealth of a country.

Wealth cannot be hoarded to any great extent in the form of money, for the total amount of the money in the country does not exceed one-fortieth part of the nation's wealth, and what there is is required for use in effecting exchanges. Wealth saved usually remains in the form of money only during that short period which intervenes before it takes the form of other property, or the form of credit. The hoarding of money causes an interruption of exchange and a disturbance of values.

It is evident, therefore, that, while one individual may provide for his own future wants by the acquisition of property or of credits, a whole people cannot so provide. The accumulations of the wealthy represent the power of a certain number of persons, necessarily limited, to command the products of the labor of other persons. Production must go on; the people must each year create that which they that year consume. One man may acquire a fortune by saving; but fortunes are possible only to a few.

Savings beyond those accumulations necessary to provide property actually used by the owner and his family are represented in rented houses, mills, or railways, the rents or profits of which command a portion of the products of other men's labor. It is from the nature of things impossible that the mass of the people should store up wealth for future consumption. They may acquire good homes, good churches, good roads, and such other durable property as they may need or desire for use; but food and clothing they must produce as they consume.

The total savings of the entire people are represented in the durable property which they use and that portion of the annual product on hand for consumption. The margin of savings is fixed within natural and somewhat narrow limits, and it follows that the greater the amount of savings which fall to the share of a few, the smaller the amount which is left for those who remain.

The wages of the laboring man are, by unchangeable natural law, limited to a sum but little in excess of the cost of food and clothing for himself and family, and that excess is measured by the additional cost of his dwelling, furniture, household utensils, and tools.

Could there be a storage of articles of food and clothing, wages might be temporarily increased, but would then vibrate as far the other way, since the limit of consumption, and not of the powers of production, determines the limit of wages.

Political economists have indulged in elaborate metaphysical disquisitions on "what determines the rate of wages." Were I required to give a short answer to this question, I should say the human stomach; but, if permitted a little more space, I should add, the intensity of the prevailing desire for the luxuries of life.

When one portion of the people spend less—that is, consume less—than they produce, less than their relative proportion of the total consumption, other people must consume more than they produce. In this manner, that part of the people who consume less than they produce draw to themselves the durable property of the country. They are thrifty at the expense, and often to the detriment, of the laboring-classes at large.

This is the principle involved in the objection to the importation of Chinese into this country, and also to the immigration of a class of Europeans who are industrious producers but more meagre consumers than the American people. And on this principle rests one of the chief objections to unrestricted commerce with foreign nations.

The standard of wages is gauged by the average consumption of the whole people who compete in a common market. While for each individual, on the principle of getting the best of a bargain, it may be a wise policy, as a competitor against his fellows, to save all he can; yet excessive savings, and resultant accumulations of credits, or of revenue-bearing property, which operate in like manner, are possible only to a relatively small number of people, and are an injury to the people at large, except that they confer certain compensating benefits elsewhere considered.

The consumption of different orders of industrial people varies greatly, and there is consequently a corresponding variation in the wages, or, what is the same, the prices of the products of the labor of these different orders. This is not necessarily detrimental to society, since a relatively large amount of savings may be left to each. But high wages for one class of workers which result in accumulations of durable property to that class greater than an equitable proportion of the permanent wealth of the whole people are detrimental to the interests of other laboring-classes, who are thereby necessarily deprived of the acquisitions to which they are entitled. Undue compensation to one class means a corresponding loss to other classes.

It is therefore not to the interest of the people to sustain a disproportionately high rate of wages to any one industrial class. A high standard of wages in general is to be desired, as by this means the share of capital is diminished; but, since the total wages must fall within the limits of the total consumption, the wages of each class should bear an equitable relation to the wages of every other class. Too high wages to one class mean too low wages to another class. Wages in skilled industries are high; but the consumption of skilled workmen and their families, as a rule, is relatively large. The savings of skilled workmen also are larger; but this class of workers occupy more costly dwellings, and use more expensive articles of durable property, and their savings in the form of credits are not excessive. The surplus which they are enabled to store up for sickness or old age does not, perhaps, go further than the surplus saved by the average laborer. Such at least is the relation which the industries ought to bear towards each other in a healthy social economy.

To illustrate the effect of savings, as well as the effect of interest accumulations, on the distribution of wealth, let us suppose the existence of an island, disconnected from all other communities, and therefore without foreign trade or exterior influence of any kind to affect the growth or distribution of wealth. To eliminate every element not essential to the illustration, we will assume the existence of conditions wholly impossible in any existing community, because of differences in intellectual capacity, physical power, the accidents of disease, the uncertainty of the seasons, and the eager graspings of avarice.

This island, we will suppose, contains eight hundred and one thousand acres of land, the soil of which is of uniform fertility, one locality affording no advantage over another. Eight hundred thousand acres is divided into five thousand farms of one hundred and sixty acres each. The remaining one thousand acres are occupied by the houses, shops, and mills of mechanics, artisans, and professional men. There are fifty thousand people divided into ten thousand families of five persons to each family.

There is one laborer or worker to each family, who engages in productive industry,—that is, in producing those things which enter into the common market. The other members of the family devote their time to domestic service, education, and the creation for home consumption of such products as are not bought and sold in the market. The annual product of each worker is equivalent to the annual product of every other worker. There are five thousand agricultural families, and five thousand mechanics, artisans, clerks, manufacturers, merchants, and professional men. Each farm of one hundred and sixty acres is valued at four thousand eight hundred dollars, and each agriculturist owns, besides, one thousand dollars' worth of other property, making a total of five thousand eight hundred dollars. Each mechanic, artisan, etc., owns an equal amount, invested in a home, machinery, tools, implements of trade, and other personal property. The total amount of the money of the country is one million dollars, which is equally divided among the ten thousand families, making one hundred dollars to each family, which amount is embraced in the total of five thousand eight hundred dollars owned by each family, as stated above. The total product each year, embracing products of agriculture and additions to, and improvements on, buildings, machinery, etc., is ten million dollars, or one thousand dollars to each family. Each family consumes, each year, an equal amount of the products of labor, and requires an equal amount of professional service. The production and consumption of each family being equal, there is neither increase nor diminution of wealth. The community has reached that stage of development where every family is supplied with all the property requisite to satisfy its wants; where no improvement or addition is needed beyond keeping property in repair and supplying the place of that which wears out. The population neither increases nor diminishes. The total wealth of the island will therefore remain fixed at fifty-eight million dollars.

We will now suppose that out of the ten thousand workers there are one hundred persons by the name of Smith, who conceive the idea of increasing their wealth beyond that of their neighbors. Since the demands of the people, as a whole, for wealth are fully satisfied, the aggregate wealth cannot be increased. The people have no use for more property, and there is therefore no demand for more labor. But the Smiths conceive the idea of acquisition by saving, by consuming less than they have hitherto consumed. They discover that, instead of expending one thousand dollars per year, they are able to subsist comfortably on eight hundred dollars per year. As the products of all labor go into and, as required for consumption, are purchased from the same market, the Smiths continue to produce, as before, to the amount of one thousand dollars per year. The product of their labor is disposed of at the usual rates in the market, and they consequently receive during the year one thousand dollars, and the product of their labor is consumed as a part of the whole. At the end of the year, Smith finds that, instead of one hundred dollars in money with which he began, he has three hundred dollars, having consumed two hundred dollars less than the amount he received for the product of his labor. As each of the one hundred families of Smiths consumes two hundred dollars less per annum, the total consumption falls off twenty thousand dollars in amount; and in order to make production and consumption equal, the remaining nine thousand nine hundred families are compelled to reduce the product of their labor to the limit of consumption or demand, or to nine hundred and ninety-two dollars per annum. If we suppose them to continue to produce, as before, one thousand dollars each, the supply each year would exceed the demand in the amount of twenty thousand dollars, thus disarranging the market. Supply and demand, or production and consumption, will always reach an equilibrium by the increase of the one or the reduction of the other. For the purpose of this illustration it is not material by which method we assume the equilibrium to be reached.

The Smith families begin the process of saving by consuming less than the annual product of their labor. They save twenty thousand dollars per year. In one hundred years they would, at this rate, save two million dollars. In two thousand eight hundred and seventy years, by the process of saving and loaning their savings, without interest, their credits would equal the total property of the island, less the amount of property which they originally owned, and they would, in effect, own the island.

However, at the expiration of ten years, the Smiths have hoarded up two hundred thousand dollars of the money of the island. The money remaining in the hands of the people is not sufficient to answer the requirements of trade. There is a demand for more money. Smith says he has money that he is not using, and that for a small compensation, eight per cent. per annum, he would be willing to loan it. So the one hundred Smiths all go to loaning at eight per cent. Loaning both annual savings and interest accumulations each year, at the end of twenty years they have accumulated seven hundred and twenty-one thousand four hundred and eighty dollars; and at the expiration of sixty-five years their credits would reach the sum of fifty-nine million dollars,—an amount in excess of the total value of the island and the accumulated wealth of the whole people.

If, instead of one hundred Smith families, there be two hundred families,—that is, one fiftieth of the entire population,—who save at the rate of two hundred dollars per year, receiving interest at the rate of eight per cent. after the tenth year, they will own the island in less than fifty years.

But, after the enterprising Smiths have accumulated a large capital, they become ambitious to engage in business enterprises, and they employ their credits in other ways. Having control of the money market, they may inflate or depress values at will. They call upon the Joneses, the Thompsons, and the Johnsons to pay their notes by a certain day. Had they called on but one or two, the necessary amount of money could be readily found; but when two or three hundred debtors are called upon at the same time to discharge a large aggregate amount of credits, money becomes scarce,—there is a tight market. The debtors offer to sell farms, mills, anything, to raise money; but, owing to the stringency in the money market, no one has money to invest, except at ruinously low prices. Prices go down; and then the Smiths buy real estate. When the pressure has been removed, business gradually recovers tone and values rise again. There is a demand for real estate. The Smiths hold on to the lands they have acquired until the pressure of a demand which has grown beyond the supply pushes prices higher than they were before the fall; and then the Smiths have real estate to sell,—on time, deferred payments drawing usual interest and secured by mortgage.

Add to the situation the uncertainty of varying seasons and fluctuating markets; introduce the cheap labor of the unfortunate or improvident poor, dependent upon the capital of others for their employment, and we have an illustration of the power of accumulated capital and the subjection of those who are without it to those who have it.

In the foregoing illustration it will be observed that the Smiths do not really *save* any of the products of their own labor. The wheat, the corn, and the cloth which they produce are not saved, but are consumed by others fully able and willing to produce all they desire to consume. But, since all products are thrown into a common market, they cannot, if they would, avoid consuming Smith's wheat and corn and cloth; and the only means they have to keep up with Smith in the race, and avoid getting in his debt, *is to limit their own consumption to Smith's standard of living.* If Smith wears wooden shoes and drinks his tea without sugar, they must do likewise. They must copy their bill of fare from that of the economical Smith, or the Smiths will own the country. They cannot get even with Smith by raising larger crops, for the supply is already sufficient to satisfy the demand.

The annual product of labor from year to year cannot be saved; but credits, the result of selling one thousand dollars' worth of labor in the market and buying but eight hundred dollars' worth, may be preserved from year to year indefinitely, and, with the aid of interest, will grow and grow till the wealth of a nation is absorbed. Had it occurred to the wily but then inexperienced Satan to sell Adam a twenty-five-cent pocket-knife, and take his note at eight per cent. compound interest, secured by a mortgage on the world, in less than five hundred years the debt would have amounted to more than the total present wealth of all the nations of the earth; and, intrenched behind the principle so often announced with long-eared solemnity, that vested rights must ever be held sacred, the devil would now own the world.

I have endeavored here to illustrate the nature and results of an industrial contest between an energetic, economical people accustomed to mean living, and an equally industrious people accustomed to more generous habits of life. When their labor is contributed to a common market, and their consumption is drawn from the same market, the more generous consumer falls behind his meaner competitor, who takes advantage of the market which he supplies, but which he does little to create.

It is true that it would not be possible to find a community in which there are two well-defined classes, such as have been described; but the principle has its illustration in many individual instances, which any one may call to mind. It has its illustration in the competition between Chinese and American labor, in the competition between convict and slave labor with free labor, and the cheap labor of the poor with the labor of the more thrifty; the parallel effect in the latter cases being obscured by the fact that the saving resulting from the small compensation of slave or dependent labor, instead of being saved to the laborer, is saved to the employer.

The operation of the principle is also further obscured by reason of the fact that the classes who are the most generous consumers are generally possessed of a higher degree of intelligence and skill, by means of which they are raised to a higher industrial level, out of contact with the immediate competition of the classes who are more meagre consumers.

Suppose that on the island which has been described, where the wages of each worker are rated at three dollars per day, and where present labor is equal to the demands of consumption, there are introduced three hundred carpenters, who are willing to work at the rate of one dollar and a half per day, that amount being sufficient to supply their wants according to their accustomed mode of living. Both wages and consumption of that class of mechanics on the island must fall to a figure approximating the lower rate of wages. A like competition in any other trade must produce like results. The effect in the end is decreased consumption; an over-supply of labor, since there will always be those who desire to increase the amount of their consumption above the enforced average; markets will be over-weighted, and yet the wants of the people be unsupplied.

· To this will come the ever-ready response that the prices of the products of labor fall in the same ratio as the price of labor falls, and that the purchasing value of a day's wages will continue the same.

But, unfortunately, values do not shrink in the same ratio in all departments of labor at the same time. Cattle have been very low for years, yet retail prices of beef have fallen but little. The fall in prices of wheat are not responded to by a corresponding fall in the prices of bread at the baker's. Low prices of agricultural produce are not soon felt in the reduction of the prices of cloth and nails. A reduction in wages is not followed by a corresponding reduction in rents. Besides, lower wages are often the effect of the introduction of a class of laborers whose habits of living have been gauged by and adapted to a smaller consumption of the products of labor, and others in the same line of employment are thereby compelled to adopt the same standard of life. The Smiths, too, are always on hand to save money, to store up credits; and the fluctuating prices and the vicissitudes of workers struggling to adjust themselves to changing conditions furnish to capital its opportunities. The interest-bearing credits of the people of the United States at this time are probably not less than twelve billion dollars. A debt of one hundred dollars contracted when labor is worth three dollars per day does not become a debt of fifty dollars when labor is worth but one dollar and fifty cents per day, but a debt of 66.6 days' labor; whereas before it was a debt of only 33.3 days' labor.

Mr. Edward Atkinson says, "If our population January 1, 1885, shall be fifty-eight million, two cents per day profit on each person's consumption would be $423,400,000, a sum of profits which would set every wheel of industry in most rapid motion. Two cents a day loss would bankrupt thousands of merchants and stop more mills and works than are even now idle." We may draw from this an inference as to the effect of fluctuating values resulting from the heated competition of seventeen million workers contending against each other in the same market. Interruptions and adjustments go on in one continuous round, and the wheels of industry are all the while more or less clogged.

The farmer sells five hundred dollars' worth of grain or stock. Naturally he would invest this money in clothing for his family or in improvements about his dwelling or on his farm. But if he has two hundred dollars interest to pay on debts, his consumption must be reduced in that amount. The mechanic whose home is mortgaged and the merchant who is in debt are each also endeavoring to save. The creditor who gathers in all this interest and principal is able to consume but a small part of it, and the result is more sellers than buyers, prices go down till consumers are found, credits are swelled in proportion, and the aggregation of wealth goes on.

A fall in prices of the products of any single industry, except where such fall is at the expense of an unreasonable margin in the profits of capital, breaks the round of production and consumption, disturbs the equilibrium of the industries, and crowds men out of employment.

While, except as considered in relation to existing indebtedness, a general and uniform fall of prices of all products produces no more harmful results than such as flow from the uncertainty which always attends a change of money values, the change of the relative values of the products of the several industries impedes and checks the current of exchange, deranges established industrial relations, compels wasteful readjustments at the expense of the working-classes, work is suspended and men thrown out of employment, but interest goes on and rents go on.

The laborer may not, and generally does not, save the difference between the amount he consumes and the value of the product of his labor, as determined by the market; the excess is saved and goes to increase the accumulations of the capitalist. The saving may be an actual saving in the form of an increase of durable wealth, or it may be only an apparent saving, in the form of credits, which, like the savings of the Smiths, add nothing to the nation's wealth, but effect a transfer of wealth from one class of persons to another.

Since, to a people as a whole, the only saving that is possible consists in an expenditure of labor in the creation of the more durable forms of property, such as machinery, tools, houses, furniture, and the like, saving may be said to be a form of expenditure. Whenever, therefore, there is a general attempt to save by checking the current of consumption and piling up money and credits, the effort defeats the purpose. But when money or credits have accumulated in amounts sufficient to invest in the creation of durable property, if so invested there is effected a saving of wealth in the only true sense of the term.

Should the people consume less expensive food, cheaper clothing, and fewer articles of perishable nature, there would be a saving of the labor required to produce these things, which labor, so saved, might be applied to the creation of durable forms of wealth. And here we meet the question, Is there any deficiency in the supply of labor which might be so employed? Is there not already an overabundance of unemployed labor, which could be used in any channel of industry open?

Releasing labor from employment and turning it idle on the market only creates greater disturbance in values. The saving of labor is no advantage except when the labor saved may be otherwise usefully employed. But when labor is so abundant that the pressing question is, How shall it be employed? there is nothing to be gained by adopting a rye-bread-and-potato diet.

It is true that, if a portion of what is consumed by some in extravagance and waste could be transferred, by some process, to those who are in need, a great benefit might accrue to the poor without loss to any. The effect, however,—at least the immediate effect,—would be of little value in the adjustment of economic forces.

To the individual, labor saved is so much gained. If one person, by means of a labor-saving device, or by superior skill, be able to perform the work of two men, he receives the full benefit of his increased labor. He enjoys an advantage measured by the inequality between himself and his fellows. But were the capacity of the entire body of American laborers to be suddenly doubled, I much doubt whether any considerable benefit or increase of wealth would result in consequence of such augmented power. With a proper adjustment of economic forces, and with fixed industrial conditions, such increase of power might bring great opportunities for leisure and culture, or for aimless idleness. Whether the result would be a market at frequent intervals choked with an overabundance of the products of labor of the kinds now in demand, or whether an improved taste might demand other articles of luxury sufficient to absorb the increased productive power of labor, it might be unprofitable to inquire and useless to predict; but, doubtless, the poor would remain, and present extremes of poverty and wealth would continue, until a remedy should be found in some modification or readjustment of economic forces.

Recognizing the necessary limitations on the creation of wealth, how is the family of the workingman to be supported during sickness or old age, or when by death they are deprived of the support of his daily earnings? By what means shall those opportunities for leisure and refined culture, so essential to the progress of society towards the higher aims of civilization, be supplied to those whose tastes and aspirations fit them to lead in that direction?

The people of a nation, interchanging the products of labor through a common market, constitute a single industrial entity; they form a social compact, with mutual interests and obligations that extend through the entire body; and the advantages which accrue are common property, in which each has a right to share according to the part which he performs, not only in supplying, but also in making the common market.

The whole people are supported by the labor of a part. The old and the infirm, and all the dependent members of society, are necessarily supported by the labor of others. This right to support, founded in natural law, in the social compact takes the form of definite obligation. Let us consider in what manner this obligation arises and in what manner it is discharged. During the period of the worker's most active industrial life, the product of his labor exceeds the amount required for the consumption of himself and family. This excess is consumed by others, and in consideration of this consumption by others he acquires money, or credits, or revenue-bearing property, such as railway stocks, mills or houses to rent, or property of like character. These constitute the security for his claim against society for payment, at some time in the future, in other labor products equivalent or more than equivalent to the product of his labor that has been consumed by others. His share of consumption is deferred to old age or to the time when needed for the support of those naturally dependent upon his labor,—a wife, children, or parents, or others having claims founded in sympathy or natural obligation. He accumulates wealth for future consumption. The course of distribution is extended so as to embrace the life of a generation or more. This is a very necessary saving for future use, a part of the social scheme, a damming of the water till it gathers sufficient volume to turn the wheel that moves the machinery of industry. This gathered wealth is consumed or distributed; and others, in their turn, enjoy like opportunity and advantage. In this manner the young and vigorous labor of the country is made subject to the burden of providing the support of the dependent classes, and secures to itself adequate compensation in the guarantee of an equivalent reward in the future. Every individual, in turn, enjoys the same opportunities and the same advantages. Civilization is the perfection of the social compact.

The limitations on the creation and use of property are such that the actual accumulations would be insufficient to provide for the wants of the dependent classes, and for the necessary requirements of society so organized, without the aid of credits. It is through credits, stocks, bonds, and mortgages, and their hold upon the property of the nation, that the dependent or non-producing classes must in a great measure, derive their support.

If the labor of one man be equal to the production of twice the amount required for the present support of himself and those dependent upon him, then one-half a lifetime spent in active labor would be sufficient to provide for the other half. One generation during its period of active labor would support two, and the next generation would, in its turn, do the same. This is possible, not by means alone of a storage for future consumption, but in the manner here pointed out. And, while debts are not to be invited, credits constitute a useful and very necessary factor in our industrial economy.

When a man has worked half a lifetime, and supported two families, or, what is the same, has contributed to the production of the country the equivalent of the support of two families, society is in his debt in the amount which the product of his labor has exceeded his consumption. The notes he holds for money loaned, his railway bonds or bank stock, or other property representing his vested capital, constitute his security for the payment of that debt. Through the consumption of himself and family that debt is discharged, and the property acquired or the title represented by the credits he holds passes to the next generation, and the process of accumulation and expenditure is repeated, and so long as society endures must continue.

The aggregation of capital or wealth to the extent here indicated is not only beneficial, but necessary. But it bears no relation whatever to that unhealthy aggregation that unduly absorbs the credits of a country, and deprives the many of this opportunity to provide for sickness and age, and for widows and dependent children. Large aggregations of capital prevent these smaller accumulations, so essential to an equitable distribution of the common benefits and opportunities which it is the purpose of the social compact to create and to preserve, by absorbing the fund out of which these small stores of wealth must be gathered.

The money which is paid to the worker in the form of wages, or as the price of the product of his labor, is merely a certificate that he has contributed so much to the support of society, and is, in return, entitled to the product of an equivalent amount of labor, valued according to the accepted standard, in whatever form he may elect. Money serves the purpose of a medium of exchange,—it is a certificate of credit. Labor in the end is paid for with the product of other labor, or with land or some of its products, which, having been appropriated to exclusive ownership, possess value by reason of their utility, and of the fact that land is limited in quantity.

A exchanges his labor for the labor of B and C, or for a part of the labor of a hundred other persons. This he is enabled to do by reason of the intervention of money as a medium of exchange. If A has received for his labor one hundred dollars in gold, that one hundred dollars represents the promise of society, which has consumed the product of his labor, that he shall be repaid in the products of other labor of any form he may select in an amount representing an equivalent value. Society stands ready at all times to cash its checks with the present products of labor. A can have flour, meat, clothing, lumber, or the product of the labor of the mechanic, or whatever else he may desire. But A is not ready to receive payment. He not only holds the obligation of society which he has received, good for all time, but he continues to contribute his own labor to the common market, which he enjoys but does not help to make, and receives more dollars. Now, by the device of a loan, a note and a mortgage, he converts this money, which bears no interest, into an interest-bearing obligation, which, by means of interest accumulations, grows and increases; and, instead of the people who consumed the product of A's labor paying the obligation given him, by returning a product of equivalent value, A's grandchildren will hold railway bonds to the amount of five thousand dollars, representing what was in the beginning but two hundred dollars and accrued interest; and the people, who had no part in contracting the debt, will pay three hundred dollars every year, without in the least reducing the principal of the debt. It is thus that the people of one generation become burdened by the obligations of a past generation, and are laid under tribute to aggregated wealth, from which there appears no avenue of escape. This transaction of A's is commonly called saving, but, in fact, A did not save anything.

The current of exchange, by which obligations are cancelled as they are made, may be thus interrupted by the economy or parsimony of a penurious young man, who, like a lodged scow in the river of trade, year by year gathers the drifting sand, develops into a sand-bar as an usurer, and finally into an island as a millionaire. The river shifts its channel to give the island room, and the surging current eats into the land along the shore and deposits its burden on the island's growing banks.

THE USE OF LIQUORS AND TOBACCO.

The value of the manufactured product of tobacco returned in the census of 1880 was $119,480,166. The exports exceeded the imports to the amount of about twenty million dollars; so that the net product consumed in the United States was about ninety-nine million dollars. The internal revenue taxes on tobacco amounted to $38,870,140, which increased the total value to $137,870,140. Sixty-four per cent. of this was cigars and cigarettes. The total value, as sold at retail, was probably three hundred million dollars.

The consumption of liquors in 1880 was as follows :

	Gallons.
Spirits consumed	63,526,694
Wines "	24,162,925
Beer and ale consumed	444,112,169

The revenue taxes paid on spirits and fermented liquors amounted to seventy-four million dollars.

These liquors brought at retail, I think, not less than five hundred million dollars. Competent authorities estimate the amount still greater. The aggregate expenditures in the year 1880 for liquors and tobacco were probably eight hundred million dollars. Of this, maybe one hundred million dollars was necessary consumption; but seven hundred million dollars of this expenditure was not necessary, in the rigorous sense of that term. Had the people refrained from the use of these articles to the extent of seven hundred million dollars, what would have been saved? The total taxes, internal revenue, State, and license, probably amounted to one hundred and fifty million dollars. This sum would not have been saved, since the people pay the taxes to themselves. Of the remainder, thirty-seven million dollars went to the tobacco raiser; twenty-five million dollars were paid out in wages to the employés of manufacturers; eighty-six million dollars were paid for materials used in manufacture of liquors, part of which went to railway companies and middlemen; fifteen million dollars paid the wages of persons engaged in the manufacture of liquors; and the remainder, three hundred and eighty-seven million dollars, went to manufacturers, transportation companies, wholesalers, and retailers, of whom there were sixty-eight thousand four hundred and sixty-one saloon-keepers and bar-tenders; and a large part went to pay the rents on buildings used. The saving which would have resulted from such reduction in the consumption would be so much labor as was required in production, transportation, and sale of the product consumed. Another effect would be to deprive capital of inordinate profits derived through this branch of industry. After paying for materials used and paying wages, capital employed in manufacture retained about sixty-three million dollars. In this amount the profits of capital employed in the transportation and sale are not included. The net contribution to capital through the consumption of tobacco and liquors probably reached two hundred or two hundred and fifty million dollars.

But there is another consideration of far greater economic importance. The expenditures of the working-people for tobacco and cigars are not distributed according to incomes. A spends nothing; B spends ten dollars per year; C, twenty-five dollars; D, fifty dollars; E, one hundred dollars; while F spends two hundred dollars per year. Because of acquired tastes and fixed habits, these expenditures become in a great measure unavoidable; and the result is that the savings of one class of men are all the while transferred to another class, and are finally absorbed in the fortunes of the wealthy. The profits are enjoyed not by those alone who are engaged in the manufacture and traffic of these articles, but by every other capitalist, whose capital is in a measure relieved from competition by the diversion of a part of the capital of the nation from employment in other industries.

From a strictly economic point of view, the chief objection to be urged against the consumption of tobacco and liquors is that it takes away the margin of savings from the workers who habitually use these articles, and is a most effective agency in the aggregation of wealth. Strange as it may appear, it is nevertheless true that, if the habit of using tobacco and liquors was universal, and the expenditure of each individual was, as compared with his income, relatively the same as that of every other individual, the margin of savings would not be affected, except to the extent that labor is diverted from other industries where it is needed; and so long as we have so much idle labor, it may well be questioned whether the employment of a very considerable number of workers in a wholly useless industry diminishes either the annual product of durable property, which represents the savings of the people, or the products of those industries which supply the necessaries and comforts of life.

The fact that a degree of opprobrium attaches to the sale of intoxicating liquors greatly increases the profits of capital invested in that business. The man who rents a building for a saloon demands more rent, and the saloon-keeper secures larger profits by engaging in a business that antagonizes public sentiment.   This unfriendly sentiment, aided by the levy of high taxes, has made the manufacture and sale of liquors in some degree a monopoly.   Capital derives pecuniary benefit and labor enjoys the moral results.

In our great cities, vice in all its forms levies heavy tribute upon the earnings of industry; but at the end of the year, when capital balances its accounts, there is always to be found to the credit of rent a liberal portion of the tribute gathered.

Individual economy in expenditure is always and everywhere to be encouraged.   That condition of society is best in which the consumption of each person bears the same relation to his earnings as the expenditures of every other person bear to his earnings, where each worker who enjoys the benefit of the common market for labor contributes his due proportion towards sustaining that market, by means of a relatively equivalent consumption.   On no other basis can this condition be so nearly reached as on the level of an intelligent, economic, and judicious expenditure by each member of society.   Parsimony is not only a private vice, but a public injury.

LIMITATIONS ON CREDIT.

Were the savings, or the accumulations of wealth, of each individual represented only by the tangible property owned by him, the power to accumulate would be confined within comparatively narrow limits.   By the intervention of credits, these limits are greatly extended.   By means of the employment of credits the control and ownership of property may remain with A, B, and C, who may be indebted to E in an amount equal to half or two-thirds the value of the property they own.   In this case E may be said, in effect, to own one-half of the property, the title to which is in A, B, and C.   A very great proportion of the accumulated wealth of the people of the United States is in the form of credits, which represent actual wealth owned and controlled by others.

Credits are a most desirable form of investment.   They bear a fixed revenue, fluctuating only within the narrow range which measures the fluctuations in the value of the precious metals; when other property depreciates, the value of credits increases;

they are readily convertible into other forms of wealth, and, in the form of notes and bonds, may be borne from place to place like money.

Within the term credits I embrace stocks of railway companies, gas companies, and the like, which, in the true sense of the word, are not credits, yet since they possess many of the characteristics of credits, for the purposes of the present discussion they may be so classed. The limits of private indebtedness are determined by the amount of tangible property in the hands of the people, and by the conditions of trade and finance, and by the rate of interest. When private indebtedness has become so great as to make it difficult for debtors to meet accruing obligations, and leads to the enforced sale of property, values become impaired, the course of trade is interrupted, the issues of business enterprises are made subject to the uncertainty of fluctuating values, and industry, in all its forms, becomes depressed; under the pressure of enforced collections property changes hands at low values, and disastrous panics are liable to occur. Property changes owners, debts are cancelled, the volume of credits is reduced, and trade resumes its accustomed channels. The net result is always a greater aggregation of wealth. While there is no destruction of property, there is a temporary depression of values, and a derangement in the relation of values, by which many fortunes are swept away, but gathered again in larger drifts farther down the stream.

Except for the accumulation of credits to an amount beyond the limit which may be borne under any fairly-regulated system of industry and trade, panics could never occur. But when the volume of credits has grown so large that accruing obligations can no longer be met in the ordinary course of trade, the way becomes blocked and panics ensue.

The growing tendency of credits is described by Dr. Wayland as follows: "When men purchase on credit, they draw upon a fund which has no definable limits. High hopes impel men to extend their purchasing power to the utmost by adding to their ready money all the credit they can command. This is the point of danger.

"This element in the market disturbs the equilibrium of prices without respect to the true standard; an artificial demand is created which finds no check, because advancing prices. and profits apparently increased, seem to warrant the further expansion of credit.

"Hence comes that excess of speculative purchases which Mr. Mill calls the prime cause of commercial crises, and which leads to the sudden recoil of prices and consequent collapse.

"The panic which follows is as rash and unreasoning as was the confidence which blew the bubble, and precludes the application of any effective relief.

"The necessity of turning all kinds of property into money to meet indebtedness fills the market with sellers, while few are ready to buy, and prices sink as far below the standard as they were previously raised above it.

"Then production must be suspended and business stand still till adjustments are made and the basis is laid for starting again by the true standard, with mutual confidence qualified and restored."

The amount of indebtedness which may be safely incurred by a state, or country, or other municipality, depends of course upon the limits of the public revenue. The amount of revenue, however, which may be raised by taxation from year to year depends to a great extent on how that revenue is expended. Where the amount collected in taxes is promptly paid out, and is at once distributed through the ordinary channels of trade, the money paid in taxes serves only as a medium of exchange; and the farmer really pays his taxes in wheat and cattle, the carpenter in the work of his trade, and the manufacturer in the product of manufacture. Where, however, taxes collected are paid out in the form of interest on a public debt, to a creditor-class who have no occasion to expend the money so received for the products of labor, but who retain it and, as opportunity offers, reloan it, perhaps in some distant locality, the round of exchange is broken, the money paid in taxes does not soon return in response to a demand for the products of the farm or the shop, and the tendency is therefore to suspend industry and depreciate values. As the public debt is cancelled, private indebtedness takes its place.

Take for illustration the revenues annually collected and expended in payment of teachers in our schools. The money quickly returns through the channels of trade, without the intervention of loans. There is but an exchange of the products of labor, or an exchange of work; the round of production and consumption is complete. But suppose the amount of money which a State pays to its thousands of teachers be paid to one individual, what is the effect? When and how does that money return to the people? The tax is paid in money which cannot long be spared; when will the necessary round of exchange be made complete by a substitution of the products of labor which can be spared for the money which cannot be?

The amount of revenue which can be raised by taxation, it will be readily seen, therefore, depends in great degree upon how it is expended. We have here another example of the evil effects of the aggregation of wealth.

The amount of credits floated in the United States cannot be very closely ascertained from statistics which have been gathered. The following is taken from the census of 1880, except where noted as estimated:

Stock and debt of railways	$5,425,722,560
" " " telegraph companies	76,068,747
" " " telephone "	13,723,119
Loans of national banks	878,500,000
Private banks and savings banks (estimated)	1,000,000,000
Public debt of United States	2,120,415,370
State and municipal bonded debt	1,117,585,546
Mortgage indebtedness of the people (estimated)	2,000,000,000
Other interest-bearing private debts	500,000,000
Total	$13,132,015,342

From this total should be deducted a considerable sum on account of railway stocks included, which yield no dividend. And there should be added stocks and bonds of street railway companies, gas- and water-works, and other joint-stock companies. Current credits between manufacturers, wholesalers, and retail merchants are not considered. Since 1880 the volume of debt has been greatly increased, and of these credits not less than eighty per cent. are owned by persons of large wealth.

In 1870 the total mortgage indebtedness of the people of Illinois was $319,864,278. In 1880 the amount of the mortgage indebtedness was $204,461,364, and in 1887, $416,379,068, an increase of over one hundred per cent. in seven years. In 1870 the farm mortgage indebtedness was $95,721,003, in 1880, $103,525,237, and in 1887, $123,733,098. In the November number (1889) of the *Popular Science Monthly*, Joel Benton asserts that the farm mortgages of the Western States amount to $3,422,000,000, but gives no authority for this estimate.

Professor Gleed, in the March number (1890) of the *Forum*, states that since 1870 one Western mortgage broker in Kansas has made nearly ten million dollars in the business of handling Western loans, and that there are probably two hundred corporations now engaged in the business of mortgage brokerage in Kansas and Nebraska alone.

The increase in railway mileage in the United States between 1879 and 1889 has been over eighty per cent., and there has been a corresponding increase in bank loans. Taking these facts as an index of the increase in the amount of stocks and credits in the United States, we may safely assume that the amount at the present time approximates close to twenty billion dollars, or about one-third of the present estimated wealth of the nation.

But of railway stocks there are about two billion four hundred million dollars that pay no dividend, and nearly five billion dollars that pay less than one per cent. dividend. Railway indebtedness and stock paying a dividend of three per cent. and over, at the present time, amounts to about five billion six hundred million dollars.

CHAPTER VI.

INTEREST ON CREDITS.

"The tooth of usury must be grinded, that it bite not too much."—BACON.

THE attitude which writers on economic science in general occupy towards the subject of interest is fairly illustrated in the comments of Dr. Wayland on usury law. Speaking of laws regulating the rate of interest, he says,—

"They violate the right of property. A man has the same right to the market-price of his capital in money as he has to the market-price of his house, his ship, or any other of his possessions.

"The real price of capital cannot be forced by law, any more than the real price of flour, or iron, or any other commodity.

"Suppose that to-day money is worth, in the ordinary operations of business, ten per cent., and it is worth six per cent. in loan. A man will as soon loan as employ it in business, if he possesses more than he wishes to use. There will be a fair supply of money in the market. But let the profits of capital rise, so that in the ordinary operations of business capital is worth twenty per cent. If, now, the rate of interest rose with the increased rate of profit, the same individual would be as willing to loan as before; and thus, the supply following the demand, there would arise no peculiar scarcity.

"But suppose that six per cent. were the highest legal rate of interest, and that he who loaned at a higher rate was liable to lose both his principal and interest, and also his mercantile character; in that case, as soon as the profits of capital in business arose to fifteen or twenty per cent., no one, who could thus employ it, would loan at six per cent. Hence, the supply would be immediately diminished; and this would, of course, cause a greater rise of interest.

"Such laws can never be enforced. Men in want of money will pay what they please for it, and they who choose to pay enough can generally borrow.

"Usury laws offer a premium for the defiance of law, and confer a monopoly on unscrupulous extortions."

John Stuart Mill says,—

"Next to the system of protection, among mischievous interferences with the spontaneous course of industrial transactions may be noticed certain interferences with contracts. One instance is that of usury laws. These originated in a religious prejudice against receiving interest on money derived from that fruitful source of mischief in modern Europe, the attempted adaptation to Christianity of doctrines and precepts drawn from the Jewish law. In Mohammedan nations the receiving of interest is formally interdicted and rigidly abstained from;

and Sismondi has noticed, as one among the causes of industrial inferiority of the Catholic compared with the Protestant parts of Europe, that the Catholic Church in the Middle Ages gave its sanction to the same prejudice, which subsists impaired, but not destroyed, wherever that religion is acknowledged. Where law or conscientious scruples prevent lending at interest, the capital which belongs to persons not in business is lost to productive purposes, or can be applied to them only in peculiar circumstances of personal connection or subterfuge. Industry is thus limited to the capital of the undertakers, and to what they can borrow from persons not bound by the same laws or religion as themselves. In Mussulman countries the bankers and money dealers are either Hindoos, Armenians, or Jews.

"In more improved countries legislation no longer discountenances the receipt of an equivalent for money lent; but it has everywhere interfered with the free agency of the lender and the borrower, by fixing a legal limit to the rate of interest, and making the receipt of more than the appointed maximum a penal offence. This restriction, though approved by Adam Smith, has been condemned by all enlightened persons since the triumphant onslaught made upon it by Bentham in his 'Letters on Usury,' which may still be referred to as the best extant writing on that subject."

Much has been said on the question whether or not interest has any foundation in equity, or whether it is not a payment without consideration. There is a theory, presented by Mr. Henry George with as much force as by any other writer, resting upon the idea that the control which a person may acquire over the productive forces of nature confers the right to special advantages, which theory is urged in behalf of the claim that interest is an equitable charge. Mr. George says,—

"Suppose I put away wine. At the end of the year I will have an increased value, for the wine will have improved in quality. Or, supposing that in a country adapted to them I set out bees; at the end of a year I will have more swarms of bees and the honey which they have made. Or, supposing that where there is a range I turn out sheep, or hogs, or cattle; at the end of a year I will, upon the average, also have an increase. Now, what gives the increase in this case is something which, though it generally requires labor to utilize it, is yet distinct and separate from labor. The active power of nature, the principle of growth which everywhere characterizes all forms of that mysterious thing or condition which we call life. And it seems to me that this is the cause of interest, or the increase of capital, over and above that due to labor."

Mr. George holds, therefore, that the return of an equal number of bees or cattle at the end of a fixed period would not be sufficient to repay the loan of bees or cattle. This argument is based upon the theory that the increased value of the wine, or the product of the bees or cattle during the period of loan, exceeds the value of labor required to secure the increased product, and the amount of risk of loss from disease or other cause incurred by keeping the wine, or bees, or cattle. In other words, the claim is made that if A has control of certain productive forces of nature, he is entitled, in equity, to receive from society, for his labor, an amount equal to that which B receives for his labor, and something in addition thereto; because he is possessed of certain property which B does not have. If this be good doctrine, it appears to me that the claim of Mr. George, that no one has a right to any special advantage growing out of the ownership or exclusive possession of land, cannot be well founded. I should say that, when a man receives the full value of his industry and skill, society is no longer in his debt.

The increase in the value of the wine, over and above cost of storage, attention, and risk, is because society has conferred upon capital an interest value. If the rate be six per cent., the value of the wine at the end of the year will be increased six per cent. above its value a year ago, with cost of storage and risk added; if the rate be twenty per cent., the value of the wine will increase in the same ratio.

If A has an article of property to-day for which he has no use, since all property is subject to deterioration in value, to decay, or to destruction, it may be greatly to A's advantage to loan that property to B, with an adequate guarantee that its equivalent will be returned when he may need it. If A is compelled to keep on hand all the products he creates, he cannot accumulate. A man cannot provide a competence for the future by accumulating hogs and cattle. He must find some one who will take them and return him an equivalent amount at some future time. The advantage is more to him who lends than to him who borrows. It is by means of credits that a man is enabled to continue to produce beyond his present needs, and avail himself of the use of his surplus product at any time in the future he may desire to do so.

In order to perfect the method by which this may be done, and enable every man to avail himself of the great benefit which results from industrial co-operation, money has been introduced, as a medium of exchange and a medium for the temporary storage of wealth, during the intervals which must elapse between the stages of a completed exchange. For the same purpose, and with the further object, among others, of providing for the storage of wealth during long periods, credits have been introduced.

The nature of money and its use is such that it is necessarily limited in amount. And when any member of the social compact appropriates the money which he receives in exchange to the permanent storage of wealth,—in other words, when he hoards it,—he does society a wrong; but, by reason of his power to monopolize the medium of exchange, other members of the industrial copartnership may be compelled to pay a premium in the form of interest, in order to secure a return of that money to its proper uses. The chief factor in determining the rate of interest is the monopoly in money.

A rate of interest sufficient to cover risk of loss, and perhaps the trouble that the lender is put to in making the loan, is founded in natural equity, and is merely compensatory; but any rate beyond this must find its justification in reasons of public policy.

If the right to interest be founded upon the theory that capital is a productive agent or power, then the amount of remuneration to which capital would be entitled would be determined by the ratio of the product to the capital employed. But where that ratio is greatest, interest is often the lowest. Common observation teaches that the rate of interest is determined by the necessities of borrowers, by law, by custom, and by the avarice of money-lenders, as well as by the supply of loans. The rate fluctuates from time to time, and varies in different localities, regardless of any equitable basis. Money, our medium of exchange, is made a subject of speculation, like wheat or corn, and usury furnishes the inducement.

Dr. Wayland says that "a man has the same right to the market-price of his money as he has to the market-price of his house." On the same theory a man would have the right to stow away a hundred millions of dollars, and hold it till the pressure of the demand was sufficient to force borrowers, whose property is jeopardized by the contraction of the circulation, to pay such rate of interest as he might choose to ask. Money is a limited quantity, and values are gauged by the amount in circulation. No man has the right to withdraw it from its legitimate uses and convert it into a commodity. He may have for it the market-price, but society has the right to determine the limit which that market-price shall not exceed, without regard to any considerations other than those which concern the people as a whole. Both Dr. Wayland and Mr. Mill speak as though, without a satisfactory rate of interest, capital might be withdrawn from production. Let us see. Capital consists, first, of money. Of this the total amount is not large. Money, to a considerable extent, may be hoarded. It then draws no interest and commands no profit. If deposited in bank, it is loaned. In the Middle Ages hoarding gold and silver was not uncommon. There were many reasons for hoarding then that no longer exist. But it will hardly be seriously contended that a low rate of interest at the present time, with our perfected banking system, would lead to a hoarding of money to any serious extent.

Second, capital consists in mills, furnaces, houses, stocks of goods, etc. How these can be withdrawn is not apparent.

Third, capital exists in the form of credits. The amount of credits is very large. It must remain in this form, or else it must be employed in production by its owners. It becomes at once apparent that the existing order cannot be changed. If the capitalist who runs an iron-mill in Pennsylvania makes gains to the amount of one hundred thousand dollars, for instance, what will he do with it? He must put it into more mills, houses, etc., or in credits. If it exists at all, it must exist in some form. And, if capitalists do not choose to avail themselves of credits as a means of storage for their wealth, they must cease to accumulate, and let go of a large share of what they now have. The idea that capital can appear and disappear at will, like the intangible substance of a ghost, does not merit serious consideration. That a low rate of interest will tend, in some degree, to lead persons to employ their own capital rather than loan it, is true; and this is one of the reasons to be urged in favor of reducing the rate.

Dr. Wayland speaks of capital being worth twenty per cent. in business. At times it is worth more. But is it to be seriously urged that the capitalist has an equitable right to appropriate the product of labor, in the ratio of twenty per cent. on the capital employed, and that a policy of legislation which would reduce this profit nearer to an equitable standard is to be condemned as an encroachment on his rights?

Finally, we are told that usury laws can never be enforced. There is no warrant for this statement. These laws, when properly framed, are as effective as other laws. It is true that there have been ineffective usury laws, and numerous instances of their evasion may be cited. The framing of these laws has not always been inspired by an earnest purpose to make them effective. But those who have had the opportunity to observe the operation of usury laws reasonably well framed with a view to enforcement, know that legislation on this subject presents no unusual difficulties. Writers on this branch of the subject of political economy have, I presume, copied from each other a statement made without adequate investigation. The policy of statutory limitations on the rate of interest has been almost universally adopted in the United States, and the views generally entertained by writers on political economy have not been accepted as the basis of legislative policy. The distinction between the right to limit the charge for the use of money, and the right to limit the charge for the use of a house or of land, is based on the peculiar character of money as distinguished from other property.

If A rent a house of the value of two thousand dollars, agreeing to pay therefor the monthly rental of twenty dollars per month, he acquires the use of two thousand dollars' worth of property. If he borrows two thousand dollars, and agrees to pay for the same two hundred dollars per annum, in this case also he acquires the use of two thousand dollars' worth of property for a stipulated consideration. In the one case the law does not interfere. The contract for rent is enforced without regard to whether the charge be reasonable or extortionate. But if A engage to pay for the use of money more than a certain prescribed interest, the law not only refuses its aid in enforcing the agreement, but also subjects the lender to the penalty of a forfeiture of all interest. The parties in either case being equally free to contract, why does the law interfere in the one case and not in the other?

In the first case, A hires a house; when the term of his lease has expired he may surrender the house. He incurs no pecuniary obligation for the principal sum involved. When he has surrendered the property and paid the rent his debt is cancelled.

But when A borrows two thousand dollars in money, the money does not remain in his possession. Money, to be used, must be spent. It is invested in other property and made subject to the contingencies of commerce; through fluctuations in value it may be lost, and, when the time for payment of principal and interest arrives, A's ability to pay may be contingent upon his success in trade or his ability to sell property at fair values. In the mean time values may have changed, or the market may have become stagnant, and sales may be impracticable. A being unable to pay the debt when it matures, the loan must be renewed or replaced by other loans at a higher rate of interest, perhaps, and the final result may be an unforeseen sacrifice of A's property.

Rent is discharged in the ordinary course of current expenditure. The amount bears a definite relation to the renter's income, and no liability is incurred which may involve him in unforeseen financial embarrassment. At the end of the month or the year he may surrender the property, and rent other property at a lower rental, if circumstances require that he should do so.

Pressed by necessity, or encouraged by hopes of profit in business which often prove delusive, the majority of borrowers are ever ready to pay a higher rate of interest than they can afford. The number of borrowers is great, and competition is strong; while the hoarded wealth of the country is in relatively few hands, and competition among those who loan is comparatively weak. They are not pressed by any peremptory necessity; they may await opportunity, and often profit most by the misfortunes of others. The rate of interest, when not restrained by usury laws, finds its only effective limitations in the ability and disposition of the workers to narrow the general margin of profits which represent the annual contribution of labor to capital.

I do not contend that the law should not, under any conditions, place limitations on rent. Rents tend everywhere beyond the limit of equitable charges. I am disposed to question the claim of capital to profits on any ground other than that of public policy and the social utility of reasonable accumulations of wealth. They are an industrial necessity, and afford a practicable means for utilizing the social and industrial energies of the people.

The details of every commercial transaction cannot be subjected to rules defined by legislative acts. The law should interfere only where it is practicable to accomplish results fully adequate to compensate for whatever inconvenience or sacrifice of individual freedom, or other evil, which the operation of the law may occasion. Otherwise, the remedy may be worse than the disease.

Ordinarily, the determination of values must be left to the law of supply and demand and to the contracting parties. There are, however, many recognized exceptions: charges for railway transportation, ferriage, hack-fare are recognized as subject to legislative control. The law of supply and demand is not in such cases fully operative. The subject here is, in its nature, such that it may be brought under the operation of legislative restrictions. Legislation is justified because it is practicable.

Ordinarily the field is left to the law of supply and demand, not because this law always fixes just prices, but because, in general, it secures a nearer approximation to equitable prices than is attainable by the operation of any law which could be formulated in a statutory enactment.

When the law of supply and demand is, from any cause, not reasonably effective to prevent extortion, then the government is justified in interfering, if in such case it be practicable to secure equitable results by means of legislation. The question then becomes one of policy and not of right. Government interference is in itself an evil. Legislative laws are clumsy remedies, and liable not only to fail in the accomplishment of the results aimed at, but also to produce unlooked-for effects not less injurious to society than the evils sought to be repressed. Commercial intercourse ought to be left as free from restraint as possible. The advantages which one man may obtain over others by reason of superior energy, skill, or foresight, or even by deceit, within certain limits, the law wisely permits. The jostling of the crowd cannot be prevented. In the great struggling mass of humanity, where the people are all endeavoring to climb on top of one another, the law cannot always keep the strong from trampling upon the weak, but it may impose restraints and establish limits.

Limitations upon rent-charges would involve a question as to the value of each lot or tract of land rented. There being no uniform standard for determining that value, every case of renting would involve an appraisement of value by some authorized agent of the government, and values being a matter of opinion, fluctuating and uncertain, a law limiting rent-charges would not only involve unusual difficulties in its enforcement, but would fail in its purpose of uniformity of price according to values.

In regulating interest-charges neither of these difficulties is met with. Usury laws are practicable and easily enforced. They are uniform in operation and certain in their effects. A law limiting the price of clothing or of provisions tends to diminish the supply. A law limiting rate of interest does not tend to diminish the supply of capital, except where the law is of local application. In the following States there is no limit on the rate of interest which may be reserved by contract: California, Colorado, Maine, Massachusetts, Nevada, and Rhode Island. In Arkansas, District of Columbia, Iowa, Michigan, Minnesota, Mississippi, Missouri, Nebraska, Oregon, South Carolina, and Wisconsin the limit is ten per cent. In Kansas and Texas the limit is twelve per cent. In Alabama, Georgia, Illinois, Indiana, Louisiana, North Carolina, and Ohio the limit is

eight per cent. In Connecticut, Delaware, Kentucky, Mary-
land, New Hampshire, New Jersey, New York, Pennsylvania,
Tennessee, Vermont, Virginia, and West Virginia the limit is
six per cent. The laws of each State prescribe a legal rate to
govern in cases where no specific rate is fixed by contract.

The right of the government to limit the rate of interest
which may be collected, and the sound policy of legislation prescribing limitations on charges for the use of money being conceded, we come to the question, what rate should be permitted?

This inquiry involves the consideration not only of the question what rate of interest can A, B, and C afford to pay, or
what are the average returns of capital, but how is society in
general affected by interest-charges? What does interest have
to do with the great economic problem, the distribution of
wealth? If the effect of a high rate of interest does not extend
beyond the borrowers, society is not so deeply concerned; but
if the effect extends to the whole people, directly involving the
welfare of the entire working population, there is then a potent
reason for the enactment and enforcement of laws limiting
interest to a low rate.

The functions of money are, first, to afford a definite standard
or measure of values; second, to supply a medium by which the
exchange of other property may be conveniently effected; and,
third, to afford a medium for the temporary storage of wealth.

To illustrate the use of money, as well as the dependence of
labor upon capital, let us suppose the existence of a community
under the conditions here described. Severed from all connection with the world of commerce, there is a community consisting of one thousand workers and their families. This community is in possession of all kinds of modern tools, devices,
and machinery, and each industry is supplied with a due proportion of workers. There is convenient access to all the materials for production. All property is owned in common, and
each worker willingly performs his part. The capacity to produce has reached that point where the labor of eight hundred
workers out of the one thousand is adequate to the production
of every species of property ordinarily consumed by the whole
community. The excess of capacity is, therefore, equivalent to
the labor of two hundred out of the one thousand workers.

But the dwellings of the people being poor, they desire better houses. They therefore propose the erection of a house of the value of one thousand dollars for each family. The productive value of a day's labor, measured in dollars, is equivalent to 1.66⅔. There are three hundred working-days in a year. Two hundred laborers working three days each perform six hundred days' labor, the equivalent of one thousand dollars. In three days, therefore, the two hundred workers will build one house of the value stated, in one year they will build one hundred houses, and in ten years they will build one thousand houses, or one house for each family. In the work of building are embraced the furnishing of materials and every stage of preparation. As everything is owned in common, the workers and their families are all the while supported out of the common fund, and no money is needed. As a result, we have in ten years the production of one hundred thousand dollars' worth of property in excess of consumption, and an equal distribution of the product.

In this scheme I have not overestimated the productive capacity of labor nor the excess of unemployed labor. In a community so organized, if such organization were practicable, money would be unnecessary, and gold and silver, except as useful in the arts, would be of no more value than in a community of beavers, that, without machinery or tools other than their teeth and tails, without any medium of exchange and without credits, manage to accumulate considerable wealth, without producing either millionaires or tramps.

But, assuming the same conditions, except as to community of goods, money or some substitute for money becomes necessary. Houses are wanted. There is a surplus of labor sufficient to build them at the rate described. There is money enough in the community to answer the purposes of exchange, but it is equally distributed, each of the one thousand workers having twenty dollars and no more. It is plain that no man can enter upon the construction of a house that will cost one thousand dollars with only twenty dollars at command. Each member of the community is already supplied with his ratable portion of the property of the whole community. There is a continual exchange of the products of labor which are consumed, and the equilibrium of wealth is all the while preserved. But A desires to build a house worth one thousand dollars; how shall he proceed? A has some property, but only such as he requires for his own use, and every other family is equally well supplied. If he would sell what he has, there are no purchasers. No one buys property to rent, because there are no renters. No man uses the property of another, and there can be no aggregation of wealth in the ordinary way. If A borrows the one thousand dollars in small amounts from each worker, how will he be able to repay it? He must do so out of the product of his labor; but the labor of each individual being sufficient for his support, though A can, during a year, perform one-fifth more labor than is required for his support, the equivalent of sixty days, or one hundred dollars, and in ten years he could repay the one thousand dollars; yet, there being no market for extra labor, the way is blocked. But, if every other man will, during the ten years, build a house of the value of one thousand dollars, there will then be a market for the surplus labor at its full value. But, since it is probable that three-fourths of the people will be satisfied with the houses they have, considering that economy consists in spending as little as practicable, no market is furnished for the extra labor.

The foregoing illustrates the condition of completed development reached by old communities, called by writers on political economy the stationary state, and shows why, with an abundance of labor at command, people continue to live in poor houses, without the luxuries, and often without the comforts, of life. The exchange of labor is limited, not only by economic conditions, but also by the disposition and habits of the people.

Now, suppose that in the community of which we have been speaking the governing power, by means of taxation, collects from each of the one thousand workers one dollar, and builds a house; then in the same manner collects another one thousand dollars and builds another house, and so on for ten years, utilizing all the excess of labor. Now, at the end of the ten years, the people have one thousand houses, have all the money they had before, and no more, and in the mean time they have enjoyed all the comforts and luxuries of life to which they were accustomed.

We have supposed one case in which the houses were built without money, and another in which money was employed much the same as bills of exchange are used. In either case the same results are accomplished by the same amount of labor. In the latter case, instead of using gold and silver, the government might have resorted to certificates of credit, or fiat money, with the same results.

The principle here illustrated is the same as that which underlies the success of building and loan associations. The effect of these associations is, first, to encourage the saving of money by furnishing an inducement by way of opportunity for immediate investment, and by supplying the stimulant which springs from the concert of many persons together pursuing a common purpose; and second, and herein lies the chief value of these associations, by furnishing a market for labor. A cannot build unless he can exchange his labor for the labor of others, and in this manner pay the cost. He cannot exchange his labor unless there be others who desire to build also. It is true that the round of exchange is not confined to building alone; all occupations are brought within the circle of exchange. But the principle illustrated is fully operative, and the building effected by the agency of these associations is largely the product of labor that would have been otherwise unemployed,—an addition to what would have been the product of all the industries had this work not been performed. No more successful agency for the distribution of wealth has ever been devised. Thousands of workingmen have secured homes of their own, while thousands more have derived advantage in the way of reduced rents.

These associations should be confined within the scope of their original design, and should not be made a mere medium for the purpose of loaning money. Aggregated capital should not be permitted to utilize these organizations of wage-earners for the purpose of absorbing the earnings of the people by an extension of credits. The way is open for the profitable investment of capital; the people may not be quick to discern the danger, and legislatures should be prompt in surrounding these institutions with the necessary safeguards to prevent the intrusion of aggregated wealth into this field of investment.

It is evident that money produces nothing. A may collect

together one hundred thousand dollars in money. That money represents so much stored wealth, and, for the purpose of transfer and of the temporary storage of wealth, money is convenient and necessary. But if A locks that money in his safe for months or years, he does society an injury. In equity he has no right to hoard it. To do so is to divert it from its legitimate use. Society is entitled to it, and that, too, without paying a premium on its use. If A does not desire to exchange it for the products of labor, society is entitled to that money without incurring any obligation other than for the return of a like sum when A may require it for the purpose of expenditure. If, then, A loans the money, he is entitled, first, to compensation for any risk of loss he may incur; and, second, to compensation for the work, care, and skill required in loaning and collecting it. To anything more he has no claim, except upon the ground of public policy, which, for the general good, permits and encourages, within proper limits, accumulations of wealth beyond the actual earnings of any individual worker.

But a question of this character must be considered in its practical bearings, and not alone from the stand-point of absolute equity as involved in a particular transaction.

At three per cent., any sum, at compound interest, will double itself in twenty-three years and one hundred and sixty-four days. At four per cent., any sum will double itself in seventeen years and two hundred and forty-six days; at five per cent., in fifteen years and seventy-five days; at six per cent., in fourteen years and three hundred and twenty-seven days; at seven per cent., in ten years and eighty-nine days; and at eight per cent., in nine years and two days.

At three per cent. compound interest, in ten years one thousand dollars will amount to one thousand three hundred and thirty-one dollars and thirty-five cents. In other words, the savings of one thousand dollars at three per cent. compound interest, in ten years amount to three hundred and thirty-one dollars and thirty-five cents; and at three per cent. simple interest to three hundred dollars.

The census reports of 1870 and 1880 show that the entire savings from the labor product of the whole people amount to less than ninety dollars per capita. This would make the savings to each average worker equal to two hundred and seventy dollars in ten years, supposing the increase of wealth to be equally distributed and the whole amount to be credited to labor. But, since, as I have already shown, more than the amount of increase in wealth has been absorbed by capital, and nothing is left to the account of labor, the account stands thus : Average savings for one laborer in ten years, nothing; savings of one thousand dollars in ten years at three per cent. interest, three hundred and thirty-one dollars. There are no statistics which furnish the data necessary to determine the total of the interest-bearing credits of the United States ; but the amount will at the present time approximate the sum of fifteen billion dollars, which, at six per cent., would in ten years, at compound interest, amount to twenty-six billion seven hundred and ninety million dollars,—a gain of eleven billion seven hundred and ninety million dollars. At three per cent. compound interest the gain would be four billion nine hundred and sixty-five million dollars. It is true that a considerable portion of these credits do not constitute a part of large fortunes ; but two-thirds of the whole amount may be set down to the credit of unduly aggregated wealth. It will be seen that interest is a most potent factor in the aggregation of wealth,—a power, in the presence of which labor is absolutely helpless. It is true to-day, as of old, that " to him that hath shall be given, and he shall have an abundance ; while from him who hath nothing, shall be taken away that which he already hath."

There is another effect of interest not yet considered. The rate of interest is everywhere accepted as a measure of the profits of invested capital. When money is worth eight per cent., it will not, as a rule, be invested in any business with a prospect of lower profit. If A has a house to rent which represents two thousand dollars of invested capital, the rent is fixed on the basis of the rate of interest which money will command. A says this house is worth two thousand dollars; eight per cent. on two thousand dollars is one hundred and sixty dollars, therefore I must have one hundred and sixty dollars per year, and enough more to cover taxes, cost of repairs, the annual wear and tear of the property, and something more for the trouble of looking after the property, collecting rents, etc.

If money was worth but three per cent., sixty dollars would take the place of one hundred and sixty dollars in determining the rental value. The manufacturer makes the interest value of money the basis of his calculations in estimating the profits which he must derive from his investment. That a certain equilibrium will always be preserved between the interest value of money and the profits of invested capital is too evident to require elaborate illustration. The enforced reduction of interest throughout the entire country would tend to a large reduction of the profits on invested capital and effect a wider distribution of wealth. Greater steadiness would be given to values, speculation would be largely eliminated, the burdens of labor would be lightened, the tightening grasp of capital on the productive forces of the nation would be relaxed, and the savings of the people, instead of being rolled into the fortunes of millionaires, would be distributed among the workers.

Mill says, "The price of land, mines, and all other fixed sources of income depend, in like manner, on the rate of interest. Land usually sells at a higher price, in proportion to the income afforded by it, than the public funds. . . . When interest is low, land will naturally be dear; when interest is high, land will be cheap."

This is true. Land being a fixed quantity, the ownership of land constitutes a monopoly; and in a country like England, where the area is fully occupied and cultivation has reached near the limit of power to produce, and the agricultural product cannot be increased by the employment of additional capital, the reduction of the rate of interest will effect an increase in the money value of land, and will not tend materially to reduce rent or the value of agricultural product. In the United States, however, where there is room for the abundant increase of capital in agriculture, the rule does not hold good. The tendency here would be to reduce rent wherever it is excessive, as compared with other values. But when in this country, as in England, the limit of the possible agricultural product is approximated, agricultural values will be pressed upward, and will require the restraint of foreign competition and statutory limitations on the ownership of land. Whenever there is a monopoly in any form of production, prices are, in a great measure, released from the effect of the laws of competition and from the economic forces to which other industries are subject. But in any case a low rate of interest tends, after a certain point has been passed, to reduce rents. Since the overflow of accumulated capital must be invested in the competing industries, and the general tribute which labor pays to capital is reduced, the portion appropriated to wages or earnings of labor is therefore greater, and average wages must be higher. From the indirect or secondary effects of a low rate of interest, rents, though intrenched behind the power of monopoly, cannot escape.

It is not necessary, and perhaps not advisable, that interest on all classes of loans should be limited to the same rate. Where loans are secured by mortgages on real estate estimated at a fair valuation, the danger of loss is reduced to a minimum ; and, except for the fluctuations in value, caused chiefly by the pressure of aggregated capital in pursuit of illegitimate profits, there need be no danger at all. The lowest limit may therefore be fixed on loans of this character. In commercial transactions, where the only security is the continued personal responsibility of the makers and indorsers of commercial paper, the rate might be somewhat higher, but the margin of difference should not exceed one or two per cent. The policy of the law should be to discourage speculative enterprise and to favor steady values. Traders burdened with heavy interest obligations are always under the spur of the necessity to make large profits, and thereby become the natural enemies of the workers, whose share of the product diminishes in the same ratio that profits increase.

Since the chief objection to a high rate of interest is founded upon the fact that interest is one of the principal agencies through which aggregated capital in the hands of a small number of persons absorbs the earnings of the people, the reason for prescribing a low limit does not hold with the same force where the lenders of money are persons of small means. It is, however, ordinarily impracticable to distinguish between lenders, and all must come within the operation of the same rule, unless special conditions shall furnish the opportunity to discriminate.

Building and loan associations—institutions which are co-

operative in character—have for several years been in effective
operation in almost every city and important town in the
country. No plan has been hitherto devised by which working-
people could combine their small savings so as to secure the
necessary capital to employ labor in constructive industry
where only considerable sums are available. The savings of
workingmen are too small in amount, too slow in accumulation,
to be available for the purpose of building a home or other individual enterprise. The organization of building and loan
associations has furnished workingmen the opportunity to co-
operate, and, by means of combination, to utilize their own
labor in building homes, without at the same time being compelled to abstain from the enjoyment of the usual comforts of
life.

How many families there are, who are now living in com-
fortable homes of their own, who, except for these associations,
would be paying rents, statistics do not inform us. The number,
however, is very large. The law has not provided for statistics
upon this subject. The curiosity of the National Bureau of
Statistics has not yet been sufficiently awakened on the subject
of the progress of the workingman to divert its attention, except
during periods of leisure, from the task of counting the people
and summing up the wealth of the nation. However, from the
statistics of the St. Louis building associations, just at hand, we
may gather an idea of what has been done. There are in St.
Louis one hundred and five associations, averaging two thousand
members each. The monthly dues amount to two hundred and ten
thousand dollars. The interest paid on loans averages five and
one-half per cent. At the date of the July statement the loans
amounted to five hundred and eighty-two thousand two hundred
and ninety-one dollars, and were increasing at the rate of two
hundred and ten thousand dollars per month, making the
volume of loans, December 1, 1889, about ten million dollars.
The average building society loan in St. Louis is two thousand
six hundred dollars. This would give three thousand eight
hundred and thirty-eight houses. The monthly savings amount
to two hundred and fifty-seven thousand seven hundred and
fifty-one dollars. These results have been accomplished within
five years. In these associations for mutual benefit the interest

accumulations are distributed on an equitable basis among the stockholders through whom they are derived, and serve merely to equalize the advantages of the early and later borrowers. An interest of six or even eight per cent. is not open to serious objection.

These associations are most effective weapons against the power of aggregated capital. They should be conducted in the interest of the working-people, and should not be given over as a field of investment for accumulated capital. If these organizations are continued, and in their operations confined to the purpose of promoting the interests of the working-people, they will soon be released from monthly tribute, in the form of rent, to aggregated wealth.

The residence and business real estate, including water-power, in the United States in 1880 was estimated at nine billion eight hundred and eighty-one million dollars. In this valuation land is included, which Mr. Atkinson estimates at from one-half to two-thirds the value of the whole. The value of dwellings alone probably did not exceed four billion dollars, or about eight-fifteenths of the annual product. The average life of a dwelling is not less than forty years; certainly not less if we allow for the greater value of the more durable ones. Five per cent. of the annual product is sufficient to duplicate these buildings in ten and two-thirds years; one and one-third per cent. will duplicate them in forty years. It is apparent, therefore, that in a short time a steady diversion of a very small per cent. of the labor of the country to the construction of dwellings would, if equitably distributed, supply the people with good homes of their own. And to three-fourths of the people of a country a good home and its furnishings must, in the nature of things, constitute the limit of individual wealth.

In order to secure the necessary diversion of labor to the creation of this form of durable property, in which the product of labor may be saved or preserved in continued use during a longer period than in any other form of product, and in which form it therefore yields a greater measure of comfort than in any other, railway freights on building materials should be limited to actual cost of carriage; capital invested in railways should derive its profit out of charges for the carriage of freights not so directly associated with the savings of the people; building associations should be encouraged, and new dwellings occupied by the owners should be exempted from taxation during a reasonable period. The policy of the law should be such as to encourage saving,—that is, the conversion of labor into durable property and the wider distribution of its ownership. Saving in the other sense of accumulating credits or revenue-bearing property, more properly described as the centralizing of capital, needs no encouragement.

This plan of co-operation, employed by building and loan associations, with such modification as experience may suggest, may doubtless be extended along other lines, in effective competition with accumulated individual wealth, thus opening the way for a practical solution of the greatest problem of the age,—the equitable distribution of the products of industry and the steady employment of labor.

The question naturally arises, If interest be reduced to a low rate and profits on invested capital be cut down, how shall adequate provision be made for the dependent classes who now rely upon the returns of a small amount of capital? How shall men no longer able to work, widows, and children derive their support?

The answer is that a wider distribution of wealth will multiply the number of small fortunes. The number of those who now are able to acquire a competence is comparatively small.

It is better to extend to the workingman an opportunity, with reasonable exertion, to acquire a small store of wealth which may constitute a fund for the support of himself in sickness, and of his family, in case by death or otherwise they should be deprived of the proceeds of his daily labor, than to pursue a policy which, while it may enable a few who may be successful under adverse conditions in accumulating wealth, to provide what will be a more adequate support for those dependent upon them, prevents the majority from making any provision at all, beyond a few months' subsistence for those dependent upon their industry. And, besides, women and children make their way far more readily in a community where labor receives its just rewards, than in a community where the earnings of the workingman are absorbed by exorbitant interest, rents, and profits, and where employment is rendered uncertain by harsh conditions prescribed by the exacting demands of capital unrestrained by the power of organized labor.

But I believe the government, as the representative of common interests, as the agent of the social and industrial compact, may well extend its functions in behalf of the dependent classes.

Suppose the State or national government should issue bonds bearing an annual interest of six per cent., or eight per cent., or ten per cent., made payable to individuals by name, in amounts not less than one hundred dollars nor more than three thousand dollars, these bonds to be issued only to dependent classes, such as widows and children left with estates under the value of, say, five thousand dollars, or such other sum as might be thought a suitable limit, and payable, if to guardians of children, when the ward should attain the age of twenty years, or if to widows, on remarriage, and under the direction of courts of probate, and through the agency of banks, let the money of these dependent classes be invested in these bonds, what reasonable objection could be urged? The benefits of such a provision might be extended to other dependent classes. The money so received could be used by the government as other funds, and replaced out of the ordinary revenues.

Or, in lieu of the foregoing, a certain amount of railway bonds might be set apart for this use, and if all workingmen whose accumulations have not exceeded a certain amount were embraced within the scope of the policy here indicated, such measure would greatly tend to reduce inequalities in distribution which result from undue aggregations of wealth. The discrimination here suggested would be a discrimination, not between individuals, which would be unjust, but between fortunes, which would be both just and practicable. The bonds might be made to bear such interest above the ordinary rate as the State should by law determine, payable out of the earnings of railways, which are in the nature of a tax upon the industries of the country, the weight of which rests upon the whole people alike.

This plan would encourage saving among the common people by holding out a special inducement, and the rate of interest would be little more than that which the people at large, through the agency of individuals, now pay to those who are already in possession of vast fortunes; for the interest paid by individuals, where it goes to swell the already overgrown aggregations of wealth, is, in effect, paid by the working-people at large.

By this method, to the extent that it should be employed, the people, as a whole, would become the borrowers. They would pay interest, not to capitalists who would reloan it, but to consumers; they would therefore pay it in the products of present industry, and the burden would be unfelt.

If, during the last five years, there had been deducted from the total product of American industry a sufficient amount to adequately feed, clothe, and house five hundred thousand of the poorer classes in this country, and this amount had been conferred upon them as a gift, the American people would have suffered neither diminution of wealth nor deprivation of the comforts or luxuries which they have enjoyed. A burden of expenditure resting upon the whole people, so adjusted as to bear equally upon all, is not felt. It is derangement of the industries and imperfect distribution that is the cause of suffering and want.

The functions of the State might be still further extended. If the interest on loans secured by real estate be limited to three per cent., the State might itself become a borrower, issuing bonds in sums of fifty, one hundred, two hundred, and three hundred dollars, and so on, and reloaning the funds so received at the rate of three and one-half per cent., payable semi-annually, secured by mortgage on real estate, the amount loaned not to exceed two-thirds the value of the security. And the State might, at the same time, become an insurer of the buildings on the real estate so mortgaged. In Germany a plan of government insurance has long been in operation, and I see no practical difficulty in the way of the government performing this service. In England the cost of insurance is little more than one-fourth the cost in the United States, the ratio being as 25 to 90. The losses paid in the United States average a little more than two-thirds of the amount of the premiums paid, indicating large expenses, as well as large profits, to insurance companies.

This plan would greatly narrow the field wherein aggregated wealth now gathers its profits.

This would not accord with the theories of political economists, of whom Professor Cairnes says their "decrees, ordinarily given to the world in the name of political economy, amount, in the main, to a handsome ratification of the existing form of society as apparently perfect;" but, without any violent departure from the existing order, would afford a practical test of the principle of industrial co-operation, under conditions favorable to success. Many States have adopted the policy of accumulating funds for educational purposes, and loaning them to citizens through official agents, and I have not learned that any but good results have followed the experiment. So long as the interest should be paid, the State would be under no necessity of requiring the principal, and depression of values occasioned by forced collections would not occur. The borrower might be permitted to repay his loan in instalments of, say, fifty dollars at any time; and the collections over the State would be sufficiently uniform in volume, so that the amount—which need not be large—necessary to be kept on hand to meet current demands could be readily determined.

The plan suggested involves no complex system of accounts, no necessary increase in the number of officials, no higher order of skill than that required by the duties of county officials at present, and need involve no considerable additional expense.

The adoption of a low rate of interest would involve the necessity of relieving credits from taxation. The tax on credits is a double tax that has no equitable basis and cannot be justified on the ground of public policy. This subject is discussed in the chapter on taxation.

I am aware that a low rate of interest, unless supplemented by some limitations on the ownership of real estate, while it would check, would not prevent a rapid growth of aggregated wealth. There must be some outlet for the overflow of profits which capitalists and their families are unable to consume, for profits must come within the limit of opportunities for investment. When interest is materially reduced, surplus capital will begin to absorb the real estate of the country at a far more rapid rate than now. High rates of interest, combined with the unprofitable condition of agriculture, have caused investments to take the form of mortgage-loans; but, when driven out of mortgages by a reduced rate of interest, capital will burrow in the earth. Even now, in the most productive counties in the comparatively new State of Illinois, from one-half to three-fourths of the land is cultivated by tenants.

Even John Bull is permitted to bore into Uncle Sam's cider-barrel, and insert his siphons at will. And our American people are foolish enough to believe that, for gold and silver, they can afford to barter away their lands and their industries to foreign capitalists. There is no consideration adequate to justify a prosperous people imposing upon themselves the obligation of perpetual tribute to foreign wealth. As I have sought to show, the wealth of the country, like its lands, is limited. If our factories and iron-mills and breweries are sold to Englishmen at a good round price, we may congratulate ourselves that we have the money to build more and better ones, but we cannot afford to build more than enough. The Englishman will retain what he gets, the American will have the remainder. After the Englishman has obtained a foothold, when the Yankee undertakes to crowd him to the wall with competition, he will discover that the economies of a people who insist on beef three times a day are poor weapons with which to vanquish a foe stolidly content with cheese and porridge. John Bull is a clever neighbor as a visiting acquaintance, but we cannot afford to pension him; we cannot afford to give him a permanent job, even in our brewery. We have ample leisure to make beer for ourselves. And, as for his capital,—his money,—we do not need it. We have enough, not very well distributed, but the amount is ample, and millions lie idle in the treasury.

CHAPTER VII.

TAXATION.

WE will now consider the manner in which public revenues should be raised, and the sources from whence they should be drawn.

In matters pertaining to taxation, history is a treasury of experience; and there ought to be no great difficulty in determining the methods best adapted to the attainment of desired results. Yet there is great apparent difference of opinion among those who assume the function of guiding the popular mind, and who profess to be seeking the same ends. I am not, however, fully assured that the conflict of theories may not be sometimes accounted for by the purpose to serve special interests, which often warps, when it does not conceal, real convictions. Nevertheless, there are wide differences of opinion sincerely entertained and earnestly supported by those who seek, regardless of special interests, to promote the common welfare.

In the levy of taxes, or the imposition of duties on imports, the direct purpose is to secure a revenue to defray the expenses of government; but in selecting the subject of taxation, in apportioning its burdens, and in prescribing the modes of collection, the leading consideration should be the manner in which any proposed measure will affect the distribution of wealth. This is the question which, more than any other, concerns the welfare of the people as a whole. There are other considerations which may not be ignored, but which, in ordinary times at least, should be subordinated to the one leading purpose of laying the burden where it will be least felt, and of protecting the weaker members of society from the pressure of those economic forces against which, without the friendly aid of a benign public policy, they are unable to effectively contend.

The necessities of government may sometimes be so urgent and pressing that little heed can be given to the ultimate equities involved in the mode of collecting a public revenue; but, in the absence of peremptory necessity, every measure and every method should find its principal test of fitness in its collateral effects, as an economic force, in the adjustment of the industries and in the final distribution of wealth.

I do not believe in the theory that the functions of government are to be considered as necessarily so limited and automatic that they should be confined to those ends alone that lie in the line of the most immediate and direct purpose which calls those functions into exercise. Government should be inspired by a guiding motive that looks to the future for the true measure of results. It is confined in grooves, in order to give certainty and safety to its operations, and not for the purpose of impairing its efficiency as a social and economic power.

DUTIES ON IMPORTS.

The sources of revenue of the United States government are customs duties and internal revenue taxes. Duties are levied on a large number of articles, but chiefly on products of manufacture and a few agricultural products which compete with the productions of our own people. These duties are levied with a view to encourage the home production of the articles taxed. Those duties which were formerly laid upon foreign products that do not compete with home products have, with few exceptions, been repealed, the revenues derived from them being no longer required to meet public expenditures. We are still, however, collecting a revenue of nearly sixty million dollars per annum from imports of sugar,—an article, the production of which in the United States, under present conditions, appears to be limited to a small part of the amount required for consumption. The duties on sugar, which amount to more than the duties on iron and steel and their products, and more than the sum of the duties on cotton and woollen fabrics combined, are paid by a larger number of consumers and in more nearly equal amounts *per capita* than any other tariff duties.

According to the theory of those who contend for a tariff for revenue only, there could be no more appropriate subject than sugar, and none so clearly falling under all the conditions involved in that theory, except tea and coffee, which are articles of universal consumption not produced at home.

If, however, in levying tariff duties, we would discriminate so that the burden of the tax may fall chiefly on the more wealthy and well-to-do classes, we must omit the food products consumed by the common people, which we are compelled to import, and, as a consequence, if duties are made sufficient to meet the demands of a necessary revenue, higher rates must be laid on articles of manufacture, and the protective character of our revenue system would still remain, though modified, it might be, so as to shift its burdens and its protective benefits, and somewhat change the relative values of the products of the various industries affected.

Tariff revenues on commodities paying $100,000 and upwards for the year ending June 30, 1887, and exhibited in round numbers, were as follows :

Articles.	Amount of Duty col- lected.	Rate of Duty. Per cent.
Animals	$933,000	20
Art-works	578,000	80
Barley	1,034,000	16.8
Books and printed matter	684,000	25
Brass and manufactures of	171,000	42.13
Bristles	174,400	15.08
Brushes	168,000	80
Buttons	898,000	25
Cement	220,400	20
Chemicals, drugs, and dyes	4,654,000	25 to 110
Chiccory root	106,700	65.17
Clocks, watches, and parts thereof	490,000	80
Coal (bituminous)	654,500	24.81
Copper-ores	104,000	49.63
Corsets	370,500	85
Cotton manufactures	11,710,000	40.17
Earthen-ware and china (mostly decorated)	8,218,000	58.02
Fancy articles	3,000,000	41.04
Fire-crackers	833,000	100
Fish	612,000	21.72
Flax, hemp, and jute textiles	9,498,000	28.10
Fruits and nuts	4,210,000	27.90
Furs	900,000	20
Glass and glassware	4,910,000	59.01
Gold and silver manufactures	132,000	80
Hats, bonnets, and hoods	1,052,000	21.44
Hay	157,500	18.89
Hops	1,830,000	42.64
Iron and steel and manufactures of	20,713,000	40.92
Jewelry	107,000	25
Lead	223,000	68.97
Leather and manufactures of	8,287,000	80.06
Liquors (spirituous and malt)	7,402,000	72.68
Marble	600,000	39 and 53
Matting and mats	177,000	20
Metals, composition, etc.	693,000	82.21
Musical instruments	403,000	25
Oils, fixed and expressed	270,000	25
	$86,178,000	

Brought forward	$86,178,000	
Paints and colors	400,000	32.73
Paper (writing) and manufactures of paper . .	425,000	21 and 25
Precious stones	1,053,000	10
Provisions (over half-cheese)	430,000	24 and 30
Rice (cleaned)	758,958	113.03
" (granulated) or rice-meal	152,460	20
Salt in bulk	284,010	79.68
" " bags	392,855	39.30
Seeds . . . . : . . .	172,000	20.36
Silk and manufactures of	15,541,000	49.71
Soap	117,000	26.89
Sugar	58,000,000	82.04
Tobacco and cigars	9,128,000	83.32
Vegetables (potatoes, pickles, and sauces)	548,000	24.05
Wood and manufactures of	1,503,000	18.28
Wool (unmanufactured)	5,900,000	36.08
Woollen manufactures . . . . ~.	29,730,000	67.21
Zinc, spelter, etc.	111,500	46.35
Total	$210,824,783	47.08
Total duties, embracing articles omitted . .	$217,286,893	

Value of articles imported on which duties were paid	$450,325,331
Average rate of duty 47.08%	
Value of articles imported free of duty	233,093,659
Total imports	$683,418,990

The imports not embraced in the above list consist of a large number of articles of which the aggregate amount makes up the difference between the totals given above.

In the above list the specific duties are reduced to *ad valorem* rates, so as to exhibit, in convenient form, the duty paid.

It will be observed that the higher rates of duty are laid upon articles of luxury, or at least upon those articles which are chiefly consumed by the more wealthy and well-to-do classes. The classes of imports from which the largest revenues are derived are barley, liquors, silk, sugar, tobacco and cigars, chemicals, fancy articles, fruits and nuts, earthen-ware and china, flax, hemp, and jute textiles, glassware, hops, iron and steel, leather and manufactures of leather, precious stones, manufactures of wood, wool, woollen manufactures, cotton manufactures, hats and bonnets. Aside from sugar and wool, beer and hops, the articles of the classes named are mostly of a high grade of manufactured articles and are not extensively consumed by the masses of the people. Many are of the class on which profits usually range higher than on articles of more universal consumption.

A high rate of duty is also laid upon articles, the home manufacture of which it was the purpose specially to encourage. Two principles of discrimination are observed; the duties on rice and sugar being the principal exceptions to the general policy on which this schedule is framed. Sugar is the product of a low grade of labor, and the industry is not, therefore, one which, under present conditions, should be encouraged.

The policy of our American system of revenue, so far as it relates to duties on imports, may be defined to be to promote the change of unskilled labor into the more productive and more valuable forms of labor, by diverting it from the more crude and unproductive industries to those industries in which the products of the same number of laborers possess a greater value, generally for the reason that it is applied to the processes of production, through the agency of mechanical devices and machinery, whereby the productive power of the same labor is greatly multiplied; and, second, subject to the first and principal aim, to so levy duties that the great burden of the revenue will rest on the wealthier members of society, who are more able to bear it, rather than the poorer classes, who are less able. That these principles are observed throughout cannot be claimed for the present schedule, but in the main it may be said that the duties conform to the policy defined.

BY WHOM ARE DUTIES PAID?

It may be well to consider here the question as to who pays the duties on foreign imports. John Stuart Mill, the leading English writer on the subject of political economy, and an advocate of free trade in the most unqualified sense, says, "The imposition of a tax on a community almost always diminishes the demand more or less; and it can never, or scarcely ever, increase the demand. It may therefore be laid down as a principle, that a tax on imported commodities, when it really operates as a tax and not as a prohibition either total or partial, almost always falls in part upon the foreigners who consume our goods; and that this is a mode in which a nation may appropriate to itself, at the expense of foreigners, a larger share than would otherwise belong to it of the increase in the general productiveness of the labor and capital of the world, which results from the interchange of commodities among nations."

I do not, however, perceive the necessity of looking for the result at the end of a route so circuitous. It is a principle universally recognized, that the price of a commodity is not determined alone by the cost of production. It is, in fact, determined by the demand for consumption. Where the demand is not sufficient to absorb a product at a price which is a fair measure of the cost of production, production tends to diminish towards the point where the values of the product rise to a fair measure of the cost of production. The change is, however, gradual, and in the adjustment the cost of production is itself lowered by a reduction of wages and profits.

If, for instance, a certain amount of wheat is raised in Kansas and shipped to New York City, and sold there for one dollar and a quarter per bushel, the freight from Kansas to New York being twenty-five cents per bushel, and the railways increase their charges by adding twenty-five cents more for each bushel of wheat, does any one suppose that wheat will rise to one dollar and a half in New York City because of increased rate of transportation? The effect would be felt chiefly by the producer, the Kansas farmer. If the people of the United States are shipping wheat to England, and wheat is selling in the market there at the rate of one dollar and twenty-five cents per bushel, and the cost of transportation is suddenly raised twenty-five cents on the bushel, it will not be contended that wheat in England will advance to one dollar and fifty cents. If, instead of an increased cost of transportation, England levies a duty on wheat of twenty-five cents per bushel, the effect is the same as though the additional charge of twenty-five cents per bushel had been made for transportation. If England is selling a certain grade of woollen goods in the United States for one dollar per yard, and an import duty of twenty-five cents per yard is laid upon that grade of goods, it is apparent that the people of the United States will at once greatly reduce their consumption of the imported cloth; and, in order to get a market, the English manufacturer must sell his cloth for one dollar and ten or one dollar and fifteen cents per yard, and he will reduce the cost of manufacture, unless his profit is sufficient to enable him to make the reduction in price without. He, like the American farmer, must have a market, if not at one price, at another. So that, in fact, duties on foreign imports are paid, in part, by the foreign producer and, in part, by the home consumer. How the rate is divided depends upon the commodity and upon the home competition. On silk and cotton and woollen goods, and on iron products and many other imports, the foreigner pays from one-fourth to one-half the duty. It occasionally happens that the American manufacturer ships his surplus product abroad and sells it for less than it is sold in the home market. He is compelled to accept the conditions which are made for him. The duty on sugar is doubtless paid nearly altogether by the consumer, since it does not have the effect to advance the price beyond the point where consumption is materially reduced, so as to limit the demand below the range of the usual quality of product.

It is true that the foreign people who receive less for their goods, to the extent that wages are reduced will be compelled to reduce their foreign purchases. The reduction, however, falls upon the markets of all countries with which they trade, and not alone on the country where the duty is imposed. Where, however, the reduction is made out of the profits of the manufacturer, the demand for foreign meats and bread-stuffs continues the same, the reduction being made in articles of luxury and such others as are not absolutely necessary.

There are other considerations involved in the theory of protective duties besides those set forth in the chapter on protection. There are industries which in themselves do not represent the most productive employment of labor, but which employ labor and capital that would otherwise remain idle, or which, because they constitute a valuable part of some general industry, require the fostering care of protective duties. Of this character of industry there is no better illustration than sheep and wool growing, which, except for considerations of this character, would not fall within the scope of any sound protective policy. A consideration somewhat in detail of the claims of this industry to the special encouragement which protective duties may afford will serve to illustrate the principles involved in the protective policy in application to other industries as well.

SHEEP HUSBANDRY.

Sheep husbandry furnishes occupation to the agricultural classes during the winter season, and thereby employs time that would be otherwise idle. It widens the field of occupation, of interest, and of intelligence. Secondly, there is in this country a large area of land adapted to grazing, but not adapted to tillage, which would be brought into profitable use through the extension of this industry. Thirdly, sheep raising is most valuable as a part of a general system of associated husbandry. It opens the way for a proper rotation of crops, and leads to the alternate use of the land for the purposes of grazing and tillage, and is the most effective means for preserving and increasing the fertility of the soil. It may be said to be an essential part of an harmonious and economic system of agriculture. It possesses a moral as well as an immediate economic value, and may be indirectly profitable to a people, and yet, in its immediate and direct results, unprofitable to individuals. But why, it may be asked, are not these considerations sufficient to promote, to the full limit of its utility, the extension of this industry without the aid of a protective tariff?

The farmer is governed by what appears to be his immediate individual interest; and this is essentially true if he be in debt, for then he is without choice.

If, during the last five years, the American farmers had raised all the sheep required to supply the home market with all the wool which has been consumed in this country during that period, even though the prices of wool had been even lower than those which did prevail, on an estimate of the total general result is there any doubt but what the agricultural classes would have been greatly benefited?

What would have been the effect? First, our product of

wheat and corn and oats would have been less, and therefore, as I have shown elsewhere, on the whole of greater value. The total value of the agricultural crop, including sheep and wool, would have been increased in an amount which cannot be definitely estimated, but it is safe to say by the amount of the value of the increased sheep and wool product; and I believe that the increase would have been greater. The labor required would have been even less than that which was required to produce the cereals that were raised during that period, and somewhat better distributed throughout the year. Second, the general average fertility of the soil would have been increased. Last, and most important in the present relation of our industries, the agricultural classes, receiving a larger sum for their total product, would have received a larger proportionate share of the general product of the whole country, and thus been put more nearly on a level with the manufacturing industries.

The direct result would have been a small increase in the value of certain grades of woollen goods and a slight advance in the price of food products. Agriculture would be to-day in a more healthy and prosperous condition, property values would be somewhat higher, making the burden of credits proportionately less, and the labor of mechanics, as well as the products of manufactures, would have been more in demand. The weakening of a great industry interferes with that steady course of production and consumption which is essential to general prosperity, and produces that condition of industrial depression by which workers in the various industries are forced out of employment, and established adjustments of wages are broken up. Manufacturers, always on the alert to keep production within the limits of the effective demand at good prices, regulate their working-force as their immediate interests appear to dictate, and the constant tendency is to drive larger numbers of workers beyond the range of steady and profitable industry. The several industries, including trade, constitute a system by which people effect an exchange of labor. Whether the number employed is one million or ten millions makes no difference as to the individual share of each. But the system is like a clock; the wheels must be adjusted with reference to each other, and all must move together. But farmers, being individually subject to prevailing conditions which they could not change, were compelled to pursue a course which many knew, but which the great majority could not well know, was detrimental to their own welfare. Had one individual reduced his grain product in order to grow sheep and wool, he would not, simply because he had raised less, have realized better prices for his grain, since the total volume of the grain product of the country would not have been perceptibly affected by the subtraction of a few bushels, and what he would have lost by his diminished grain product he could not have gained from his wool, it being in itself less profitable than grain. To effect a profitable substitution of wool for grain, such as would reduce the grain product in sufficient amount to advance the price, required the combined action of the farmers of the nation, which could be secured only by a policy that would lead farmers in general to substitute wool in place of a part of the grain crop. Farmers, as a class, cannot be expected to be governed by the incidental value of an industry, as to its improvement of the soil or its effect in distributing labor throughout the seasons, and, when disposed to give such considerations full weight, present necessity compels them to pursue those branches of agriculture promising the largest immediate returns.

There is no industry which, in the levy of duties or taxes, demands more consideration than that of agriculture in its present condition in this country. For there is no industry so helpless against destructive competition; none, the annual returns of which fluctuate through so wide a range. The principal factor in modifying the effect of these fluctuations is a diversity of production, whereby the loss on one article is made up by the gain on another.

The time is coming, however, after this country shall be more thickly populated than now, when this capacity to overweight the markets will be subjected to the limitations on the agricultural area, and the farmer, as the owner of a natural monopoly, instead of needing the aid of protective duties, will become a power against which other classes may require the protection of foreign competition as they do in England to-day. But policies must be adapted to prevailing conditions; and one reason for guarding agricultural interests now is that the accumulation of lands in large bodies, owned by single individuals, which must result from the long continuance of present conditions, may be prevented. It is the special interest of the American people at the present time to guard against monopoly in land. And, aside from express limitations, no remedy can be made so effective as properly-adjusted revenue laws.

PASTURAGE OF THE PUBLIC LANDS.

The rapid growth of the cattle industry on the public lands of the West has not been productive of good to the farmers as a class nor to the people as a whole. This appropriation of the public domain to the use of the ranchmen for grazing purposes constituted a most effective attack of accumulated capital on one of the chief branches of agriculture, in consequence of which that industry has been much disorganized. Destructive competition compelled a change in the relations of the different branches of agriculture as a properly-organized system of husbandry, in the interest of capitalists, many of whom were not American citizens,—a change disastrous to the greatest American industry in its immediate results, and to all other industries in its secondary effects. Had a sufficient tax been laid upon the cattle grown upon the public lands to have prevented demoralizing and destructive competition with a leading product of an industry which the whole body of agricultural people were directly, and other classes were indirectly, interested in maintaining, all would have enjoyed the benefit of a more healthy industrial condition.

It is true that most of this land is fitted only for grazing, and that it must be appropriated to that purpose. But the growth of the cattle industry in the public lands of the West should have been restrained to a pace consistent with the continued prosperity of agriculture in the States. The notion, so generally inculcated, that cheap bread or cheap food or cheap clothing is to be desired, even at the expense of industrial derangement, is doubtless responsible for the neglect to guard agriculture, as an organized industry, against the raid of ranchmen and cowboys.

Changes even in the direction of cheaper production, in whatever manner they may be brought about, whether by machinery or by the stocking-up of the wild Western ranges, are to be encouraged; but the more steady and gradual the change, as a rule, the better for the greater number of people. The shifting of labor from one form of industry to another is always a slow process; and the adjustment of the different branches of the agricultural industry proceeds more slowly, and is effected with greater difficulty, than industrial changes in general.

Cattle, horses, and sheep require years to mature them; and an overstocked market cannot, as in the manufacturing industries, be relieved by a sudden diminution of the product. In agriculture it is not possible to determine beforehand what the product is to be, for statistics do not furnish the required information. The statistical information furnished by the Agricultural Department is generally too late to be of use to farmers in regulating production according to the measure of the demand.

Writers on political economy usually proceed on the theory that all industries will promptly adjust themselves to the effects of competition, however violent that competition may be. Nothing could be further from the truth. Labor is a heavy commodity, not susceptible of rapid changes of form, or of being promptly shifted from one locality to another to meet the fluctuating demands of trade. Professor Fawcett says, "During the winter months an ordinary agricultural laborer in Yorkshire earns three dollars and twelve cents per week; the wages of a Wiltshire or Dorchestershire laborer, doing the same kind of work, and working a similar number of hours, are only two dollars and sixteen cents a week. This great difference in wages is not counterbalanced by other considerations. Living is not more expensive in Yorkshire than in Dorchestershire; and the Dorchestershire laborer does not enjoy any particular advantages or privileges which are denied to the Yorkshire laborer."

Of the freedom of movement from one industry to another, says Professor Walker, "Professor Cairnes sought to reach a measure of the rate of this movement in England. His result was substantially, that only loss by death or disability could be relied on to relieve the labor market in any branch of industry which was overdone; and the sole disposable fund for supplying new laborers to new and growing branches of industry was to be found in the body of persons each year coming of age, industrially speaking.

"It would be easy to show that the play thus given to the labor market is far within the limits of the great oscillations of industry which labor must meet fully and promptly, or suffer because it cannot meet them."

Professor Walker dwells much more at length upon the sluggishness of labor in adapting itself to changing conditions. The remedy, he thinks, must be found in some plan by which these movements of labor may be accelerated. It appears to me, however, that the policy of the law should be, so far as practicable, to protect the working-people from the rush of events by which the relations of the industries are deranged. The speed of genuine progress is gauged by the mobility of labor. Competition, to the extent that it is useful, should be free; when destructive, it should be restrained, where restraints may be applied under the operation of general and practical laws, that permit free play to the ordinary movements of industrial enterprise. Because competition is an essential factor in production and distribution, the ready inference is that competition should never be restrained. Thus we fall into careless generalizations, that take no account of important distinctions to which exceptional occasions may give rise.

If it be the chief aim of civilization to gather wealth into the hands of a few, to build palaces for princes, and adorn their walls with the works of highest art, the political economists are right, and their doctrines need no amendment; but if the purpose be to lift the common people to a higher level of thought and refinement and comfort, their theories have not been verified by results; the march of civilization has left too many behind; there is too much truth in the statement made by Mr. Carnegie, that the contrast between the palace of the millionaire and the cottage of the laborer measures the change which has come with civilization.

THE BURDEN OF TAXATION.

Taxes are a public necessity, and, to the extent that they may be required for legitimate expenditures, cannot be avoided. There is always a limit within which taxes may be confined,

without withholding funds which may be considered necessary
for public uses, and beyond which the question is always open
for discussion as to whether the best interests of the people are
subserved by the collection and expenditure of public revenues.
The burden of taxation is a theme entering into the discussions
of every important political campaign, and the inquiry arises, To
what extent are taxes a burden upon the people, and what
degree of relief might be expected from a reduction of taxation?
It is all-important that industrial evils should be traced to their
true sources, and that we should measure correctly the causes
to which they owe their origin.

Mr. Atkinson is accustomed to refer to taxation as though the
amount of taxes paid represented so much taken from the
pockets of the people which they would otherwise have and retain to add to savings. The view is plausible, and generally
goes unquestioned, but is it true?

The taxes paid represent a certain portion of the annual
product; according to the estimate I have made of the total
amount, apparently a little more than one-twelfth. Since, however, a considerable portion is spent for public buildings, river
and harbor improvements, and in other ways embracing a part
of the labor which has already been included in the total
product, the proportion is something less, say one-fifteenth.
This amount may be said to represent so much wheat, so much
corn, so much clothing, iron, carpentering,—in short, so much
labor. We may say, therefore, that one-fifteenth of the labor
of those engaged in productive industries was consumed in
public works, and in food and clothing, and other comforts for
government employés, pensioners, public creditors, and others.
The whole matter resolves itself into a question of the consumption of labor. To what extent did the people deprive themselves of what they otherwise might have enjoyed, by expending one-fifteenth of their labor in this manner? It is a question,
first, as to whether the people have that amount of labor to spare.

Among the employés, whose services were paid for out of the
public revenues, were two hundred and twenty-seven thousand
teachers, two-thirds of whom were women. It is not probable
that the corn crop was short, that the iron and steel product
was less, or that even the supply of muslins and jeans was defi-

cient, because of this diversion of labor. But a large number of
men were also employed in government service, who, had they
not been so employed, would have engaged in productive industry, in agriculture, manufacture, or trade. If, under such
conditions, our product had been greater, which I doubt, who
would have consumed it? Suppose the agricultural product
had been increased, who would have been benefited? Was
there any demand for labor to make nails, or to weave cotton
and wool? Was there any want, not supplied, of book-keepers
and clerks? Would it have assisted the poor to have added
to the number of those who were competing in the market for
work? or would the fiercer competition have blocked the way
to increased production and better distribution?

According to Mr. Atkinson, in the cotton and woollen industry, where employment was certainly as steady as in any other,
the average term of employment was not over ten months in
the year.* The report of the Bureau of Labor Statistics for Illinois for the year 1886, which gives the record of the number of
weeks' work performed by eighty-five thousand three hundred
and twenty-nine mechanics, railway employés, coal-miners,
workers in manufacturing establishments, barbers, tailors,
bakers, and brewers, all belonging to organized labor associations, shows an average loss of twenty-eight per cent. of time
during the year. Bricklayers and stone-cutters average twenty-
seven weeks of work; brickmakers, twenty-five weeks; plumb-
ers, twenty-eight weeks; carpenters, thirty weeks; hod-carriers,
thirty-five weeks; plasterers, forty weeks, coopers, metal-
workers, and upholsterers, thirty weeks; tailors, wood-workers,
terra-cotta workers, and half the iron-moulders, thirty-five
weeks; and seventy-three per cent. of the coal-miners, twenty-
six weeks or less for the year. In 1885 the census of Massachusetts shows that persons engaged in manufacturing were
unemployed 3.9 months during the year at their principal occupations. If we add to this the number of those who may be
said to have no regular occupation in villages and towns, the
per cent. of idle labor will appear still greater.

---

* The blast-furnaces ran on the average but eight months, and the steel-
works but nine months during the census year.

If, working but three-fourths of the time, we produce all that, under the present system of distribution, we are able to consume, all the market will accept, cannot the girls be spared to teach school?

Extravagance and wastefulness of expenditure are certainly to be condemned, since they are always unnecessary and are in themselves, as well as in the demoralizing effects of example, detrimental to the public welfare. But it must nevertheless be borne in mind that our government expenditures are simply the expenditure of so much labor, of which we have an abundance left and running to waste.

The question of the *reduction* of the amount of taxes is therefore of little moment. They who strive in that direction to obtain relief from existing evils are wasting time. If our government could be run without a dollar of expense, there would be nothing gained. Industry is the life of the nation. An invention that would make labor unnecessary would be a curse upon the people. The real question is how to distribute the burden of taxation that it may be lightly and cheerfully borne; how to relieve those who are overweighted, and to distribute the rewards of industry according to merit.

The question is not the *amount* of taxes, but the sources from which they shall be drawn. It is a question of how taxes shall be laid so as not to interrupt the course of industry and distribution. The yoke is light enough when properly adjusted.

It is not a question as to how much shall be withdrawn from the total product of the nation's industry and distributed through the channel of public expenditures; and all the rattle and noise about high taxes is but the pow-wow of the Indian medicine-man, who understands neither the pathology nor therapeutics of the disease.

Our public schools have everywhere suffered from the false notion that taxes necessary to secure good schools are a public burden. Good schools cost nothing but labor, and generally female labor at that, which would be otherwise unemployed, and, when they are made universal, they add no weight to the burden that oppresses industry. It is only where good schools and poor ones, high taxes in one community and low taxes in another, generous living and niggardly saving compete with each other in a common market, that taxes for purposes of education are felt.

It is the conflict between Chinese habits and American habits. The man who keeps his children out of school, in order to obtain a larger share of the common market than his more liberal and enlightened neighbor, is a public enemy, and should be subject to the penalties of the law.

The present product, equitably distributed, and consumed without necessary waste, would be adequate to meet the reasonable wants of the whole people; and, if that product were increased by the employment of one-fourth of the idle labor and machinery, it would be abundant to supply the comforts and luxuries necessary to satisfy the demands of our present civilization.

The problem is how to secure that distribution; since a prompt and equitable distribution, conforming to the requirements of social demands, would bring into steady employment the labor necessary to meet the demand.

Of food products there is already an abundance; but improvement is much needed in the direction of more economic consumption and improved domestic cookery. And, in devoting his attention to the latter branch of economic and sanitary science, Mr. Edward Atkinson is rendering a public service fruitful of practical results, and altogether worthy of his superior talents. He should be encouraged to continue, only now and then laying aside apron and cap to find needed recreation in occasional rambles through the fields of statistical romance.

With all this burden of taxation upon us, we have filled the country with railroads, factories, furnaces, and mills and dwellings. Better dwellings, it is true, are needed, but the labor that could have supplied them has been sitting on dry-goods boxes, whittling pine sticks, waiting for work, and all because the round of distribution has been continually interrupted by obstructions interposed by the efforts of aggregated wealth, in continual struggle to maintain its margin of profit and extend its mortgage upon the future product of the labor of the country, and also by the fierce conflict among the working-people trampling over each other to gather the coin that is tossed among the crowd, where, since all cannot be in the middle, many are on the outer edges picking up stray pieces that roll beyond the usual range. This chaotic mass of workers and capitalists must be reduced to order by some system of limitations and restraints that will give free play to individual industry, by protecting it from the avarice of wealth, and thereby, at the same time, secure it from the mad rush of the surging crowd, who, pressed by daily needs, are forever trampling opportunity under foot.

PENSIONS.

Since 1863 we have paid in pensions to old soldiers, their widows and orphan children, a billion of dollars. We have paid it, but how? First in money, which was soon expended for the comforts of life. We have therefore paid it in the products of the field, the workshop, and the factory; paid it out of our abundant harvests, and out of the products of machinery run by steam. We have paid it with the labor of farmers, carpenters, clerks, merchants, factory employés, bakers, barbers, ministers, and teachers; we have paid it in new houses, in corn, potatoes, and meat, in flour and bread, in clothing, in hair-cuts and in sermons. We have paid it chiefly in perishable products which we might neither keep nor otherwise consume, and which, when consumed, are promptly replaced by like products, all of which we have abundant power to create.

During the same period we have paid over two billion three hundred million dollars interest on the public debt. How have we paid it? In the first instance in money, as pensions were paid. A certain portion of this money was expended for the perishable products of labor, which, being gone, do not stand in the way of further production. Another part was expended in the construction of business houses, factories, mills, and railroads, which maintain themselves out of their own profits; so that the demand of the country, except as increased by the growth of population, has been substantially supplied, directly for years, and indirectly, considering the profits on capital, forever. The demand has been supplied, and the common people have divested themselves of the opportunity to acquire the interest of ownership in the great body of the revenue-producing wealth of the nation.

The farmer furnishes wheat to the consumer, who eats it and

returns for more. When the barber shaves his customer he does not close his shop, for he knows that beard will grow again and his customer will come back; the bar-tender knows that his patron, who has drunk his fill, will soon return as thirsty as before; the shoemaker is comforted with the thought that half-soles wear out; and even the minister may find consolation in the worldly knowledge that souls once brought to grace are prone to backslide and return to be saved again; but when rail-roads are built, railroad building is at an end, for railroads pay their own way, and the capitalist is never called upon to expend his gathered fortune either to repair or build them anew.

We have paid the interest by expending our heritage of opportunity!

But a large portion of this enormous sum paid in interest has not been expended even in constructive labor, by capitalists themselves, but has been returned to the people in the form of loans to farmers and mechanics. We have paid the interest on the public debt in promises to pay more interest, in mortgages that will never die till strangled by the iron grasp of an un-friendly law. They will remain, continually urging the people into the hurry of wasteful endeavor. They will ride production and distribution with whip and spur, till the whole people are joined in one wild race for the prizes of wealth which are re-served to the swift and strong alone. It is under such condi-tions that speculation thrives, and wealth is amassed in millions, and the common people grow poor. We have not paid the in-terest; we have but renewed the bond, and chained labor to the chariots of millionaires.

The relation of the government of the United States to the public debt is that of an intermediary, an agent to collect the money from the people and transmit it to the bondholder. The people are the debtors, and, instead of paying the interest on the bonds in the products of labor,—the only real payment there can be,—the people have reborrowed the money at a higher rate of interest than before.

He who imagines that only the particular debtors whose names are on the notes are concerned, fails to consider the effect which a large amount of individual indebtedness owing to a class of wealthy capitalists constantly exerts on production and distribution, and the manner in which values are necessarily affected through the operation of such indebtedness on the distribution of money. The debtors represent only the particular spots where the leeches are applied; the blood by which they are distended is withdrawn from the entire industrial system.

When fortunes grow so large that their gathering gains can be no longer consumed in the products of the labor of the people of the country from which they are drawn, they block the way to general thrift; check the growth of small savings among the people, by which are gathered those small fortunes which yield a competence to many families, endure for a generation, and are then dissolved and distributed among the people of the generation that follows after, in such amounts as are sufficient to give assistance and encouragement to the building anew of like fortunes, thus gathering and dissolving again, as they serve their purpose, yielding opportunity for leisure and culture to many families distributed among the people at large as centres of moral force and refined social influence.

That selfish maxim, "Look out for number one," cannot always be successfully observed, without a considerate regard for numbers two, three, and four. A people are bound together by common ties and common interests often liable to be overlooked in the struggle for individual advantage. A man cannot live a civilized life among Indians, for the simple reason that the people about him are Indians. He may have the necessary capital to start a bank, or a merchant-tailoring establishment, or an Italian opera; but a bank would not flourish, and even an Italian opera might fail of appreciation. Individual welfare depends on general thrift; and every man has a selfish, if not a humane, interest in the welfare of his neighbor, of which he cannot divest himself.

It is too late now to mend the mistakes of years ago, errors of policy now too long past to require special attention, and which, for the most part, were but the natural, perhaps unavoidable, results of economic conditions which had grown up through the course of centuries, and for which no set of individuals and no political party may be held accountable. The only purpose, in bringing these measures and their results into view at the present time, is to gather from experience a knowledge of the route that must be travelled in order to escape from the swamp into which we have wandered.

INDIRECT TAXATION.

It has been the experience of all nations that taxes in the form of duties on imports are more willingly paid, and meet with less opposition from those who pay them, than direct taxes. Some writers have regarded this as a reason why this mode of raising public revenues should be discouraged, placing their objection on the ground that taxes drawn from the people in this manner do not sufficiently challenge their attention to cause them to properly guard their own interests, and that this mode of collecting taxes therefore leads to extravagance in expenditure.

But there is something more to be said in favor of indirect taxation than merely that it does not arouse opposition among the people. The burden not only seems to be lighter; it is so in fact. It is a tax which is paid according to consumption, which every man regulates more or less, both as to time and amount, according to his ability and convenience. It is paid at no stated time. Money is all the while being collected and returned to the people. The stream is constant; there is no interruption of trade or of industry. The amount of trade determines the amount of tax. The tax is a part of each day's expenditure, whereas direct taxes are paid in bulk at a certain season of the year. The people of a whole State are required to store a requisite amount of money, from five dollars to ten thousand dollars in amount, each; sellers become numerous and buyers become few; it becomes more difficult for each one to raise money, because his neighbors are all endeavoring to do the same thing; trade is interrupted and values are impaired. Sometimes the depression in values, particularly of farm-stock, is very marked, and the period of depression may be protracted for months. The demand for money for the payment of taxes at a particular time is so great that, where the volume of currency is gauged by the average amount of business in a country, as in the nature of things it must be, a disturbance of the course of distribution necessarily follows. Production is reduced in corresponding degree, and there is a consequent waste of labor.

It may be said, also, that the burden of a direct tax often bears very unequally on different members of society accordingly as they happen to be prepared to meet the stress of the demand or be compelled to make sacrifice of property in order to do so.

The fact must never be overlooked, that the *real burden of taxation is not measured by the amount, so much as by the degree of disturbance to the even run of production and distribution.* Its weight depends upon how it is adjusted; upon the direction taken by the public revenues in their distribution after they are collected, and the degree of promptness with which moneys collected are returned to the people. A surplus in the treasury, beyond that which is required to meet accruing demands, is not, under any circumstances, to be justified or excused. Values are gauged according to the volume of money in use; and a withdrawal of a large amount of money from the people at any one time, to lie in the public treasury, forces a readjustment of values corresponding to the amount of money remaining in circulation, and readjustment of values is only another name for robbery. It is true that an entire readjustment of values does not at once follow. The place of the withdrawn currency may be, to some extent, supplied by an extension of credit, or the volume of trade may diminish. But, however the pressure may be relieved, and whether or not the consequences are made manifest in clearly-defined results, many people must suffer loss.

INTERNAL REVENUE TAXES.

The internal revenue taxes of the United States for the year 1887 were as follows:

Spirits	$65,829,322
Fermented liquors	21,922,187
Tobacco	30,108,067
Banks and bankers	4,288
Oleo-margarine and dealers	723,948
Penalties	220,205
	$118,808,017

The tax on spirits, fermented liquors, and tobacco was, when levied, justified by the necessity for a large revenue, these articles being considered suitable objects of taxation because of the large revenue they may be made to yield and the facility with which the tax may be collected. Since, however, the necessity out of which these taxes originally sprung no longer continues, the question now arises as to whether there remains any good reason for maintaining them. If it were true that the tax on spirits tended greatly to diminish their consumption, there would be little question as to the wisdom of continuing the tax. That the large consumption of intoxicating liquors is a grave social evil admits of no controversy. But it is unfortunately true that people who use these articles pay little heed to the price; and I believe the opinion is generally entertained by careful observers that the increased cost resulting from high taxes tends in no marked degree to diminish their use.

The taxes on liquors and tobacco are frequently defended on the ground that these articles are luxuries. Taxes are laid on the luxuries rather than on the necessaries of life, for the reason alone that taxes on luxuries are supposed to fall upon the more wealthy members of society who are able to pay them, rather than on the poor who are less able. The distinction drawn is not to be determined by the definition of words; it is a practical distinction relating to a clearly-defined economic principle.

Tobacco is an article of almost universal consumption; and the greater part of the spirituous and malt liquors which are consumed are drunk by working-men, the majority of whom can ill afford the indulgence; and large numbers deprive themselves and families of the necessaries of life in order to gratify an appetite which they are unable to restrain. To impose upon these people, and especially upon those already impoverished through the indulgence of an unfortunate habit, a special tax, in addition to the burdens which they share equally with other members of society, is only another exhibition of that spirit of injustice which takes advantage of the weak because, having no power to resist, they become the easy prey of those whose interest it may be to despoil them. And then to justify the robbery on the ground that the tax is a tax upon luxuries is to offend intelligent sincerity with transparent pretence.

In favor of the license tax, it may be said that it is a measure whereby the evil of indulgence in intoxicating liquors is restrained. But the revenue received from this tax, instead of being appropriated exclusively to public uses in general, should be, in part at least, converted into a fund for the education and support of the necessitous and dependent poor, to whom in equity it belongs. The money which should be used to purchase food and clothing for women and children is gathered into the revenues of a great city and expended for public uses, thus relieving property owners from burdens which they could not otherwise escape. As ever, the weak and defenceless are the prey of the heartless and the strong. A part of this fund might be employed to a good purpose in providing places of respectable resort, free from the demoralizing influence of vicious surroundings, where working-men might find opportunities for amusement and social intercourse, which they must now seek in drinking-saloons, for the reason that they may not be found elsewhere at prices which they are able to afford.

There is a further objection to the internal revenue tax on liquors because of the fact that the necessary conditions imposed on the manufacture are such as to make a monopoly of the trade, thus affording opportunities for the aggregation of wealth which should find no favor in the policy of the law.

INCOME TAX.

In the United Kingdom of England, Scotland, and Ireland a large portion of the annual revenue is raised by a tax on incomes; the amount of this tax in 1881 being fifty-three million two hundred and fifty thousand dollars.

The United States collected an income tax from 1863 to 1872 inclusive. The largest amount raised in any one year was about sixty-one million dollars in 1866, assessed on four hundred and sixty thousand one hundred and seventy persons. The law was a departure from the methods with which the people were familiar, and met with much opposition. Its enforcement was attended with difficulties, which experience would no doubt, in time, greatly modify. The chief objection to this mode of taxation lies in the inquisitorial character of the assessment, which requires disclosures that many people are reluctant to make. But the tax is an essentially just one, and, if levied on incomes of not less than two thousand dollars, much of the friction occasioned by the operation of the law would be relieved without a corresponding reduction in the amount of revenue.

Taxes should, in the main, be collected out of that excess of income over necessary expenditures which may be spared without inconvenience, and which, since it generally represents gains accruing from the advantages of superior skill in trade, or profits on capital, is the product of the labor of other people, may be justly taken for the common benefit. The only reasonable objections which may be interposed are such as arise out of public policy. If the tax were graded according to the amount of income,—if, say, two per cent. were the rate on the amount over two thousand dollars and under three thousand dollars, three per cent. on the next thousand, four per cent. on the next, and so on until the amount of the tax would absorb the excess of income,—the law would be most effective in modifying inequalities of distribution and equalizing opportunities among the people. Such a law would impose no burden upon industry, nor would it interfere with the operations of trade. It would meet with opposition from those who would be most affected by it, but even they would cease to complain after it had become fully established as a feature of the revenue system of the country.

DIRECT PROPERTY TAXES.

The taxes collected by States and minor political divisions are direct taxes laid almost wholly on property without distinction as to character or amount. However, in some States exceptions are made of amounts under a certain sum; and since assessors are accustomed to place very low valuations on household goods, those persons who own little else enjoy the benefit of an exception in practice not allowed in theory.

In a country where the right of suffrage is exercised by all, and where, in theory at least, every man possesses equal authority over the disposition of the public revenues, public policy would seem to require that all, unless it should be the exceptionally poor, should feel the touch of the public burden. The payment of taxes tends to enhance the interest of the citizen in public affairs, while entire freedom from pecuniary responsibility places in the hands of the voter who may be exempt a power without the restraint required to hold that power in check.

Taxes are paid from the annual product of labor; and property which yields no revenue ought not to be taxed, if it were practicable otherwise to rate taxes according to incomes. There is no good reason for taxing household goods, or a homestead, except that the amount of property of this class may be considered as an index to the amount of the owner's income, or to his ability to pay. But, since it is impracticable to gauge the amount of the earnings of individuals, or their ability to contribute to the public revenues, by any more accurate system of measurement, the method is adopted of assessing each according to his property, regardless of its character.

Church property is not taxed, for the reason that it neither yields a revenue nor represents an income. Revenue-bearing property of churches, however, should not be exempt, unless, considered as contributing to a worthy object, the State may properly allow an exemption below a reasonable limit fixed by constitutional law. This policy, however, is one which is liable to abuse, since it does not have the support of any clearly-defined principle marking the limit which may not be passed. Churches may be educational institutions of great public benefit, or they may be narrow sectarian establishments whose influence is pernicious. The Legislature cannot assume the function of deciding.

TAXES ON REAL ESTATE.

Mr. Edward Atkinson is of the opinion that a tax on real estate should constitute the principal source of public revenue, holding that such a tax would so diffuse itself that the burden of its payment would be more widely and equitably distributed than that of any other form of taxation. And if taxes are to be collected from a single source only, a tax on real estate would come nearer filling all the requirements of an equitable tax than any other. But it is not true that the revenues raised by direct taxation, where the amount is large, can be confined wholly either to real estate, or to personal property, or to any species of property, without causing the burden of taxation to press very unequally. Theories of political economy are generally framed on the assumption of the complete mobility of capital

and labor, and of the prompt adjustment of inequalities by
means of the levelling power of competition. But, since the fact
is that labor is most sluggish in its movements as regards
changes both of occupation and locality, and the movements of
capital in many departments of industry are subject to natural
limitations prescribed by the form of investment, as well as
other obstructing causes, the theory fails to conform to actual
conditions, and is without value as a test of practical measures.

A tax levied upon real estate, occupied for the purposes of
trade or manufacture, quickly diffuses itself among consumers,
without hinderance from any strong counteracting tendency.
To the amount of the original cost of his goods, the merchant
adds cost of carriage, rents, clerk-hire, and a margin of profits;
the total determines his retail prices, and the consumer pays the
whole. The trade of every merchant is subject to the same
conditions. The manufacturer fixes his prices by the same rule.
When prices become too high, consumption falls off, and the
reactionary effect is seen in a corresponding reduction of each
of the several items of cost, subject, of course, to causes which
disturb the ratios of reduction as between profits, rents, wages,
and transportation. Here the conditions approximately conform
to the facts assumed by the general theory.

But suppose the cost of an agricultural product be increased,
say, twenty per cent. by the levy of high taxes or transportation
charges, the price of the agricultural product may not be advanced
in the least. The farmer does not say, rents are so much, wages
so much, and taxes are so much, therefore this grain or these
cattle must bring a certain price, and in this manner determine
what the consumer shall pay. The purchaser fixes the price
according to the supply. When prices of a particular agricultural commodity are low as compared with other agricultural
commodities, the farmer produces less of the particular commodity, but more of something else. When prices of all commodities are reduced, he only endeavors to produce more, in
order to make up in quantity what he loses in price. His
capital is fixed, his occupation is fixed, and he cannot relieve
himself from the pressure of taxes or of railway charges by
shifting the burden on consumers.

Agricultural labor is to a great extent unskilled labor. While all cannot do equally well, everybody can farm, and surplus labor tends to drift into agriculture. All the lands of a country will be occupied and cultivated. There is a counter-tendency, it is true, but it is not effective to put agriculture on a level of advantage with other industries.

When the agricultural area is all occupied, and the limit of cultivation without material increase of capital and skill shall have been reached, and the demand for agricultural products begins to press against this limitation, then a tax on real estate will diffuse itself among consumers, and the higher the tax the higher the relative price of agricultural products. Then the theory of Mr. Atkinson will more nearly define the operation of an economic principle.

Taxes in different States and in different localities greatly vary; and a tax on lands might, in some sections, not only destroy all the profits of agriculture, but also force wages far below the average general standard. It would be like a special tax on a single merchant in a village, or on a woollen-mill in one locality. By, in the first instance, through the direct operation of law, distributing the burden of taxation over all classes of property, these inequalities are reduced to a minimum.

There is no good reason, however, why taxes on real estate should be made absolutely uniform in proportion to value. The man who owns and cultivates forty acres of land ought not to pay the same rate of tax as the man who owns five thousand acres, which he rents to other people. Lands included in one individual ownership to the value of, say, five thousand dollars, aside from dwelling-house, might be taxed at the same rate; but on values in excess of that amount the rate should be gradually advanced to the point of making ownership unprofitable after a certain limit has been reached. The operation of a revenue measure of this character, in preventing the aggregation of real property, might be more satisfactory than that of a law prescribing an absolute limit on the amount.

The homesteads occupied and owned by widows and minor children and of men above, say, sixty years of age, under the value of, say, one thousand dollars, should be exempt from taxation, for the reason that they neither are revenue-bearing property, nor do they, as a class, measure the income of the

owners. This property, by the conditions of its use and ownership, may be readily distinguished and excepted, and there is no
good reason why it should bear any part of the burden of the
public revenues.

TAXATION OF CREDITS.

The attempt to tax credits has everywhere proven a failure.
Being intangible, they elude the assessor, and not one-fifth of
the credits of a State where the attempt is made to tax them
are ever listed for taxation. In the country and in small towns
the proportion of credits taxed is much greater than in cities.
There is no uniformity, and there never can be. The burden
falls most heavily on honest people, who pay a penalty for being
more truthful than their fellows.

In the year 1884 the valuation of credits, other than those of
banks, bankers, etc., in Cook County, Illinois, which contains the
great and wealthy city of Chicago, was only $209,476; while in
the county of Knox, with a population in 1880 of 38,344, the
same class of credits were valued at $793,819; in the county of
La Salle, with a population in 1880 of 70,403, the valuation was
$632,681; in the county of Winnebago, with a population in
1880 of 30,505, the valuation was $725,218; in the county of
McLean, with a population of 60,100, the valuation was $591,286.
In the year 1888 the valuation of the same class of credits was, in
Cook County, which then had a population of 1,000,000, $119,990;
in Knox County, $346,541; in La Salle County, $532,070; in McLean
County, $554,184; in Winnebago County, $636,688; while in the
county of Edwards, with a population not one-hundredth part as
great as that of Cook County in 1888, the valuation was $119,200,
only seven hundred and ninety dollars less than that of Cook
County. Clay County had $28,064, while the much larger
county of Wayne adjoining had but $19,248, and the adjoining
county of Effingham, with a greater population and more
wealth, had but $7813. In the same year the credits of banks,
brokers, etc., of Cook County, are returned at $67,800, while the
same class of credits in the county of Clay, with a population
only about one-fiftieth part as great, are returned at $19,463;
those of the larger adjoining counties of Wayne, Effingham,
and Marion, at $3609, $315, and $12,117 respectively. There is,

indeed, no approximation towards a true valuation of credits of any kind.

The tax on credits, so far as it is effective. is a double tax. B owns two thousand dollars' worth of property; A has one thousand dollars in money. Here then is three thousand dollars' worth of taxable property. But B borrows A's one thousand dollars, and gives to A his note for one thousand dollars; the assessor lists the two thousand dollars' worth of property which B had at the start, and also one thousand dollars more in money or other property in which B may have invested the money he borrowed from A, and also the note for one thousand dollars given to A, making a total valuation of four thousand dollars. By this transaction between A and B the amount of the assessment has been increased in the sum of one thousand dollars, although the amount of property remains the same. Here is an injustice, the weight of which must fall on either one or the other, or on both the parties. It in fact falls upon the borrower; the effect of taxation of credits is to raise the rate of interest. The money-loaner generally escapes the tax, the amount of which he saves as compensation for risk, or wear and tear of conscience in dodging.

The rate of taxation varies greatly in different localities. In one village, or city, or school district it may be double the rate which is collected in another district or village near by. The rate of interest cannot be made to vary to correspond with these varying rates of taxation. The lender of money will therefore either conceal his credits or adopt for his residence a locality where the rate is low.

The borrower may reside in one State and the creditor in another, thus subjecting credits in the same locality to different rates of taxation.

The tax on money should be retained, since such a tax, particularly if credits are untaxed, tends to prevent hoarding.

Banks should not be taxed on their circulation or their credits; they should be reached by reducing the rate of interest they may be permitted to collect.

The rate of taxation on money should be uniform,—everywhere the same,—so as to present no obstacle to its free circulation. A tax on money will always be more or less evaded;

nevertheless, the value of such a tax, as a measure to prevent hoarding money and thus withholding it from circulation, justifies the imposition of such tax, notwithstanding the frequent evasions to which it would be subject.

The only reason that can be urged for the policy of taxing credits is that such tax yields a revenue. It is, however, a revenue unjustly drawn from the borrower, who really pays the tax by way of increased interest.

Instead of persisting in the ineffectual attempt to reach credits through revenue laws, we should reach them by means of usury laws. Let B pay the taxes on the tangible property which he owns, and let every other person do likewise; and, when all tangible property is taxed, there is no more property to tax. The sum of the tangible property of a country comprises its total wealth. When a government taxes credits it enters into partnership with the creditor to compel the debtor to pay the higher rate of interest necessary to satisfy the demands of both the creditor and the government.

Continuing the foregoing illustration, the property which A did have, one thousand dollars in money, having been transferred to B, in order to equitably apportion the burden of tax, B should have the benefit of a reduction in the rate of interest, which is now fixed on the assumption that A will be required to pay taxes on B's note. Under the present policy, A gets the interest, but, by evading the law, escapes the taxes. The tax on tangible property cannot be evaded; therefore let the tangible property, which is all the property owned by both A and B, be taxed; but allow B to withhold a part of the interest which he now pays, in order to make sure that A does not escape from his just obligations.

The present system is wholly in favor of the capitalist, and against the borrower and against the working-people. If Hodge be not too dull, he will change his tactics, and catch the coon at the other end of the log.

In 1881 the Legislature of the State of Massachusetts passed an act exempting mortgages on real estate from taxation. The effect was an immediate decline in the rate of interest on mortgage loans of nearly one-half of one per cent., and the decline which measures the full effect of the law amounts to about one per cent. in the rate of interest on mortgage loans. There followed the enactment of this law a remarkable increase in building operations in Boston. The new buildings and alterations in 1881 amounted to $3,144,260, in 1882 to $8,918,969, and in 1889 they had increased to $17,120,779. The total value of real estate improvements in the period from 1882 to 1889 was $77,855,884 more than if the average of the two years preceding the passage of this act had been maintained.* That this increase in building is wholly attributable to the reduction in the rate of interest consequent on the enactment of the law exempting mortgages from taxation may not be claimed; but the reduction in the rate of interest was no doubt a principal factor in producing the result shown.

The distinction made in the legislation of Massachusetts between mortgage loans and other credits is wholly arbitrary and not marked by distinction in principle.

Taxes represent a certain portion of the annual product which is diverted to a designated use. The working-people, who create this product, pay the taxes. Those whose names appear upon the tax-list are the persons through whom the taxes are paid. The amount which they in fact pay is measured by the amount of their contribution to the total product and the rate of tax to which property is subject.

The manner in which taxes are levied has much to do with the distribution of products, and the diversion of wealth and the prosperity of particular industries depends in great measure on the revenue policy of a country.

The working-people, and particularly the poorer classes, who are erroneously supposed to pay but little tax, have a vital interest in the question as to how public revenues shall be raised. Revenue systems should be judged by their effects upon the distribution of wealth, as well as by their effectiveness in accomplishing those ends which are supposed to lie within the scope of the direct purpose which they are intended to serve.

By means of properly-adjusted revenue laws, supplemented by the necessary limitations on rates of interest, it is practicable to prevent those gross aggregations of wealth which have

---

* See *Quarterly Journal of Economics*, April, 1890.

grown up under existing policies. In many States constitutional amendments would be required, in order to admit of the introduction of the necessary revenue reforms. But present conditions will not be remedied without some radical departures from the course of legislation hitherto pursued.

CHAPTER VIII.

INTERNATIONAL TRADE—PROTECTION.

IN all ages and in all stages of civilization the habit of ex changing the product of one form of labor for the products of other forms of labor has existed. To the North American In dian, the African barbarian, and the wild Australian, trade is as habitual as with the civilized European. But to a civilized people, among whom there exists the utmost subdivision of labor, so that one individual consumes only a small part of the product of his own labor, and every person consumes a resultant product of the labor of many persons, exchange becomes an absolute necessity. Merchants, wholesale and retail, agents, factors, and traders of all classes become necessary in the business of distribution. The value of the services which they render to society is added to the price of the product which passes through their hands, and their wages are paid by the consumer. It becomes the interest of this class to promote ex· change, even beyond the demands of society. The greater the volume of trade, the greater the quantity and value of the products exchanged, the larger their profits.

The service performed by this class requires a high degree of intelligence and skill. They constitute, therefore, one of the most influential classes of society, not only because of superior intelligence, but because, also, of acquired wealth. Their interests are always well guarded; their influence upon legislation is prompt, persuasive, and effective. The earliest writings upon the subject of political economy relate to commerce. How to promote commerce is a question that never retires from the arena of debate, nor withdraws from the chamber of legislative council. The highest moral considerations yield it precedence; and violated law and outraged humanity await their turn in patience and in silence. When trade makes its demands, it is not with the hesitating words of modest diffidence, nor in the subdued tones of unpractised timidity, but with the loud assurance of accustomed command. And the popular mind appears to be thoroughly imbued with the idea that national prosperity is gauged by the volume and extent of commerce, and that whatever is done that promotes trade, promotes national prosperity. To such an extent has this idea been cultivated, that boards of trade, whose principal business it is to speculate in future values, and conduct a seeming trade without any accompanying exchange of products, are rated as men of business, and rank, in general esteem, as promoters of public interests.

In the popular mind there seems to be a tendency to overlook the fact that the usefulness of trade has its limitations in the needs of the consumer and not in the needs of the merchant who conducts the business of exchange; that it is possible to promote and carry on a commerce that serves no good purpose, except to yield revenue to merchants and traders and transportation companies; that a demand for products may be cultivated in the interests of those alone who derive a profit from buying and selling.

America is a great country, with a variety of people, and possessing a capacious and hungry market that, with ostrich-like avidity, seizes every shining bauble that falls within its range. We are a people of generous consumers, with liberal purses. When John Bull rings the door-bell and calls for the lady of the 'ouse, he receives a civil answer; and when he opens his pack and displays his wares, "missus" is sure to find something she wants,—and so cheap. There is no doubt but that if the products of foreign nations had free entrance to our markets, we should buy freely some things which we can do equally well without, and many more that we can more cheaply produce at home. We would ship back agricultural and manufactured products in payment; trade would be promoted; traders, merchants, and transportation companies would make good profits; but would the American people, as a whole, be benefited or injured thereby? This is the question involved in the issue.

There always is an appearance of prosperity attending the

interchange of commercial products, and it is clear that the merchants who handle foreign trade in those cities which are its chief avenues enjoy opportunities for increased profits, which they do not neglect to improve; but what are the advantages, or disadvantages, to the people at large? Does the prosperity of the artisan, the mechanic, the farmer, and common laborer depend upon crowded docks, or may it be estimated by a count of masts in the harbor?

To a country of small area, or a country of limited natural resources,—to a country like England or France, whose food-products are not adequate to the wants of the people,—foreign trade is essential. Trade between nations rests upon the same necessity as trade between individuals. If A has that which he does not require for his own use, but which B needs for his use, and B has that which he does not require for his own use, but which A does need, an exchange may be made which will be profitable to both. If A be a farmer, and B a blacksmith, it is more profitable to both that A should raise wheat for B, and that B should shoe horses for A, than that both should attempt to perform labor for which they are unfitted, and supply their own wants without exchange of the products of their labor. But if, instead of A, we suppose a community of one hundred farmers, having interests and property in common, and contributing their labor to a common fund, and the labor of one blacksmith yields an annual product one-third greater in value than the labor of one farmer, then it would be to the interest of this community, instead of employing a smith outside of its own members, that one of themselves should learn the trade of blacksmith and thereby save the equivalent of one-third of the labor of one man. If England has that which the people of the United States need, and the United States have that which the people of England require, beyond the demands of home consumption, then there may be profitable trade between the two countries. If there are two articles, one of which may be produced at less labor-cost in England, and the other may be produced at less labor-cost in the United States, then a mutual exchange may be profitable to both. But if the reason of the higher cost in one country be because of the want of skilled labor, or the natural inertia of unskilled labor and its disposition to adhere to its accustomed pursuits, then it may be to the interest of that country to develop its unskilled into skilled labor, and save to itself the extra labor-cost required for the purchase of the product of skilled, with the product of unskilled, labor. The rule, that every nation should buy in the cheapest, and sell in the dearest, market, is subject to the more important rule of political economy, that it is the first duty of every nation to cultivate the highest capabilities of its own labor.

The reason why we should buy our coffee from Brazil and our tea from China is sufficiently apparent. We are able to produce neither at home, without the most unprofitable expenditure of labor. We buy silks from France and ivory from Africa for the same reason. By so doing we may procure silk at one-half the labor-cost that would be required to produce silk in the United States. But why should we buy coal and iron in England? The coal-merchant in a city on the coast of Maine or Massachusetts may be able to purchase a supply of coal for less money than he could procure it from Pennsylvania. (We import nine hundred thousand tons annually.) We import annually over fifty million dollars' worth of the products of iron and steel This is nearly all brought from England. The trader who imports it pays for it with gold and silver,—so much money. The price is less than he would pay at home. The traders who buy this coal and iron do not ask, "What will you buy in return?" they do not stop to inquire in what way the balance of trade will be preserved. Their interest begins and ends with their own transaction. When the farmer purchases one hundred dollars' worth of dry goods, he pays one hundred dollars in money; but he must sell to some one one hundred dollars' worth of agricultural product to cover that purchase of dry goods. He may not sell to the same merchant, nor in the same village; but he must sell somewhere and to some person, and preserve his "balance of trade."

In the year 1887 the people of the United States purchased in Brazil commodities amounting to $52,953,176, but sold in that country products to the amount of only $8,127,883. But during the same period the exports to Great Britain amounted to $366,310,679, while the imports from Great Britain amounted to only $165,067,443. This account balanced would show the people of Great Britain in debt to the people of the United States in the sum of $201,243,236. But the exports of Great Britain are in excess of its imports in its trade with Brazil, Germany, Italy, Holland, Central America, Mexico, and other countries. In the trade between two countries exports and imports may differ widely in amount, as in the case of the United States and Brazil; but the excess of imports from one country is balanced by an excess of exports to another country. The United States buys coffee in Brazil; sells wheat and flour to England, which ships iron and steel and cotton and woollen fabrics to Brazil. The entire trade may be conducted without shipment of any very large sums of money, by means of bills of exchange.

The statistics of British trade show that her annual imports are greatly in excess of her exports. During the twenty years ending December, 1880, there was imported into Great Britain, in excess of exports, $7,540,000,000 worth of products, of which $4,680,000,000 worth was imported during the decade ending December, 1880, which is equivalent to $468,000,000 per year. We must not infer from this showing that the people of Great Britain incurred debt for the amount of this excess of imports, nor that they sent abroad $7,540,000,000 in gold and silver to pay the account. This excess of imports means that British capital is invested abroad in large amounts, and that it yields an annual revenue of $468,000,000. The yield of British foreign invested capital in the form of dividends or interest in 1883 was as follows:

Colonial loans	$37,000,000
Indian "	31,000,000
Indian and colonial railways	46,500,000
Foreign loans and railways	128,500,000
Total	$243,000,000

To the above should be added moneys loaned on mortgage in Australia, Brazil, and other countries, and much capital otherwise invested.

The exports and imports of American commerce at the present time are nearly equal in amount, the excess of exports in 1887 amounting to about twenty-four million dollars. There has been an annual excess of exports over imports since 1873, except the year 1875. From 1850 to 1873, inclusive, imports exceeded exports, the balance against the United States being met by the export of bullion. The excess of exports during the last twenty years is explained by the fact that large amounts of American bonds are held in Europe, and we have been paying interest with wheat, corn, and meat.

Some product of American labor must be sold abroad to pay for the coal and the iron which we import. What shall it be,—our principal export, bread-stuffs? of which in 1887 we exported one hundred and sixty-six million dollars' worth. In 1887 we exported one hundred and two million bushels of wheat at a fraction less than ninety cents per bushel at the port of shipment. Saying nothing about railway freights, it required sixty million bushels of wheat delivered at seaboard to pay for that iron and coal, without including the cost of transportation. The production of this sixty million bushels of wheat, estimated on the basis of the cost of agricultural products in this country as shown by the census of 1880, represents a year's work of one hundred and ninety thousand laborers; and, according to the same census the products of iron and steel, which were imported to the amount in value of fifty-four million dollars English prices, or eighty million dollars American prices, required the labor of less than one hundred and fifteen thousand laborers. In the round of exchange we have traded the labor of five men for the labor of three men; and yet we have bought in the cheapest market and sold in the dearest. The same relation exists between the labor-cost of the products of agricultural labor and the products of skilled labor and machinery in other manufacturing and mechanical industries.

The same year we imported $7,300,000 worth of glass and glassware, which at American prices amounted to $10,950,000. This product represents the labor of twenty thousand four hundred persons, of whom one-third were women and children. It may be said, therefore, to represent the labor of about seventeen thousand men. We paid for it in agricultural products with the labor of twenty-four thousand three hundred men, and paid transportation charges on agricultural products besides. We imported $44,000,000 worth of manufactured woollen goods, of which sum $17,000,000 was the product of labor in manufacturing, allowing $27,000,000 to the credit of materials. A product of $17,000,000 in the woollen goods industry at English prices, or $28,390,000 at American prices, represents the labor of forty thousand four hundred and fifteen persons, of whom one-eighth are children under fifteen years of age, and over one-third are women,—more than three-sevenths are women and children. We may say this product represents the equivalent of the labor of thirty-two thousand men. To pay this seventeen million dollars in agricultural product required the labor of more than fifty-six thousand men, and we paid the cost of transporting agricultural product to seaboard besides. To the extent that we pay in manufactured products, the foregoing deductions do not apply. But our imports of manufactured products are nearly all paid for in the products of agriculture.*

In arriving at the results here given, I have not taken into consideration the capital employed in the production of manufactured products, nor the capital employed in agriculture, which is relatively much larger than that employed in manufacturing, for the respective products contrasted. Nor have I considered the wear and waste of machinery, buildings, etc., in either industry. There is probably no great difference, comparing the two branches of industry, in proportion to value of product. I have estimated the agricultural product at three hundred dollars per year for each full hand. The basis of this estimate will be found in the chapter giving statistics of productions of agriculture. The figures may be varied somewhat by the actual facts, could they be ascertained more accurately; but the relations of the industries are substantially as shown.

Had the rate of duty been low our imports would have been greatly increased, making it necessary to export a correspondingly increased amount of agricultural product. And, since the price falls as the supply increases, the price received for the exported

---

* In the manufacturing industries the average annual product in 1880 was seven hundred and twenty-one dollars and ninety-three cents per worker, while in agriculture it was two hundred and eighty-eight dollars and forty-five cents per worker, the product per worker being two and one-half times as great in the former as in the latter. If we pursue the policy of purchasing manufactured goods abroad it will at once appear at what expense of labor we must do so.

product would have been still lower, and the cost of imports, measured in labor, would have been relatively higher, thus increasing the ratio, already great.

The question, then, that confronts us is, Shall we continue to use the products of foreign manufacture, and pay for them with the products of agriculture, or shall we do our own manufacturing? Shall we plough corn and hoe potatoes two days, or work one day in the mill, the factory, or the mine?

So long as we continue our foreign importations, the diversion of labor from agriculture to manufacturing industries, the conversion of common into skilled labor, will proceed but slowly. The agriculturist will struggle on, year by year, endeavoring to increase his income by raising more wheat and corn and cattle, and continue to defeat his aim by overweighting an already overburdened market. He may attempt to reduce the price of manufactured articles by unlocking our ports to foreign trade; but it has always been true, and will remain true, that skilled labor employed in manufacturing industries will command higher prices than the unskilled labor that finds employment in the field of agriculture; money will flow to manufacturing centres, and go out again in the form of investments in stocks and mortgage-loans, drawing interest at a rate that absorbs the savings of the people.

The remedy must be found in the conversion of unskilled into skilled labor, a low rate of interest on capital, and other measures of a kindred character, suggested in other chapters. Wages may be thereby forced nearer to a common level, while the general average of wages will be raised, and the power of capital diminished. What is required is a tariff that will preserve to our own people the American market for those articles of manufacture or of agriculture which may be produced at home, at a labor-cost not greater than that which is required to effect their purchase by means of the exchange of the products of unskilled labor. I am able to perceive no other means by which this most desirable result may be accomplished. The history of the relations between the industries, and between capital and labor, in all nations, goes to show that leaving industries free and untrammelled does not accomplish it.

·If we seek—as we must, if we find a remedy for existing

evils—to establish a national policy which will, in a measure, control the distribution of labor in the interest of a more equitable distribution of its rewards, we must dissever ourselves from the influence of economic conditions which direct the industries of foreign nations, whose policy is shaped by no such aims, where no such purpose is entertained, and where old-established conditions, indurated customs, and long-stifled aspirations obstruct the way to industrial reform.

Mill, in his "Political Economy" (vol. ii. page 532), says,—

"It was shown, however, in our analysis of the effects of international trade, as it has been often shown by former writers, that the importation of foreign commodities, in the common course of traffic, never takes place, except when it is, economically speaking, a national good, by causing the same amount of commodities to be obtained at a smaller cost of labor and capital to the country. To prohibit, therefore, this importation, or impose duties which prevent it, is to render the labor and capital of the country less efficient in production than they would otherwise be, and compel a waste of the difference between the labor and capital necessary for the home production of the commodity and that which is required for producing the things with which it can be purchased from abroad.

"The amount of national loss thus occasioned is measured by the excess of the price at which the commodity is produced, over that at which it could be imported. In the case of manufactured goods, the whole difference between the two prices is absorbed in indemnifying the producer for waste of labor or of the capital which supports that labor. Those who are supposed to be benefited—namely, the makers of the protected articles (unless they form an exclusive company, and have a monopoly against their own countrymen as well as foreigners)—do not obtain higher profits than other people. All is their loss to the country as well as to the consumer."

The foregoing is a statement, in general terms, of what is known as the doctrine of free trade, as held by writers of that school of political economists. It is not unusual for advocates of this theory to preface their remarks with some such language as that employed by Mill, "as it has been often shown by former writers." Had Mill been able, by a satisfactory analysis

of the principles of international trade and the laws of production, to show the truth of the doctrine which he embodies in
such broad generalizations, he doubtless would have done so,
instead of tendering the conventional excuse which is here
offered in lieu of a clear analysis of principles.   Mill's reference
to his analysis of the effects of international trade does not assist
us.   He does show, as he claims, that in one sense the importation of foreign commodities does not take place, except when
such commodities may be obtained at a smaller cost of labor
and of capital than that for which they may be produced by the
country importing.   But in what sense, and according to what
measure of cost?   The answer is, When capital is measured by
prevailing rates of interest, and the value of labor is measured
by the *money standard of wages of the class of laborers employed
in the production of the commodities imported.*   For instance,
suppose the United States to be an agricultural country, and
England to be a manufacturing country; the wages of persons
engaged in agriculture in the United States to be one dollar per
day, and the wages of persons engaged in manufacture in England one dollar and fifty cents per day; the interest value of capital in the United States to be six per cent., and the interest value
of capital in England to be four per cent.; the wages of persons
engaged in manufacturing in the United States to be two dollars
per day.   Fix the number of working-days at three hundred
per year.   We will take a manufactured product that consumes
the labor of one hundred men working one year, and requires
one hundred thousand dollars capital.   The cost and value of
the product (omitting materials) in England will be as follows:

Labor of 100 men one year, at $1.50 per day each . .	$45,000
Interest on $100,000 one year, at four per cent. . . .	4,000
Waste of capital (to replace machinery, etc.)	4,000
Total value of product of labor and capital .	$53,000

The cost of the same product manufactured in the United
States will be as follows:

Wages of 100 men, at $2.00 per day, for one year . .	$60,000
Interest on $100,000 capital, at six per cent.	6,000
Wear and waste of buildings, machinery, etc. . . .	6,000
Value of product	$72,000

Here exist the conditions which, according to Mill, render the importation of the English product of manufacture into the United States profitable to both countries. A higher rate of interest and a higher rate of wages in manufacturing industry has increased the cost (measured in money, but not the cost as measured by amount of labor expended) of the American over the English product.

Let us carry the doctrine of Mill into the field of practical operation and observe the result. Since, in agriculture, a part of the capital employed is land, which is not the product of labor, we will assume that only one-half of the capital employed is the product of labor, and the other half land, the total capital being the same as that used in manufacturing as compared with product, although it is in fact much greater.

The result of the labor of one hundred men employed in agriculture, and working one year at the wages stated, would be as follows:

Wages of 100 men one year, at $1.00 per day	$30,000
Interest on $50,000 capital, at six per cent.	3,000
$50,000 capital in land, interest value six per cent. .	3,000
Waste of capital per annum	3,000
Total value of agricultural product	$39,000

Now, if we desire an agricultural product sufficient to purchase the $53,000 worth of English manufactured goods, since $53,000 is 1.359 times $39,000, we must multiply each of the above items by 1.359. We obtain as the result:

135.9 men one year, at $1.00 per day	$40,770
$67,950 capital, at six per cent.	4,077
Waste of capital	4,077
Six per cent. on $67,950 (value of land)	4,077
Total value of product	$53,001

Now, if we exchange this agricultural product for the English manufactured product, the market value of each being the same, there is a loss to American labor of twenty-six per cent.,— that is, it requires 135.9 men to produce what is exchanged for the product of one hundred men.

This labor that is lost, rated at one dollar per day, amounts to $10,770; valued at $1.50 per day, the price assumed for English manufacturing labor, it amounts to $16,155.

By reason of the use of land in production there is a saving of the use of $32,050 of labor-created capital, which at six per cent. amounts to $1830, and the net result is a loss to the people of the United States of $8940, or $14,325, according to which standard of wages we adopt as the measure of the value of labor. The true measure, however, of the loss or gain is the amount of labor saved or lost. Stated in terms of labor, there is a loss of twenty-six per cent.

To purchase of the American manufacturer the same product (that is, the product of the labor of 100 men) as was purchased from the English manufacturer for fifty-three thousand dollars, would require, on the basis of the wages and interest assumed, seventy-two thousand dollars, which would require the product of the labor of 184.6 men employed in agriculture. It would, therefore, apparently be to the interest of the agricultural class —regarding those engaged in agriculture as a distinct class, and ignoring the movement of labor from one industry to another— to purchase of England; and yet it is nevertheless clearly in the interest of an increased total production of American wealth to purchase of the home manufacturer. The increase of the wealth of a nation depends upon production, but the increase of the wealth of any class of producers depends not only on production, but also on distribution.

But that which may be to the apparent interest of a class, and which may be to their immediate interest, may be far from their true interest. If the exchange of the products of American agriculture for the products of English manufacture be not interrupted in some manner, the conditions which bring about such exchange on unequal terms tend to perpetuate themselves indefinitely, as the history of these two classes of industry abundantly shows.

Adam Smith, speaking of the wages of labor, says, " The wages of labor in a great town or its neighborhood are frequently a fourth or a fifth part—twenty or twenty-five per cent. —higher than at a few miles' distance. Eighteen pence (36 cents) a day may be reckoned the common price of labor in

London or its neighborhood.   At a few miles' distance it falls to
fourteen and fifteen pence.   Ten pence may be reckoned its
price in Edinburgh and its neighborhood.   At a few miles'
distance it falls to eight pence, the usual price of common
labor through the greater part of the low country of Scotland, where it varies a good deal less than in England." And
yet, at the time of which he wrote (1775), he says, " Grain,
the food of the common people, is dearer in Scotland than in
England."

In 1835 the average wages of a day-laborer in agriculture
were, in England twenty pence, Scotland sixteen pence, Ireland
eight pence; in 1880 the rate was, England thirty pence, Scotland twenty-eight pence, Ireland eighteen pence.   The average
annual earnings of the working-class in 1882 were, in England
$305, Scotland $247.50, Ireland $121.75.   In 1882 the wealth of
England was $35,890,000,000, that of Scotland $4,950,000,000,
that of Ireland $2,760,000,000 (Mulhall).   The foregoing statis-
tics illustrate the relative power of manufacturing and agriculture in accumulating wealth.

Now, suppose that, instead of buying the products of manufacture abroad with the products of agriculture raised at home,
we convert the necessary amount of agricultural labor required
to produce the fifty-three thousand dollars' worth of manufactured product into manufacturing labor.   The land we cannot
convert into other forms of capital, so we have the labor of 135.9
men and $67,950 of capital to employ in manufacturing.   To
make up the requisite amount of capital corresponding to the
number of men, it will require the sum of $135,900.   We already
have $67,950, and we must create or borrow $67,950 more,
to replace the land which we may suppose to lie idle.   The
result will be,—

Labor of 135.9 men one year, at $1.50 per day . . .	$61,125
Interest on capital, $135,900, at four per cent. . . .	5,436
Wear of machinery	5,436
Total value of product (English prices) . . .	$71,997
Subtract additional cost of American capital, which would be two per cent.	5,436
Net product of labor and capital	$66,561

Brought forward $66,561
Value of the agricultural product of same labor and
   capital before it was converted, measured in English manufactured product for which it exchanged
   $53,000, to which we add $4177, six per cent. on
   the additional capital called into use, and we have .   57,177
                                                          ─────────
Net gain from conversion of labor $9,384

I have carried the element of interest on capital into the
foregoing analysis, not because it belongs there, but because we
are accustomed to regard interest as a part of the cost of production. Interest, however, when we are considering the cost
of production to a whole people, is not a part of the cost of
production, unless capital borrowed from a foreign people be
employed. When regarded in any problem embracing the
nation at large, interest is an element of distribution, and does
not represent consumption of capital, but merely a transfer of
product from one person to another. The wear and waste of
buildings and machinery in either country, measured in labor,
is the same. So that the real gain is the labor that is saved,
which, measured by the value of the product, is $16,125.

Now, while the value of a certain amount of labor in one
country, measured by the quantity of product, is the equivalent
in value of a like amount of labor of the same grade in another
country, except as natural advantage of location or climate may
somewhat increase the productive power of the labor in one
country above that of an equal amount of labor in another
country, yet, in the conversion of the cheaper into the more
productive, and therefore more valuable, forms of labor, there
is a very great gain.

The mistake of writers on this branch of political economy
consists, first, in ignoring the facts that the value of labor depends upon how it may be employed; that the value of different
classes of labor, when measured in the price of the product,
varies widely, and that the cheaper forms of labor may be
readily converted into the more valuable forms; and, secondly,
in treating interest as an element of the cost of production
(which as between individuals it is), and not as merely a factor
in the process of distribution.

Reducing these deductions to the form of an abstract generalization, I would say that it is not to the interest of any people to produce a commodity requiring an amount of labor relatively large in proportion to value of product, for the purpose of export and exchange for the product of another form of industry representing an amount of labor relatively small according to value. Whenever a necessity exists which compels the exchange of the product of two days' labor for the product of one day's labor, true economy requires a policy that will remove that necessity.

Labor does not readily transfer itself from one industry or form of production to another. Common labor and labor employed in agriculture will continue to be so employed until converted by capital into other forms of production. The fact that it may be to the interest of a people, *as a whole*, to create and carry on a particular industry, is not alone sufficient to divert labor and capital into such new industry. Capitalists must first be convinced that such industry will yield the usual profits on the capital invested; or else a reduction must first take place in the profits on capital invested in the industries in general, by which the average rate of profit on capital is brought below that which the industry sought to be introduced may be made to yield.

While it was clearly to the interest of the people of the United States to do their own manufacturing, yet so long as capital could be more profitably employed in other ways it was not to the interest of capital to engage in manufacturing; or, rather, it was not to the interest of any particular capitalist to do so. The imposition of a high tariff on cloth, and on iron and steel, brought the profits of capital employed in the manufacture of these products up to or above the general level of the profits of capital otherwise invested.

The result of a high tariff was a phenomenal growth of all protected industries. By the transfer of labor from one industry to another the productive power of American labor was wonderfully increased. There followed a corresponding increase in national wealth, and also a corresponding aggregation of wealth. This great increase of wealth represents so much labor saved by changing it into more productive forms.

The natural effect of this great increase of wealth would have been, by force of the competition of accumulated capital, employed and seeking employment in manufacturing industries, to force profits to a much lower rate than has been reached. But the building of railways, the issue of a large amount of government, State, and municipal bonds, the disposition of the agricultural classes to employ borrowed capital to invest in agriculture and increase the volume of the product already equal to the demand at a fair price, and other openings for the investment of capital at a high rate of profit, have enabled manufacturers to maintain a margin of profit much greater than they otherwise could have done.

The equilibrium of the industries has been disturbed by causes growing out of the late war, the rapid introduction of machinery, and the extension of the agricultural area. The rapid growth of wealth, instead of weighing down the profits of manufacturing, as it must have done under other conditions, has been absorbed by other industries and other enterprises; and manufacturing has been relieved from a burden of competition that of its own weight would have borne down prices of the products of manufacture to a point more nearly approximating the value of the product of an equal amount of capital employed in agriculture.

The amount of capital accumulated in other industries, and aggregated by speculation, which has been loaned on farms, much of it at a high rate of interest, has of itself been large enough to so increase the product of agriculture as to greatly reduce the value of the product of that industry in the market; and thus, by lowering the price of food, relatively enhancing the value of the products of manufacture.

The rapid extension of the cultivated area, for which unoccupied public lands furnished the opportunity, is largely attributable to the effect of investments of accumulated capital in the form of mortgage-loans on agricultural lands.

There has been a glut of wealth which has not been properly assimilated by the various industries, and agriculture has been the principal sufferer. A more healthy condition will, in time, be brought about by the unaided and unhindered operation of economic forces; but the present condition tends greatly to aid the process of aggregating the wealth of the country.

So far, we have considered the effect upon production of a diversion of labor from one form of industry to another. We have shown that the product is greatly increased by a conversion of cheap labor into labor of a higher grade, or by the conversion of labor engaged in the production of low-priced commodities into labor producing high-priced commodities. It remains to consider the effect upon distribution.

Withdrawing labor from any industry tends to reduce the product, and thereby to increase the price of the product of such industry; while increasing the amount of labor employed in an industry increases the product and reduces the price. Prices in the several industries, therefore, tend to approach a common level; and the prices of labor in all industries would attain a common standard if the operation of this tendency were not obstructed by certain causes. What are they? First, different forms of production require different degrees of intelligence and skill, and skilled labor does not come in direct competition with unskilled labor. Common labor cannot be converted into skilled labor at will, but must await the slow process of education and training. The immediate interest of skilled laborers is to prevent the increase of skilled labor. The process of education and industrial training is therefore hindered, not only by the natural difficulties that attend the education of a people, but also by the opposition or indifference of those who already occupy the field of employment in the higher grades of industry.*

There is another more potent influence. Capital employed in agriculture is fixed. Much of it—indeed the greater part—cannot be withdrawn at all, and the remainder cannot be readily withdrawn. It is chiefly in the hands of those whose labor is employed in production, and it is impracticable to greatly reduce the labor force employed, so as to keep production within the limits of the effective demand, at a price sufficient to yield a

---

* The mistaken policy of discouraging the apprenticeship of boys and young men in the mechanical trades with a view to maintaining wages has been generally pursued, and in consequence we have been receiving annually from Europe large numbers of skilled artisans to occupy the places which should be filled by artisans educated at home. The true policy is to encourage industrial training.

liberal compensation for the labor employed and a fair profit on the capital invested.

In manufacturing industries, when prices tend downward, the labor force, as well as the capital employed, may be readily reduced. As the capitalist and the laborer are not, as they generally are in agriculture, the same person, the labor-force may be reduced without serious detriment to the controlling force, capital; and the requisite amount of capital may be withdrawn, and invested whenever an opportunity for greater profit may invite.

To the individual agriculturist, production varies with the changing seasons, and values are unstable. The amount of the product cannot be regulated to meet a known demand, nor estimated beforehand. When the product is ready for the market, it must be sold at a price fixed by conditions not within the control of the producer. While the manufactured product is often sold before made, the price fluctuates within narrow limits, and when the market is heavy the manufacturer may hold his product longer to await a more active demand; for his commodities will keep, and may be cheaply stored. When the farmer's hogs or horses or cattle are matured, they must be sold; for the cost of keep will always soon outrun an advance in market values. When the farmer sells his wheat, corn, or cattle, he asks, "What will you give?" The manufacturer and the merchant says what he will take. While, therefore, agriculture, as an industry, possesses many advantages, it is also attended by disadvantages inherent in fixed conditions.

When laborers are thrown out of employment in other industries, they resort to the field of agriculture, where they may produce at least their own food and a small surplus for the market. This is to the advantage of those who would otherwise be without means of subsistence, but a detriment to agriculture, the industry on which at any time may be precipitated the unemployed labor of other industries which, when prices go down, relieve themselves of a superabundance of labor at its expense. Land, however, is a limited, fixed quantity. The area of cultivation will soon reach the limit beyond which it may not extend. The demand for food-products will begin to approximate the limit, beyond which production can be increased only by an active demand for more food. Agricultural values will then acquire greater stability, and, while they will continue to fluctuate, it will be within more narrow limits. Ordinary economic forces will then operate, with effect, to restore a greater equilibrium of values, except in so far as prevented by the power of aggregated capital to restrain or pervert natural tendencies.

It is with a view to the destruction of the power of aggregated wealth to control values that many are turning their attention towards the abolition of protective duties. But should they accomplish their purpose, it will be but another instance of Samson pulling down the temple to destroy the Philistines. The abolition of protective duties would undoubtedly to some extent reduce the prices of the products of manufactures. This reduction of prices, it is claimed, would be brought about by the importation of the products of foreign manufacture. But what would be the ultimate results? What we buy abroad we have no need to produce at home. The product of American manufactures would therefore fall off, and the weaker establishments now doing business on a narrow margin of profit give way. We would in time, in some measure, divide the foreign trade with England and other countries, at prices below those at which foreign markets are now supplied. In a foreign trade England enjoys this advantage: she needs that which her foreign consumer has to sell,—food,—while, except as to a few commodities, our home food-supply is already more than adequate to the demand. A sale of the products of our manufactures in foreign countries, beyond the amount of our present sales, means the purchase of an increased amount of foreign products to be placed on our markets in competition with our established agricultural industries, and a consequent fall in prices. The reduction of duties on products of foreign manufacture means, in the first instance, a reduction of the labor-force employed in manufacturing at home, and an increase of agricultural laborers; it means the conversion of labor of high productive value into common labor of low value; it means a disarrangement of values, doubt, hesitation, and distrust, until after such time as may be required for a readjustment; it means the reduction of all wages and of all values to a lower level, and a consequent relative enhancement of the value of credits; it

means more labor and more property to pay the same debt; it
means a wreck, from which the strongest will gather the salvage,
—a wreck in which labor will lose and from which capital will
gain. When the *débris* is cleared away, Samson will be found
buried beneath the pillars of the temple, and a few Philistines
will be found alongside; but a crowd of Philistines will view
the ruins and rejoice that Samson is dead.

If there be any remedy for the present inequitable distribution
of the products of labor, for the absorption by capital of the
savings of labor, that remedy must be found in legislative restrictions, modes of taxation, and in industrial training.

The control which the people of the United States may exercise by means of legislation over social and economic tendencies is confined to the limits of our own country. But if American labor is compelled to compete, in an open market, with all
grades and classes of labor throughout the world, then American
labor must rest content to accept a scale of prices determined
by conditions which exist in other countries, and which we have
no power to change. The less we are subject to the influence
of economic forces, determined by inequalities of wealth and
social condition that exist abroad, the more effective will be the
measures upon which we must·rely for an escape from that
bondage of eternal poverty which is the fate of laboring millions in Europe. Foreign trade we need, *to the extent that we
need the products of foreign countries*, but not for the purpose of
carrying on a war of competition between American and European labor. In such a contest, as I have shown elsewhere, the
gain is to the people whose production, measured by the amount
of labor employed, is relatively large, and the loss is to the
people whose consumption is relatively great.

It is frequently asserted that the immigration of foreign
laborers has the same effect upon American labor as the free
importation of the products of foreign labor. This is, in a
measure, true; and there should be some restriction upon immigration. We cannot afford to permit the United States to be
made a dumping-ground for the paupers and criminal classes of
Europe. But the average European in America soon becomes
an American. He adapts himself to his new environment, and
is subject to the laws of production and of distribution which

prevail here; and legislation that could not reach him in Europe will reach him as an American citizen.

When, in any year, the number of immigrants is very large, the equilibrium of labor values is disturbed, wages are reduced, or labor is idle. In order that absorption and assimilation of foreign labor may keep pace with immigration, we should in some manner guard against the too rapid increase of our foreign population. During the last two decades immigration has been invited and encouraged in a manner which ought not to have been permitted. But the American people have always appeared in haste to see their unoccupied lands settled and under cultivation. Whatever measures would stimulate the growth of the country and swell the census roll it has been considered good statesmanship to adopt. The resounding platitudes of Fourth of July oratory have not been without effect in shaping national legislation.

In England, until after the time when manufacturing industries in that country had reached a stage of development that made protective duties unnecessary and ineffective, the policy of protection was rigidly adhered to. The agriculturist was protected by duties on corn and meat, and the manufacturer by various duties and restrictions designed to place him in the position of greatest advantage in competition with foreign products. The agricultural area of Great Britain was not, however, sufficient to supply the food-products required by the large and growing population of that densely-populated country; and owing to the limited land area the effect of protective duties on agricultural products was not marked by a corresponding increase of the product protected,—a result which it is one of the chief objects of a protective duty to accomplish; and, since the lands were in possession of a few landlords, the duty was necessarily at the expense of the working-people, and in the interest of those who were already enriched by means of an oppressive monopoly, and to whom a protective duty afforded the opportunity for still greater exactions, such a policy could be maintained only until its effects were oppressively felt and clearly perceived.

By the aid of protective duties, far less needed in that country than in this, the manufacturing industries of Great Britain were rapidly developed and carried to the highest degree of perfection. When this result had been reached, the protective policy had served its purpose and was no longer required. The interests of the English people demanded foreign trade; the sale of manufactured products abroad was absolutely necessary, in order to enable them to procure the food which the agricultural area of that country was not adequate to produce. England had become able to compete with every other country in foreign markets; no other people could successfully compete with her in her own. Protective duties were no longer necessary; nor could a policy of restraining the importations of the same class of products that the English manufacturer was offering for sale in every foreign mart be pursued, without sanctioning a doctrine which had ceased to be useful to the English people, and which it had become their interest by every means to discourage.

The conditions which make protective duties available to promote the industrial welfare of a people have in England long since ceased to exist. The protective policy of other countries is of course detrimental to English interest, since by it the market for English manufactures is restricted, and manufactures which represent the highest and most valuable form of labor are the only products of considerable value which England has to sell.

It is not, therefore, surprising to find English economists, with scarcely an exception, insisting that absolute free trade is the only policy consistent with the true principles of economic science, and as far as England or English interests are concerned they are undoubtedly right. With the development and growth of manufacturing skill throughout the world, the prosperity of England, and of every country whose food-product is limited below the requirements of her population, must decay. Her position depends on inequalities of industrial development among the nations of the earth.

In the United States the policy of protection was inaugurated immediately after the organization of the government, by the levy of duties on imports ranging from ten to fifteen per cent. These duties at the beginning of the war of 1812 were doubled. In 1816 an act was passed reducing the rate and establishing what was regarded as a moderate protective tariff. The sudden transition from the high duties that had prevailed to comparatively low rates occasioned a serious disturbance of industry, which had been greatly stimulated by the high tariff that was repealed. The act of 1816, with few substantial changes, remained in force until 1824, when what was known as the Clay tariff act was passed, imposing new duties and raising those on most woollen goods. In 1828 there was an increase of duty on many articles, and in 1832 an act was passed reducing the rates on some articles and raising them on others.

In 1833 what was known as the Clay compromise tariff was adopted. This act provided for a reduction of all rates in excess of twenty per cent. to twenty per cent. *ad valorem*, by remitting one-tenth of the excess after December, 1835, one-tenth after December, 1837, one-tenth after December, 1839, one-half the remaining excess in December, 1841, and the remainder in December, 1842.

In 1842 the Whig tariff was adopted, establishing high protective duties on most articles of domestic manufacture, making an average rate on dutiable goods of 33.47 per cent. This act continued in force until 1846, when it was repealed, and what is known as the Walker tariff, from the name of the Secretary of the Treasury, was adopted. This act reduced the average rate on dutiable goods to 26.22 per cent. Reductions on most of the articles in the tariff schedule of 1846 were made in 1857, lowering the average rate to 20.12 per cent.; but on many articles the tariff of 1846 remained in force till 1861, when the Morrill tariff was adopted. This was a highly-protective tariff, and many rates were subsequently reduced. Since 1861 rates have been reduced, but there has been no change of policy. The present schedule is made up largely of specific duties, but the average rate at the present time is equivalent to 47.08 per cent. *ad valorem*.

During the period from 1810 to 1815 many mills and furnaces were built; but after the reduction of the tariff in 1816, the manufacturing industry being exposed to a degree of foreign competition it was unable to withstand, many proprietors were ruined, and large numbers of workers were turned out of employment. From 1828 to 1831 manufacturing industries

revived, mills were again erected, and there was a rapid growth
of manufacturing industry; but in 1833 the protective policy
was again abandoned; the ruin of manufacturers ensued, agriculture was extended, the agricultural product grew in excess
of the demand, and the fate that overtook the manufacturer
pursued the farmer.

From 1842 to 1847 there was again a revival of manufacturing industries; mills and furnaces were again constructed
and again closed, when the protective policy was abandoned for
the Walker tariff of 1846.

From 1850 to 1852 the price of flour fell below the lowest
prices that had ever been known before. From that time
forward to 1861 few mills were erected, the old having depre-
ciated in value below the cost of production.

The effect of the low tariff of 1846 upon the general prosperity
of the country was greatly modified by certain occurrences,
among which was the discovery of gold in California and an
inflation of values resulting from an increase of metallic currency.* The great famine in Ireland, following soon after the
enactment of the Walker law in 1846, and short crops in Europe
in the ensuing years, created a greatly-increased demand for
the product of agriculture. Industrial disturbances in Europe,
occasioned by the revolution of 1848, and followed by the
Crimean war, which began in 1853 and ended in 1856, which,
while it increased consumption, greatly reduced the agricultural
product, and shut off the grain-fields of Russia from competition
with the United States, stimulated the foreign demand for
agricultural products and greatly relieved the depression naturally occasioned by the adoption of a low tariff policy; yet, notwithstanding these favorable conditions, there followed in 1857 a
disastrous panic, involving all interests alike, suspending industrial progress and producing general stagnation in business.
Henry C. Carey, in his book on political economy, written in 1858,
says, " The history of industry in no civilized country of the world
presents such a scene of ruin as is found in the manufact-

---

* The gold product of the United States during the period from 1847 to
1860 was over $600,000,000. The circulation, which in 1850 was $265,000,000,
in 1860 had increased to $487,000,000.

uring, mining, and railroad history of the United States. The farmers," says he, "are poor, and with each successive year the land is being more rapidly exhausted, and the country exhibits many other evidences of declining civilization."

The repeal of the high-tariff schedule of 1842 was in great measure owing to the efforts of Robert J. Walker, a Mississippian, who had been made Secretary of the Treasury under President Polk. He claimed that manufacturers were deriving exorbitant profits from the protected industries, to the detriment of the agriculturist and mechanic. He was no doubt right in the claim that the profits of manufacturing were relatively large. Wealth has always accumulated in manufacturing centres. Skilled industry is always the most profitable; skilled labor, reinforced by machinery, is the most productive. This fact constitutes the principal reason for converting crude labor into skilled labor, and employing it in manufacturing industries in preference to buying manufactured products abroad and paying for them in the products of agriculture.

Prior to the abolition of slavery, the South had no interests to be subserved by a protective policy. Her labor was not susceptible of conversion into skilled labor; the market for her principal product was in London and Liverpool rather than in the cities of the American Union; and it was to her interest to pursue a policy that would insure the lowest possible prices for food and clothing, neither of which constituted a leading product in the cotton-producing States.

The same argument advanced by Walker in 1842 may be urged to-day. The relatively large increase of wealth among those engaged in manufacturing industries, while it does not constitute a sound reason for a modification of the protective policy, affords a most plausible pretext. If the industrial co-partnership is continued, it must be on the condition of a more equitable distribution of its advantages. Manufacturers, mechanics, agriculturists, and miners constitute a single industrial entity. One class cannot exist without the others; and notwithstanding the diversity of interests of the several classes, they together constitute a system of interdependent parts, operating together both in production and distribution, and the prosperity of each depends upon the general prosperity of the whole. The values of the products of one class are measured by the products of other classes, and are therefore relative, and not absolute. All are therefore alike interested in maintaining the common market to which all products must be contributed, and in which all values are measured.

Says Mr. Hoyt, in his work on " Protection *vs.* Free Trade,"—

" Professors in colleges, the capitalists whose money is invested in banks, railroads, farms, and plantations, worked by tenants, go abroad. In London, Paris, and Berlin they purchase many articles of *vertu*, household decoration, and personal adornment, which we either cannot make at all, or make as cheap as the foreign artisan, and our travellers soon acquire an air of condescension towards Americans and American products; they are fond of reckoning the cost in pence and pounds sterling. On their return they are landed at the custom-house, and the wealth they are bringing into the country in the shape of gloves, corsets, and the like, is intercepted long enough to enable the government to collect the share of taxes which they ought to contribute to the common revenue. The professors and the capitalists are hurt as to their feelings, and proceed at once to join a free-trade club."

The wages paid in America for labor and the salary paid for professional service are gauged by the American standard. When measured in money, and generally when measured in any product of labor, the compensation of labor here is higher than that made for like services in Europe, because of American institutions, because of protection to American industries, because our market is preserved to our own people. He, however, who enjoys the benefit of the American market, has discharged only a part of his obligation when he has contributed the product of his own labor to that market; or rather, it may be said, when he has sold his labor in that market, and enjoyed its special advantages, he has entered into an obligation to do his part in maintaining that market. If he sells, he is under obligation to buy. For his own labor he is entitled to an equivalent amount of the products of other labor, measured by the same standard. He takes upon himself the obligation of a citizen to promote the common interests of the industrial co-partnership into which he enters. He is not entitled to enjoy

a distributive share without complying with conditions imposed
on his copartners.

BESSEMER STEEL.

The steel industry in the United States has been made the
subject of frequent discussion by both the advocates and
opponents of protection. The friends of protection point to the
phenomenal growth of this industry under the protection of high
duties, while the advocates of a tariff for revenue only point to
the phenomenal profits which manufacturers of steel rails have
derived from capital invested in a protected industry.

Statistics of the Bessemer Steel and Open-Hearth Steel-Works
in the United States, from census of 1880, covering the year
ending May 30, 1880, show the following:

Total number of establishments	36
" amount of capital invested (real and personal)	$20,975,999
Average capital to each establishment	$582,777
" number of hands employed (of these there were females, 1; males below 16, 621)	10,835
" wages of skilled workmen per day	$3.21
" " " unskilled " " "	$1.25
Total wages paid during the year	$4,930,349
Average yearly wages of skilled workmen	$751.14
" " " " common "	$292.50
Number of months in active operation	9
The number of skilled workmen would therefore be	3,840
" " " unskilled " " " "	6,995
Total value of all materials used	$36,826,928
" number of tons of product	983,039
" value of all products	$55,805,210
Average value of product per ton	$56.76
Net value of all products, deducting materials and wages	$14,047,933
Per cent. of capital represented by net value of product	66.9
Number of tons of Bessemer steel rails embraced in this product	741,475
Value of steel rails included	$37,408,625
Value per ton of steel rails	$50.40
Cost of labor and material entering into a ton of steel	$42.47
Value of pig-iron used in total product	$22,521,098

Other materials used and embraced in the foregoing total
were as follows:

Iron - ore, $59,997 ; spiegeleisen and ferro-manganese, $2,868,519 ; old steel rails, $2,435,463 ; Bessemer ingots and blooms, $2,300,988 ; open-hearth ingots and blooms, $1,129,662 ; scrap-iron, $295,074 ; scrap-steel, $2,257,053 ; hammered iron-ore bloom, $889,136 ; pig- and scrap-bloom, $10,500 ; anthracite coal, $348,752 ; bituminous coal, $1,087,731 ; coke, $471,618 ; charcoal, $3461 ; other materials, $138,076.

It will be observed that all these materials represent labor performed. But, starting with the ore or crude material, capital derives a profit at each stage of progress towards the completed product. Profits, however, are comparatively moderate until the last stage is reached,—the conversion of pig-iron into steel. Here the amount set apart to the credit of capital is 66.9 per cent. on the capital invested. What proportion of this large margin is required to maintain capital—that is, to repair and replace worn-out machinery, buildings, and fixtures—we have no means of ascertaining. But if we allow fifteen per cent. for maintenance of capital, and 1.9 per cent. for taxes, there remains fifty per cent. to the credit of profits or interest on capital. The pig-iron used in making steel is made in blast-furnaces, of which accurate statistics are given. As pig-iron represents more than half the cost of materials entering into the steel product of which the statistics have been given, the statistics of the production of pig-iron and spiegeleisen are here presented :

STATISTICS OF BLAST-FURNACES, 1880 (PIG-IRON).

Number of establishments	490
Total amount of capital (real and personal)	$105,151,176
Average capital to each establishment	$214,594
Total hands employed	41,875
Males above sixteen years	40,688
" below " "	1,183
Females	9
Total wages paid	$12,680,703
Average day's labor, twelve hours.	
" " wages, skilled mechanic	$1.90
" " " ordinary laborer	$1.17
" time of work during the year (months)	8
" annual wages to each worker	$304.27
" " earnings of skilled laborers	$395.20

Average annual earnings of common laborers	$244.06
Total value of materials used	$58,619,742
" " " product "	$89,315,569
Net " " " (deduct materials and wages)	$18,015,124
Per cent. which net product is of capital	17.13
Value per ton of product	$23,62
Cost of labor and material per ton	$18.87

It will be observed that in the steel industry the average employment was for nine months, and in the blast-furnace industry the average time was eight months of the year, showing a capacity for production, without increase of capital or number of workers, in the former industry, of one-fourth, and in the latter industry of one-third, in excess of the demand for the products of those industries.

The number of establishments engaged in making pig-iron is four hundred and ninety; and the number of establishments engaged in making Bessemer and open-hearth steel is only thirty-six. The average capital to each establishment in the former industry is $214,594, and in the steel industry the average is $582,777.

Had all the blast-furnaces been operated with full force throughout the year, the excess of product would have destroyed values; no profit could have been realized, but great loss of capital must have ensued. The same is true of the steel industry.

Where the number of establishments is small, and particularly in industries where the sale of the product is generally contracted before the product is manufactured, there is little difficulty in avoiding destructive competition. And where the number of establishments is so small, as in the steel industry, and the average capital employed so great, combinations, either tacit or express, to advance prices beyond a reasonable profit, are easily effected and adhered to.

Since 1880 the price of steel rails has fallen below what was then the cost of material.

In 1860 the United States produced but 821,223 tons of pig-iron. In 1886 the product amounted to 6,365,328 tons. The number of tons of steel rails in 1880 was 741,475, and in 1886, 1,763,667.

The reduction in the price of steel is the result of improved methods and machinery and of increased competition. This industry, since 1861, has all the while been in a course of development. In the end it must reach the status of other industries, and yield its excessive profits to the effect of competition. And if, from the necessity for the concentration of large amounts of capital, the number of establishments shall be limited within the range of effective combination to maintain unreasonable prices, there should be no hesitation in applying the remedy of foreign competition, by making a special reduction in the rate of duty on steel.

Iron and steel cannot be produced as cheaply in this country as in Europe, for two reasons. The first is, that wages in this country are comparatively much higher; and the second reason is, that in Europe the materials are found in much closer proximity than in the United States.

In 1881 the price for puddling was fixed for one year, by agreement between employers and employés, at a minimum of $5.50 per ton, the price to be advanced when bar-iron advanced beyond two and one-half cents per pound. In 1880 the minimum price was fixed at $4.00 per ton, to be advanced to $4.50 per ton when bar-iron advanced to two and one-half cents per pound. While in North England, the principal seat of iron industry in that country, the price fixed for the same work was $1.75 per ton.

In the United States materials are sometimes transported as far as one thousand miles. Connellsville coke is taken six hundred miles to the blast-furnaces of Chicago, and seven hundred and fifty miles to those of St. Louis. The average distance over which iron-ore is transported in the United States is about four hundred miles, and the average distance of the transportation of fuel used for smelting about two hundred miles, while in Great Britain the materials are seldom required to be transported over one hundred miles. A considerable part, therefore, of the cost of production in this country is the cost of transportation.

The following table shows the fluctuations in price of steel rails in England and in the United States during the period from 1871 to 1882, inclusive:

Year.	Price in England.	Price in the United States.	Difference.
1871	$54.99	$91.18	$36.19
1872	67.64	98.43	30.79
1873	80.05	103.91	23.06
1874	68.75	85.76	17.01
1875	44.28	59.75	14.97
1876	32.12	44.97	12.75
1877	29.20	42.08	12.88
1878	25.55	42.00	16.45
1879	26.88	48.25	21.37
1880	34.36	67.50	33.14
1881	31.53	60.00	28.47
1882	31.10	57.00	25.90

The duty, during that time, was twenty-five dollars per ton.

There will be observed a corresponding fluctuation in English and American prices, the price being determined by the American market, and not by a fixed cost of production in England. Had the duty been less, English prices would have been higher and American prices lower.

The steel used in the United States, in the form of steel rails, during the period named, cost the people of the United States, at the prices paid, $159,312,216 more than the cost would have amounted to at the English prices. And therefore Mr. John G. Carlisle, in a recent number of the *Forum*, says that this sum was *received by the manufacturers for their private use.* In making this statement Mr. Carlisle ignores, first, the cost of transportation of all this steel from England to points in America as convenient for distribution as the several locations of the American steel-works; second, the far greater cost of materials in the United States; and, third, the far greater cost of labor in this country; the wages paid to skilled workmen in America being about twice as much as the wages paid in England. So, while it is true that American manufacturers made large profits, the amount is not expressed in the sum stated. The cost of labor and materials alone entering into the manufacture of a ton of steel rails in this country, for the year ending May 30, 1880, was $42.47; while in England, for the year 1879, the price of steel rails per ton was but $26.88. In 1880 the English price advanced to $34.36; the American price having advanced from $48.25 to $67.50. As the price of the product advances, the

cost of material and the price of labor advances, the manufacturer, however, getting the larger share of the increase in value.

If, instead of stimulating the manufacture of iron and steel
in this country by means of high duties, we had been compelled
to import our iron and steel from England, where we would
have purchased it, not at the prices shown above as the prices
that did prevail in England, but at that advanced price which
would have resulted to the English manufacturer from the
demand in America, the effect of that demand, as it increased
or diminished, is fully illustrated in the table above. When the
demand was reduced, as compared with the capacity to produce,
which was all the time increasing, prices went down; when the
demand increased, prices advanced. In 1877 the number of
tons made in the United States was 432,169, and the price per
ton was $42.08. In 1880 the product was 968,075 tons, and the
price was $67.50 per ton; in 1881 the product had increased to
1,355,519 tons, and the price was $60.00 per ton. In 1882 the
increase was but small, the product being 1,460,920 tons, and the
price fell to $57.00 per ton. Since then prices have been going
down. The capacity to produce has increased, and the pressure
of the demand is no longer effective to maintain the high prices
that formerly prevailed. The price in 1887 fell to $27.50 per
ton, and is now no higher than in England.

Who paid for these rails? The railway companies, in the
first instance. And from the railway companies the cost is
gradually distributed, through freight and passenger traffic
charges, among the whole body of the people.

The statement of Mr. Carlisle, that the entire cost of transportation is deducted from the price of the agricultural product,
is inconsistent with the theory maintained by the free-trade
school of political economists in this country, that the consumer
pays the entire amount of the duty on foreign imports. Charges
for transportation, as well as the amount of duty levied on imported goods, are divided between producer and consumer. No
principle of economic science is better established.

Suppose that, instead of manufacturing our own steel rails,
we had pursued the policy of importing largely from England,
how would the account now stand?

First, as the demand pressed upon the English market, prices would have advanced. Second, as our agricultural export required to pay for the increased imports grew in volume, it must have fallen in price. The consumption of food-products by the English people could have increased only within narrow limits, and only as prices fell, or as wages in that country advanced. Third, a considerable portion of those engaged in the iron and steel industries would have been compelled to seek employment elsewhere, as soon as the demand for the product of their labor fell off, the market being supplied by the English product. The persons of the personal-service class, mechanics and others supported by those released from the manufacturing industry, would also have been compelled to look elsewhere. The effect would have been an increase in the number of agriculturists,—a class already relatively too large.

The American price of steel rails per ton during the census year was $50.40. The total value of products in the steel industry (deducting materials) was $18,978,282; the value created by each worker being $1751.50, the amount of capital employed to each worker being $1860. In agriculture, the average capital to each worker was not much less; the average product was three hundred dollars. If we assume the English price of steel rails, with cost of transportation added, to have been thirty dollars per ton, which is about the true amount, the labor of one man in agriculture, assuming that the product in England would sell for enough more than the farm-price here to pay for transportation, commissions, etc., would purchase ten tons delivered in New York; while one man in this country can produce with his labor 34.7 tons equal in quality to those of English manufacture. But, allowing for greater waste of capital in the iron and steel industry, we may say that the labor of one man in the iron and steel industry, measured by English prices, is equal in value to the labor of two and one-half men in agriculture. Can we then afford to trade two and one-half days of American labor for one day of English labor?

This basis is on the estimate of values *as they stood.* But, had we largely increased our importations, and paid for the increase with our agricultural product, the difference would have been much greater, for we would have paid more for rails and got less for our agricultural export, while agricultural prices in general would have fallen. We paid still a higher price to the American manufacturer, measuring prices in money, but a less price as measured by labor, and the increase of wealth resulting from the employment of our own skilled labor remains at home. The distribution of the increased wealth is in favor of capital, it is true; but it is a question of distribution and not of production. The remedy will not be found in abandoning our protective policy and transferring the profits to England, but in a more equitable distribution among our own people.

In the rapid development of a great industry like that of the production of iron and steel in the United States, these inequalities of distribution necessarily arise. The large profits are in part attributable to the employment of patented processes and machinery, the same cause which so long unduly enhanced the profits of the manufacture of agricultural machinery. Enormous profits have likewise been made in railway building, in land speculation, in the mining of precious metals, and also in trade. We ought to be able to find a remedy, without the assistance of England. The lion would no doubt be pleased to drive the wolves away, but how shall the lambs be protected from the lion?

In Great Britain, notwithstanding low prices of steel and of other products of manufacture, the agricultural laborer is not only absolutely, but relatively, far poorer and more meanly paid than in the United States.

In England, as well as in the United States, the capitalist manages to secure large profits. If prices are low, he pushes down the price of labor, but always preserves a good margin for himself.

The great American people can never promote their own prosperity by buying the products of skilled labor in England, and then, in payment, shipping wheat and cattle and corn across the ocean to the markets of Liverpool and London, already crowded with the products of cheap labor from South America, Australia, Russia, Africa, and India. Western Europe is the only country importing wheat for home consumption, and Western Europe produces three-fourths of the wheat required for home consumption. India produces from ten to fifteen per cent. in excess of the home demand, and South

America, Australia, Russia, and Africa all grow wheat for export. In 1889 the area of the wheat crop in the United States was about ten million acres in excess of what is required for home consumption. The prices of late in Liverpool have been the lowest that have prevailed during the century. South America possesses an unlimited area of fertile lands not yet brought under cultivation, and an abundance of cheap labor. By means of the construction of railways, the cultivation of wheat for export, on the fertile lands of India, has been greatly increased. Owing to the habits of the laboring-people of India, who, like the Chinese, are content to subsist on a few cents per day, the cost of production in that country does not exceed forty cents per bushel, and Indian wheat can be put on the London market at sixty cents per bushel. There is no foreign demand for our corn and oats, and our export trade in meats is subject to competition with the cheap products of South America and Australia.

The European market for the products of American agriculture, unless the quantity of our export be relatively reduced for at least fifty years to come, must continue, as a rule, to be a market of low prices. The industrial development of South America, India, and Africa will proceed but slowly. They will continue to be fields of crude, cheap labor, devoted chiefly to agriculture, and they will fill the markets of Europe with their surplus.

European agriculture has suffered from the same ruinous competition that has destroyed the profits of farming in the United States. The lands of Germany, France, and Great Britain are covered with mortgages, and the distress of the agricultural classes in those countries has been a subject of grave concern.

According to Mulhall, real estate in the United Kingdom in 1883 was mortgaged to forty-one per cent. of its value, the mortgages amounting to eight billion three hundred million dollars; in France to seventeen per cent. of its value; in Germany to forty-nine per cent. of its value; and in Italy to thirty-seven per cent. of its value. According to Lord Reay, the landed properties in England in 1883 were mortgaged to fifty-eight per cent. of their value. In Prussia the land mortgages in

1869 were fifty-one per cent. of the value of the lands, and the
house property in Berlin was mortgaged to sixty-eight per cent.
of its value.   In Egypt the mortgages registered from 1878 to
1883 amounted to thirty-two million dollars.

Later statistics show a large increase, and the mortgages of
France are now estimated at forty per cent. of the value of
the lands.   The amount is about four billion dollars.   The
mortgages of Ireland amount to fifty per cent. of the value of
lands, and about two-thirds of the real estate of Russia, Italy,
Spain, and Switzerland is mortgaged.   Universal competition,
with its resultant fluctuations in values, has opened the way to
an aggregation of wealth in all the countries of Europe that
absorbs the profits of agriculture and weighs heavily upon the
middle classes.

All countries trading together, or whose labor and capital
compete in a common market, are exposed to financial convul-
sions and industrial depressions caused by events and conditions
affecting any one or more of the countries so united.   Industrial
depressions in the United States have been quite contempora-
neous with like depressions in Europe.   The following table,
which I quote from the Report of the Commissioner of Labor
of 1886, shows the dates of industrial depressions and countries
affected.

YEARS OF DEPRESSIONS.

COUNTRIES.	YEARS.										
United States	...	...	1814	1818	1826	...	1837	1847	1867	1873	1882
Great Britain	1803	1810	1815	1818	1826	1830	1837	1847	1866	1873	1883
France	1804	1810	1813	1818	1826	1830	1837	1847	1866	1873	1882
Belgium . . .	...	...	...	...	...	...	1837	1848	1864	1873	1882
Germany . . .	...	...	...	...	...	...	1837	1847	...	1873	1882

To the extent that any of the leading industries of the United
States are made dependent upon foreign markets, to that extent
do our people impose upon themselves the risk of industrial
depressions arising from conditions prevailing in foreign countries which they are unable to control or prevent.   Unrestricted
trade means an industrial copartnership with the nations of
Europe, by virtue of which all the industrial evils established in
those countries shall become factors in determining the fate

of our own people. Industrial independence, so far as natural conditions will admit, should be the aim of every people.

Mr. Edward Atkinson, in a recent article, which he entitles "Common Sense and the Tariff Question," in the *Popular Science Monthly* (September, 1890), in advocacy of the principle of free trade, says, "On the plea that this branch of industry should be sustained, the consumers of iron and steel in this country have paid a sum in excess of the price paid by the consumers who have been supplied by Great Britain and Germany, ranging from fifty millions to eighty millions of dollars a year for the last ten years. *The excess of price has not been paid over to the workmen by the owners of the mines and works;* it has been bestowed upon private individuals to aid private enterprises. One has only to examine the average wages of the workmen in iron-mines and works of this country to be convinced that they are much less than the wages of those who are engaged in the conversion of crude iron and steel into machinery, tools, beams, bars, and other forms of use." Mr. Atkinson seeks to show that, by reason of the tariff, manufacturers of iron enjoy excessive profits.

In 1884, Mr. Atkinson published his book on "The Distribution of Products," the leading purpose of which appears to be to demonstrate that, in the division of product between capital and labor, labor receives its full share. Speaking of the iron industry, and particularly of data gathered from the accounts of an Eastern furnace, employed to illustrate the industry in general, he says, "If we consider the period from 1860 to 1880 historically, it has been one of singular progress in improvements for converting ores into iron, both in the construction of furnaces and in the saving of labor. To whom the benefits of these inventions and improvements have inured the table shows.

"1st. The margin between the selling price of iron and the cost of materials has decreased $83\frac{78}{100}$ per cent. *The share of capital has been reduced both absolutely and relatively.*

"2d. Labor has been rendered less arduous, while the wages of the laborer have been increased $37\frac{68}{100}$ per cent. *The share of the laborer has been increased both absolutely and relatively.*

"3d. The price of iron to the consumer has been reduced 31$\frac{88}{100}$ per cent."

Mr. Atkinson follows these statements with a graphic table demonstrating and illustrating the propositions announced with a full array of figures, and says, "This table might well be named ' The indicator of progress from poverty of the workman, and *progress towards poverty of the capitalist.*'"

Taking the conditions of 1860 to 1864, inclusive, and comparing these conditions with those of 1875 to 1879, inclusive, Mr. Atkinson illustrates, by means of a second graphic table, the changes which have occurred in a blast-furnace used for the conversion of iron-ores and coal into pig-iron. The changes exhibited are as follows :

" Product per head increased from 776 tons to 1219 tons.

" Total product increased from 58,959 tons to 86,546 tons.

" Wages increased from $353 per year, in a depreciating currency, to $486 per year in an appreciating currency.

" Gross value of product increased from $1,627,268 to $1,651,298.

" Number of hands employed decreased from 76 to 71.

" Price of iron decreased from $27.95 to $19.18 per ton.

" Margin between the value of the product and the cost of materials and labor, from which margin taxes, general expenses, and profits are to be derived, *depressed from $9.55 per ton to $1.09 per ton.*"

He then says, "It will be apparent that, while the profits of capital may have been much more than ten per cent. in the first period, and must have been much less in the second; yet such facts can seldom be correctly ascertained, and, if given, would not be as useful as to assume a certain uniform rate of profit. *It is an absolute rule that if profits rise above a certain rate in any art which is open to free competition, capital will be immediately applied thereto in ample measure so as to bring them down to an average at any given time.* If an excess of profit is gained for any considerable period, an excess of capital will be invested, and presently what is called an over-production will occur."

The italics in the foregoing quotations are my own.

This is a clear case of *stare decisis.* Mr. Atkinson first writes a book, the product of painstaking investigation, in which he demonstrates to his satisfaction the equitable division of product between labor and capital, and that "it is an absolute rule that if profits rise above a certain rate in any art which is open to free competition, capital will be immediately applied thereto in ample measure so as to bring them down to an average at any given time;" and the industry he cites, and from which he obtains his statistics for his final and conclusive demonstration of this proposition, is the iron industry.

He now contributes to a leading magazine an article showing careful preparation, and accompanied by the usual object-lesson in the shape of a graphic illustration, the purpose of which is to demonstrate the advantages of free trade, in which he assumes, with the confidence of one accustomed to speak with authority, that the truth does not accord with the statistics or the deductions which served his purpose in a discussion of the relations between capital and labor, but that what he then announced as an absolute rule is no rule at all.

The readiness with which Mr. Atkinson abandons his former position in order to place himself *en rapport* with the spirit of free-trade logic indicates no common aptitude for the adjustment of his views to meet the requirements of the argument in hand.

In other chapters of this book I have endeavored to show that, in the division of the product between labor and capital, capital obtains an undue share. I now desire to examine the statement to which Mr. Atkinson lends his later endorsement in the article above mentioned, in which he abandons the doctrine which he has hitherto maintained.

In one sense it is true that "the consumers of iron and steel in this country have paid a sum in excess of the price paid by the consumers who have been supplied by Great Britain and Germany." Whether that sum reached the figures named by Mr. Atkinson, from fifty million to eighty million dollars a year, it is not important to determine. The purpose of the statement is, I presume, to convey the idea that by reason of the tariff the iron and steel consumed by American consumers during the last ten years has cost them from five hundred million to eight hundred million dollars more than it would have cost had there been no duty.

If Mr. Atkinson's figures correctly measure the difference in the cost of iron and steel consumed at American and at English prices during the ten years, and if we assume that, had there been no duty and we had imported largely, as we would have done, no advance would have been made in European prices; that, contrary to all experiences, an increased demand for the foreign product would have had no effect in raising prices; and if we assume further that the export of agricultural products could have been increased in amount sufficient to have paid for the increase of importations without reducing the price in the foreign market of the bread-stuffs, meat, etc., exported, then Mr. Atkinson's statement, in the sense in which he employs it in his argument, would be apparently true; but still, in fact, untrue, for the reason, as I have already shown, that it takes at least three days' work in agriculture, at the prices which prevailed, to purchase the product of two days' work in manufacturing iron, measured by European prices and cost of transportation. It is altogether a question of the exchange of labor.

It is true, as Mr. Atkinson and others contend, that many leading manufacturing industries no longer require the support of a high tariff on the theory of encouraging infant industries. Intelligent advocates of a high protective duty do not rest upon any such claim. Many of our manufacturing industries, with such reduction in the price of labor as free trade would bring, are prepared to compete in foreign markets, sell their goods, and force in return the importation of the products of foreign agriculture, or of foreign manufacture, to compete with and cripple other weaker industries, to the advantage of many capitalists engaged in manufacture and others engaged in trade; but such foreign trade would be no advantage, but an injury to the American people as a whole. What concerns us now is not an extension of the field for the exploitation of capital, but a better adjustment of industrial forces and a more equitable distribution.

The average wages in the iron and steel industries of the United States during the census year were $2.59 per day for skilled labor and $1.24 for unskilled labor. The average annual wages of both skilled and unskilled labor in the industries referred to by Mr. Atkinson were as follows:

Industry.	Wages.
Anthracite coal mining	$321.00
Bituminous " "	326.00
Iron-ore mining	301.00
Coke (manufacture of)	381.50
Iron rolling-mills	424.35
Bessemer and Open-Hearth Steel Works	455.00
Blast-furnaces	310.25
Cutlery and edged tools	472.70
Iron nails and spikes	431.80
Iron-works, architectural	406.40
Iron forgings	414.00
Steam-fittings	378.80
Tools	472.60

The low average annual wages as compared with daily wages results from the fact that these industries were, during part of the year, either wholly or partly suspended.

Mr. Atkinson, in his statement that "the excess of price" (of the American over the English product) "has not been paid over to the workmen by the owners of the mines and works; it has been bestowed upon private individuals to aid private enterprises," wholly ignores not only his former deductions, but also the well-known fact that the wages of workmen in American mines and in the American iron and steel industries are very much higher than the corresponding wages of English workmen. And while it is true that the whole amount of the excess of the money cost of American iron and steel has not been paid out in wages, about two-thirds of it has been paid out in wages to working-men directly and indirectly employed in these industries. The profits of capital, not only in these, but in all American industries, and on money loaned or invested in trade, have been greater than the profits of capital in England. The profits of capital in new and rapidly-growing countries are always greater than in old countries whose industries are developed and whose wealth has accumulated near to its approximate limit.

It is true, as Mr. Atkinson says, that the average wages of those engaged in converting crude iron into machinery, tools, and so on are higher than the wages of those engaged in mining and the manufacture of pig-metal, for the reason that the wages of skilled labor are higher than the wages of unskilled labor in this and in all other countries, and this fact bears no relation to the question of protection or free trade.

AN INDUSTRIAL BUREAU.

Manufacturing industries are among the most potent factors of civilization. They develop in the highest degree mechanical and industrial skill; they stimulate invention and discovery, excite mental activity, widen the scope of human energy, and bring into the fullest play the powers of the educated mind. They at the same time furnish to agriculture the implements of an improved husbandry, and make a market for the increased product of the farm; they arouse the people from the dull lethargy of a plodding, uneventful life, create new opportunities, and open up new avenues of wealth.

Combining the productiveness of skilled labor, aided by every ingenious mechanical device that invention can supply, with the powers of machinery operated by electricity and steam, they multiply the capacity of labor from ten- to a hundredfold; and, as production is increased, the wages of the laborer, which are the measure of his share of the product, are increased in like ratio from a few cents a day, as in India and China, where production is limited to handicraft, to the highest wages in the civilized world, which are paid in the United States, where improved implements and machinery are employed in agriculture and in all departments of industry.

Not only have manufacturing industries increased production and advanced wages, but, at the same time, they have extended the limitations of wealth. The wealth of a purely agricultural people is measured by their farms, their cattle, horses, and implements of husbandry, a temporary supply of perishable products, and the property employed in transportation and trade adequate to the distribution of the annual product. Beyond these subjects of wealth there is no field for investment, no room for growth. But a nation of diversified industries, in addition to these, has its mines, its factories, its furnaces and mills, an accumulated product in the form of fabrics and the various manufactures of wool and iron, which, being more durable than potatoes and corn, and less expensive to keep than cattle and hogs, give storage-room for wealth; and, in addition to those, there are more railways and more of everything required in the pursuit of many industries and the distribution of the larger product. Hence it is that manufacturing countries grow rich, while agricultural countries remain poor. Hence it is that in manufacturing countries wages are high, while in agricultural countries wages are low.

Wealth accumulated is a power that controls commerce, determines the conditions of trade, and commands perpetual tribute from every industry that competes in the market where it holds sway.

A people who, like Africans exchanging ivory for cotton cloth, or Indians trading venison for beads, exchange, in a foreign market, the fruits of husbandry or the products of handiwork for the products of machinery, who trade the work of muscle for the work of iron and steam, build up a power beyond their reach to control; while, at the same time, they divest themselves of the opportunity for acquiring and storing that wealth at home which is the source of a nation's strength and the measure of the prosperity, intelligence, and culture of a people.

The relative wealth and prosperity of England and Ireland or India furnish the only illustration needed of the effect of a policy limiting the industry of a people to the pursuit of agriculture and the productions of handicraft, and compelling them to purchase in a foreign market the products of manufacture made by skilled labor with machinery run by steam and controlled by capital.

But, on the other hand, it will be said, with equal truth, that the contrast between the rich and the poor in England is a measure of the evils that spring from the centralization of wealth, and that the advantages which accrue from manufacturing industries are not distributed among the people. Yet the English working-man is infinitely better off than the Irish peasant or the Indian ryot. Besides, evils at home, by means of intelligent concert among the working-people, and by wise legislation, may be modified and corrected; but the wealth that is gathered in an unequal exchange of the products of crude for those of skilled labor, carried away and piled up in a foreign domain, will not return, unless in the form of credits or investments in revenue-bearing property to carry abroad the perpetual tribute of labor to an alien people.

In the United States not only will duties on foreign imports continue to be a principal source of national revenue, but-the policy of so adjusting these duties as to foster the growth of those industries which it is to our interest as a people to encourage, and, by preserving our own market for the products of our own labor in those industries which combine skill with the power of machinery, promote the conversion of crude into skilled labor, thereby increasing its productiveness and its value, will be maintained. Rates of duty, from time to time, will be readjusted to meet the requirements of the demand for public revenue and conform to changing industrial conditions. These adjustments can be effected only by statutes enacted by the national Congress, but framed by committees who are appointed, and who must complete their work, during the sessions in which bills reported by them are enacted into laws.

Imported articles which are subjected to duty under our system of revenue are numerous and varied in character, and the rate of duty upon each article must be fixed, not only with reference to cost of production, but also with reference to rates of duty on related articles. Thus if the duty on wool is ten cents per pound, the duty on manufactured woollens, in the various forms of manufacture, must be so adjusted as to conform to the cost of wool to the American manufacturer, or else foreign fabrics will crowd the home product from the market. The same principle applies to the iron industry and all other industries where imports are received, both in the form of raw material and in the various stages of manufacture up to the completed product. The cost of production, involving both the prices of labor and the profits of capital, is involved in every adjustment of the tariff schedule. A congressional committee can have neither the time nor the opportunity to secure and digest the information essential to the making of a schedule adapted to the requirements of the revenue and adjusted to the policy of protecting, in equal degree, the various industries affected so as not to disturb them in their proper relations, and at the same time conforming to the true principles of taxation ; and being composed of individuals of whom some, at least, possess little qualification for the work of adjusting the details of a tariff schedule, and of politicians concerned for their own political future, such a committee is not always able to disregard considerations of personal interest which ought, so far as practicable, to be removed from influence on legislation so directly affecting the industries of a nation.

Not only is the information on which these committees and Congress are compelled to act necessarily incomplete and often erroneous, but the people are not advised concerning the industrial facts which are supposed to form the basis of tariff rates, and they are unable to judge of the acts of their representatives, or to hold them to account.

Errors and omissions are liable to occur in tariff schedules, and unforeseen effects sometimes result from a want of knowledge of the industrial uses of articles of commerce, or from not fully comprehending the exact meaning of commercial terms, and from a lack of knowledge concerning industrial conditions.

There is need, therefore, of a permanent industrial commission which shall be charged with the duty of collecting and collating statistics necessary to exhibit fully and in detail the cost of production, the wages of labor and the profits of capital, and other facts the knowledge of which may be essential or useful in shaping legislation affecting industrial interests or social conditions.

Such commission should have the power to examine witnesses and to require the production of books and papers, so as to obtain full disclosures concerning every industry and trade sharing the advantages of the American market and enjoying the protecting care of the government.

The advantages which secrecy often affords to capital as a cover for its operations in securing an undue share of the products of industry are not advantages which rightly belong to any individual in the industrial copartnership of a commonwealth, and the enforced disclosure of the cost of production or the profits of trade is no invasion of any private right.

Such commission would be able to ascertain and make clear many facts the knowledge of which is essential to sound legislation touching industrial relations or affecting economic conditions which determine the welfare and shape the progress of a people. And the statistics required cannot be gathered by the agencies and methods now employed; but a commission, properly constituted and clothed with the necessary authority, would be able to obtain the information needed in shaping legislation, and which might also, independent of legislation, greatly aid in securing and preserving a well-balanced adjustment of the various industries, and, in a measure, eliminate speculation as a principal factor in the distribution of wealth, and lead to that steadiness of industrial growth which is the best guarantee of reasonable prices and sure but not exorbitant profits.

The institution of such a commission would meet the active opposition of that class of persons who make free use of the word "paternalism" as a term fitly characterizing all legislation designed for the protection of the people from the industrial wrongs and commercial frauds which enable aggressive and not over-scrupulous individuals, in the name of "business," and without legal hinderance, to build fortunes for themselves at the expense of others.

The word "paternalism" is the English antipodes of *laisser faire*, and those who are now opposing the progress of industrial legislation are the successors of those who in the past opposed, as an unwarrantable interference with the right of private contract, those salutary laws which effected the reform of the factory system in England, and whose theory was tersely epitomized in the phrase *laisser faire*. Their successors, laying less stress upon an affirmative declaration of a somewhat discredited doctrine of economic science, now employ the word "paternalism" to express their repugnance to the policy which has established itself in opposition to their views and against their vehement protest.

But, whether we desire it or not, the evident drift of public opinion and the general trend of events is in the direction of the employment of legislative restraints as a protection against industrial wrongs; and one of the most useful as well as least objectionable of legal remedies is the collection and publication, by competent authority, of social and industrial statistics which may serve as a basis for sound theories and a guide to safe action.

Industrial reforms must be pursued along the line of social progress and worked out as a natural product of existing tendencics. Legislation may aid the process of evolution, and, as one of its leading factors, in a great measure control results. And, since changes in industrial conditions are inevitable, and the tendency in the direction of radical legislation in some form is everywhere apparent, the establishment of an industrial bureau would be a wise and conservative measure, by means of which public opinion and the legislation which shall proceed from it may be moulded into conformity with sound principles of economic science.

We have already a Commissioner of Agriculture and a Commissioner of Labor. These two offices should be united in one department, so as to co-ordinate their work; and such department should be clothed with the power necessary to secure a complete collection of social, industrial, commercial, and agricultural statistics; and its duties should be enlarged, so as to embrace the work of exhibiting the statistics so collected and deductions derived therefrom in convenient form to serve as a guide in framing or modifying measures affecting the revenue or directly touching social and industrial relations. The work of such a department would necessarily be so conducted as to be little affected by partisan bias, and the domain of science would be gradually extended over much of the territory now in dispute between contending political factions. The organization of a bureau of this character would lead the people in the direction of scientific investigations and deductions, correct false theories based on defective information or erroneous suspicions, and moderate the intensity of that radical spirit which feeds on *a priori* reasoning in fields unexplored by science.

FOREIGN IMMIGRATION.

In 1880 the total foreign-born population of the United States was 6,679,943, and the number of native-born population of foreign parentage was 8,316,053, making a total population that was either foreign-born or of foreign parentage of nearly 15,000,000, or thirty per cent. of the total population. The per cent. of foreign-born population in several leading cities was as follows:

Boston	31.8	Detroit	39.2
Cincinnati	28	Milwaukee	39.8
Chicago	40.5	New York	39.7

The per cent. of persons of foreign birth of the whole number of workers engaged in all occupations in fifty leading cities was forty-two and six-tenths; of the number engaged in trade and transportation, thirty-four and three-tenths; and of those engaged in manufacturing, mechanical, and mining industries, forty-nine and three-tenths.

Assuming that in the industries of these cities the general ratio of native-born persons of foreign parentage is maintained, the percentage of population that was either foreign-born or of foreign parentage would be as follows:

Boston	71.58
Cincinnati	62.8
Chicago	90.8
Detroit	87.9
Milwaukee	89.3
New York	89
In all industries in fifty cities	95
In trade and transportation in fifty cities	76.1
In manufacturing, mechanical, and mining in fifty cities	110.6

It will be observed that the percentage so obtained is impossible as to "manufacturing, mechanical, and mining" industries, and too large as to the industries combined. We may therefore conclude that a larger percentage of the children of foreign than of native parents leave these cities; also that the ratio of the number of persons of foreign birth to the number of the native-born of foreign parentage engaged in manufacturing and mining is greater than in other industries.

Of those classified as of foreign parentage, there were a fraction over one-seventh, one of whose parents was native-born.

Since 1880 the ratio of immigration has greatly increased, and the ratio of foreign population in 1890 will be still greater than that shown by the census of 1880.

In the State of Massachusetts, in 1888, the number of alien males above the age of twenty-one years was 197,861, of whom 99,131 were unnaturalized. The number of native-born males over twenty-one years of age was 343,886, including those who were native-born, but of foreign parentage. The number of foreign-born was 36.5 per cent. of the whole.

In 1880, when our foreign-born population was but thirteen per cent. of the whole population, nineteen per cent. of the convicts in our penitentiaries and forty-three per cent. of the inmates of work-houses and houses of correction were of foreign birth.

That the importation of an alien population, many of whom are grossly ignorant and most of whom are extremely poor, injuriously affects our people, socially, morally, and economically, there can be no question.

The lower portion of Manhattan Island, on which stands the City of New York, is a delta, formed of the detritus dropped at the mouth of the turbid stream of foreign immigration that is steadily pouring into this country through Castle Garden. A large portion of these people, now crowding in upon us, are not only without any true conception of the dignity and the obligations of American citizenship, but they are ignorant and morally depraved; they are the stunted and misshapen products of ages of degrading servitude, and their deformed physiognomies make constant proclamation of mental and moral defects that have acquired the character and permanence of inheritable traits, which it will require generations in contact with more generous environments to eradicate.

While it would not accord with the genius of our institutions to deny admission to any European immigrant whose moral and educational attainments are such as to bring him into harmonious and sympathetic accord with the spirit of American civilization, and fit him for the duties and responsibilities of a citizen of a free and progressive republic, we are under no moral obligation to degrade any American industry by admitting into our midst a horde of ignorant, non-progressive, morally degraded foreign competitors, to divide with the poorer and more defenceless of our own people the advantages of that generous market for labor, in the making of which the higher standard of living of American working-men has been the chief factor. We are not impelled by any sentiment of humanity or by any patriotic impulse to destroy the value of our free schools—fountains of learning and culture which are the resort of the children of the whole people—by making them places of infectious contact with social depravity, nor to permit the current of social life

among the common people in this country to be converted into
a lavatory, into which thousands of ignorant immigrants may
plunge and cleanse themselves from the gross impurities that
incrust the lower grades of human character in many sections
of Europe.

Foreign immigration has been considered only in its relation
to the interests of capitalists looking to immediate pecuniary rewards.   Indiscriminate immigration has been invited and aided,
in the interest of great railway corporations, in haste to enhance
the value of the lands conveyed to them by a generous government as a bonus for the construction of railways; the owners
of mines, the proprietors of furnaces and factories, railway con-
tractors, builders, and other employers of labor have encouraged
and often directly aided the importation of foreign labor, in
order that they might increase the margin of profit in the particular enterprises in which they were at the time engaged,
without regard to future results, or the moral and economic
effect upon the nation at large.

Foreign immigration has an economic bearing in relation to
the distribution of wealth which is of concern to the whole
people; and it has also a moral bearing of equal concern to
those whose vision is not bounded by the horizon of dollars and
cents.   Our national policy on this subject should be framed on
a broader basis than that of subserviency to the interests of
capital in its struggle to appropriate a still larger share of the
product of labor.

CHAPTER IX.

MONOPOLIES AND TRUSTS.

MR. HENRY GEORGE portrays with great strength and clearness the condition of poverty and dependence of a numerous
class of working-people,—a class that is constantly increasing,
and whose condition every year grows more and more hopeless.
Looking about for an explanation of this phenomenon,—for in
a country like the United States, where wealth is abundant, and
where the power of the people to produce greatly exceeds their

power to consume, such a state of affairs may well be regarded as a phenomenon,—he finds the explanation, as he believes, in the monopoly in the ownership of land. Finding here what is undoubtedly one of the chief sources of the evil which he so eloquently portrays, he permits himself to overlook other co-operating causes in his earnest pursuit of the one to which his attention is mainly directed, and which he so vigorously assails.

Land is not the only subject of ownership the quantity of which is limited. Every other species of property is also limited by economic conditions; and the amount of the total wealth of a country is likewise limited.

The limitation on land is a natural limitation on the quantity of the subject-matter. As to other classes of property, the limitation rests in economic conditions which determine the quantity that can be used. The limitation is a limitation on values, which, as effectually as any other, sets bounds to production. The amount of money (omitting all consideration of foreign commerce) which a country may have, while not as definitely, is as effectually prescribed by economic conditions as the quantity of land is fixed by the limitation of nature. The nominal amount of money may be increased; but beyond the demands of trade, while the number of dollars or of pieces may be multiplied, the total value cannot be increased. And the economic necessity for preserving a definite and unchanging standard of value makes it essential that the volume of currency, measured by the number of nominal dollars, as well as the total value of the whole, shall conform to conditions which change but slowly. The limitation on the quantity of land is modified by the employment of an increased amount of capital and improved skill in agriculture; so that, practically speaking, it may be said that the limit on land fluctuates over a margin as wide as that which covers fluctuations in the amount of money.

The necessary limitation on the number of railways is apparent; it is, however, a limitation of precisely the same character as that which determines the number of factories or mills in a country. The differences are those of degree, not of principle. The conditions which give rise to monopoly in land make monopoly possible in every species of property. Great wealth, regardless of the form of its investment, is a monopoly.

It will be seen, therefore, that the remedy proposed by Mr. George strikes at only one of the causes of the evil which he seeks to cure. And if we are to apply the principle of his remedy throughout, we must not only abolish property in land, but all property, and organize society on the communistic principle.

The causes from which evils spring are, however, productive of good. We do not put out the fire in the furnace because by fire cities are consumed; we do not abolish steam-engines because they sometimes explode, nor prohibit railways because they are dangerous to operate. We employ safeguards to diminish the evils which we cannot wholly prevent.

If we learn by experience that the aggregation of a large amount of land in the ownership of single individuals is detrimental to the interests of society, this is not a good reason why we should proceed at once to abolish all ownership. The remedy need go no further than an evil we seek to prevent or to mitigate.

If we are justified in preventing one species of monopoly from which society suffers injury, we are also justified in preventing every other species of monopoly from which society suffers harm, provided only that we find efficient and practical means to accomplish our purpose without doing violence to natural rights or harm in other ways that may counterbalance the good we accomplish. But, in applying measures of relief, we may not ignore human nature, which in the end will always assert itself and render ineffective any scheme for social or economic reform evolved by abstract reasonings from assumptions that run counter to the current of human aspirations and desires.

Railway companies, telegraph and telephone companies, gas companies, and street-railway companies are classed as natural monopolies, for the reason that they are not effectively subject to control by means of competition. They are therefore considered as proper subjects of legislative control. In behalf of these institutions, it was at first earnestly insisted that, being private corporations, any attempt by legislation to regulate their charges is a violation of property rights and a pernicious intermeddling with private affairs. This view has been practically abandoned; but the measures by which these charges are to be finally regulated have not yet been brought to a high degree of efficiency.

The policy of governmental ownership has been adopted in Continental Europe and, to some extent, in Great Britain, and appears there to be an improvement on private management. If the policy of public ownership of natural monopolies be not adopted in this country, their management and control will, at least, be made subject to the supervision of government officials, under a system of laws which necessity and experience will develop. A long step has already been taken in that direction, and further advance will be made at the usual pace which must govern movements of this character. The wisdom gained by experience is learned but slowly; and the problem is complicated by the fact that powers which should be centred in one governing body are divided between the general government and the governments of the respective States, resulting in a divided management of the same subject-matter.

Nevertheless, the policy of limiting by law the maximum charges of natural monopolies has become fully established. The reasonableness of such charges must be determined by some ascertained standard of measurement. What shall that standard be? The only answer that can be made is, a fair profit on the capital invested, after the payment of customary wages and reasonable salaries and cost of maintaining the property employed. A reasonable profit is the average profit which may be permitted to capital in general. But how shall the amount of capital be measured? The amount of stocks and bonds set afloat by railway companies is evidently not a reliable basis. This amount may be, and often is, two or three times as great as the amount actually invested in construction and equipment. And in many cases, where it fairly represents the original cost, with improvements added, owing to depreciation in values it has ceased to be even a near approximation to what would be the present cost.

The value of the lands of the farmer is subject to depreciation which results from unlimited competition; the value of houses, mills, and machinery is limited to the amount which it would require to construct like machinery or build like houses, the present value of labor being the gauge of value for all products of labor which do not exist in excess of the demand; but, where the demand is exceeded, the value of property of this character falls below what would be the cost of reproducing it. The property of natural monopolies not being in like manner subject to competition, its value is determined by the rate of profit it may yield. Unless this class of property shall be, in the interest of capitalists, made an exception to the operation of the general rule which determines the value of other property, and the profits of capital otherwise invested, the only true gauge of the capital of railway, telegraph, or gas companies, on which a profit should be permitted, is present value, as determined by what would be the present cost of construction.

It therefore follows that it is the duty of the government to ascertain present values of property of this class, upon the basis of present cost; and that such value, when ascertained, should constitute the basis of established charges for the services or the products of natural monopolies. No advantages resulting from the necessary absence of competition in any industry can legitimately belong to any individual. Progress in the direction of fixing an equitable basis for legislation determining maximum rates of railways for freight and passenger carriage has been impeded by the opposition of aggregated wealth, which is always a most potent factor in shaping legislative action, where its interests are concerned.

In the census of 1880 the total permanent investments of railways per mile is reported at $59,718. The cost of construction of roads is set down at $47,387 per mile, and the cost of equipment at $4817; the value of lands owned, including buildings, at $1191; the value of telegraph lines, etc., at $2361; and stocks and bonds owned (issued by other companies) at $3962 per mile. This would make the cost per mile of construction and equipment of roads, with lands and buildings used for depots, etc., $53,395, which is double what would be the present cost of the same railroads economically built and equipped, taking the right of way at the amount which was actually paid for it. Most of the railways in the United States, through the greater part of the length of line, are built over level lands, where the cost of grading is light. The rails now in track are not worth more than thirty-five hundred dollars per mile, and the ties from six hundred to one thousand dollars, according to location.

Railway property should be subject to the same reductions in value as other property; for otherwise the equilibrium between different interests is destroyed. If railway property were owned by the government, this question would not arise. The profits arising from railway traffic would then assume the character of a tax to be expended for the common benefit.

Owing to the great danger to life and limb to which workers in the employ of railway companies are exposed, resulting in the creation of a class of persons who have been by accident deprived of the ability to support themselves and families, a part of the revenues derived from railway traffic ought to be applied to the support of employés who have been crippled in the service, or to the support of those naturally dependent upon them. The distribution of this fund might be regulated according to the principles and methods of life and accident insurance companies. A measure of this character would be in accord with sound public policy, and would impose no hardships on the people, whose chief concern it is to see that natural monopolies be not made agencies for the undue aggregation of wealth.

Another form of natural monopoly is the ownership of land. The ownership by one individual of a certain tract of land means the exclusion of all others from any right or title to, or control of, such tract; and the ownership of a limited number of persons of the entire area signifies that other people must do without. Social and economic conditions do not permit that land be equally divided, nor that every man be the owner of a part. When ownership of the entire area is so widely distributed among the people as to confer no excessive advantages upon any one individual, or class, thus preserving an approximate equality of opportunity to all, the conditions conform to the demands of justice and the practical requirements of industrial prosperity and social progress.

But, because a man may own land, it by no means follows that he has the right to own all he may be able to acquire. The right of the state to prescribe a limit to the ownership of a limited gift of nature is obvious; and that public policy requires the exercise of that right, in order to prevent the evils

which have grown up in Europe and are now establishing themselves in this country, appears equally clear.

Heretofore, in this country, there has always been land open
to settlement; but we are now rapidly nearing the time when
the supply of raw lands will be exhausted and all the desirable
land in the nation will be in the hands of private owners.   The
demand, which then can no longer be supplied out of an unappropriated public domain, will increase, and prices will advance;
and those who have had the misfortune to be born too late, of
parents who have failed from inability or neglect to adequately
provide for their coming, will find the task of securing a farm
one of great difficulty; and, in time, land will be wholly beyond
the reach of the common laborer.

Then the owner of land will have an obvious advantage over
him who owns none.   He will be in possession of a kind of
property for which the demand will exceed the supply, which
labor cannot create, and which no human power can increase.

The amount of unappropriated public lands available for
agricultural purposes is very much less than is commonly supposed.   It is true that there is a wide expanse of territory
reaching from the longitude of Western Kansas to California,
which, with the exception of a few spots, is unoccupied.   Owing
to the want of sufficient rainfall, there is but little of this land
which is arable without the aid of irrigation, and that which
there is is already taken and in cultivation.   Irrigation appears
to be limited to the valleys among the mountains, and those
lands which are susceptible of irrigation without great expense
are practically all occupied.   By means of expensive dams and
canals the area of irrigated land may be somewhat extended;
but the limit of the annual rainfall is such as to forbid a wide
extension of the cultivated area.   The Missouri River, which
drains a basin of five hundred and eighteen thousand square
miles, annually discharges only about one-tenth more water than
the upper Mississippi River (from the Missouri north), which
drains a basin of only one hundred and sixty-nine thousand
square miles, less than one-third the area drained by the Missouri,
which embraces three-fourths of Montana, about two-thirds of
Northern and all of Southern Dakota, three-fourths of Wyoming,
one-third of Colorado, Nebraska, part of Iowa, the northern half

of Kansas, and two-thirds of Missouri. In part of this territory, embracing Missouri, the greater part of Kansas and Nebraska, and part of Iowa, there is about the average rainfall; from this an inference may be drawn as to the remainder. A great part of the lands of both Northern and Southern Dakota, Western Nebraska, and Western Kansas, without irrigation, cannot be profitably employed for purposes of tillage, and a very small per cent. of the lands of Wyoming, Idaho, Nevada, Arizona, and New Mexico can be used for any purpose except grazing. There are rich valleys in Utah and Nevada; but the per cent. of arable land is very small. The same is true of Montana, Eastern Washington, and Oregon. The truth is, our valuable public lands are gone. What some new scheme of irrigation may accomplish it would be unsafe to predict, but I have little faith in any great addition to the amount of arable land by means of irrigation.

Mr. Josiah Strong, in "Our Country," says, "Driven from the plains east of the Rocky Mountains, the 'Great American Desert' seems to have become a fugitive and a vagabond on the face of the earth." And it is true, that if an individual travelling through this country were required to locate the "Great American Desert," he would find little choice in territory. Most any of it would make a respectable desert, or a good mountain resort. The American Desert *is* a vagabond in the great West, equally at home wherever he finds himself, on the arid plains between Kansas and the Rocky Mountains; and he appears somewhat familiar with Western Kansas.

Soon the tide of emigration will turn backward; the injustice of large ownerships will then begin to be felt, and before many years have passed will press heavily upon the common people. Then the evil will be corrected. In Great Britain land monopoly stands intrenched behind venerable titles and caste distinctions. The people, divested of power, their customs, habits of thought, social relations, and religious opinions all cast in the mould of fixed conditions, and developed through the course of many centuries of a slow-growing civilization, are slow to feel the need of new conditions unknown to their experience; and they move on in the ancient grooves. The American people, trained to independent thought, animated by the belief that the rights of all men are equal, feeling no regard for mere class distinctions, their ideas and habits of thought, their aspirations and ambitions developed and nourished in an atmosphere of universal freedom, will never consent to be shackled by conditions which they know to be unjust. They hold the ballot; when awakened to action they control legislatures; and when constitutions are in their way they alter them. But since a change must come, it is better that it begin now with conservative measures, and while we may proceed with caution. After a time the people may get in a hurry; and people in a hurry seldom do things well.

A limitation might be fixed on the amount of land one individual shall be permitted to own. I am, however, of the opinion that the operation of well-adjusted revenue laws, as suggested in the chapter on taxation, would afford the relief required. But some adequate measure should be adopted now. Large bodies of land ought not to be held, so as to enable the owners to speculate out of the advance in values which the pressure of events must soon compel.

ARTIFICIAL MONOPOLIES.

Artificial monopolies exist where an individual, by means of the employment of great wealth, or several individuals, by means of combination among themselves, restrict competition in production, or in buying or selling, and thereby fix prices of commodities either above or below the natural standard which is determined by the result of unrestricted competition. The number of natural monopolies is large; but their success in controlling or modifying the effects of competition varies according to the wealth which they may control, or the thoroughness of combination which they are able to effect.

These combinations are not necessarily, and perhaps not generally, made in the form of an express agreement. Where the number of competitors is not too large, tacit understandings are often almost as effectual as express agreements to restrain competition. But in the absence of an express agreement, or a marked effect on prices, the term monopoly is not applied. The principle is, however, the same, whether the combination be extensive and organized on the basis of an express agreement or confined to a few individuals acting with some degree of concert to promote a common object. It is a principle which cannot be eliminated from business transactions. Hence results a difficulty in the application of direct legislative remedies. One of the most powerful monopolies ever organized in this country is the Standard Oil Company, which controls almost the entire coal-oil product of the United States. In behalf of this company it is claimed that it furnishes oil to the consumer cheaper than it could otherwise be furnished. The claim may be true; and if the only question involved was a question as to the price of coal oil, this monopoly might perhaps justify itself on the plea of cheap oil. The question involved, however, is one which relates to the aggregation of wealth through an accumulation of large profits in the hands of a small number of persons, resulting in the building of immense fortunes which absorb the savings of the people. While the people are being cajoled with the assurance of cheap oil, they are being bound in fetters of iron, which they may neither break nor unloose. They are entering upon an everlasting servitude to the Crœsus in whose doubly-locked vaults are stored the gold that moves and controls a nation's commerce, who draws to himself houses and lands, and by insidious stealth robs the nation's poor.

PATENT RIGHTS.

As a means of absorbing and aggregating the wealth of the people, there have been no more potent agencies than patent rights. The evil does not lie in the mere fact that the prices of patented articles to the consumer have been high; for, as measured by the increased power of the new device or machine over the old, prices have always been low. Patented articles which sell, as measured by utility or convenience, are always cheaper than those which they displace, and it is for this reason that they supplant them. The evil lies in the power that is conferred upon the owner to aggregate wealth.

To illustrate. Suppose that A has an entire monopoly on the trade in sewing-machines, and that on each machine sold he is able to make a clear profit of twenty dollars. He sells two million machines each year for ten years. As a result, four hundred million dollars of the nation's money pass into his hands over and above what he pays out to defray the cost of manufacture and distribution. Rating the interest value of capital at six per cent., at the end of ten years A has accumulated over six hundred and fifty million dollars. The entire amount passes into his hands as money. The money leaves his hands, first, in payment for what he consumes in food, clothing, a residence, personal service, and so on. We will suppose that in this manner he expends fifty million dollars. The remaining six hundred million he may either loan on mortgage notes, or he may invest it in lands, houses, railway stocks, and mills. It is immaterial what form this vast amount of accumulated capital may assume. The result is that A owns and controls six hundred million dollars' worth of property used by other people, and for which those who use it pay him tribute. He has a permanent and rapidly-growing mortgage upon the future labor of the nation, a mortgage which can never be discharged. For how can the people pay it, so as to relieve themselves from tribute? In money? Money must not be withdrawn from circulation; and, besides, money merely expresses the obligation of the people to pay on demand so much of the products of labor. Can they pay it in foods, clothing, or personal service? A and all the non-producers dependent on him for support can consume only a small part of the annual increase. No: A has possession and absolute control of six hundred million dollars' worth of the permanent property of the country, in which alone savings can be stored, and the opportunity of the people to save and accumulate property has been diminished in that amount, and will continue to diminish in the ratio of the increase of A's fortune. The wealth of A means the dependence and the poverty of B, C, and D. Wealth, when it reaches beyond the property which the owner makes use of, lays its hands on that which must be used by other people; it means the power of one man over another.

Give to A six hundred million dollars' worth of houses and lands, and A is a millionaire; then give to every other man an equal amount, and none are rich. A could reside in but one house, and there would be no renters to occupy the others. His property would cease to bring tribute; it would cease to be power.

Great wealth is merely power centred in one man to derive revenue out of the necessities of other people. Great wealth cannot exist without corresponding poverty, any more than a king may exist without subjects, or a creditor without a debtor.

It is beyond the power of the people to pay to A the debt which they have contracted. They have bound themselves in perpetual bondage. Their ears are bored and they are servants forever.

What is the remedy? Repeal the patent laws? No: the inventor should be protected and recompensed. He should receive liberal compensation as a reward for his genius and perseverance. But he is not entitled to the earth. He is not entitled to ride forever on the back of impoverished toil. He invented a machine; the people made the market.

THE VITAL QUESTION.

The public mind is often agitated on the subject of a cheap railway service, as though it were merely a question of rates. The important question always is, What becomes of the profits? Are they distributed in the hands of a great number of consumers, or gathered and stored in the great and growing fortunes of a few? When one man accumulates a fortune of millions by depressing the values of railway stocks by ruinous competition, or skilful bad management, then by bringing up the values of stocks so depressed and restoring their values, or by manipulations of the market, the people look on with little concern. It is to them merely a battle between the bulls and the bears, in the result of which they have no concern. It is a grave mistake. After a time the people will realize that they are weighted with a burden too heavy to be borne, and they will cast it off in violence and wrath.

The shipment of cattle to foreign ports is at present under the control of a trust or syndicate of persons who control the trade and enjoy the profits. If any one outside the combination seeks to make a shipment, he finds the vessels employed in the transportation all engaged.

The meat-trade of the nation has become an overgrown monopoly, with the power to move prices up or down at will. The "Big Four" stand at the gate-way of commerce and exact their toll from producer and consumer alike. To what extent prices are affected cannot be told. The Senate committee now making ·investigation of that subject will not be able to determine. But that a few men are piling up mountains of wealth and robbing the people of their inheritance we already know.

Though the price of cattle and hogs to the producer be not lowered, and though the price of meat to the consumer be not raised, a few are enjoying opportunities that should be the common privileges of many, and building fortunes that can serve no purpose but to lay the people under tribute to themselves and those who shall succeed them. When the rich grow richer, the poor grow poorer. The figures that stand in *bas-relief* on the face of the embossed shield may be traced in corresponding depressions on the other side.

Statesmen should concern themselves less about the price of pork and beef and more about the absorbing power of aggregated wealth. The profits of trade, widely distributed, furnish continuing opportunities for the growth of those small accumulations of wealth which make provision for sickness and old age and dependent children, and furnish opportunities for the culture that refines and purifies social life,—fortunes the incomes from which are returned to the people again in exchange for the products of labor,—small reservoirs giving out a steady supply, emptied and replenished again from the ever-flowing stream of trade. But when the golden stream of profit is poured into the Dead Sea of a millionaire's fortune, there is no outward flow.

The number of persons engaged in trade and transportation, aside from banking, insurance, and newspapers, as shown by the census of 1880, was 1,700,385. Of these, 1,122,481 were engaged in trade, and 557,904 were employed in transportation. The cost of transportation added to commissions and the percentage of merchants amounts to about fifty per cent. of the value of the product distributed. The number of persons engaged in transportation is not in excess of the number required for this service. But the number of persons engaged in trade is much in excess of the number necessary.

It is a common delusion that competition always tends to reduce prices. In trade it is necessary for each merchant to obtain a profit sufficient to pay rents, interest on capital, cost of advertising, and clerk hire, and to furnish a living for himself and family. These are fixed charges, which cannot be avoided, and which increase as trade is subdivided. Therefore, while the direct effect of competition in trade is to lower prices, after a certain point has been passed the tendency is to maintain prices above the necessary cost of distribution. The evil, however, which grows out of this tendency is not of serious consequence. A far greater evil is the monopoly of trade by persons or corporations of great wealth.

The fierce competition in trade is a war at the expense of the consumer, and from which the consumer does not always derive sufficient advantage to pay the cost of the war. It is a competition in which the strong destroy the weak; a competition in which cunning schemes and petty deceits are most effective weapons.

The skill of the mechanic is exercised in perfecting and adding value to the product of his labor. The skill of the merchant is employed in contesting with his neighbor for a larger share of trade. The skill of the mechanic creates property; the skill of the merchant increases his own share of profit chiefly at the expense of his competitor.

It is true that the people may be better served by an intelligent and competent merchant; they may also suffer loss from the superior skill of the successful merchant. Skill in trade is not always to their advantage. The skilful angler who catches the most fish is a more useful man than his shrewd companion who outwits him in dividing the string.

The large accumulations of middle-men are not always the rewards of a proportionate service rendered the people, but are often only the measure of the ability of the merchant to help himself. The risks of trade, against which the merchant insures himself by large profits at the expense of the consumer, are often the results of manipulations in the interest of capital. Speculation, disguised under the name of "enterprise," is everywhere, with its hands in the pockets of the people gathering together hoards of wealth.

Gambling on boards of trade, in stocks or in provisions, is a public evil loudly condemned by religious teachers and theoretic moralists because of the "sin" of it. The sin, however, is not ordinarily apparent to laymen, few of whom would be restrained by scruples of conscience from engaging in this form of speculation could they feel assured of success. Public opinion on this subject is loud-mouthed rather than earnest. The evil is respectable and does not shock the public conscience.

Speculation enters into most business transactions, and is considered legitimate, since it is unavoidable. It is not, however, productive of good to society, and pure speculation unconnected with the transaction of legitimate business is unnecessary. It creates nothing, and is employed solely as a means of aggregating wealth. It is at war with a sound social economy. The evil lies in the fact that it disturbs actual values along the lines of legitimate trade; that it demoralizes the people and builds up colossal fortunes. It should be assailed on economic grounds, as an enemy of labor, and suppressed by legislative restrictions. It is a waste of words to condemn men who deal in futures and corner markets. Their conduct may afford a theme for the rhetorician, but it does not shock the public conscience. This evil cannot be successfully assailed from the stand-point of religion or morality; it must be dealt with as a question of economics which concerns the material welfare of the people. Trade monopolies might perhaps be successfully dealt with by means of a progressive tax upon gross sales above a certain amount, or by the employment of graded income taxes. When, however, the public is fully awakened to the wrongs which are perpetrated in the name of "business," and to the extent of the injury to the working-people, no great difficulty will be experienced in discovering and applying adequate remedies.

The people must learn that great wealth is necessarily a monopoly, and that the right to limit the extent of trade that may be controlled by any one individual belongs to the people who furnish the market.

Every State constitution should be so amended as to leave the power in the Legislature, restrained by judicious limitations, to employ taxation as a means of restricting monopolies, and the growing aggregation of wealth.

TRUSTS.

Trusts are combinations of capitalists engaged in manufacture, trade, or transportation, by means of which the profits or products of each are divided upon some agreed basis, for the purpose of regulating and restricting competition. There are many combinations entered into for this purpose, without any sharing of common profits. Sometimes the combination effects its purpose by arbitrarily fixing prices, and sometimes by restricting production. But, aside from such combinations, capital engaged in production is always careful to gauge its product to the effective demand.

In many branches of manufacturing industry the capacity to produce greatly exceeds the demand. For instance, during the census year of 1880, blast-furnaces were in operation, on an average, but eight months out of twelve; and the steel-furnaces were run, on an average, but nine months during the year. During the year 1886, seventy-five per cent. of the coal-miners in Illinois were employed but one-half the time. The Massachusetts census of 1885 shows that the capacity of the manufacturing establishments in that State was equal to the advantageous employment of 438,229 hands; yet the total of the highest number employed in each industry, at times of the largest employment, was but 304,159, while the lowest number employed was but 177,381; showing that, during part of the year, the working-force was curtailed nearly fifty per cent. below the number of highest employment.

In gauging the number of its working-force, capital necessarily consults its own interest. It is by this means that prices of manufactured goods are kept steady and maintained at a figure sufficient to yield a good margin of profit.

In agriculture, where worker and capitalist are generally combined in the same person, where production is subdivided among over four million farmers, no such power to regulate the quantity of product exists. The amount of the product varies from year to year, and prices fluctuate over a wide range varying as much as fifty per cent. within the limit of two or three years.

The manufacturer employs his labor at stated wages, and makes his product out of materials which he purchases. He is therefore under the necessity of keeping within the demand of the market, at prices sufficient to cover a fixed cost of production. When the prices of farm produce go unexpectedly low, the farmer, who, relatively, hires but little labor, deducts the loss from his own wages, which are not paid until the product is sold, and are represented by the price received.

If, in manufacturing, the price of labor and materials yielded promptly to a fall in price of product, and consisted merely of a certain proportion of the price received for the product, this absolute necessity for restricting production would not exist. But the manufacturer buys both his labor and materials at a stated price. They cost him, on an average of the industries, about three-fifths of the value of the finished product. The cost of materials and labor must be paid, no matter what price the product may bring. We have here one of the effects of the subdivision of labor and of the severance of the interests of capitalist and worker.

This necessity, which controls manufacturing industries, com pels a frequent curtailing of the working-force, and leads to frequent suspensions.

The amount of manufactured product is not dependent upon the seasons, or other like circumstance, that affect the agricultural product; and the employer of capital gauges his product according to the market,—not according to the demand at *some* price, but according to the demand at the figure which he fixes as his selling price.

This power over production, necessary for the protection of capital, is employed to maintain or to advance prices, and is subject to constant abuse.

It is to the common interest of all classes that labor be universally and constantly employed, and that the total product should be as large as it can be made, or as large at least as can be consumed. But it is important that labor be properly distributed and that production in each industry be relatively large. If this condition could be established and maintained, there would be no occasion for poverty, except as the result of accident, disease, or wilful idleness. But under the conditions which actually prevail, poverty is unavoidable; it is a necessary result of the present industrial arrangement.

While industry in general is most prosperous when production is greatest, provided there be at the same time an equilibrium of production between the industries,—that is, a production in each industry relatively large,—yet any particular industry, by restricting its production, and thereby enhancing the value of its product, may gain at the expense of the other industries.

Let the number 100 represent the product of the cotton-goods industry that may be sold for an amount which covers a fair margin of profit, and which we will also designate as 100. Now, if this total product be reduced to 90, the price of cotton goods will advance, the supply having fallen below the demand at the old price. A product of 90 will not only bring a higher price, but the total value may be more than that of a product of 100. But if the product be increased to 110, the price will fall, and the total value of the whole may be less than 100. Thus the margin of profit may be increased by restricting production. What is true of one industry is true of every other industry. The principle here illustrated is well understood.

There is, therefore, at all times, independent of express combinations, a strong tendency towards the restriction of the product. The manufacturer of cotton goods is on the alert to maintain prices and to prevent the market from being overstocked. He employs only the labor required to meet the demand at certain prices; the manufacturer of woollen goods does the same. If the demand weakens, he reduces his working-force. Men out of employment must limit their consumption; consumption being reduced, weakens the demand. Thus, as production is restricted at all points, the demand is likewise restricted, and the contest between capitalists, to preserve the margin of profit, has the effect to reduce the demand for their product. The workers who are thrown out of employment, crowded out of the circle of production and distribution, are kept out, because there is no demand for more product; and there is no demand for more product for the reason that labor is unemployed and unable to supply its wants.

Formerly, when the amount of capital required to make labor available was small, and most workers were their own employers, creating their product and getting their wages out of the price that product brought in the market, the present condition was not possible. Labor distributed itself through the several industries according to a demand which was steady and subject to only slight vacillations; and the product of one industry was not liable to a sudden increase out of proportion to the products of other industries. The employment of machinery run by steam, combined with the use of large amounts of capital in single establishments, has brought about a condition leading to frequent disturbance of the equilibrium of the industries, and making the worker dependent upon the interests of aggregated wealth which now controls production.

The worker can no longer employ himself. He must find an employer or lie idle. The interests of the employer compel him to limit his production; and, in the contest to maintain prices, large numbers of working-men are kept out of employment. The less competent are the ones who suffer most; and since, relatively, there must always be a weaker class, that class must bear the principal burden of competition, and many are continually pressed to the extremes of poverty. One individual may rise above his class; but some other person is crowded into the place he leaves vacant. As a class, the poor are powerless to extricate themselves from the condition made for them by agencies over which they have no control. They are a product of our industrial civilization. They are the victims of a fate from which they cannot escape. Paupers are the industrial correlatives of millionaires.

The prevention of trusts and combinations, it will be seen, while it may remedy, cannot eradicate the evil. The problem is one of extreme difficulty, requiring time for solution. But when the theory that capital can do no wrong, and that all competition is legitimate, is abandoned, and the idea of promoting the welfare of the working-people takes control of legislation, the way will be opened; there will be light enough to mark the pathway to each advancing step. What is most needed now is a clear understanding of the causes of existing evils. If, in addition to remedies of a general character, suggested elsewhere, more special legislation be required, no insurmountable obstacle will be met with. The principal obstruction that stands in the way of remedial measures is the lack of knowledge among working-men of the causes of industrial evils.

The doctrine that "whatever is is right," so persistently maintained by writers on economic science, has been generally acquiesced in, if not sanctioned; but working-people must learn that labor and capital have interests that conflict as well as interests in common, and that legislation whose policy is shaped by representatives of aggregated wealth alone is not always best adapted to promote the welfare of the people.

The conditions of industrial oppression which prevail in all old countries, where, with great wealth in the hands of a comparatively small number, the masses are deprived of all opportunity to gain a competence, and many are unable to obtain the ordinary comforts of life, is proof enough that the wheels of evolution need to be lifted out of the old ruts.

CHAPTER X.

WHAT MAKES THE RATE OF WAGES.

WRITERS on political science have devoted considerable space to abstract reasonings regarding the "law" of wages, in search of a definite and concise formula for the expression of that law, with the result that cheap generalizations, arrayed in the uniform of so-called scientific thought, have been successfully paraded as "laws" of economic science.

Of this order is the wage-fund theory, until recently quite generally accepted and adopted by even as profound a writer as John Stuart Mill. The theory is that wages are paid out of a certain limited fund, which consists of the amount of capital which, at any one time, may be devoted to the purchase of labor; and that therefore the rate of wages depends upon the ratio of the number of workers to the amount of capital devoted to their payment. Mill says, "Wages depend, then, on the proportion between the number of the laboring population and the capital or other funds devoted to the purchase of labor;" and again, "Since, therefore, the rate of wages which results from competition distributes the whole wage-fund among the whole laboring population, if law or opinion succeeds in fixing wages above this rate, some laborers are kept out of employment; and, as it is not the intention of the philanthropists that these should starve, they must be provided for by a forced increase of the wage-fund by compulsory saving."

This theory has been exposed to elaborate analysis by different writers, who have made plain its fallacy. It has ceased to be of interest except as a part of the history of the growth of the science of political economy. It is difficult, however, to comprehend how an able student and author like Mill could fall into an error so transparent.

Ricardo, speaking on the subject of wages, says, "The natural price of labor depends on the price of food, necessaries, and the conveniences required for the support of the laborer; so that with a rise in the price of food and necessaries the price of labor will rise, and with a fall in the price the natural price of labor will fall."

Dr. Wayland says, "By free competition wages are adjusted to the ratio between the amount of capital seeking labor and the number of laborers seeking employment; competition itself being modified by some regard to the cost of living, the productiveness of industry, established custom, and the promptings of good-will between man and man." Speaking of demands of workers for higher wages, he says, "A claim is reasonable when the necessities of the laborers require, and the actual profits of the industry permit, the increase of wages or what of better terms is insisted on."

It will be observed that the theory here advanced is that the worker is not entitled to anything beyond what his necessities require. A claim to that much is reasonable, when the profits of the industry are sufficient to justify it. The claims of the horse to his keep, and the working-man to his subsistence, it will be seen, are, in the eyes of political economists, defined according to the same rule.

Professor Walker, who rejects the wage-fund theory, and recognizes the obvious fact that wages are a portion of the product created by labor by which the wages are said to be earned, seeks to define a rule or law by which the proportionate amount due to labor and the proportionate amount due to capital may be determined. He makes a new application of Ricardo's law of rent, and constructs a sort of metaphysical mitre-box, by the aid of which the total product may be cut in two at the right place and at the proper angle.

Ricardo's law of rent appears to be a formula devised as a justification of the rapacity of landlords. Concisely stated it is: "The rent of land is determined by the excess of its produce over that which the same application can secure from the least productive land in use." Assuming that, from the effect of competition, wages, as well as profits on capital, are necessarily reduced to the same level, this rent theory would be true. It is, however, only approximately true; and as a rule of practical application it is misleading. Take, for instance, agricultural lands. Here is one section of country where the lands are poor and unproductive. Such lands may be occupied in large bodies for grazing purposes, deficiency in quality being made up in quantity. But we will suppose that portions of this poor land are used for tillage, and occupied by poor people who obtain a mean and precarious subsistence; near by may be fertile lands many times as productive. According to the theory of Ricardo, the renter of the fertile land, after paying his rent, would have nothing left above the mean subsistence of the people on the poor lands near by. Yet every person of observation knows that tenants or renters on the most productive land fare much better than those on poor lands. If the theory were true as a practical rule of action, an individual about to rent a farm would need feel little concern about the fertility of the soil, since all above a certain stated amount would belong to the landlord. The average reward of agricultural workers varies greatly, within the limits of short distances. In one part of a country lands will be quite thoroughly cultivated, which will not yield one-half the reward to labor that is enjoyed by renters in other sections of the country. People adapt themselves to surrounding conditions, among which is the measure of the soil's fertility. In the same neighborhood, the better tenant gets the best lands; and, while it is true that there always is a strong pressure forcing the wages of labor of any class to the level of the demands of the most im-

poverished members of that class, there is also a strong counter-
tendency. But this theory of rent approximates the truth so
nearly that it should be regarded as a most sufficient reason for
the adoption of such policy of legislation as will tend to the
abolition of landlordism. The use which political economists
are accustomed to make of Ricardo's law of rent is to demonstrate the fitness of things as they now exist.

Professor Walker's theory of wages and profits is that, in a
state of perfect competition, the profits of the manufacturer are
not deducted from the wages of the mechanic, any more than
rent is obtained through a deduction from the prices of agricultural labor. He holds that profits are measured from the
level of those employers who receive no profit, as rents are
measured from the limit of the product of those lands which
yield no profit, and embrace the whole excess of the product of
the more valuable lands over the product of the poorest lands
in cultivation; so he holds that profits embrace that excess of
product, created by the exceptional skill or opportunities of employers, over the amount of product which is created with the
same amount of labor, by that class of employers who are able
to produce nothing beyond the amount required to pay wages,
or who, in other words, make no profit.

To illustrate: The demand for woollen fabrics is of a certain
degree of intensity. To supply this demand industry is organized, under the requisite number of employers of labor, and
capital, or *entrepreneurs*, as Professor Walker terms them, who
will naturally be of different degrees of capacity; those of the
lowest capacity will be able to make no profits at all, or at most
a meagre living for themselves and families, amounting only to
a moderate compensation for their work as managers. As the
demand may increase, and thereby push prices of the product
upward, still other and lower grades of *entrepreneurs* will be
brought into the field of production, until the no-profit line is
again reached by the lowest grade of *entrepreneurs*. Since the
same wages must be paid by all employers, the part of the product that remains, after paying wages of the workers and cost
of maintaining capital, will represent profits; and the quantity
of this product that remains to the credit of profit, under the
management of the most skilful *entrepreneur*, will be measured

by the excess of product, under his management, over the amount of product created by the least skilful *entrepreneur* who makes no profit; in short, the profit of each *entrepreneur* will, like any other quantity, be measured by its excess over nothing, —ten is ten more than nothing. It will be seen that Professor Walker's reasoning is verified by the result, which corresponds with a most familiar principle of elementary mathematics.

But, to permit him to explain his own theory: "The price of manufactured goods of any particular description is determined by the cost of production of that portion of the supply which is produced at the greatest disadvantage. If the demand for such goods is so great as to require a certain amount to be produced under the management and control of persons whose efficiency in organizing and supervising the forces of labor and capital is small, the cost of production of that portion of the stock will be large, and the price will be correspondingly high; yet, high as it is, it will not be high enough to yield to the *entrepreneurs* of this grade any more than that scant and difficult subsistence which we have taken as the no-profit line. The price at which these goods are to be sold, however, will determine the price of the whole supply, since, in any one market, at any one time, there is but one price for different portions of the same commodity. Hence, whatever the cost of those portions of the supply which are produced by *entrepreneurs* of higher industrial grade, they will command the same price as those portions which are produced at the greatest disadvantage. The difference so measured will go as profits to each individual *entrepreneur*, according to his own success in production, whether that be due to exceptional abilities or to exceptional opportunities, or to both in one proportion or another."

Professor Walker, therefore, concludes that profits do not come out of wages. The no-profit employers must pay sufficient to hire laborers, and the wages of these laborers constitute an essential part of the cost of production. The *entrepreneurs* of the higher grades will pay the same wages,—"they will clearly pay no less, they need pay no more."

This is a somewhat circuitous statement of the industrial fact that, whatever remains to the employer, after paying the wages of his employés at the customary rates, may be set apart as profit. And if by reason of superior skill, or because of exceptional opportunity, this remainder be large, his profit will be large; if small, his profit will be small. The amount of his profit depends on competition. If there be numerous competitors possessing a high degree of skill, and equal opportunities, the profit will be less; if he be without competition, he may advance his prices and his profit will be large.

I admit that the relative profits of different *entrepreneurs* are measured in accordance with the theory here advanced; in short, the ratio of profits is determined by the ratio of capacity and opportunity. Yet I am unable to perceive in this elaborately-stated theory a solution of any practical question in economic science. It does not therefore follow, as claimed, that the working-man has no cause for complaint. The fact is not, as assumed, that profits are the measure of skill in production. The larger profits are to be accounted for in many ways. There are, first, the advantages of large aggregations of capital, by which a larger volume of business is controlled in proportion to the expense of management and cost of distribution. Second, there are the advantages of established trade which enable a manufacturer to shape his product to the requirements of known demands, and dispose of his goods with little delay and at fair prices, and at the minimum cost of getting such goods on the market. This is not skill in production, but the skill of the merchant in promoting his individual interests. Third, there are the advantages which, as suggested by Mr. Carnegie, are not the least, "of those economies which are exercised by the employer in the rate of wages paid to labor." Large profits are the result, in great degree, of economy in getting the best labor for the particular work done at the lowest prices, and in getting the largest amount of work for the smallest pay.

The rate of wages in two factories may be the same; but the skill of employés in the one is often of a higher order, work is pushed with greater energy, and less time is lost by the workers.

There is no lack of competent managers who may be brought into the field. And it is not true that the degree of competence of the most unsuccessful *entrepreneurs* is a measure of the demand for the product. There will always be some managers who make little or no profit, or who even lose the capital invested, continuing in business for a time, until their competency is tested, and until competent persons may be found and selected to take their places. In the adjustment of men to their proper positions in the industries it must be that there will be those who for a time occupy positions they are not competent to fill.

For the purpose of a starting-point Dr. Walker locates an *entrepreneur* at the no-profit line, on the theory that a manager of the assumed grade is put in such position by force of the demand and from necessity, there being a lack of efficient managers; whereas, in fact, the no-profit manager in charge of any considerable amount of capital and labor is only a temporary accident; but he is able to hold his position longer than he otherwise might by reason of low wages, which are in part the result of the "economies" of the skilful *entrepreneur* in securing labor without equitable compensation.

It is not true that "the price of manufactured goods of any particular description is determined by the cost of production of that portion of the supply which is produced at the greatest disadvantage." The price of any product is the resultant effect of many economic forces. The total amount of the supply, as measured against the demand, is the most potent factor operating directly in determining prices. To say that any particular part of a total product determines the price of the whole is to mistake the fact of a correspondence between price and amount of wages paid for a cause. In a business, where some must fail while others succeed, there will always be a point somewhere along the line where the amount of wages paid in production corresponds with the commercial value of the product.

The position of Dr. Walker appears to be this: If there be found an *entrepreneur* running a woollen-mill over in Connecticut, who takes advantage of women and children by paying them but a niggardly pittance for their labor, and who practises various other mean economies to the disadvantage of his employés, who yet, being a stupid fellow, succeeds merely in making a subsistence for himself and family, then every manager of a woollen-mill in the whole country is justified in paying his employés the same rate of wages, and subjecting them to the same mean exactions, and pocketing the profits, no matter how large they may be; and working-people have no right to complain; for, says Dr. Walker, "Why, in equity or in economics, should a laborer who works for a strong, prudent, and skilful master receive higher wages than one whose fortune it is to work for a vacillating, purblind, inefficient, or reckless *entrepreneur ?*"

In short, if there be one miserable ruffian in town who kicks his dog, every good citizen is justified in administering to his own dog the same rude treatment, *since one dog has no right to greater consideration than any other dog.*

A more pitiful exhibition of that heartless indifference to the interests of the working-people, which pervades the theories of political economists who hold it their mission to defend the existing order, will not be found in any treatise on economic science.

Mr. Attgeld, in "Live Questions," speaking of the wages of women and girls in certain manufacturing establishments in the city of Chicago, says, "They are at starvation's edge, and they never get below that in Europe. For example, two, three, and four dollars per week, and board oneself, for ten hours' toil a day. So, the wages paid in the cigar manufactories and other establishments of the East, as shown by congressional investigation now in progress, are below what is possible for an American to live on. . . . It is almost the lowest European standard. Establishments that used to pay ten dollars a week to American laborers now pay three or four dollars to imported Europeans for doing the same work. It is true that all establishments do not employ imported laborers, but enough do to fix the standard of wages. If only a few establishments in the same line get their work done for four dollars a week by foreigners, this will become the standard all along the line, even in houses employing Americans, for the latter cannot pay ten dollars and compete with the former; and as it has been shown that there is scarcely a line of industry in which these imported laborers have not been introduced, it follows that the standard of wages has been largely fixed by what these imported people will work for.

" For years we have heard of the Italians, Poles, Hungarians, etc., who were imported constantly into Pennsylvania, and in many cases where these people refused to submit to further reduction of wages they were simply discharged, and their places filled with fresh importations. So that now Mr. Powderly claims that almost all American citizens, both native-born and naturalized, have been driven out of the mines and manufacturing establishments of that great State."

We see here, as an evident effect of the ignorance, poverty, and dependence, and an established habit of mean living, of a class of laborers, a low rate of wages, not to themselves only, but to other laborers who come in competition with them.

It is to such conditions that Professor Walker would have the American working-man resign himself, as to a decree of providence; because he is able to make it clear, by the application of a logical formula, that such must be the result of unrestrained competition.

The fixing of the wages of an individual worker, or of a class of workers, is a part of the complex general adjustment of the wages of all classes of workers in the various industries by which are produced all the commodities exchanged in the common market. The wages of a class, or of an individual even, cannot be changed without affecting the adjustment of the whole. Wages, though first paid in money, are finally and truly paid in commodities or products. For this reason wages are not readily changed, except within the narrow limits allowed by those oscillations which disturb values, and which are occasioned by variations in the supply of natural products, fashion, and temporary over- or under-production of particular commodities.

Wages, therefore, may not be arbitrarily fixed by the contracting parties. But wages in a particular industry may be slowly and gradually pushed up or down, and related conditions and values will adjust themselves accordingly.

To illustrate. Let the total product of all the industries of a nation be represented by one hundred. Let us then assume labor to be divided into five different classes, though the divisions in fact are as numerous as the various occupations; and, besides, workers may be classed also with reference to intelligence and indigence or independence. But to simplify the illustration, we will divide the workers into five classes.

Let us suppose, in the first instance, that one-tenth part of the product is set apart as the share of capital, and that the remaining ninety parts are equally divided among the five classes of workers. This will make the share of each class eighteen.

The statement will stand:

Share of capital	10
Share of Class 1 workers	18
" " " 2 "	18
" " " 3 "	18
" " " 4 "	18
" " " 5 "	18
Total product	100

Now, if, without increasing the product, we increase the wages of Class 1 of the workers thirty-three and one-third per cent., and of Class 2, sixteen and one-third per cent., it is evident that the increase in the wages of Classes 1 and 2 must be drawn either from capital or from the other classes of workers. But an increase in wages reduces but little, if at all, the aggregate profits of capital.

The gain of Classes 1 and 2 will be at the expense of the other classes, and the statement will stand:

Share of capital	10
Share of Class 1 workers	24
" " " 2 "	21
" " " 3 "	15
" " " 4 "	15
" " " 5 "	15
Total product	100

We have here assumed, what is not in fact true, that the shares of Classes 3, 4, and 5 would be equally affected by the increased wages of Classes 1 and 2. The other classes would be unequally affected, according to the direction of the pressure and the difference in capacity to resist reduction.

If we now increase the share of capital, the increase will be drawn from the shares of labor, and the loss to labor will, in the end, so adjust itself as to fall principally on the most help-. less class. After the competing forces have had free play in adjustment of wages, we will suppose the following statement to represent the result.

Share of capital	15
Share of Class 1 workers	25
" " " 2 "	21
" " " 3 "	16
" " " 4 "	13
" " " 5 "	10
Total product	100

So far we have supposed the product to remain the same, and we have disregarded money as a medium of exchange and measure of wages.

In the beginning the wages of Classes 4 and 5 amounted to thirty-six per cent. of the product, and they were therefore consumers of that proportion. Their shares having been reduced to ten and thirteen respectively, they now consume but twenty-three per cent. of the product. The demand therefore has, in this direction, been reduced in the amount of thirteen per cent. by reason of reduced consumption, and in another direction increased in like amount by the increased consumption of other classes.

This increased consumption would be, necessarily, to a great extent, not only of a different class, but of a different grade or quality of articles. And, the industries of a whole people having adjusted themselves to the conditions arising out of this division of the product, the shares of the several classes of workers are fixed by the conditions and habits of a whole people, and an increase of wages in any department involves the necessity of a change in these conditions and habits.

The division of the product is not made direct, as we have assumed, but through or by means of the employment of money as a measure of values and a medium of exchange. Money is employed first in the payment of wages, and second in the purchase of commodities. The completed payment is not effected until labor has been paid for in the products of other labor.

Capital, whose immediate interest, in order to maintain its margin of profit, is to purchase labor at the lowest price for which it may be procured in money, exerts a continual pressure in the direction of lower wages.

The total product in the United States might be readily increased, say, twenty-five per cent.; and there might be a considerable reduction in the consumption of articles of luxury and a corresponding increase of other classes of products. But consumption is measured by wages, and consumption must keep pace with production.

Increasing production without increasing wages in corresponding ratio reduces prices, and falling prices are resisted by restricted production. If the wages and the consumption of Class 5 could be simultaneously advanced to eighteen, absorbing the increased product, there would need be no change in prices of commodities if the increase in product corresponding with the increase of wages did not exceed eight per cent. In this event the workers would gain and no one would lose.

The competition which prevents this represents the struggle of individuals for immediate personal gain at the expense of the interests of the community in general. Half a dozen large manufacturing establishments engaged in the manufacture of ready-made clothing, for instance, each seeking the largest possible immediate gain, and finding opportunity in the general helplessness and dependence of a large class of sewing-women, may push prices of labor in that department down to or below the equivalent of the measure of the actual necessaries of life. Competing establishments must manufacture as cheaply or lose their trade, and thus the selfish greed of a few may fix the compensation of great numbers of working-people. By this course the general market for labor is restricted to the extent of the reduced capacity of these poorly-paid workers to buy the commodities of labor which they would desire to consume, and the community gains nothing. The community is abundantly able and willing to pay these workers liberally in food, clothing, and shelter; but the system of exchange, under the pressure of that selfish competition in which each endeavors to advance his own interests at the expense of society, prevents it.

The existence among the poorly-paid classes of numbers of those whose tastes are uncultivated, and whose wants are few, who have little ambition, or who, from that necessity which attends an impoverished condition, are compelled to accept what is offered, strongly operates to fix the status of the entire class of workers of whom they constitute a part, both as to wages and condition in life.

Those combinations of labor which sustain and advance the wages of Classes 1 and 2 are necessarily more or less at the expense of Classes 4 and 5, who, because of their numbers, their ignorance, and their poverty, or because of the competition of an indigent and helpless minority among themselves, are unable to contend against the competing forces that oppose them.

While, therefore, it is not true that all employers of labor, who pay wages that are too low, are responsible for the fact that the workers in their employ are inadequately compensated, since the employers are subject to conditions fixed by others, it is true that the greed of many who employ labor is responsible for the hard conditions that are forced upon large numbers of working-people.

While those who control capital cannot pay what they choose, they can, if they have in general the disposition to be just, assist poorly-compensated working-people in a gradual advance to fair wages, or, what is the same thing, to a reasonable share of the total product. They can at least refuse to lend weight to the downward pressure; and they can lend their assistance to those gradual changes of condition essential to a proper adjustment of the several shares of workers and capital.

Mr. Henry George, following in the wake of the illumined streak poured from the bull's-eye lantern of his logic, explores the realms of economic abstractions, and discovers in the mists the following:

"The relation between wages and interest is determined by the average power of increase which attaches to capital from its use in reproductive modes. As rent arises, interest will fall as wages fall, or will be determined by the margin of cultivation."

This formula, subjected to a careful assay, will be found to contain these general truths: First, as profits of capital in general increase, the rate of interest tends to advance; as profits diminish, the rate of interest is reduced. Second, as rent advances, interest and wages both go down. Neither of these propositions are universally true, and the latter is not generally true. When profits are large, neither the landlord nor the money-lender fails to secure a liberal share; when profits are small, they must both be content with less. There are conditions, such as the limited area of land suitable for the purpose for which it is required or the scarcity of capital, that affect the relative shares of the lender of money, the landlord, and the worker; but these conditions cannot be exhibited within the compass of a formula. Propositions like this, made up by the mere juxtaposition of related truths, afford little aid in the solution of economic questions.

Of a somewhat similar character is a proposition announced by Bastiat, and quoted by other writers on political economy, and recently by Mr. Atkinson, who says that, by its application, he has been able to observe the phenomena of wages with much clearer insight. It is as follows:

"In proportion to the increase of capital the absolute share of the total product falling to the capitalist is augmented, but his relative share is diminished; while, on the contrary, the share of the laborer is increased both absolutely and relatively."

Generalizations of this character, declaring the concurrence of certain phenomena, without the exhibition of any principle of sequence, or philosophy of relation, may be manufactured at will; and, possessing the quality of ponderosity, are frequently accorded recognition as principles of science.

Let us examine the proposition just quoted from Bastiat. We are met at once by the question, What is here meant by "the increase of capital?" If, by this expression, is meant simply an increase in the quantity of the tools, machinery, and materials employed in agriculture and manufacture, and of the store of food and clothing on hand to maintain the worker, we have one meaning; if credits are embraced, we have another; and if by increase of capital is meant not only the actual increase, but also that aggregation of wealth which is generally included in the description "an increase of capital," we have still a third meaning. Taken in the latter sense, the proposition is not true.

From British statistics, as given by Mulhall, we learn that in 1688, when the gentry and middle classes of Great Britain together comprised one-tenth of the population, this one-tenth enjoyed four-tenths, or forty per cent., of the total amount of the incomes of the British nation. In 1800 these classes together constituted twelve-hundredths of the population; they then enjoyed thirty-seven per cent. of the amount of total income; in 1883 these classes remained relatively the same as in 1800, but enjoyed forty-five per cent. of the total income; showing that from 1800 to 1883 the relative share of capitalists had increased. In 1800 the working-people (not including trades-people) were less than two-thirds of the whole population; their share of the total earnings was a fraction over one-third of the total earnings; in 1883 their number had relatively increased a very little, but their share of the total earnings had not kept pace,—we may say, in round numbers, that the proportion of numbers and earnings had remained the same; yet the proportionate increase of wealth was fifty per cent. greater than the increase of population. These statistics do not take into account the much larger proportion of earnings, or of production by means of domestic manufacture, in 1800, that are not counted in the estimate of earnings.

Nor is it true that, in the United States, the proportionate share of earnings, absorbed by capital in the form of profits, interest, and rents, has grown smaller, or that the proportionate share of the worker has grown larger.

It is true that, with the wonderful development in our industries and increase in the productive capacity of labor, the average earnings *per capita* have increased. It is also true that the worker has become more dependent, that the number of those whose living is precarious and the number who are exposed to penury and extreme want have increased absolutely and relatively. The proportion of those without homes has increased and is still increasing.

It is not claimed that capital absorbs all the increase of the products of labor. But capital is absorbing the principal portion of the *savings or durable products of labor;* and the aggregation of wealth in the ownership of a relatively small number of persons is rapidly bringing the American people to the condition of European people, and is making impracticable that general distribution of wealth which is essential to the prosperity and happiness and to the moral and social well-being of the people of this country.

Against the increase of capital there is no complaint. The objection lies to the undue aggregation of wealth, and to the subordination of production to the purpose of building fortunes for a few at the expense of interrupted industry, unemployed working-men, and the oppression of a large and growing class of helpless and dependent poor. If it were true that the average earnings of a working-man are sufficient, the fact that there are large numbers whose compensation is neither adequate nor just still remains. Justice is not satisfied with general averages.

It is no answer to the claims of the working-people to say that the earnings of labor have increased, and are more now than formerly.

There are admitted evils. It is not the principal duty of political economists to hunt excuses for them; their efforts should be expended rather in seeking the cause and the remedies.

It is not the purpose of this chapter to formulate a "law" of wages or a "law" of profits. The statement of the principle or causes by which the relative shares of capital and labor are determined, and the definite results of their operation, can no more be compressed within the limits of an economic formula than the law which determines the force of the wind or the height of a wave. Wages constitute one part of the product of labor, profits of capital another part. The relative sizes of these shares are the resultant action of many conflicting forces. What these forces are, the influences that limit and control them, and determine their power and intensity, I have sought to make clear in the several chapters of this book. The purpose of this chapter is to exhibit the tenor of doctrines held by writers of acknowledged merit on economic science.

As an author whose views have had much influence in shaping modern doctrines of political economy, T. R. Malthus, A.M., who wrote in 1803, holds prominent place. The following quotations from his writings indicate their tenor:

"The increase of population is necessarily limited by the means of subsistence.

"Population invariably increases when the means of subsistence increases, unless prevented by powerful and obvious checks. These checks, and the checks which keep population down to the level of means of subsistence, are moral restraint, vice, and misery. It has appeared from the inevitable laws of human nature some human beings will be exposed to want. These are the unhappy persons who, in the great lottery of life, have drawn a blank."

He quotes approvingly Arthur Young, as follows: "If you would see a district with as little distress as is consistent with the political system of the old government of France, you must assuredly go where there are no little proprietors at all. You must visit the great farms in Beauce, Picardy, part of Normandy, and Artois, and there you will find no more population than what is regularly employed and regularly paid; and if in such districts you should, contrary to the rule, meet with much distress, it is twenty to one but that it is in a parish which has some commons, which tempt the poor to have cattle, to have property, in consequence misery. When you are engaged in this political tour, finish by seeing England, and I will show you a set of peasants well clothed, well nourished, tolerably drunken from superfluity, well lodged and at their ease; and yet among them not one in a thousand has either land or cattle."

Malthus, continuing, says, "The specific cause of the poverty and misery of the lower classes of people in France and Ireland is that by the extreme subdivision of the property in the one country, and the facility of obtaining a cabin and potatoes in the other, a population is brought into existence *which is not demanded by the quantity of capital and employment* in the country. And the consequence of which must necessarily, therefore, be . . . to lower in general the price of labor by too great competition, from which must result complete indigence to those who cannot find employment, and incomplete subsistence even to those who can.

"The desirable thing, with a view to the happiness of the common people, seemed to be that their habitual food should be dear, and their wages regulated by it; but that in scarcity or other occasional distress, the cheaper food should be readily and cheerfully adopted."

The idea that the poverty of the Irish people is caused by the facility for getting cabins and potatoes, rather than by the want of facility for getting anything better, has the genuine ring of classically orthodox political economy.

CHAPTER XI.

THE profits of capital in the same field of competition, whether invested in one industry or many, tend to a common level. Capital always seeks that form of investment affording the largest returns with the least risk of loss; and, when readily convertible into money, it flows from one industry to another until an equilibrium is attained. Such is the universal tendency, checked and restrained by the constant operation of hindering causes. This general tendency is well understood, and requires no comment. The obstructing conditions or causes arise out of the fact that capital invested in certain forms, as shops, mills, furnaces, and lands, cannot be withdrawn and diverted to other purposes, and from the immobility of labor. It hence results that the profits of different industries greatly vary, and that through long periods of time.

But the question to which, in this connection, I desire to direct special attention is, What are the principles that determine the relative shares of capital and labor, of the product of labor; what are the economic forces, by the operation of which capital is enabled to say, "So much is mine, and so much I leave to you"? Wages, we are told, are the remainder after the share of capital has been taken out; the residue after capital has drunk his fill; the cold meats for the waiters after the banquet is over. "Wages," says Atkinson, "therefore, are apparently deferred to profits; but, on the other hand, wages constitute *all that there is left.*" It is not my purpose to question this view. It correctly expresses the existing relation between capital and labor. But why the relation of dependence implied in this form of statement?

Again, it is an accepted dogma of political economy, until recently rarely questioned, that the rate of wages is determined by the relative amount of capital, which constitutes the fund from which wages must be drawn. I do not quote this doctrine to sanction it, but to show the utter dependence of labor upon capital according to the views entertained by standard authorities upon the subject of political economy. According to this view the wages of labor, and therefore the profits of capital, which are the correlative of wages, are determined by conditions over which the laborer exercises no control. Current and generally accepted dogmas of political economy appear to regard the worker merely as an inanimate factor, whose wishes and whose necessities do not at all enter into the problem. I do not claim that such conclusion has been announced or formulated, but only that it is the logical sequence of doctrines embodied in the orthodox code of economic science.

This merely illustrates what every one familiar with standard authors must have observed, that writers upon political economy have been accustomed to view the subject from the standpoint of the interest of capital rather than that of the interest of labor, and that the policies of the past have been shaped without due consideration of the rights and interests of the working-people.

It is true, in a measure, that these writers have treated facts as they found them, and estimated social forces as they existed; but it is also true that they have persistently overlooked the open way through which imprisoned humanity might escape from the bondage of perpetual poverty.

Much ingenuity has been wasted in shaping idle theories that explain no phenomenon of economic science, and contribute nothing to the store of useful information. Belonging to this class of unprofitable speculation is what is known as Ricardo's law of rent, the formal declaration of which may be found in every standard work on political economy. But, until Henry George put it into the foundation of his peculiar doctrine regarding land, it was without value, except as an *a priori* spring-board to assist learned professors in feats of intellectual gymnastics.

The "doctrine," as by conventional courtesy it is called, is formulated, in the words of John Stuart Mill, as follows: " The rent which any land will yield is the excess of its produce beyond what would be returned to the same capital if employed on the worst land in cultivation." Mr. Mill devotes several pages to its elucidation. The proposition is true enough as a statement of abstract principle applicable to assumed conditions, being merely an indirect statement of the well-understood and universally-observed fact, that the productiveness of land is the measure of its value. Land that will produce no more than the amount requisite to pay for the labor and capital required in production is worth nothing, since it contributes nothing beyond cost of cultivation; and just in proportion as the product increases beyond that point, and there is a margin above cost of cultivation, land possesses commercial value. But no principle is here elucidated; there is no contribution to political science,— merely a commonplace fact in uniform, taken for a law, on the same principle that small boys are liable to mistake drum-majors for generals.

In comment, Mill says, " This is the theory of rent, first propounded at the end of the last century by Dr. Anderson, and which, neglected at the time, was almost simultaneously rediscovered, twenty years later, by Sir Edward West, Mr. Malthus, and Mr. Ricardo. It is one of the cardinal doctrines of political economy; and, until it was understood, no consistent explanation could be given of many of the more complicated industrial phenomena."

This "doctrine" may have been unknown to scientists, and may have been discovered, as Mill says, by West, Malthus, and Ricardo. Nevertheless, landlords and tenants had known it all the while, only they did not know a name for it.

If some industrious far-fetched individual should chance to invent an elaborate and ingenious formula, in which the little fact that two plus two are four could be wrapped so as to require considerable mental effort at each undoing, he would incur great risk of being embalmed by fame as the discoverer of a new principle in addition.

The total product of a country may be said to be divided into two parts: one part, being the share of labor, represents the wages or earnings of workers; the other part, being the share of capital, represents the amount appropriated by the owners of capital, as their compensation for its use. But who decides, and how is it determined, where the dividing line shall be drawn? Is there any rule of right and wrong, or any economic law, by which this division is determined?

Should fifty pounds of meat be tossed to two lions, it would be impossible to determine by *a priori* reasoning just how much of that meat each lion would get. The factors in the problem would be the quantity of meat, the relative appetites of the two beasts, the strength of their respective jaws, the length and sharpness of their claws, and the relative fierceness of their dispositions. He who should attempt to determine the result of the competition by estimating these factors might be regarded as proceeding according to scientific methods; but if a reliable answer be desired, the only way is to wait and see the animals eat. This we have done in the chapter on "Production and Distribution."

We have observed that the lion Capital gets the larger share; while Labor growls and shows his teeth, Capital eats the meat. Capital is a valuable lion, and we cannot afford to slay him; and if we could but trim his claws or file his teeth, and in this manner compel him to observe the golden rule and do unto others as he would have others do unto him, he might become a most exemplary lion. But the veterinary chiropodist and dentist possessing the requisite strength and skill to perform this service has not yet come forward; nor is he to be looked for in the form of a professor of the orthodox school of political economy.

To generalize the truth which I have sought to illustrate, I may say that the division of the product, which constitutes the sum of the wages of labor and the profits of capital, between the workers and the owners of capital, into wages and profits, is the combined effect of two opposing and ever-varying forces, which spring out of changing social and industrial conditions, and which cannot be measured, except in their results, as manifested in the division which actually takes place. Neither wages nor profits can be ascertained by rule; nor may they be fixed by legislative law, except in so far as the conditions by which they are determined may be slowly modified by the effects of legislation, or economic forces may be restrained from producing their ordinary results by the limitations of law. The only exception to this general proposition that need be noted, and that is an apparent rather than a real exception, is in the case of natural monopolies, where by law charges may be limited below a maximum rate, and limitations on rates of interest, which rest upon special grounds, and do not fall within the reason of the general rule.

It is a habit of writers on economic science to assert with loud emphasis that there is no conflict between capital and labor. The most ignorant working-man knows better. He may not comprehend the precise nature of the conflict, nor be able to see where it begins or where it ends; but that there is a conflict, in which he is continually worsted, he knows full well. He knows that every stone in the palaces of the rich was lifted and laid in place by the hands of working-men. He knows that the dwellings of the poor, for which they pay monthly tribute to capital in name of rent, are the product of labor. He knows that silks and satins and gauzy laces, that lend enchantment to the beauty of fine ladies, are not gathered from trees, but are the products of ill-requited toil; and why attempt to deceive him? The day has gone by when gross public wrongs may be successfully defended by denying the existence of facts that lie clearly exposed to the view of whoever may choose to look. There is a conflict between capital and labor; and it is the duty of the political economist to define its nature and character, that society may be protected against the growth of doctrines that may endanger social order.

In production the interests of capital and labor are combined, they are mutual; but in the division of the joint product into wages and profits, terms which describe the respective shares of the worker and the owner of capital, these interests become two antagonistic forces; and the owners of capital and the workers contend in opposition, each for the larger share of the same thing.

The tendency of capital is, therefore, to force wages down to the "minimum fixed by what is called the standard of comfort, —that is, the amount of necessaries and comforts which habit leads the working-classes to demand as the lowest on which they will consent to live." While the tendency of the opposing force, the interests of the workers, is to force the profits of capital down to the minimum which the owners of capital will consent to accept as necessary to maintain them in the style of living prescribed for them by custom or fashion and social ambition, or to augment their fortunes by accumulations of additional wealth.

LIMITATIONS ON PROFITS.

As I have already said, we cannot measure these forces, except by their results. Their character, being inherent in the nature of things, may not be altered by the force of legal enactments. But there are certain limitations upon their operation to which I desire to call attention. These limitations are, first, natural limitations; second, limitations imposed by law.

First, as to natural limitations.

The total product may be regarded as divided into two parts, the first part consisting of perishable products, such as food and clothing, which, being of such a nature as to require that they be consumed within the limits of a short period, the amount of wealth which can be saved or stored in this form is limited by the amount of the product which may be on hand at any one time; the other part, consisting of durable products, such as machinery, houses, furniture, horses, carriages, paintings, statuary, and other form of property that endures through a considerable period of time. The two classes, it will be observed, merge into each other. What are designated as the savings of labor, or the savings of capital from year to year, must take the form of durable property. There may be a temporary saving in the form of perishable property, subject to the necessary limitation, both as to amount and period of duration. Being so limited, the perishable product is not usually embraced within the meaning of the term savings, as employed in the discussion of the subject of wealth.

The total product, including both that which may be classed as perishable and that which may be termed durable, is limited by the total demand of consumption, as well as by the capacity of labor to create.

The total profits of capital are represented by that portion of the total product set apart to the credit of the owners of capital, and which must consist of either perishable or durable property or of both. The portion of profits which is paid in the form of perishable products is limited to the amount of food and clothing and things of like character which the owners of capital and their families can directly consume, and which they

may indirectly consume in the form of personal or professional
service, such as the services of domestics and coachmen in
livery, brass bands, theatrical players, ministers and mission-
aries, music-teachers and dancing-masters, and so on through
the list of occupations classed under the head of personal and
professional service. It will be seen that the amount of perishable products which the owners of capital may consume, though
large, is necessarily limited.

The amount of durable property, in the form of dwellings,
horses, carriages, paintings, statuary, and the like, which the
owners of capital can appropriate to their own use, or which
they may indirectly employ through the personal and professional service classes, has like limitations. The boundaries are
still farther out; and, under the pressure of improved tastes,
vanity, or love of luxury, keep expanding, limited only by the
reach of human desire. But when, at any time, the supply
of durable property has approximated somewhat closely the
amount required to satisfy the more reasonable demand, property of that character increases but slowly; since people of
wealth do not readily abandon or pull down good houses, that
come near the measure of their desires, in order to build better
ones; they do not discard the old paintings to make room on
the wall for new. Conditions become fixed; a stationary point
is reached; and the demand for new buildings travels but little
in advance of the increase of population.

The other forms of durable property which absorb the investments of the profits of capital embrace railways, ships,
factories, tools, and other revenue-bearing property, including
houses to rent. This form of property has its limitations in the
demand, which grows but slowly from year to year. In England, and also in this country, the demand for this class of
property is already well supplied.

There is not room for the expenditure of a great amount of
constructive labor in any one year, in creating durable revenue-
bearing property. The supply is apace with the growth of
population. We cannot keep on at the old speed, building
factories and mills and railroads; and, in consequence, that part
of the product which we call savings, and which represents the
increase of wealth from year to year, must fall off.

The principal effect of the conditions now reached is a reduction of the savings of capital; and the savings of capital being a part, and the greater part, of the profits of capital, the profits of capital must fall. The savings of labor will suffer less, since labor saved but little hitherto, and, since something cannot be taken from nothing, the quotient will not suffer violent diminution.

But capital has one other resource, the folly of farmers. By loaning their surplus capital on farms, capitalists bring about this result: at the end of a year, or, say, a period of five years, the farmers have consumed in food, clothing, or investment in stock or buildings a larger share of the total product than that which is represented by their own labor during the same period, or, if the same amount, at prices maintained on a higher scale as to manufactured products, and on a lower scale as to agricultural products, and the profits of capital have been kept up. Except for this, and other like fields of investment, profits of capital and rates of interest would have gone down from the effects of natural causes. In England, and in all old communities which have reached a state of completed development, rates of interest go down, because the margin of savings is reduced, and would go much lower, except that they are kept up by investments in credits in other countries or other sections of the same country, where a fixed status has not yet been reached and there is more rapid increase of durable wealth. English capital confined on English soil would not command a rate of interest above two and a half or three per cent., and I believe not above two per cent., and New England capital would subsist on lean profits, except for the rapidly-developing West.

But, while the interest and profits go down, as the margin of savings narrows, it is because of the fact that the margin of savings grows small that profits do go down, and the opportunity of labor to save disappears at the same time. A low rate of interest indicates low wages, though it does not cause low wages. When two horses in the same pasture grow lean at the same time, we do not infer that one is lean because the other is, but that both are poor because the pasture is short. This is a distinction which some writers on political economy have not always observed.

Adam Smith apparently entertained the opinion that reduction in profits of capital is to be attributed to the competition of capital growing out of its increase. John Stuart Mill does not fall into this error, but offers the explanation of Mr. Wakefield, which is as follows: "On a limited extent of land only a limited quantity of capital can find employment at a profit. As the quantity of capital approaches this limit, profit falls; when the limit is attained, profit is annihilated, and can only be restored through an extension of the field of employment." While the explanation embraces a general fact, it is founded on reasoning that is unsound, and leads to the false inference, that the tendency to lower profits finds its entire, or even its principal, explanation in the limitations of agriculture. The true explanation must be found in the limitations of wealth.

It has already been stated that credits constitute an outlet for the savings of capital. The volume of credits, however, has its limitations in the fact that they may not exceed a certain relative ratio to the property of the country.

It will be seen, therefore, that the natural limitations on profits are, in part, the same as the limitations on wealth; and that, except for the agency of credits, the margin of profits would tend rapidly to the minimum, which would represent the annual consumption by capitalists of perishable products, and the maintenance and annual increase of durable property directly owned by capitalists. Limitations on the rate of interest, or limitations on the amount of real estate which may be owned by any one person, will operate as a limitation on profits, and will have the effect to increase wages as compared with profits.

My purpose in pointing out these limitations on profits is to lead the way to some avenue through which it may be practicable to reach excessive profits by means of effective legislative limitations, general in character, practical in operation, and free from the objection of a tendency to hinder production.

The first measure that suggests itself as fully complying with these conditions is a low limit on the rate of interest. The effect that would follow would be to take from capital the power to absorb that portion of the product which is represented by interest accumulations effected by the present excess of the rate of interest over the rate that might be fixed. Should the rate be fixed at three per cent., the annual share of the product set apart to the credit of capital would be reduced in the amount of about three hundred million dollars, which sum, deducted from the profits of capital, would go to the credit of wages, and the wages of each worker would be proportionally increased. But, since the tendency of the rate of profit on capital, in all forms of investment, is towards a common level, a reduction in the rate of interest would be followed by a corresponding reduction in rents of dwellings and other forms of profits; and the indirect effect of lowering the rate of interest would be as great as the direct effect; and the portion of the annual product which would be thereby withdrawn from profits and added to wages would not be less than six hundred millions of dollars, or an increase of thirty dollars to each worker.

The immediate effect of thus impairing the value, by limiting the absorbing power, of credits would be an attempt on the part of capitalists to convert a large portion of credits into real estate; and agricultural lands would be in demand as a safe form of investment, not subject to the full force of restrictions on profits of capital otherwise invested, for the reason that land, being limited in area, the profits of agriculture are forced up by the demand for food, the supply of which is confined within bounds that may be extended only by improved methods of agriculture, and that gradually, and within limits unalterably fixed by physical laws. It would, therefore, be advisable, if not necessary, to limit the amount of land which any one person may own. This latter limitation would have its direct effect upon the limitation of profits of capital, and is to be commended as an independent measure; but, in conjunction with the reduction of the rate of interest, it would be an essential part of a successful scheme to restrain the omnivorous propensities of capital, and secure to labor, in the form of increased wages, a larger share of the total annual product.

I name a particular rate of interest in this connection only as a matter of convenience in illustration. The rate that ought to be adopted should be a matter of independent consideration.

No other limitations of general character would be required. There are some special limitations to be hereafter considered.

The objections to the scheme here suggested are embraced in the following propositions:

First, capital would be deprived of its equitable share of profits.

Second, production would fall off, because capital would be withdrawn.

Third, a low rate of profit would not induce people to save.

I am able to conceive of no objection which might be urged other than those here stated.

To the first objection, the other chapters of this book furnish such answer as I have to make.

As to the second, how can railways be withdrawn? how can factories, mills, and tools be withdrawn? If credits are withdrawn, the amount must be invested in other industries,—in other words, in production, under direct control of the owners of capital. The only way capital can be withdrawn from an industry is to transfer it from one industry or subject-matter to another. It may take the form of credits; but credits represent capital invested in tangible property. When one industry is depressed, or is relatively unprofitable, capital may be withdrawn to another industry, but it cannot be withdrawn into the air; a withdrawal of capital means a transfer of capital to another form of investment. A measure which affects all industries alike can have no tendency to drive capital from one industry to another. If any one should imagine that capitalists might convert the thirty or thirty-five billions of productive capital in this country into money, and lock it up in the banks, it is only necessary to remember that the total amount of money in the United States is only $1,405,018,000.

If the profits of capital were less, capitalists, who cannot escape the expenses of living, would be under the necessity of keeping their capital still more actively employed that their incomes might be increased.

As to the third objection,—it is the objection urged by writers on political economy,—John Stuart Mill says, "There would be adequate motives for a certain amount of saving, even if capital yielded no profit. There would be an inducement to lay by in good times a provision for bad; to reserve something for sickness and infirmity, or as a means of leisure and independence in the latter part of life, or a help to children in the outset of it. Savings, however, which have only these ends in view have not much tendency to increase the amount of capital permanently in existence. These motives only prompt persons to save at one period of life what they propose to consume at another, or what will be consumed by their children before they can completely provide for themselves. The savings by which an addition is made to the national capital usually emanate from the desire of persons to improve what is termed their condition in life, or to make provisions for children and others independent of their exertions. Now, to the strength of these inclinations, it makes a very material difference how much of the desired object can be effected by a given amount and duration of self-denial; which again depends on the rate of profit. And there is in every country some rate of profit below which persons in general will not find sufficient motive to save for the mere purpose of growing richer, or of leaving others better off than themselves. Any accumulation, therefore, by which the general capital is increased requires, as its necessary condition, a certain rate of profit; a rate which an average person will deem to be an equivalent for abstinence, with the addition of a sufficient insurance against risk. There are always some persons in whom the effective desire of accumulation is above the average, and to whom less than this rate of profit is a sufficient inducement to save; but these merely step into the place of others whose taste for expense and indulgence is beyond the average, and who, instead of saving, perhaps, even dissipate what they have received."

Further on he says, " A profit or interest of three or four per cent. is as sufficient a motive to the increase of capital in England at the present day as thirty or forty per cent. in the Burmese empire, or in England at the time of King John. In Holland, during the last century, a return of two per cent. on government security was consistent with an undiminished, if not with an increasing, capital."

In a work recently published, entitled "Premises of Political Economy," by Patten, I find the following enigmatic declaration: "Both a high rate of interest and high wages are necessary to preserve a high standard of life, and any plan of

social improvement which would secure a high rate of wages by
lowering interest is defective. A reduction of the rate of interest can only be accomplished by such a diminution of the inducement to save as will cause all capital to be concentrated in
the hands of a few persons. A class of laborers who do not save
for themselves will always be so deficient in intelligence as to
lack those qualities necessary to maintain high wages, and they
will necessarily sink to as low a social level as the surrounding
natural conditions will allow. What is needed is that every
one be required to do his part, and that each should obtain the
whole reward which nature gives for labor and abstinence. So
long as interest is low, and cheap labor is allowed to compete
with skilled labor, the benefit of low interest does not come to
the laborers, nor that of cheap labor to the capitalist; but the
loss of both classes goes to the landlords, who reap all the benefits of low interest and cheap labor, no one receiving the whole
of that reward which nature offers to those who save and those
who labor. If intelligent laborers, who would save, had only to
compete with the ignorant, who would not, the former could
win in the contest everywhere; it is only when the latter are
reinforced by low interest that they obtain the victory."

The evidence that this is a bit of German metaphysics, with
lucid intervals, does not need the corroborating testimony of the
dedication of the book, from which we learn that Mr. Patten
was a student of Dr. Johannes Conrad in the university at
Halle. German metaphysics is the art of mounting common
ideas in stained-glass cases, and exhibiting them by moonlight.

What Mr. Patten seems to say, in the first sentences of the
quotation, in which he declares for both high wages and a high
rate of interest, is that the yard of product should be cut into
two large pieces, so as to give three-quarters of a yard to the
laborer for his wages, and one-half a yard to the capitalist for
his profits; but I am disposed to acquit the author of an intention to make such violent assault on an inoffensive rule of
division. What he means to say is, I presume, that if the price
of manufactured products is relatively reduced, the price of
agricultural products will remain relatively high. Since the
landlords have a monopoly in the ownership of land, the
agricultural product is a limited quantity, and therefore the

benefit of low prices in manufactured products will accrue to the owners of land, for the reason that they will be able to purchase a greater quantity with the same quantity of their own products. So stated, it is an argument in favor of applying legislative limitations to the ownership of land, the force of which I admit. But the theory that capitalists should continue to rob labor by means of excessive profits on capital, since if they do not do so the landlords will, is the political economy of freebooters and pirates.

The position of Mill, plainly stated, is that if people who save a part of their own earnings cannot, by the device of interest or profits, acquire a part of the earnings of other people, they will not have the necessary encouragement to save at all, except to meet the pressing necessities of sickness and age, and the support of helpless children. But, if people generally were to save so much, the aggregate savings of the country would not be less than they now are. Mr. Mill appears to overlook the important fact that increasing the power of capitalists to save diminishes, in like ratio, the power of laborers to save. Only so much of the total product may be saved; the more capital gets the less labor retains. That it is important that there should exist inducement to save must be admitted. But who most needs encouragement, the capitalist or the working-man? Is it he who is beginning, and who is without money to loan, or capital to invest, or a house to live in, who needs aid and encouragement in his effort to save, or he who has houses and lands and money to loan? The question is, Shall the policy of the law be such as to place in the way of labor the opportunity to save its own earnings, or to give to capital the power of absorbing them?

The chief difficulties to be overcome in the way of saving lie at the beginning; it is the struggling poor who need the encouragement of better wages. Lower rates of interest, lower profits, make it easier for the working-man to save, and the best encouragement that can be given is opportunity.

Accumulations of capital are discouraged by the disorganized conditions of society, prevalent in semicivilized countries, which take away the protection of law, and expose property to the dangers of robbery or confiscation; but I know of no in-

stance in modern history, in a civilized community, where property is secure, of the development of a disposition on the part of
the owners of capital to consume their whole income, and cease
to save, because they could not save rapidly. On the other
hand, I believe the statement will be borne out by general observation that the disposition of the wealthier classes in the
direction of economy and providence grows as their incomes
diminish.   The popular idea, embodied in the vulgar proverb,
" Come easy, go easy," expresses a truth of economic science that
eminent authors seem to have overlooked.

But Mr. Mill answers his own argument by citing the case of
Holland, where he says that, " during the last century, a return
of two per cent. on government security was consistent with an
undiminished, if not with an increasing, capital." The theory that
a high rate of interest is necessary in order to induce people to
save rests wholly on *a priori* assumption. It has not been verified
by the history of any people, and has seldom been put to the
test of experience. It is merely the formula for the defence of
existing conditions which it is to the interest of a class to
maintain.   It is quite to be expected that writers on the subject
of political economy should assume that the industrial conditions by which they are surrounded, and which prevail throughout all nations, rest on sound principles of economic science.
Slavery, serfdom, feudalism in their day prevailed. They were
condemned when the march of civilization had left them behind.
Civilization continues, as it has done throughout the ages, to
present the spectacle of the masses of mankind slowly struggling upward, nearer and nearer, to the level on which stand the
more favored classes of society. Every proposed advance is
condemned beforehand and applauded afterwards. Orthodox
maxims of political economy may keep them in line, but cannot
long retard their advance. Patiently, slowly, and steadily they
move forward, hindered and delayed sometimes by an army of
conventional ideas and doctrines intrenched behind statutes and
constitutions and venerable customs ; but they never surrender
nor turn back.

As to other limitations : The pressure of the interest of the
owners of capital, in the direction of constantly-diminishing
wages to the working-man, is met by resisting tendencies

springing out of the desires and the interests of the working-classes, aided by education, custom, and the common instincts of justice, which assert themselves with increased vigor as they gather strength from improved social and moral conditions. The maxim, that wages are regulated by the law of supply and demand, is subject to many qualifications and partial exceptions, which may, perhaps, be considered as embraced within the rule when liberally interpreted, but do not lie within the scope of its direct meaning.

For instance, the supply of carpenters, painters, masons, and other artisans is, on the average, in excess of the demand. This excess is, perhaps, proportionately as great as that of the number of domestic servants in excess of the demand for the service of persons of that class ; and yet wages of artisans are, in general, three or four times as high. To say that the services of the latter are three times as valuable as the former is only another form of saying that they bring three times as much in the market. The true reason will be found in the higher average intelligence and consequent superior social position of artisans as a class, and in the independence and self-assertion growing out of these conditions, as well as the general recognition of the claims of superior industrial skill to more than an average share of the rewards of labor.

Wages in the lower forms of industry will always be relatively low ; the result of the competition of the ignorant, the dependent, and that large class of persons whose coarser physical needs constitute the measure of their demands. Illustrations of this truth may be found on every hand ; and in special illustration the low intellectual condition, and the correspondingly low wages, of the common laborers in the Southern States of the Union may be cited. The wages of those engaged in agriculture in Georgia, North Carolina, South Carolina, Alabama, and Mississippi, during a series of years, average not more than one-half the wages of the same class of laborers in the New England States.

The education of the masses must be recognized as one of the most effective remedies for low wages.

LABOR COMBINATIONS AND STRIKES.

The demands of workers for higher wages, everywhere operative, and in a measure effective, if not to secure an advance, at least to retard reduction, often take on the form of violent assertion in strikes. That labor strikes are, in a measure, effective is shown by carefully-collected statistics.

In Illinois, during the years from 1881 to 1886, inclusive, there were 1805 strikes, or 65.2 per cent. of the whole number of strikes during that period, whose object was to secure an increase of wages. Of these, 1215, or 67.3 per cent., are recorded as successful. There were 580 strikes for the reduction of the hours of labor; of these, 167, or 29 per cent., succeeded. The success of strikes in Illinois is a fair average of the success of strikes throughout the country during the same period, 66 per cent. of which were successful. The success of these strikes is not the full measure of the power of organization to maintain wages. The mere fact of organization stands in the way of reduction, and often compels an increase without resort to extreme measures.

The loss of wages sustained by the seventeen thousand nine hundred and twenty-two persons who engaged in the successful strikes amounted to $286,472, and the gain was an average increase of twenty-six cents per day. In the partially-successful strikes, involving three thousand three hundred and three men, there was an aggregate wage-loss of $125,674. In the range of the United States, in successful and partially-successful strikes, involving two hundred and two thousand eight hundred and eight workers, the direct wage-loss was $5,921,151. This estimate does not include losses from unsuccessful strikes, idle machinery, or indirect losses. While it will be seen that labor organizations and strikes may not be without value as a remedy for low wages, they constitute an unsatisfactory and expensive remedy.

When wages are advanced by measures of this character, capital maintains its margin of profit by demanding higher prices for products, and, in the end, the burden of the increase of wages in one industry is borne by the workers at large in the form of higher prices for the commodities which they consume. Labor only shifts his load on to the other shoulder. These organized efforts for the advance of wages do, in the end, no doubt result, in some degree, in lowering the margin of profits; but they are, in the main, but long-range contests between different classes of labor, in which unorganized labor, being at the greatest disadvantage, suffers the loss of what is gained by other classes. The Knight of Labor gets a more generous allowance, but Hodge goes hungry.

The total amount of wages falls within fixed limits. An increase of wages in all departments of industry means simply an increase in the prices of the products of all industries, and nothing is gained except that products at a high price go further in the discharge of existing debts. An increase of wages in one industry advances the price of the products of that industry to the people in general, to the advantage of a class of workers.

Let us assume that the total product is equivalent to 100, and that of this product eighty per cent. goes to labor and twenty per cent. to capital; that the share of labor is divided as follows: twenty per cent. to agricultural workers, twenty per cent. to workers in manufacturing industries, twenty per cent. to mechanics, miners, clerks, railway employés, etc.; ten per cent. to day laborers, and ten per cent. to personal service and professional classes. Now, suppose that the wages of agricultural workers be increased, so that they shall receive thirty per cent. of the entire product, from what source will this additional ten per cent. be drawn? A very small proportion, if any, will be drawn from the share of capital. The owners of capital will pay more for meat and flour, but prices of commodities handled by capital will be advanced, and rents and interest will rise. The great body of working-people will pay more for the products of agriculture, and, though their wages may remain as before, by reason of higher prices for what they buy their shares of the total product will be reduced, so that the ratio will stand:

	Per cent.
Agricultural workers	30.00
Manufacturing "	16.33
Mechanics, etc., "	16.33
Personal service classes	8.66
Day laborers	8.66
Capital	20.00
Total	100.00

If the wages of workers in manufacturing industries be increased in like proportion, the wages of other classes remaining the same, the ratio will stand:

	Per cent.
Agricultural workers	16.33
Manufacturing "	30.00
Mechanics, etc., "	16.33
Personal service classes	8.66
Day laborers	8.66
Capital	20.00
Total	100.00

The changes in ratio would not correspond with any definite mathematical exhibit which can be made, for the reason that the consumption of different classes is affected in different degrees by a rise or fall in prices. The problem is a complex one. I have merely sought to illustrate a governing principle in the division of the total product among different classes of workers, and to show the effect of an increase in wages of one class of workers upon the wages of other classes.

If we increase the money wages of all classes of workers by an addition of twenty per cent., the result as compared with former wages will be as follows:

	Per cent.
Agricultural workers	24.00
Manufacturing "	24.00
Mechanics, etc., "	24.00
Personal service classes	12.00
Day laborers	12.00
Capital	24.00
Total	120.00

An increase in wages without increase of quantity of product means a corresponding increase of prices. The total product, measured in money, would be increased in like ratio, and the relative share of capital would remain the same. The total product, though not changed in quantity, measured in money, instead of remaining at 100, would then be represented by 120.

The only advantage gained by labor would be that existing credits, as measured by the value of commodities, would depreciate, and what was 100 before the rise would be 83⅓ after the rise, since one hundred dollars would purchase only 83⅓ per cent. of the product which it would have purchased before the advance in prices.

Let us examine further the effects of an advance in wages of a class of workers. Take for illustration the artisans in the building trades. If the wages of carpenters and masons be increased there will be less building, and a smaller number of families of limited means will be able to secure homes of their own, and rents will be maintained or advanced to the advantage of capital, and building being restricted, artisans themselves, while securing higher wages for the work they do, will do less work, the total product will be correspondingly diminished, and the share of the workers, as a whole, will be less.

What is required is not an increase in the rate of wages of any class of workers whose wages are already relatively as high as the wages of other classes, but the adjustment to a fair and equitable standard of wages, interest, rents, and profits in trade.

When wages are so adjusted that, in the various occupations, they are relatively equitable and just, an increase of the wages of one class of workers is secured chiefly at the expense of other classes; capital takes care of itself.

In these wage-contests the classes who suffer most are the agricultural classes, day laborers, and workers in those industries where special skill is not required, and where the number seeking employment is greater than the demand.

As an organized force capital is far more effective than labor. While the workers are numbered by the million, capitalists are counted only by hundreds or thousands. Large amounts of capital owned by many individuals are employed under the management of a single representative or a board of directors; interests are readily combined. An intelligent understanding of mutual interests enables a small number of capitalists operating together to maintain their profits against the disconcerted efforts of large numbers of workers to whom effective organization is impracticable.

Adam Smith, writing upon this subject, says, "We rarely hear, it has been said, of the combinations of masters, though frequently of those of workmen. But whoever imagines upon this account that masters rarely combine, is as ignorant of the world as of the subject. Masters are always and everywhere in a sort of tacit, but constant and uniform, combination not to raise the wages of labor above their actual rate. To violate this combination is everywhere a most unpopular action, and a sort of reproach to a master among his neighbors and equals. We seldom indeed hear of this combination, because it is the usual, and one may say the natural, state of things, which nobody hears of. Masters, too, sometimes enter into particular combinations to sink the wages of labor even below this rate. They are conducted with the utmost silence and secrecy till the moment of execution; and when the workmen yield, as they sometimes do without resistance, though severely felt by them, they are never heard of by other people. Such combinations, however, are frequently resisted by a contrary defensive combination of the workmen, who sometimes, too, without any provocation of the kind, combine of their own accord to raise the price of their labor. Their usual pretences are, sometimes the high prices of provisions, sometimes the great profit which their masters make of their work. But whether their combinations be offensive or defensive, they are always abundantly heard of. In order to bring the point to a speedy decision they have always recourse to the loudest clamor, and sometimes to the most shocking violence and outrage. They are desperate, and act with the folly and extravagance of desperate men, who must either starve or frighten their masters into an immediate compliance with their demands. Their masters, upon these occasions, are just as clamorous upon the other side, and never cease to call aloud for the assistance of the civil magistrate, and the vigorous execution of those laws which have been enacted with so much severity against combinations of servants, laborers, and journeymen. The workmen, accordingly, very seldom derive any advantage from the violence of those tumultuous combinations, which, partly from the interposition of the civil magistrate, partly from the superior steadiness of the masters, partly from the necessity which the greater part of the workmen are under of submitting for the sake of present subsistence, generally end in nothing but the punishment or ruin of the ringleaders."

But labor organizations are more powerful and effective now than in the time of Adam Smith. It cannot be said that they now end in nothing but the punishment or ruin of the ring-leaders. They very often accomplish the objects at which they aim. They are able to secure an advance of wages and shorter hours; but they push up prices along with wages, and the advantages gained by one class of workers are mainly at the expense of other classes of workers. They do not prevent, if indeed they even check, the aggregation of wealth. These labor contests not only suspend industry for the time being, but greatly hindering the regular movement of production and distribution, they make employment more irregular and uncertain, diminish the total product, and *thereby reduce wages*.

When the wages of miners are advanced, the price of coal advances also; the price of iron responds to advance of wages in the iron industries; and the price of the product in all industries, where labor is hired by capital, keeps well in front. A man cannot outrun his own face, nor can wages overtake prices.

One class of laborers may secure substantial advantages by means of organization and strikes, but chiefly at the expense of the workers at large, and particularly of unskilled laborers.

In the United States, during the six years from 1881 to 1886, inclusive, there were two hundred and fifteen strikes against the employment of non-union men, and one hundred and sixty-seven lock-outs against the demand for the observance of union apprentice rules. And recently the green-glass blowers have expended two hundred and fifty thousand dollars in a protracted strike, the purpose of which was to limit the number of apprentices in each factory to two for any one year.

In the time of Adam Smith the various trades were generally in the hands of corporations, and the term of apprenticeship as well as the number of apprentices was regulated by by-laws of these corporations. The statute of apprenticeship, 5th Elizabeth, which was construed to apply to market towns only, provided that no person should exercise any trade, craft, or mystery at that time exercised in England unless he had previously served to it an apprenticeship of seven years. The silk-weavers of London enacted a by-law prohibiting any master from having more than two apprentices at a time. The cutters of London limited the number to one apprentice at a time to each master-cutter. No master-hatter could have more than two apprentices anywhere in England.

On the Continent, seven years was the usual term fixed for the duration of apprenticeships. In Paris, five years was the term required in many trades.

The principal object of this long term of apprenticeship was to restrict the number of artisans by adding to the expense and the time required in acquiring a trade. The purpose and the effect of the general policy pursued was to restrict competition.

The law no longer seeks by means of onerous restrictions to limit industrial education, or to confer upon any industrial class the advantages of a monopoly. But trades unions, labor organizations, and the general disposition to promote individual interests at the expense of the public are still operative and effective in limiting industrial education, restricting production, and denying to many those opportunities which should be open as common privileges to all working-men. Strikes which have for their purpose the restriction of the number of apprentices or the exclusion of any working-man from the privilege of pursuing any industry he may choose should be prohibited as criminal conspiracies. Strikes in general have had the excuse of a legitimate purpose, and no doubt have frequently accomplished much good; but when strikes are organized by any class of working-men for the purpose of advancing their own interests at the expense of the weaker members of society, and appropriating to themselves the special advantages which the monopoly of any industry is supposed to confer, they are not only destructive of the public welfare, but they are in direct subversion of private rights, and cannot be justified according to any principle of economic or moral law.

It should be the policy of the state to encourage industrial education, and to this end technical schools should be established and maintained at public expense. The advantages of such schools should not be restricted to those who may have the means and disposition to pursue an elaborate course of study; the purpose should be, rather, to widen the opportunities and stimulate the ambition of the masses of the people while affording special facilities to such as may seek a high degree of proficiency in any art or calling.

LIMITATIONS BY STATUTE ON RATE OF WAGES.

So far we have considered limitations upon the margin of profit interposed by the force of economic laws and legislative restrictions, operating for the most part indirectly and with uniform effect upon the profits of capital, in whatever form or industry invested. It remains to consider another class of limitations by means of legislative law operating in a manner more direct, or applied to particular forms of industry.

Attempts have been made, but without success, except in particular instances, or under special conditions, to fix by law minimum or maximum rates of wages and maximum prices of commodities. One reason why the rate of wages may not be prescribed by legal enactment is that the value of the product may not be determined beforehand for a whole state, nor for a fixed period of time, and wages fixed by law might amount to more than the product or else they might amount to so much less than the product as to be wholly out of proportion thereto, and laborers might refuse to work for the wages allowed. Both wages and profits must vary somewhat in different localities, and in different years and different seasons. No general law could be framed that would be equitable or practicable. Nor is it policy, if it were practicable, by arbitrary enactments to attempt to limit the free play of social forces within too narrow bounds. It is the province of the law to restrain the strong and to assist the weak, but not to impose restraints upon individual freedom that may not be fully justified by public necessity.

Attempts to regulate the rate of wages, and also the price of products, were not infrequent in the earlier history of legislation in England.* Adam Smith says, " That though anciently it

---

* " Another relic of mediævalism was the regulation of wages by justices of the peace, a practice enjoined by the Act of Elizabeth already referred to. Adam Smith speaks of it as a part of a general system of oppression of the poor by the rich. Whatever may have been the case in some instances, this was not generally true. The country gentry were on the whole anxious to do justice to the working-classes. . . . The justices often ordained a rise in wages, and the workmen themselves were strongly in favor of this method

was usual to rate wages first by general laws extending over the whole kingdom, and afterwards by particular orders of the justice of the peace in every particular county, both these practices have now gone entirely into disuse." "By the experience of above four hundred years," says Dr. Burn, "it seems time to lay aside all endeavors to bring under strict regulations what in its own nature seems incapable of minute limitation; for if all persons in the same kind of work were to receive equal wages there would be no emulation, and no room left for industry or ingenuity.

"Particular acts of Parliament, however, still attempt sometimes to regulate wages in particular trades and in particular places. Thus, the 8th of George III. prohibits, under heavy penalties, all master-tailors in London, and five miles round it, from giving, and their workmen from accepting, more than two shillings and seven pence half-penny (sixty-three cents) a day, except in case of a general mourning." The early history of New England discloses legislation of similar character. There were statutes prescribing the prices of victuals, drink, and bread-stuffs. A meal at an eating-house was six pence, and one penny additional for a quart of beer. A statute of Connecticut fixed the wages of carpenters, ploughwrights, wheelwrights, masons, joiners, smiths, coopers, and mowers at twenty pence per day from March 10 to October 11, and eighteen pence thereafter, and prescribed eleven hours for a day's work in summer and nine hours in winter. The wages of other workmen were fixed at two pence less. In Massachusetts the lawful hire of a steer was nine pence per day, or twelve pence for a grown ox; of a horse, sixteen pence. Master-carpenters, joiners, coopers, bricklayers, plasterers, and rivers of clapboards were allowed two shillings in summer and twenty pence in winter. Other mechanics, "experienced and diligent," were allowed eighteen pence in summer and fourteen pence in winter. In 1650 the prices of cereals were fixed by law as follows: wheat, four shillings six pence; peas, three shillings six pence; rye,

---

of fixing them. The employers, on their part, also often approved of it. In fact, we have an exactly similar system at the present day in boards of arbitration."—*Industrial Revolution of the Eighteenth Century in England.*

three shillings six pence; Indian corn, three shillings,—all per bushel.

NATURAL MONOPOLIES.

In many, if not most, of the States there are still in force statutes limiting the amount of toll that may be taken for grinding flour, and requiring the miller to assist in loading and unloading. The limitation by law of the amount of toll before the day of railways was justified by the fact that flouring-mills were, in a measure, natural monopolies. One mill was sufficient for the people who resided within convenient distance, and mills were necessarily too far apart for competition to have its full effect. People could not well protect themselves from over-charges by driving to distant mills, since the expense of the longer drive would exceed the amount of overcharge. Legislative limitation was the only protection adequate to prevent extortion. And the cost of grinding was so nearly uniform throughout the country, and from year to year, as to present no great obstacle to the application of a maximum limit that would, at the same time, leave room for reasonable profit and protect the people from any considerable extortion. When, however, through the agency of railways, mills were all brought into close competition with one another, there remained no reason for legislative restriction; and laws regulating toll of flouring-mills, though still carried on the statute-books of many States, are no longer needed, and they only remain from neglect to repeal them. They have become inoperative by reason of competition, which has reduced the cost of grinding below the old prices and confines the margin of varying charges within narrow limits.

The limitation of charges for hack fare is everywhere recognized as within the proper scope of legislative supervision. Not because of any lack of competition among hack-drivers, since the supply has always been in excess of the demand; but people, if inclined, do not have the time to stipulate beforehand as to hack charges, nor will they protect themselves against extortion by disputing a fare, at the risk of an altercation with an impertinent clown, in a public place. In this case the chance for extortion grows out of the smallness of the amount involved in any one transaction and the frequent recurrence of the opportunity, the necessary lack of knowledge on the part of the travelling public of the individuals with whom they are compelled to deal, and the circumstances of time and place which enable those disposed to take advantage to enforce extortionate charges. Here the power to extort money beyond a reasonable compensation, as in case of natural monopolies, arises out of the peculiar conditions.

No difficulty is here found in applying legislative restrictions; since, although the effect of limiting fares is to reduce the number of hackmen, the number that survive is always adequate to the demand.

While the effect of limiting fares is to lessen the number of those who engage in the business, the compensation of those who continue is not reduced; the smaller amount which is paid by the travelling public is divided among a smaller number, the earnings of each remaining the same.

The limitation of freight charges and passenger fares on railways, and of fares on street railways and ferry-boats, is founded on the public necessity of restricting charges for services rendered by natural monopolies which are not fully subject to the limiting power of competition. The charges of telegraph companies, telephone companies, and gas companies are embraced in the same necessity, and ought to be, and will be, made subject to limitations fixed by law; since they are subject to none other that are operative within the range of gross extortion.

Here, again, no great difficulty is experienced. The volume of business, which expresses the amount of the total product, varies between limits that may be readily ascertained; so that the effect of a proposed limitation of rates may be estimated with approximate accuracy. It will be observed that this form of legislative restriction involves no direct limitation of either wages or profits.

If, in addition to limitations by the imposition of fixed maximum charges, the business were further subject to the varying limitations imposed by competition unrestricted by natural conditions, capital might thereby be exposed to the hazard of doubtful results, from which it would be restrained from protecting itself by expedients permitted in the management of other business enterprises; but when capital is invested in any business beyond the range of effective competition, legislative limitations of the character imposed on the charges of railway companies and similar natural monopolies may be applied without endangering reasonable profits; and the necessity of some restriction in cases where, without legislation, there are none, fully justifies the imposition of legislative restraints.

PATENT RIGHTS.

Patent rights are artificial monopolies created by law for the encouragement of invention. As a reward for industry, perseverance, and talent, the patentee, in the event of success, is assured in the absolute control of the market during a limited period of years. It may be that, on the whole, the compensation of inventors has not exceeded a reasonable reward for exceptional perseverance and talent. But the monopoly, designed for the benefit of inventors, generally falls into the hands of shrewd capitalists, who have done little to give them title to it except to drive a hard bargain with some poor inventor who has wasted his years and his means in pursuit of a possible fortune, which, in the hour of his success, his hard necessities compel him to relinquish to the grasping avarice of one of those whose trade it is to thrive on the misfortunes of others.

The law is deficient in two things: first, in such provisions as would prevent the inventor and his family from being wholly deprived of the royalty of his own invention, even by his own act; second, in not protecting the people, by in some manner limiting the maximum profits which may be derived through any patent. The extent of the aggregation of wealth through the agency of patent-right monopolies cannot be ascertained; but in many departments of manufacture profits have been enormous. No other single agency perhaps, except interest on money, is more responsible for the present inequitable distribution of wealth. The wrong done to the masses of common people, and especially to the agricultural classes, has been flagrant and gross; and yet there has been no great outcry against it, for the reason that the people have never understood, nor do they now understand, that great profits in one industry mean the robbing of some to build the fortunes of others; that wealth and poverty are correlative conditions, even in the closing decades of the nineteenth century, when the power to produce has far outrun the power to consume, and the workers in our manufacturing industries, with the aid of machinery, electricity, and steam, can, in one day, do more than a like number of workers could have done in a month, eighty years ago.

LIMITING THE RATE OF INTEREST AND THE OWNERSHIP OF LAND.

The theory that a reduction of the rate of interest, or of profits on capital, would tend to the aggregation of wealth, springs from a mistaking of effect for cause. It is true that small profits and small accumulations of wealth are, as a rule, found only in conjunction. The same may be said of low wages and small savings. But it is not therefore claimed that small savings are the cause of low wages. On the other hand, it is clear that low wages are the cause of small savings. So it is equally plain that a small amount of general savings, or a small product of durable property, is the cause of both a low rate of interest and low wages. The same cause which reduces the share of the worker reduces the portion of capital. The necessary effect of lowering profits by limiting the rate of interest is not to reduce the total savings of the country, but to bestow a larger share upon the workers in the form of wages, or the earnings of labor. Thus the opportunity to save would be distributed among a greater number of people, and, instead of aggregating wealth, would divide it among those who create it, and who are entitled to enjoy it. At present, the working-man who saves even a home must do so at the expense of a degree of self-denial that deters many from the effort, and defeats many more in the attempt.

When, by extreme self-denial, shrewd cunning, or by lucky chance, one succeeds in accumulating a small capital, he may then climb upon the necks of his fellows and ride into fortune; and, if he succeeds, the world applauds, for "there is nothing like success." This vulgar maxim is the plebeian brother of the phrase "the divine right of kings," born of the doctrine entertained by titled nobles, that it is a part of the scheme of Providence that the common people should be by them saddled and ridden at will, and then turned out like donkeys on the common, to feed and renew their strength for the morrow's journey.

The equal right of all men to life, liberty, and the pursuit of happiness must be admitted in practice as well as theory; and it is the duty of every government, so far as practicable, to preserve to all its people alike an equality of opportunity. Its efforts should be to give every man a chance, not to get other people's earnings, but to keep his own; and to see that the weak, by the encroachments of the strong, are not deprived of those things which are by nature the common heritage of all "I got here first" may be a good claim to a reasonable share of land, but not to a State or county or town, to the exclusion of those who come after. There is no divine decree commanding that the world shall be parcelled out among a chosen few who shall exact tribute from the rest of mankind for the privilege of enjoying a share of nature's gift.

And, on the other hand, the sense of individualism, the promptings of desire, and all the finer instincts of human nature unite in protest against any scheme to destroy competition, tame human endeavor, stifle the leaping aspirations of youth, and dull the sense of keenest joy, by drowning emulation in the Dead Sea of communistic equality. In order to correct social abuses and industrial wrongs, it is not necessary to tear down the old-established institutions and build anew according to plans revealed in dreams.

Our social structure has been slowly and gradually evolved, under the shaping hand of time, by the forces of human nature. We cannot tear it down if we would; its foundations are deep, its walls are lofty and strong. Civilization will never consent to abide in a habitation artificially constructed, arranged, and decorated, according to the elaborate specifications of artisans who, through success at scroll-saw fancy work, have acquired the reputation of social architects.

But reforms are needed, and sooner or later they will come, and demand admission with an authority that cannot be questioned. Better to make way for them and bid them welcome. Much may be done. Obstructions may be removed; economic forces may be assisted, modified, or hindered; currents may be turned into new channels; industrial laws may be conformed to the demands of justice and equal rights; and the struggling poor may be assisted upward into the sunlight of a warmer social life, where the destroying blight of poverty may not reach, and kindlier feelings and nobler aspirations will be nourished into growth.

The remedies here suggested do no violence to social order; they involve no destruction of property rights, no overthrow of established institutions, no chimerical scheme of communistic equality, no artificial reconstruction of human society, no untried experiment freighted with possibilities of extreme disaster. They conform to the principles of tried legislation embodied in existing statutes, and may be subjected to the test of experience without any rearrangement of the industrial programme. They involve no temporary expedients; and yet, I believe them to be effective and, in conjunction with revenue measures elsewhere suggested, sufficient. Full scope is left for the free play of the desires, hopes, and ambitions of men. The acquisition of property is aided and encouraged, and not restrained, except from those excessive accumulations by which are built up great fortunes that represent booty gathered from the people by the use of an unjust advantage, which accumulated capital possesses, in competition with labor. Talent and skill will still be left free to contend for the prize of fortune honorably won; and, in plain view of every man who toils, the future will display the promised reward of a home, a competence for old age, and a little store of wealth for dependent wife and children. Where to-day he is loitering on the way, weary of the burden of unrequited toil, now and then, perchance, quickening his sluggish pace as he catches the gleam of distant gold, only to resume his lagging step as he reflects that his vision extends beyond the goal where the journey of his years must end, then, encouraged and buoyed with the hope of generous recompense, he will march forward with strong and steady tread to the achievement of possible aims.

Competition is one of the vital forces of all social and industrial life. But competition unrestrained enables the strong to trample the weak underfoot; by it monopoly may be built up as well as destroyed; by means of competition the great capitalist crushes small competitors, and everywhere the strong override the weak. How far the government should interfere is always a question to be determined relative to existing conditions, the stage of civilization, and of moral, intellectual, and industrial development. No universal formula can be devised. We cannot abolish human passions, nor eliminate selfishness and avarice as potent factors in commercial life; we cannot change the elemental forces, but we can restrain and limit their action; and this is the purpose of nearly every law that is enacted. It is not at all necessary that industry or commerce should be fretted with limitations that interfere with that free play which is essential to general prosperity; nor should unlimited license be permitted to the strong to despoil the weak in the name of free competition and unrestricted trade.

That it is practicable to arrest the centralization of wealth in this country, and to secure and maintain a more equitable distribution of wealth than that which now exists in this or any of the nations of Europe, is certain. That this result may be accomplished by means of general legislation, conforming to clearly-defined principles, is also evident. The people, however, do not much concern themselves about dangers that lie some distance in the future; they are disposed rather to pursue what appears to be present interest, and secure immediate results. And so we shall drift forward much like a whaling vessel on the high seas, often shifting our course and crossing our own track in pursuit of the whale we may for the time be chasing.

However, education is more nearly universal now than at any other period in history, and more nearly so in this country than in any other. There has been awakened an interest in economic science, and the masses of the people realize, to an extent which they have never realized before, that the general frame and policy of the laws of a country have much more to do with the prosperity of the people than is apparent to casual or superficial observation.

CHAPTER XII.

EDUCATION OF THE PEOPLE.

IMPROVEMENT in the condition of the working-man necessarily depends, in chief measure, upon his ability and disposition to help himself. The law may secure to him opportunity, and may protect him from the encroachment of superior power; but being himself the maker of laws, the source of the policies by which his destiny is shaped, it is to himself that he must look for whatever measure of relief may be found in constitutions or in the operation of friendly statutes. Those who are unable to help themselves, must be 'content to occupy such position as may be assigned to them, and enjoy such advantages as may be conceded to them by others, whose chief effort it must be to promote their own individual welfare. It is therefore evident that the working-man must possess the degree of intelligence and information required in order to enable him to comprehend his own interests, and the measures by which they may be preserved and promoted. And it is, perhaps, still more important that the great body of working-people should possess that degree of loyalty to principle that is essential to secure united effort in the promotion of common interests. Without conforming to these requirements that steady concert of action necessary to achieve results cannot be secured; and the welfare of the working-people, as a whole, will be lost sight of in the selfish individual pursuit of immediate temporary advantage, or of cunningly-devised policies designed for the promotion of special interests under the cover of a seeming purpose to promote the general welfare.

In this connection may be mentioned a great and growing evil, in the suppression of which working-men have a special interest. I refer to the use of money in elections.

The commercial vote of the country, already large, is steadily increasing. The number of those whose votes may be purchased, in many communities, will exceed ten per cent. of the total vote. While there are no statistics on the subject, every person who is well informed concerning the manner in which elections are conducted is cognizant of the fact that large numbers of American citizens make merchandise of the elective franchise. Where the evil prevails, these persons are known, and their names may be found alphabetically arranged on the lists of local political managers. And, if necessary, the executive force of either of the great political parties of the country, when in perfect organization for practical campaign work, could in thirty days ascertain, by a close approximation that would do credit to the census bureau, the number of American citizens who, for a consideration of from fifty cents to twenty-five dollars, the amount depending on the individual and the state of the market, can be persuaded to cast their ballots for the candidates of either of the contending parties.

To be elected to any office frequently costs the successful candidate more than the emoluments of the office amount to; and he who gets through at the expense of a year's salary may congratulate himself; while the unsuccessful candidate, who loses both his money and the office to which he aspires, is liable, in consequence, to become involved in that financial ruin which frequently marks with painful emphasis the disappointment of defeated ambition.

The degree of demoralization varies greatly in different localities, and many counties are almost wholly exempt. But, in the aggregate, the amount of money expended for venal purposes in contests for nominations, and in elections, is very great.

"How much money has he to put into the fight?" is one of the most common inquiries made concerning an aspirant for nomination to a public office. And, where contests are close and the floating vote is large, it is the usual thing to select a candidate with distinct reference to his bank account.

It is the custom to refer the responsibility for this evil to politicians, and to candidates who are frequently, in fact, but the unwilling victims, unable to ignore prevailing conditions. Personal interest, laudable ambition, an honest belief that certain principles or policies ought to prevail, and a public opinion that howls for success, compel men to yield to the demands of those who are moved by no consideration higher than a desire for money,

and whose demands are always accompanied by the certainty
that, unless complied with, their votes will count on the other
side. A candidate for office is considered the legitimate prey of
every political black-mailer in his district, and his success generally depends to a great extent upon the manner in which he
complies with the demands upon his purse.

As a rule, those who interest themselves in public affairs, and
conduct the management of political campaigns according to
the terms prescribed by an established usage, are less to be
censured than may be supposed. If they who are most prone
to visit censure upon politicians were themselves to enter into
this branch of a necessary public service, they would find it
somewhat difficult to get through the heat and dust of a political campaign, wearing robes of spotless white, without showing
a few unseemly smudges at the close.

The drawing-room moralist who, that he may preserve his
virtuous innocence untarnished and his reputation unscarred,
stands aloof from the battle, and who,

" But for these vile guns, would himself have been a soldier,"

may be a very proper and circumspect individual, but he is not
one of the most useful members of society.

The blackened face of the miner, the calloused hands of the
mechanic, the grim visage of the engineer are pledges of work
performed ; and in the moral and political field there are con-
taminating contacts that cannot always be avoided by those
who achieve results.

The demoralization of the people is to be condemned not only
as a great moral evil, but the working-men, who are most exposed to the danger that lurks in corrupt elections, have special
interest in the preservation of the integrity and dignity of the
American voter. Wealth is already a potent factor in elections.
Political managers, politicians, legislators are brought under
obligation to a power which they dare not offend. Those who
are most able, and most inclined to serve the interests of the
people, are often deterred from seeking political preferment.
Legislative action that would promote the interests of working-
men to the injury of monopolies, or to the detriment of aggre-

gated wealth, is prevented; for a political party must take care
not to arouse the angry antagonism of those who hold the power
to defeat it. The evil, at present, is not that votes are bought
for the special purpose of subserving the interests of wealth.
It lies rather in the fact that political parties, being largely dependent for success upon contributions from men of great
wealth, must so shape their policies as not to give offence to
those who, by withholding their aid, or by contributing to the
opposing party, have it in their power to prevent success.
When a party assails the evils of aggregated wealth, it awakens
an enemy whose opposition it cannot withstand.

The masses of honest voters naturally divide in nearly equal
numbers between the two great political parties of the country.
Each side is always intensely desirous of success. Aggregated
wealth holds the power to control the commercial vote, and
give success or bring defeat to either party,—to either cause.
Thus wealth is able to dictate to either party, and neither
party dare venture far enough to give serious offence. They
come to the lion in the pathway, and then prudently turn back.

The ballot is the working-man's only protection. The elective franchise must be guarded as the most sacred privilege of
freemen. If votes are to be bought and sold as an article of
merchandise, then truly money is king, and every politician
and every citizen seeking political preferment must do the king
homage. And there are six millionaires in the United States
Senate to-day to attest the measure of their loyalty.

Legislatures, manifesting double zeal in the pursuit of abstract
justice, and none at all in the pursuit of practical results, have
generally enacted laws punishing alike the man who buys and
the man who sells his vote; and thus, closing the mouths of all
witnesses to the transaction, have protected both parties from
exposure to the censure of public opinion by making secrecy a
necessity alike to each.

If those alone who barter their votes should be made subject
to penalty, all others could be required to testify; and grand
juries would need have no great difficulty, by following the contributions of candidates and others to the point of ultimate expenditure, in discovering those who have sold themselves. The
evil can be reached and broken up when there is developed a

disposition to resort to practical measures. Disfranchisement is a natural and appropriate penalty.

A system of balloting, like that known as the Australian System, that leaves the voter to select and deposit his ballot, without the presence and free from the espionage of any who may have an interest to see that a vote has been delivered according to promise, will, in time, greatly modify the evil. But the only remedy that can be relied on as effective and complete is universal education and the higher standard of manhood which intellectual and moral training alone can secure.

Improvement in the condition of the working-man depends upon his intelligence; upon his having a true conception of his relations as a moral and social being; upon his sentiments of equity and justice; upon the strength of his affections; and upon his reverence for worthy ideals.

Our public schools afford fair opportunity for secular education and a certain amount of moral training and social culture; but the number of children who, because of the poverty or indifference of parents, are not permitted to enjoy the opportunities placed before them is very large. That mass of crude, untrained humanity, without aspirations, without worthy ambitions, without sentiment, that lives but to eat and drink, competes for the lowest wages, and drags to the level of its own standard all those pursuing occupations that lie within reach of its sullied hands, grows day by day. Occasionally are seen persons of refinement and education, by accident or misfortune, thrust down to the lowest industrial level, compelled to measure their necessities by the standard of this vulgar herd.

It is from this crowd that capital draws constant supplies of labor with which to beat down wages, in the interest of higher profits; for there are few who, though their intelligence be of a low order, may not be utilized to feed a machine, and thereby displace some worthy man who is not content with the bare necessities of food and raiment and squalid shelter.

The intelligent working-man cannot afford to compete with a human automaton. And he must see to it that the people who stand upon this low plane are lifted to a higher level. If they were exclusively confined to one industry, and were wholly out of the line of direct competition with working-men of other

orders, their influence might be little felt beyond their own industrial circle. But they spread through the industries; and
everywhere their competition is more or less felt in reducing
the standard of living, and thereby lowering the standard of
wages.

Every measure that may be effectively employed to promote
the education of the people is a measure in the interest of
working-men who aspire to a degree of comfort and refinement
above the coarse and meagre subsistence that satisfies the more
urgent wants of those who have not learned to live.

Every available agency should be employed to get children,
whose education is being neglected, into school, and to keep
them there; and, when necessary, compulsory measures should
be employed. From an economic stand-point alone, general
education is a necessity in the interest of working-people. He
who seeks to share in this great social and industrial copartnership should be required to comply with the conditions necessary
for the general welfare of the people and in no way hurtful to
himself.

Care should be exercised in the management and control of
our public schools. They at present fall far short of that degree
of efficiency which should be required, and which is readily attainable, except for the prevailing popular indifference as to the
more important results of educational training. As aids to the
moral and social refinement of the people, they lack the support
and hearty co-operation of parents, as well as the efficiency of
thoroughly-competent teachers. Yet they nevertheless constitute the strength of our civilization, and the power on which
we must rely for still further progress in the direction of a wider
intellectual and moral culture.

If railways, street railways, telegraphs, water-works, gas-
works, coal-mines, and timber lands could be owned by the
government and efficiently managed through government officials, and if branches of the various manufacturing industries
requiring large amounts of capital could be established and conducted by government agents in different localities, so as to
employ labor otherwise unemployed, at reasonable but moderate
wages, so as to protect that class of workers who are oppressed
by the grasping avarice of those disposed to take advantage of

the necessities of others, and by protecting this class relieve the
labor market from that unhealthy competition which steadily
depresses the value of labor; if fire insurance could be furnished
by the State; and if the State, as the representative of the people, could receive their small savings and erect for them suitable
homes, following the principle on which building and loan associations are conducted, but exacting a lower rate of interest,
very much might be accomplished in aid of those who suffer
from industrial conditions. But how would it be possible to
secure and retain in position intelligent, competent, and faithful
officials to conduct railways and manage telegraphs or manufacturing industries, conducted under government supervision?

The ignorance, selfishness, cupidity, dishonesty, and prejudice
existing among the working-men themselves constitute the
principal barrier to the success of any scheme of the character
here pointed out, or indeed of any other effective measure for
their relief. When the great majority of the working-people
shall have become intelligent enough to understand their own
needs, and to comprehend the measures by which their common
welfare may be promoted; when they shall be willing to relinquish temporary selfish advantages in order to share in the
benefits to be derived from community of labor and capital;
when they can be trusted in the selection of competent officials
of the State or of corporations organized in their interest; when
they shall learn to abate somewhat the fierceness of individual
competition, and submit to regulations looking to the common
welfare of all classes, it may then be practicable to secure to
every man the opportunity for steady employment and fair
remuneration.

The industrial condition of a people may be gauged by their
intelligence, and by their social and moral culture. And any
remedy for industrial evils that does not include education as a
principal factor is radically defective. An individual with little
education may succeed; another of the highest attainments
may fail. But an educated people, or an educated class, always
succeed; and the industrial position of an uneducated class is
always inferior.

The wages of any industrial class are equivalent to, and
limited by, the consumption by that class of the products of

labor. Consumption is determined by habit, by intelligence, by refinement; in short, by education. Thus it is education of the class that determines the wages of the class. The status of the individual worker is determined by his industrial class, and every working-man is concerned for the improvement of the condition of society in general from which he cannot disassociate himself.

THE WORK OF THE CHURCH.

During one day of each week ordinary industry is suspended, and the people rest from their accustomed pursuits. With this day comes to the masses of the people opportunity for leisure, social intercourse, the pursuit of useful knowledge, and the cultivation of those refining and ennobling sentiments that shrink from the harsh contacts of every-day life. To cultivate these sentiments in the hearts of the people, to awaken and strengthen their better thoughts and impulses, I conceive to be the chief mission of church associations, and the purpose which justifies large expenditures of money in the erection of church buildings and the employment of an educated ministry.

As an organized institution firmly established in the customs, habits of thought, prejudices, and beliefs of the people, the Church has appropriated this day for its own special work. It is possessed of advantages and opportunities enjoyed by no secular institution; and, in great degree, it must be judged by results, as measured by the moral and religious condition of the people. May it not have failed to fully grasp the true conception of its mission? Religious organizations are one of the natural outgrowths of human society. There is no civilized people without them. They vary in form and character according to the people who compose them. They are as perfect as other social institutions, and no more so. They may be most effective agencies to promote, or most effective obstructions to hinder and delay, the moral growth of society. Being, in their nature, fashioned by ancient traditions and long-established ideas, they are essentially conservative. It is in the nature of things that they should change but slowly, and operate as a constant check upon the tendencies of advancing thought. But their advance movements are liable to be too long delayed, while the people go from them and their influence is weakened.

The fact that they everywhere exist, and always have existed, is quite sufficient evidence that they are to continue as one of the principal agencies in moulding popular ideas and impulses. That they perform a useful and necessary service ought to be apparent even to those who find nothing to commend in the special mission which they assume. Whatever we may think of any formulated system of theological beliefs, nevertheless there are certain sentiments that cluster around the faiths of religion, and which, among the people at large, under the influence of defined ideals fashioned in the mould of venerable traditions, are nourished into growths that no people can afford to neglect.

It is, of course, unreasonable to expect that all the world may be driven to accept any one form of speculative theological belief; or that there is any principle of ethics involved in believing or not believing this or that, or in believing nothing at all. Fancies with regard to the unseen world naturally shape themselves into beliefs, and certain accepted ideals become current among the people of a nation or an age; and the realist who conceives it a duty to subject this poetry to the test of philosophy has no true conception of the nature and needs of the human mind. Whether Satan be an absolute physical reality of definite specific gravity, or the conception of a boisterous fancy, the Gulliver of religious romance, it is not necessary to inquire. He has enacted a leading part in the drama of human life, and is still doing service in the field of ethics as a vivid personification of evil. His period of usefulness has not yet expired; and though bearing the scars of many wounds from the spear-thrusts of modern science, he is still abroad dodging in and out across the pathway of human life, in the dim twilight of uncertainty that hangs on the edges of the day.

The higher Christian ideals, which exhibit the best conceptions of divine character, are most valuable aids in subduing the selfish instincts of human nature, and in purifying and refining human thought and feeling. To preserve these noble conceptions and mould character into correspondence with these lofty ideals is peculiarly the function of the Church and its ministry. But these ideals are not to be subjected to the tape-line measurements of prosaic logic, nor tested by the rules of material science; and the minister who conceives it to be his duty to stake the claims of the Christian religion upon the correspondence of these conceptions with absolute realities understands little of the philosophy of human thought and feeling. He who conceives it to be his mission to be continually pulling down the fancy-woven drapery that adorns poetic ideals, in order that he may count the meshes and exhibit the texture, is but a clumsy realist out of place. He who makes the test of religious virtue the belief, or professed belief, in some grotesque metaphysical distortion, instead of pure and noble sentiment, is a destroyer of faith and an enemy to the cause he assumes to espouse. When metaphysical beliefs are exalted into virtues, and honesty, purity, nobility of sentiment, and refinement of feeling are degraded to the rank of secondary merit, religion loses its power and its worth. The prevailing apathy, to say nothing of the open antagonism, towards the Church at the present time can be accounted for only by the natural repugnance of the human mind to the idea of a compulsory acceptance of a code of distorted metaphysics as a test of religious merit. If the energy of the Church were directed to the teaching of the saving power of the Christian virtues instead of the saving power of beliefs which are to-day professed only in a perfunctory sort of way by many of the most intelligent and enlightened leaders of the Church itself, then the influence of genuine religious faith would take hold of the hearts of the people, and the minister would become a more effective teacher and leader.

The hope of immortality springs perennially in the human heart. Mind cannot be chained to matter; the imagination will never stay its flight within the bounds of material vision, but will continue to soar into the realms of poetry and romance, and gather flowers of beauty with which to adorn the realities of life. It will continue to fashion ideals, and the human heart will do them reverence. Beliefs concerning supernatural things have their origin in the nature and constitution of the human mind; they are irrepressible, and no philosophy can extinguish or supersede them. But it is not the function of the Church to stereotype these beliefs into unchanging forms, and compel

poetic fancy to travel a beaten path; or to put reason on the
rack to extort confessions of beliefs not honestly entertained.

There is no class who so much need the support of a warm
and generous faith in the saving power of Christian virtues, or
who are more in need of the inspiriting influence of an awakened
religious sentiment, than the working poor, who, for the most
part, are beyond the range of effective church influence. The
Church is a social power, and its best influences arise out of its
organized social relations. People form in groups about a
centre of conventional ideas, and enjoy the warmth of sympathy
that springs from community of thought and feeling. Religious
doctrines are little more than solemn passwords, the answer
to the "Who comes there?" of the sentinel. The value of these
social influences is not to be disparaged. But it is to be re-
gretted that the direct teaching power of the pulpit should be
sacrificed to the demands of a conventional theology that brings
religion itself into disrepute, and to which men of mature
thought yield only a formal assent, as a mode of paying respect-
ful obeisance to social law.

How, where, and by whom are the masses of the people to be
educated and trained in the ethics of social life? by whom are
they to be taught the art of living aright? how are they to be
instructed in the principles and methods of the domestic training of children? how are they to be made to comprehend the
nature and value of moral worth? The task of instructing the
people in the philosophy of social life would appear to be
peculiarly the work as well as the opportunity of the minister;
but his special training is not to that end. As a practical guide
and teacher, when he has sought to make his influence felt in
the direction of moral purity, it has too often been as an advocate of some mistaken policy that demoralizes and destroys.

It was the pulpit, dominated by theologic dogma, that
banished amusements from the fireside and the home-circle, and
drove many into drinking-saloons, and into the by-ways and
dark corners of iniquity. And the young men and boys and the
working-men in our towns and cities have followed after. In
our great cities the task of furnishing amusement and social
recreation to the laboring poor has been commonly left to the
retailer of whiskey and beer, who has learned the art of enhanc-

ing the profits of his trade by gratifying the love of music, the natural desire for amusement and recreation, and the yearning for social sympathy that abides in the human soul. And thus, in his leisure, when most subject to the influence of surrounding conditions, the working-man is lured to his ruin.

Cards and billiards and tenpins and social dances have been driven from the shelter of religious influence as worldly outcasts; when the devil goes gunning for souls, he can have no more faithful assistant than an intolerant, unthinking minister to beat the bushes and start the game.

On every hand may be observed ministers, the scope of whose thought is confined within the narrow limits of traditional dogma, who, ignoring practical and common-sense methods of reform, deliver conventional sermons on the depravity of the human heart, or the sin of vanity, in fashionable churches that vie with the palaces of millionaires in luxury of adornment and splendor of architectural display, or, varying the character of the entertainment, give æsthetic sparring exhibitions on Sunday with the intangible devil of ghostly romance.

The result of these efforts is misshapen character; an abnormal pietism on the one hand and a lack of reverence on the other; the world is filled with cant; religion is divorced from ethics; and the most earnest and sincere religious devotees are often found most deficient in moral worth, uncharitable and ungenerous, wanting in a sense of justice, wanting in a sense of honor, while they maintain respectability by observing conventional standards, and deceive themselves, as they deceive others, by assuming those artificial virtues which a false theology has set in place of genuine worth.

What is here said is not with the view of reflecting censure upon the minister. He performs the difficult part assigned him with fully as much zeal and loyalty to duty as any other member of society. But he is under the bondage of an exacting conventionalism; and, like a pet squirrel in a revolving cage, he may whirl the wheel, but he cannot advance. Ostensibly he occupies the place of a leader, yet he dare not lead. He may only stand still and exhibit the ancient relics of mediæval theology, of which he is custodian; and when he essays to vary his accustomed routine, it is too often only to beat the snare-

23

drum for some squad of visionary reformers. He is confined
within the narrow limits of prescribed formulas of faith handed
down from an ignorant and credulous age, and is denied the
opportunity to do the most effective service to the cause of
either morality or Christianity. If he does become a student
of social philosophy, and attempt to put his ideas in harmony
with the laws of human nature, and range himself in line with
advanced thought, he incurs the suspicion of the awful sin of
unbelief in some shaky old dogma which it is the special care of
theological seminaries to guard from dangerous proximity to
any useful or practical knowledge.

In order to better serve the interests of the Church itself, in
order to promote the cause of genuine Christianity, and to advance the moral culture of the people by interweaving into the
fabric of common thought and feeling strands of pure and noble
sentiment, the minister must be released from the idle task of
crocheting the filmy threads of theological metaphysics into
conventional fancy work for the special pleasure of those who,
from habit or perverted taste, have acquired an interest in these
specimens of a useless art.

The prevailing theology conceives of God as a jealous and intolerant being, who requires of man that he disregard the
verdicts of his own reason, and that he accept, as his belief,
dogmas which to some appear incomprehensible and to others
absurd; a God who, instead of esteeming man according to the
measure of his manhood and real worth, attaches the penalty
of everlasting punishment to disbelief; while the vilest of men,
through the agency of that humility and mellow penitence that
besets cowards when they stand face to face with death, may
win his eternal love. Such degraded conception of the God of
the universe is unworthy of a civilized people; it is at war with
morality and with noble religious sentiment.

Such conception is no part of the Christian religion. But it
appears to be the fate of all great religions to become submerged
beneath the gross superstitions of the people among whom they
are promulgated. Barren theological speculation soon displaces
the plain and simple utterances of ideal sentiment and maxims
of pure morals in which these messages of truth are delivered
to the world; superstition resumes her sway and, in the name

of the divine commission she professes to hold, perpetuates her power,

The Vedic religion of India was a simple code, giving expression to the sentiments of integrity, charity, and faith in lofty ideals, free from gross superstition or any artificial system of theology. But there came to the front a class of men called Brahmins, who laid claim to special powers, and built upon the Vedas a "huge artificial system by which to rule every moment of a man's life." The Vedas were made to say that " when Brahma created man, the Brahmins or priests came from his mouth, the soldiers from his arm, and the farmers from his thigh, and the Sudras (the conquered race) from his foot. The Brahmins thus set themselves above all. They laid down rules so strict about prayers and sacrifices, and made the favor of their gods to depend on such trifling things, that every one was glad to secure their help to do these duties aright. The people believed that the Brahmins alone knew what foods might be eaten, what air might be breathed, what clothes might be worn, and what was the proper length of the ladle in which the offering was to be put."* Thus were the people brought in bondage to an artificial system of ceremonials appealing to superstition alone, fraudulently devised for the benefit of an unscrupulous priesthood. In a manner somewhat similar have other religious faiths been prostituted to unworthy ends.

In the earlier centuries of the Christian religion the priests promulgated their doctrines, and built up their power by proclaiming eternal damnation to those who refused to believe the things which they taught. Perhaps civilization may have derived some advantage from the use of this device. Perhaps in an ignorant and superstitious age it may be impossible to control and lead the ignorant masses, even in the direction of their own welfare, without appeals to superstition. Ignorant people are not readily swayed in moral or religious matters by reason alone, or through appeals to the higher emotions. The oracles of Greece and Rome may perhaps be justified. But the utility of such devices lies wholly in the past. The coarse theology of the Middle Ages is not adapted to the present era.

---

* The Childhood of Religions.

Its effect at the present time is demoralizing; and, instead of aiding the Church, it is weakening the influence of the ministry. It is as much out of place in a religious code adapted to the nineteenth century as would be a stone god of the Aztecs in a modern church. The sacrifice of cattle and sheep was a useful ceremony among a race of semicivilized people; among an enlightened people it would be a coarse burlesque.

The theology of a people cannot remain stationary. And it is a mistake to attach the quality of virtue to an act of belief, and thus obstruct intellectual growth and erect a false standard of ethics.

Religion is essentially progressive and cannot be imprisoned forever in the hard dogmas in which lie dormant the reason and conscience of an unenlightened age. After a time the vital germ within, warmed into life, will demand air and light, and the shell will be broken or the germ must die. What is the condition to-day? Are the ancient faiths of the people growing into strong, deep-rooted plants, filling the moral atmosphere with the aroma of a fragrant bloom, rich in the promise of ripened fruit, or do they lie dead in the mould of decaying creeds? The Church points to her thousands of splendid edifices, to her long roll of membership, counts the cash in the contribution-box, and serenely answers that all is well. But there is another answer. Ministers are preaching to vacant benches; sermons falling on listless ears awaken only the cold, half-cynical response of formal assent; the human heart, that "harp of a thousand strings," attuned to another key, no longer makes music for the soul in answer to the rude touch of the unskilled master who forever strums his medley of resounding platitudes; the weary twang of discordant notes is sweet only to those who sleep and dream.

It is not to be expected or desired that human thought shall ever cease to range the field of theological speculation. Theological beliefs possess their value, and even the grosser superstitions of a barbarous people may be sometimes utilized to good ends. But theology is not of the essence of religion; and as a people advance in knowledge and culture, the influence of fixed beliefs concerning supernatural things loses sway. As they advance in knowledge, they cease to be controlled by superstitious fears, the influence of theological dogma declines, and, instead of relying upon the will of an unseen Deity, revealed in dreams, or formulated into creeds by quibbling priests, they learn that the laws of ethics and religion have their origin in the constitution of the human mind, in the impulses of the heart, in the nature of man.

A religion that does not make men better or happier here and now serves no good purpose. It is a vulgar conception that men's souls are to be saved from punishment in a world to come by espousing certain beliefs concerning things unknown, and that substitutes for the laws of natural ethics the arbitrary commands of an unseen Deity, whose wrath may be stirred or appeased by observing, or neglecting to observe, prescribed modes or ceremonials. Such doctrines do not have their origin in the lofty teachings of the great founder of the Christian religion; they are the remnants of Jewish barbarism and pagan superstition, useful, perhaps, in their day as devices for the control of an ignorant populace, but altogether unworthy of a place in the religious code of an enlightened people.

It is not essential to the faithful performance of the proper work of the ministry that the pulpit should array itself in offensive antagonism to fixed theologic faiths, or even to vulgar religious prejudices; but the interests of the great mass of working-people require that the influence of the pulpit should be extended over a wider field, that its teaching should have broader scope. To be effective it must be able to instruct and to entertain. Its function is to educate the people in whatever pertains to social philosophy, ethics, or religion; to hold up worthy ideals, to awaken and cultivate pure and refined sentiment; in short, to help make the world better here and now.

The question is, Shall the minister apply himself and the agencies under his control to the culture of the people in that broad sense essential to the development of a perfect manhood? shall it be his work to lead them into better ways of living and to fashion character in the mould of ideal conceptions? or shall he continue, along with fortune-tellers and interpreters of dreams, the professor of a mediæval and mysterious art by which, through the device of a combination of ceremony and faith in things unseen, the soul is made happy in the belief that it has escaped the wrath of an angry Deity in the world to come?—a peculiar scheme of salvation devised in the cloister, remarkable chiefly for the fact that it is instantaneous in its results and dispenses with the necessity of both mental culture and moral refinements as conditions of divine favor.

An able writer, M. Maurice, in a recent article truly says, "There are few happy people. And why? The answer is a plain one, and goes straight home to our civilization : we do not educate for happiness. In no direction do we find our Church or our school system permeated with the idea that a young person to be permanently happy must understand and be true to the laws of nature. The Church, as a rule, has given over any effort to construct a happy life, and bends all her energies to point out a possible happy hereafter. The state has constructed a system of education which never refers to happiness as an end. Moral purpose and our dependence upon ethical principle is left to our schools. The parochial schools confuse religion and a noble life, and aim for the most part only to save souls after death. In all directions the young are not trained to know how to be happy.

"The end of all education should be to create (1) character, (2) homes, and (3) citizens. When we point the enthusiastic to education as the only possible remedy for ills of any sort, it is sure to be a disappointment. One-half the world is either concocting a panacea or is swallowing one. Our social panaceas are exactly as valuable as our medical cure-alls. You *must* live rightly to be whole or healthy; you must learn rightly and be made rightly in order to be good and happy in your own soul and your relation to yourself, in your family, in your relation to your children and partner, and in the state as a citizen."

The ministry, as a body, lack neither earnestness nor zeal. They are, however, the victims of an established routine that cramps educational growth and in no small degree impairs their capacity as leaders in any field of modern thought. Those among them who possess more than average ability or independence of character are often disposed to disregard the narrow limitations that restrict their influence and their usefulness within a prescribed sphere, and become, in a broader sense, educators of the people; and gradually, but slowly, the work of the ministry takes wider scope. But they labor under the embarrassment of being compelled to introduce new ideas by stealth, arrayed in the unbefitting attire of conventional phraseology already worn threadbare in the service of a superannuated theology. The hold of the pulpit upon the masses grows weaker and weaker. Its success in diffusing religious sentiments, and in establishing a high standard of ethics among the people, falls far short of the measure of expended effort.

The Church must get its dead theology out of the way. It must cease to antagonize demonstrated truths; it must cease to magnify absurd dogmas and to belittle ethics. While it has in a measure ranged itself in line with modern thought, it is not yet in a position to do the work that belongs to it to do. The sooner the ministry in general are awakened to a clear perception of the true condition of affairs the better it will be for the Church, considered merely as a temporal organization, and the better it will be for the growth and spread of Christian sentiment and for the good order of society.

The social and moral training of the masses of the people cannot be effectively carried forward without the aid and active co-operation of an intelligent ministry. The economic forces which determine the material welfare of the people do not operate independent of ethics. Improved physical conditions are in great measure dependent upon improved education, and an advance in moral and religious sentiment depends upon improved physical conditions. The mental and physical cannot be divorced; ignorance and immorality beget poverty, and poverty begets ignorance and vice.

Any system of economics that fails to take account of the moral and intellectual education of the people, and of the influences and agencies by which education is promoted or retarded, rightly or wrongly directed, omits a leading and controlling factor in the problem.

We readily recognize in the Mormon, Moslem, or Hindoo religions forces that stimulate, retard, or modify industrial civilization. The institutions in our midst exercise a corresponding influence; and improvement in industrial or economic conditions of the people of our own country depends also in great measure upon the Church, and the manner in which it may perform its part in promoting the general culture of the people.

Even where the Church has in great measure lost its potency as a direct moral force, and where it neglects its proper work as the chief agency in promoting the education of the people, it still remains a leading factor in our civilization, if for no other reason because of the ground it occupies and from which it in great measure excludes other agencies. The Church is a power by reason of its inertia alone. It is interwoven with every fibre of the social fabric, associated with the ancient traditions and popular conceptions that unite a people into a society of common ideas, faiths, and tendencies; and the great problem of economic reform and social development cannot be worked out without regard to the Church and its teachings.

INDEX.

THE END.

PRINTED BY J. B. LIPPINCOTT COMPANY, PHILADELPHIA.

www.ingramcontent.com/pod-product-compliance
Lightning Source LLC
Chambersburg PA
CBHW051115120726
47905CB00005B/1283